Querying MySQL

Make your MySQL database analytics accessible with SQL operations, data extraction, and custom queries

ADAM ASPIN

www.bpbonline.com

Group Product Manager: Marianne Conor

Publishing Product Manager: Eva Brawn

Senior Editor: Connell

Content Development Editor: Melissa Monroe

Technical Editor: Anne Stokes

Copy Editor: Joe Austin

Language Support Editor: Justin Baldwin

Project Coordinator: Tyler Horan

Proofreader: Khloe Styles

Indexer: V. Krishnamurthy

Production Designer: Malcolm D'Souza

Marketing Coordinator: Kristen Kramer

First published: July 2022

Published by BPB Online
WeWork, 119 Marylebone Road
London NW1 5PU

UK | UAE | INDIA | SINGAPORE

ISBN 978-93-5551-267-3

www.bpbonline.com

About the Author

Adam Aspin is an independent Business Intelligence (BI) consultant based in the United Kingdom. He has worked with MySQL for over 20 years. During this time, he has developed several dozen database and analytical systems based on different databases. He has applied his skills for a range of clients in industry sectors across finance, utilities, pharmaceuticals, telecoms, insurance, retail, and luxury goods.

A graduate of Oxford University, Adam moved into IT early in his career. Databases soon became a passion, and his experience in this arena ranges from dBase to Oracle, and Access to MySQL, with occasional sorties into the world of DB2, Informix, and PostgreSQL.

Adam is a frequent contributor to SQLServerCentral.com and Simple Talk. He is a regular speaker at SQL Server User Groups, SQL Saturdays, Power BI Meetups and conferences such as SQL Bits. He has written numerous articles for various French IT publications. A fluent French speaker, Adam has worked in France and Switzerland for many years.

He is the author of SQL Server 2012 Data Integration Recipes (Apress, 2012), High Impact Data Visualization in Excel with Power View, 3D Maps, Get & Transform and Power BI, Second Edition (Apress, 2016), Business Intelligence with SQL Server Reporting Services (Apress, 2015), Pro Power BI Desktop, Third Edition (Apress, 2019) and Pro Pro Power BI Theme Creation (Apress 2021).

About the Reviewer

Roni Levy is a software development team manager with the French education ministry, where he and his team are using SQL and MySQL to develop applications for users in the field of education.

Roni has extensive database experience having worked for many years with Informix, DB2 and MariaDB as well as MySQL. He also has extensive systems integration experience and a wide-ranging project management background.

Roni is now acting as director for development of new projects at the Information Systems Department (DSI) of the Académie d'Aix-Marseille.

Acknowledgements

Writing a technical book is an arduous project at the best of times. Fortunately, the author was lucky to have help and support from a great team.

Above all, I owe a deep debt of gratitude to Roni Levy, who kindly accepted my offer to be the technical reviewer of this book. Roni brought a wealth of experience to this role, and his experience as a database developer shone in the way that he helped me ensure that the code worked exactly as it was intended. Roni went far beyond the call of duty in his efforts to help me deliver a book that would help readers master SQL with MySQL.

I also would like to thank Natalie Heger for letting me make use of her wide-ranging Linux expertise.

Finally, I have to thank the production staff at BPB for all their help. Their professionalism in guiding me through the publication process was much appreciated.

Last—but not least—I need to thank my wife and son for putting up with my obsession with writing a book on a subject like SQL. Their good humor and encouragement have helped me considerably on this particular journey.

Any source code or other supplementary material referenced by the author in this book is freely available for readers to download.

Code Bundle and Coloured Images

Please follow the link to download the
Code Bundle and the *Coloured Images* of the book:

https://rebrand.ly/lhnbff8

The code bundle for the book is also hosted on GitHub at **https://github.com/ bpbpublications/Querying-MySQL**. In case there's an update to the code, it will be updated on the existing GitHub repository.

We have code bundles from our rich catalogue of books and videos available at **https://github.com/bpbpublications**. Check them out!

Errata

We take immense pride in our work at BPB Publications and follow best practices to ensure the accuracy of our content to provide with an indulging reading experience to our subscribers. Our readers are our mirrors, and we use their inputs to reflect and improve upon human errors, if any, that may have occurred during the publishing processes involved. To let us maintain the quality and help us reach out to any readers who might be having difficulties due to any unforeseen errors, please write to us at :

errata@bpbonline.com

Your support, suggestions and feedbacks are highly appreciated by the BPB Publications' Family.

Did you know that BPB offers eBook versions of every book published, with PDF and ePub files available? You can upgrade to the eBook version at www.bpbonline.com and as a print book customer, you are entitled to a discount on the eBook copy. Get in touch with us at :

business@bpbonline.com for more details.

At **www.bpbonline.com**, you can also read a collection of free technical articles, sign up for a range of free newsletters, and receive exclusive discounts and offers on BPB books and eBooks.

Piracy

If you come across any illegal copies of our works in any form on the internet, we would be grateful if you would provide us with the location address or website name. Please contact us at **business@bpbonline.com** with a link to the material.

If you are interested in becoming an author

If there is a topic that you have expertise in, and you are interested in either writing or contributing to a book, please visit **www.bpbonline.com**. We have worked with thousands of developers and tech professionals, just like you, to help them share their insights with the global tech community. You can make a general application, apply for a specific hot topic that we are recruiting an author for, or submit your own idea.

Reviews

Please leave a review. Once you have read and used this book, why not leave a review on the site that you purchased it from? Potential readers can then see and use your unbiased opinion to make purchase decisions. We at BPB can understand what you think about our products, and our authors can see your feedback on their book. Thank you!

For more information about BPB, please visit **www.bpbonline.com**.

Table of Contents

Introduction

> *If you are looking at this book, it is probably because you need to use data from a MySQL database in some way. Perhaps you need to create lists of client information, maybe you want to carry out analysis of financial facts and figures, or it could be that you want to prepare the data for corporate dashboards or visualization in one of the many applications that can present MySQL data.*

Whatever the motivation, you know that the data is stored in MySQL, and you want to access this information and learn how to slice it, filter it, tweak the presentation, and deliver the output you need.

This book is the first step on this journey. It aims to teach you the essentials of SQL (Structured Query Language) querying using data stored in a MySQL database. It presumes that you have no previous knowledge of SQL or MySQL and introduces you to the core concepts, structures, and approaches that you will need to write basic SQL queries.

Why Learn SQL?

Most of the data that fuels businesses throughout the world is stored in relational databases. Nearly all of these databases are queried using a variant of Structured

Query Language (SQL). So, simply put, SQL is key to data analysis. A mastery of SQL will help you to delve deep into the data that is stored in corporate databases. You can apply SQL to analyze the data and then present it in a clearly understandable form.

SQL can usually serve a vital role in preparing the data for final delivery, whatever the output application that you are using to present your analysis. Most end-user tools have an option for entering SQL to help derive meaning from the underlying data sources. Consequently, a knowledge of SQL can help you analyze data faster and more clearly. The aims of this book are to give you the necessary mastery of SQL to enable you to get the most out of your data and to deliver the insights that will drive your competitive advantage.

Why MySQL?

MySQL is one of the world's leading databases and has an ever-growing user base. That's why learning the MySQL flavor of SQL has the immediate potential to be a career-enhancing move. As the data store for innumerable corporate, commercial, and web-driven databases, this mature and impressive system is used to power data analysis across the globe.

What Is SQL?

SQL (pronounced Ess-Queue-Elle) is the standard computing language for managing and querying data in relational databases. Every database has its own flavor of SQL, and these variants are subtly different. MySQL uses its own dialect of SQL. While the core elements are the same as those found in other databases, there are many subtle differences between the SQL used by MySQL and other flavors.

This means that learning "plain vanilla" SQL will soon leave you struggling with queries that use MySQL. It can also mean that you will find yourself unable to extract the deeper insights that a mastery of SQL on MySQL can provide.

So, right from the start this book takes you into the world of MySQL and SQL. This way you will learn to use the MySQL dialect of SQL to its full capacity, not limiting yourself to underperforming queries and not missing out on features that other flavors of SQL simply do not have.

However, the MySQL flavor of SQL is, fortunately, close to the SQL used by rival databases. Therefore, learning SQL with MySQL will set you on the path to applying standard SQL query techniques in most of the available relational databases currently deployed.

Who This Book Is For

This book will help anyone who wants to know more about using SQL to deliver analysis. This means you could be any of the following:

- A data analyst
- A student
- A database developer
- A finance professional
- A business analyst
- A job seeker looking to get ready for a technical interview
- A trainee preparing for a SQL exam

Indeed, this book is for anyone who needs to deliver accurate analytics from the data stored in a MySQL database.

What This Book Will Bring You

This book was written to help you, the reader, to become proficient in querying databases using SQL. It will help you to master a language that might seem arcane or even weird at first sight. To overcome any initial reticence you may have, it progresses step-by-step through all the core concepts and techniques that you need to master. This way, you learn the essential keywords that you need to query MySQL databases progressively, without "information overload." To make SQL comprehensible, the book introduces each new concept or keyword individually so that you can learn each element in isolation. As the book progresses, you will learn how to combine SQL keywords to extend the power of SQL as you learn to create more powerful queries.

However, no one queries databases purely for fun, so each query that you apply in this book also has a purely practical purpose. You also see how to develop real-world queries that deliver essential data analysis. You can then adapt these queries to your own requirements using your own data.

How to Read This Book

You can use this book in several ways, depending on your knowledge of SQL and your real-world requirements. Some examples of how you could choose to read it are discussed next.

SQL Novices

If you are a complete beginner, then you can begin with Chapter 1 and progress through the book until you feel that you have attained a level of SQL skills that matches your needs. This book is designed to be a complete SQL querying course that allows readers with no previous SQL experience progressively to gain the skills and experience they need.

Refreshing Your Knowledge

If you are coming back to SQL after being away for a while, then you should probably skim through the first few chapters until you start meeting techniques and approaches that are less obvious. Then you can slow down and concentrate on progressing through the book and consolidating as well as refreshing your knowledge.

Coming from Another SQL Database

If you are proficient in another SQL database and are used to writing SQL queries, then you can probably skim through the first few chapters fairly quickly and concentrate more fully on the later chapters. The later chapters contain information that is specific to the flavor of SQL used by MySQL. This variant of SQL might be slightly different from the version you are used to using.

In-Depth Querying

If your needs are more advanced, then you might want to begin by skimming through the initial chapters in this book and use them to provide inspiration on how best to solve your specific problems. You can then take a deep dive into the later chapters to make quite sure that your advanced SQL querying knowledge is up to scratch.

The Structure of This Book

This book is aimed at true MySQL beginners. It presumes no previous knowledge of SQL or MySQL and helps you progressively to acquire the core knowledge that is required to carry out basic SQL queries.

It consists of the following 21 chapters:

Chapter 1, "Writing Basic SQL Queries": This chapter introduces the basic concepts of SQL and MySQL and shows you how to write simple queries.

Chapter 2, "Using Multiple Tables When Querying Data": This chapter extends your knowledge by showing you how to join tables to return data from more than one table at a time. It also explains many of the ways that you can join tables.

Chapter 3, "Using Advanced Table Joins": This chapter discusses how to use more advanced table joins.

Chapter 4, "Filtering Data": This chapter introduces a fundamental concept: filtering the data that you want to use.

Chapter 5, "Applying Complex Filters to Queries": This chapter shows you how to combine filters to produce more complex queries.

Chapter 6, "Making Simple Calculations": This chapter shows you some of the ways that you can apply basic math to the data in a MySQL database.

Chapter 7, "Aggregating Output": This chapter explains how you can use SQL to group and aggregate data to deliver analysis.

Chapter 8, "Working with Dates in MySQL": This chapter introduces you to some of the essential ways that SQL handles dates and can use dates to deliver analysis over time.

Chapter 9, "Formatting Text in Query Output": This chapter shows you some of the key ways that SQL can be applied to format queries.

Chapter 10, "Formatting Numbers and Dates": This chapter introduces a series of techniques that you can use to change the way that dates and numbers appear in the final output.

Chapter 11, "Using Basic Logic to Enhance Analysis": This chapter concludes the book with an introduction to using SQL to analyze data and deliver added value.

"Chapter 12: Subqueries". This chapter shows you how you can use independent SQL queries inside other queries.

"Chapter13: Derived Tables". This chapter teaches you how to compare data at different levels of aggregation or carry out calculations that mix and match different ways of grouping data.

"Chapter14: Common Table Expressions". This chapter explains a powerful way to simplify working with complex datasets.

"Chapter15: Correlated Subqueries". This chapter shows you how you can use certain kinds of subquery to filter the data in the outer query in a specific way.

"Chapter16: Joining and Filtering Datasets". This chapter introduces methods of handling data spread across a series of tables with similar or identical structures.

"Chapter17: Using SQL for More Advanced Calculations". This chapter teaches you how SQL can go much further than simple addition, subtraction, division, and multiplication and how SQL handles numbers.

"Chapter18: Segmenting and Classifying Data". This chapter introduces ways of prioritizing and classifying lists of data in order to analyze the elements that really matter.

"Chapter19: Rolling Analysis". This chapter covers ways of discerning trends, tracking growth, and establishing a solid factual base that you can use for your analysis.

"Chapter20: Analyzing Data Over Time". This chapter goes deeply into techniques that you can apply to track the evolution of sales, profits, or, indeed, any metric over any time period: from years to days to hours and seconds.

"Chapter 21: Complex Data Output". This chapter concludes the book with a look at ways of shaping output so that the essence of your analysis is immediately comprehensible. These techniques will also help you to present your analysis in various ways that can make the results easier to read and understand.

The Sample Data and Sample Queries

To help you learn SQL, the sample data as well as all the SQL queries in this book are available on the BPB Publishing website. You can download and install the sample data into a MySQL database on your PC and practice SQL querying using this data to help you learn SQL.

If typing the queries is a little laborious (though I do recommend it as an excellent way of learning), then you can also download all the queries in the book and simply copy them into the querying application that you are using to see the results.

You can find the sample data and essential query snippets at www.BPB.com/XXX.

MySQL Versions

The queries in this book have been written using version 8.0.12 of MySQL. However nearly all of them should all work on most previous versions of this database.

Time to Get Started Querying MySQL

That is enough about the theory! It is time to get up close and personal with MySQL.

The first thing you will need is a working copy of the latest version of MySQL. This book was written with MySQL 8.0.12, and I strongly advise you to install this version of the database, as described in Appendix A.

Once you have a functioning database, you will need an application that you can use to test your queries. Many such apps are available, but I advise that you use MySQL Workbench. Indeed, this is the application I have used throughout this book. You can find out how to download and install this tool in Appendix B.

Finally, you will need some sample data to work on. For this (and especially if you want to test your SQL using the examples in this book), you will need to download and set up the sample database PrestigeCars. This is described in Appendix C.

You are now ready to start on your journey toward becoming a SQL querying maestro.

Have fun!

Chapter 1

Writing Basic SQL Queries

Welcome to MySQL and the new world of data and analytics that you are about to experience. As you are standing on the threshold of this voyage into the realms of databases and data analysis, you could be feeling a little apprehensive. Well, don't worry, your journey will be as simple and comprehensible as I can make it. This chapter will start you on your adventure first by outlining the software that you need to install and then by explaining what a database is. Then I will show you how to look at the data itself. As you progress, you will learn how to be more selective about the data that you analyze.

Prerequisites

It may seem obvious, but you will need some data in an accessible database before you can start your analysis. So, throughout this book I will be asking you to develop your analytical skills with the aid of a sample database named PrestigeCars. This database contains a small amount of data concerning sales of vehicles by a fictitious British car reseller. If you want to try the examples in this chapter, you will have to download the sample database from the BPB Publishing website and install the database into a version of MySQL. So, it follows that now could be a good time to set up the sample database as described in Appendix C, unless you have already done so. Of course, you can install the sample database only if you have a version of MySQL already installed and available. So, if you are not in an enterprise environment where MySQL is already accessible, you will need to install a version of the database software before anything else. This is described in Appendix A.

Once MySQL is up and running, you will need somewhere to enter and run your queries. I am presuming that you have also installed MySQL Workbench (or one of the other interfaces that are available for MySQL) as the tool to query the sample database. Installing this piece of software is described in Appendix B. I presume that you will be trying your queries using this particular application.

MySQL Workbench is not the only tool that you can use to query databases. There are indeed many excellent apps that you can use to analyze MySQL data. So, if you prefer to use another application to test the queries in this book, then that is entirely up to you. However, you will have to handle the specifics of installing and working with that application yourself; there are simply too many of them for us to explain every one!

Whatever the tool that you use to write your queries, this chapter will teach you how to

- Query MySQL databases using MySQL Workbench
- List the contents of tables
- Select only certain fields in tables to display
- Display only a few records from a table
- Give columns new names in your query output
- Sort your output

When you have all the prerequisites in place, it is time to move on to the core focus of this chapter and start querying MySQL data.

Note: If you know a little about the standard MySQL data tools and if you have a basic knowledge of databases, then feel free to skip past the first few sections of this chapter until you find the parts that are new to you. However, I realize that the first steps for a novice are important. Consequently, I prefer to start from the beginning and provide all the information that you are likely to need to get the most out of your SQL learning experience

1. Relational Databases

As you have decided to learn to analyze data using SQL queries, you need to know a few basic concepts to begin with.

To start, what is a relational database (or a relational database management system, RDBMS)? At its simplest, a relational database is a method of storing data in a clearly defined way. A database consists of tables (sometimes thousands of tables) that each contain rows of data. All the rows in a table consist of the same number of columns. So, a table is really nothing more than a well-structured list—rather like the ones that you have probably encountered in Excel.

In a well-designed database, tables will be organized to avoid duplicating data. The tables in the database can then be linked together to present the data in different ways.

To resume, then, a relational database is a collection of lists (tables) containing columns (fields) of data in a set of rows (records). These elements can then be accessed independently or joined together to deliver the analysis you are looking for.

Conceptually, a database looks something like Figure 1.1.

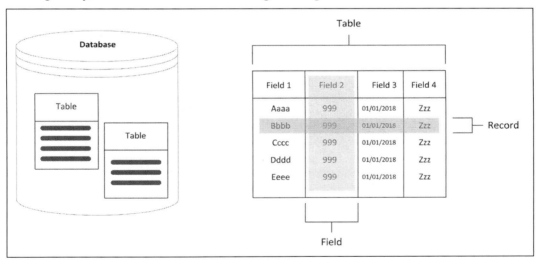

Figure 1.1: Conceptualizing a relational database

Note: Please note that all the exercises in this book use a sample database named PrestigeCars. If you need to install this database, then please consult Appendix C.

2. Running MySQL Workbench

The time has come to start putting the theory into practice. As relational databases can require considerable IT horsepower, they will nearly always reside on powerful servers either on-premises or in the cloud. They are rarely installed on PCs or laptops unless they are being used for learning.

So, what you will nearly always do is connect to the database using a separate piece of software that is, itself, installed on a PC. This is called a client-server model, where you use one application (the client) to connect to the database (the server). While there are many applications that can read data from MySQL databases, there is one that tends to be used by most analysts and developers. This is MySQL Workbench. It is an application currently distributed by Oracle and is (at least at the time that this book went to press) free to install and use. As befits a piece of software that has been evolving for many years, it is both efficient and reliable. Indeed, it is the standard tool that is used by hundreds of thousands of analysts and developers. Consequently, this is the tool that we will be using throughout this book.

I will assume that you have MySQL Workbench installed on your PC. If this is not the case, then please consult Appendix B to learn how to find and install this tool. Otherwise you will have to run the application that you have chosen to work with. Indeed, you may prefer not to use a graphical user interface at all, but to query MySQL using a command line client. The choice is entirely up to you.

To open MySQL Workbench, follow these steps (exactly how you do this will depend on the actual operating system as well as the version of the operating system that you are working with):

1. Under Windows 10, you can open the Start menu and expand the MySQL folder, where you will find the MySQL Workbench option. You can see this in Figure 1.2. (On a Macintosh, open the Applications folder and double-click MySQL Workbench).

Figure 1.2: Running MySQL Workbench

2. Select MySQL Workbench.

3. MySQL Workbench opens and displays the Welcome screen with the server details, as you can see in Figure 1.3.

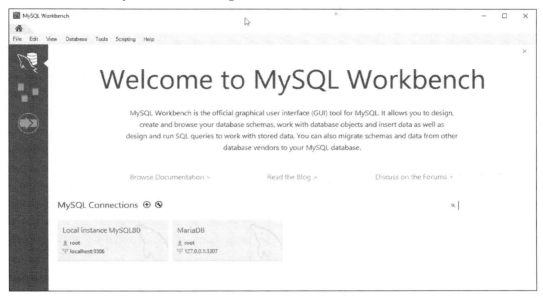

Figure 1.3: The MySQL Workbench Connect to Server dialog

4. Select the server name from the available connections. If you are in an enterprise environment, you can always ask a system administrator which database to use. If you have just installed a stand-alone version of MySQL on your laptop or workstation (this is described in Appendix A), then just select MySQL from the available connections. You might see a warning dialog like the one shown in Figure 1.4.

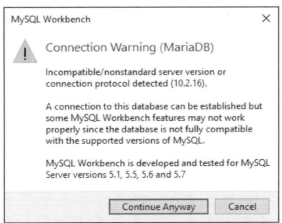

Figure 1.4: The MySQL Workbench connection warning

5. As this warning is largely irrelevant when querying MySQL just click "Continue Anyway". You will see MySQL Workbench, ready for you to begin working, as shown in Figure 1.5.

Figure 1.5: *MySQL Workbench*

6. Expand the PrestigeCars database in the list of databases in the Navigator window on the left by clicking the small triangle to the left of the database name. You will then see all the elements (or "objects" as geeks call them) that are contained in this database, as shown in Figure 1.6.

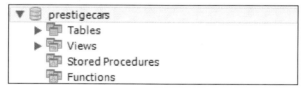

Figure 1.6: *The PrestigeCars database*

There are, of course, many other GUIs (graphical user interfaces) that you can use when querying MySQL. So feel free to install the one that suits you best. The SQL that you will enter and the results that you will obtain will be the same.

3. Connecting to a Database

Before you can do anything at all with MySQL, you need to tell MySQL Workbench (or the GUI that you are using) which database you want to work with. After all, you could be using a corporate or educational system with hundreds of available databases.

To connect to a database:

1. Double-click on the database that you want to connect to (PrestigeCars in this example) in the Navigator window of MySQL Workbench.

    You will see that the active database now appears in boldface in the MySQL Workbench Navigator window.

Now that you have connected to the database, you are ready to start analyzing the data it contains. I realize that the first time you carry out this sequence of instructions the process may seem a little laborious. However, you will probably launch MySQL Workbench only a couple of times a day when you start working with MySQL. So, it is not really any different than opening desktop applications when you first start creating documents or editing spreadsheets. In any case, this routine will certainly become second nature in a short time.

4. Displaying the Tables in a Database

All the data in a MySQL database is stored in tables. A database can consist of dozens—or even hundreds—of tables of data that have been carefully designed and created by database professionals. The first thing that you will have to do when faced with any database that is new to you is to take a look at the tables it contains. To do this, follow these steps:

1. Expand the Tables folder by clicking the small triangle to the left of the Tables folder in the PrestigeCars database. You should see something like the list of tables shown in Figure 1.7.

Figure 1.7: Displaying the tables contained in a database

As this sample database is small, it contains only a handful of tables. You will learn what they all contain as you progress through this book.

5. Finding All the Views in a Database

SQL-based databases do not just contain tables. Indeed, they can contain hundreds of different items (that are collectively called objects). One of the aims of this book is to introduce you progressively to the essential objects that you will need to learn to manipulate when querying data.

Apart from tables, one kind of object that you need to know about is the view. Quite simply, although all data is stored in tables, you could frequently find yourself querying not only tables but views too. This is because views are a way of looking at data that is filtered or combined in some way, essentially making life easier for users by doing some of the work for you.

In SQL queries you can treat views exactly as if they were tables. The first thing to know is how to find the views in a database. Fortunately, this is similar to what you just did when looking at the database tables.

1. Expand the Views folder by clicking the triangle symbol to the left of the Views folder in the PrestigeCars database. You should see something like the list of views in Figure 1.8.

Figure 1.8: Displaying the views contained in a database

As you can see, there are even fewer views than tables in the PrestigeCars database. Indeed, there is only a single view named SalesByCountry.

6. Using the Command Line Client

Although we live in an age of graphical user interfaces, you can also query MySQL using a command line client if you prefer (or if you have no other options). Here is how to connect to a database and list all the tables and views using the command line client for MySQL that is installed by default with the product.

1. Launch the command line client. Exactly how you do this will depend on the operating system and the version of the operating system that you are working with. Under Windows 10, you can open the Start menu and expand the MySQL folder, where you will find the MySQL 8.0 Command Line Client option. You can see this in Figure 1.9.

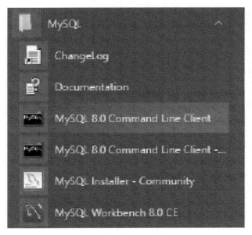

Figure 1.9: Running the MySQL Command Line Client

2. Click MySQL Client (MySQL 10.2). A window will open asking you for the MySQL password. If you have installed your own MySQL instance on your computer this will be the password that you set when installing the database software.

3. Enter the Password and press [Enter]. The screen will look like the one shown in Figure 1.10.

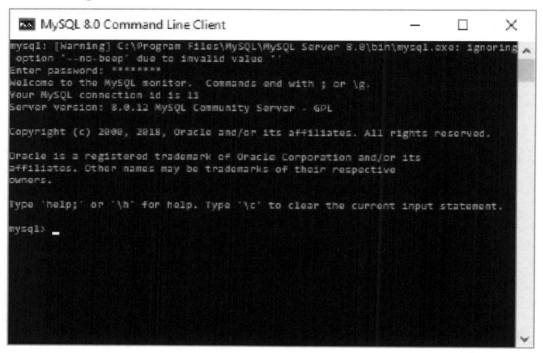

Figure 1.10: The Command Line Client with a successful database connection

4. Enter the following command to select the database to query
   ```
   use prestigecars;
   ```

5. Press [Enter].

6. Enter the command to list all the tables and views in the database:
   ```
   show tables;
   ```

7. Press [Enter]. The screen should look like the one shown in Figure 1.11.

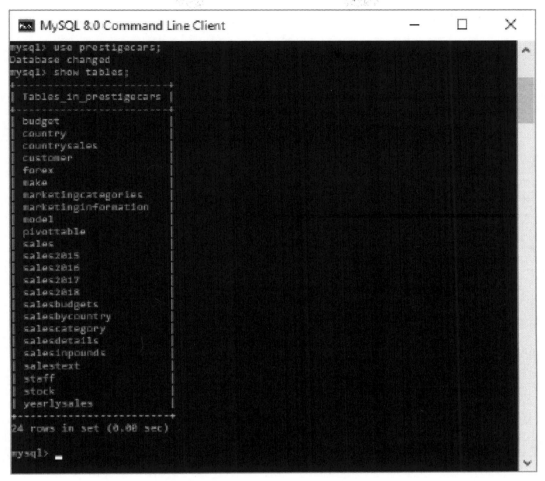

Figure 1.11: Displaying tables and views using the Command Line Client

When you have finished using the Command Line Client simply enter:

- Quit
- followed by [Enter]

Then close the command line window.

Tricks and Traps

There are a few comments to make about the command line interface.

- A Command Line interface may seem a little old fashioned, but it is certainly extremely efficient.

- Each separate SQL statement that you write must end with a semi-colon.

- The SQL that you enter at the command line is absolutely identical to the SQL that you enter using a graphical user interface. A command will be run, however, when you enter a semi colon and press [Enter].

- A GUI may be easier to use (and is certainly prettier) but the end result of a query is exactly the same.

7. Displaying the Data in a Table

Now that you have learned how to look inside a database, it is time to look at some actual data. For your first query, let's suppose you want to see what makes of vehicle are sold by Prestige Cars Ltd.

1. In the query window, type in the following short piece of SQL:

```
SELECT   *
FROM    make;
```

2. Select Query⇒Execute (All or selection) from the MySQL Workbench menu to run the code and show the results. A new pane will open under the code, and the results of the query will appear as shown in Figure 1.12.

MakeID	MakeName	MakeCountry
1	Ferrari	ITA
2	Porsche	GER
3	Lamborghini	ITA
4	Aston Martin	GBR
5	Bentley	GBR
6	Rolls Royce	GBR
7	Maybach	GER
8	Mercedes	GER
9	Alfa Romeo	ITA
10	Austin	GBR
11	BMW	GER
12	Bugatti	FRA
13	Citroen	FRA
14	Delahaye	FRA
15	Delorean	USA

*Figure 1.12: Displaying all the data in a table with SELECT ***

How It Works

In just five words you have said to MySQL, "Show me the complete contents of the Make table, including all the rows and all the columns of data." All you needed to know is which table you wanted to look at. SQL did the rest.

This code snippet is incredibly simple—five words in all—but that is enough to show you how SQL works in practice. If you issue the right command, then you will get back the data you want to see.

As you can see, this command did more than just list the makes of car. It also showed any other elements that are present in the table, but that is exactly the point of the command. This way you get to see everything that is stored in a table of data.

Of course, you will need to know which table contains the data you want to display when you are dealing with your own data. If you are working in an enterprise environment, this may involve talking to the people in your organization who developed or maintain the databases. Alternatively, there may be documentation that you can read to find the information you require.

If there is no one you can ask and no documentation available, then you can still acquaint yourself with the data by running the SELECT * FROM clause with each data table that you can see in the Tables folder. However, before actually carrying out this operation I advise you to continue a little further with this chapter and learn how to limit the number of records returned by a query.

So, what exactly have you done here? Let's take a closer look at what you have written. Figure 1.13 breaks down the SQL statement into its constituent parts.

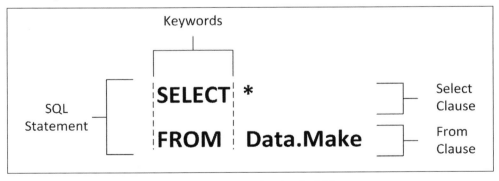

Figure 1.13: The anatomy of a simple SQL statement

These constituent parts are:

Keywords: SQL is built using a set of keywords that you combine to produce commands. These commands (or snippets or phrases if you want to call them that) are in English and follow a fairly rigorous syntax. Learning to understand and apply the "grammar" of SQL is what this book is all about.

Clauses: These are a set of short phrases composed of keywords and data elements that make up a SQL statement.

Tricks and Traps

This was a simple SQL command, but the following are nonetheless a few key points that you will need to remember:

- As I mentioned, each MySQL instance can contain (or host if you prefer) dozens of databases. This means you always have to tell MySQL which database you want to interrogate. One easy way to do this is to double-click the appropriate database in the Navigator before opening a new query window (by selecting Query⇨New Tab to Current Server, for instance). Alternatively you can enter the command

  ```
  use prestigecars;
  ```

  And then execute this piece of code.

- If you do not indicate the right database to use, MySQL will either return no data at all or, worse, return the wrong data from another database.

- All SQL commands in MySQL must end with a semicolon.

- As an alternative to using menu commands, the Windows [Shift]-[Control]-[Enter] keyboard combination runs (or *executes* if you prefer) the SQL code that you have typed or copied into a query window. On a Macintosh, pressing [Command]-[Enter] will do the trick. Another alternative is to click the Execute button (the yellow lightning bolt) in the toolbar.

- It can happen (even when you are an experienced data analyst) that executing a query returns nothing more than an irritating error message like this:

  ```
  17:38:50 SELECT ** FROM  Make  Error Code: 1064. You have an
  error in your SQL syntax; check the manual that corresponds to
  your MySQL server version for the right syntax to use near '* FROM
  Make' at line 1 0.000 sec.
  ```

This probably means you have made a typo or entered a wrong keyword, and so will have to check and correct the SQL that you entered and re-run the code snippet.

- In this book I will explain the data tables that you need to use as you meet them. Here you have seen the first of the small set of tables that make up the core tables in the sample database. As its name suggests, the Make table contains the makes of cars that are stocked and sold by Prestige Cars Ltd.

Note: Make sure you have *not* selected any of the SQL text before you execute the query. This guarantees that MySQL Workbench will run the entire SQL snippet.

8. Displaying Data from a Specific Field

A MySQL table can contain hundreds of columns. Most of the time you will want to display data from only a few of the available columns in a table. The next piece of SQL shows how you choose a single column to display instead of all the available columns in a table. More specifically, it shows how to list only the customer names.

```
SELECT CustomerName

FROM    customer;
```

Executing this piece of code (using any of the techniques that I pointed out at the end of the previous section) will show you something similar to the output shown in Figure 1.14.

CustomerName
Magic Motors
Snazzy Roadsters
Birmingham Executive Prestige Vehicles
WunderKar
Casseroles Chromes
Le Luxe en Motion
Eat My Exhaust Ltd
M. Pierre Dubois
Sondra Horowitz
Wonderland Wheels
London Executive Prestige Vehicles
Glittering Prize Cars Ltd
La Bagnole de Luxe
Convertible Dreams
Alexei Tolstoi
SuperSport S.A.R.L.
Theo Kowalski

Figure 1.14: Choosing a column from a table

How it Works

By replacing the star (or *asterisk* if you prefer) in your SQL with a specific column name, you have told MySQL that it is this column—and this column only—that you want to display. This example also makes the point that SQL is an extremely modular and extensible language, and you can easily extend or modify a simple command to make it more specific.

Of course, this approach relies on your knowing the exact name of a column and also typing it exactly as it appears in the table. Fortunately, MySQL Workbench has ways of displaying column names and using them in your SQL, as you will discover in the next section.

Tricks and Traps

Even simple SQL commands have their subtleties. When listing data, you need to remember the following:

- You can write short SQL commands like this one on a single line of you prefer. That is, you could write the following instead of placing each clause on a separate line:

```
SELECT CustomerName FROM customer;
```

This is entirely a question of personal choice. As I am presuming that you are new to SQL, I will keep the core SQL statements on separate lines in this book to accentuate the underlying logic of the language. In your queries, you can write the SQL any way you want, as long as it works. All that MySQL wants is that the "grammar" of the command is technically accurate and that keywords are separated by spaces, tabs or returns.

9. Finding the Columns in a Table

You may well be wondering how on Earth you can be expected to remember all the columns in each table so that you can type them into your SQL queries. Fortunately, MySQL Workbench (like most graphical user interfaces) can help you here by displaying all the columns in a table in a single click.

1. In the MySQL Workbench Navigator, expand the PrestigeCars database and click the triangle symbol to the left of the table whose columns you want to see (we will use the Country table in this example).

2. Click the triangle symbol to the left of the Columns folder. You should see something like Figure 1.15.

Figure 1.15: *Displaying the columns in a table*

10. Displaying Data from a Specific Set of Fields

SQL does not limit you to displaying all the fields—or only one field—from a table. You can choose not only the fields from a table that you want to display but also the order in which they will appear in the output from the query. The following piece of code shows you how to select two fields (Country Name and Sales Region) from another table in the database—the Country table:

```
SELECT CountryName, SalesRegion

FROM   country;
```

Executing this piece of code will show you something similar to the output in Figure 1.16.

CountryName	SalesRegion
Belgium	EMEA
France	EMEA
Germany	EMEA
Italy	EMEA
Spain	EMEA
United Kingdom	EMEA
United States	North America
China	Asia
India	Asia
Switzerland	EMEA

Figure 1.16: *Displaying multiple fields from the Country table*

How it Works

Here again, you have extended the base SQL that you used at the start of the chapter. Specifically, you have developed the SELECT statement to include the field names containing the data that you want to view. All you had to do was to separate each field name with a comma and place the field names in the order that you want to see their data in the output from left to right.

Note: The data that you see might not be in the same order as the data shown in Figure 1.16. You will learn how to apply a specific sort order in a few pages.

Tricks and Traps

There is only one major trick to remember when listing a specific set of fields.

* Remember *not* to add a comma after the final field in a list of fields in the SELECT clause.

11. Using the Command Line to Show the Structure of a Table

Another way to visualize the structure of a table is from the command line. To display the essential information about the fields in a specific table use the desc keyword—as you can see in the following piece of sql:

```
desc country;
```

Press [Enter] to execute this short snippet and you will see something similar to the output in Figure 1.17.

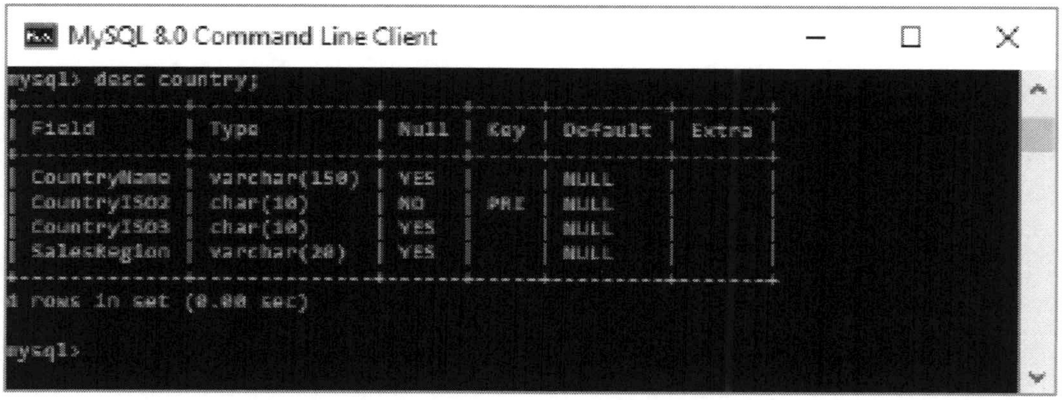

Figure 1.17: Displaying multiple fields from the Country table

How it Works

The *desc* command followed by a table name and a semi-colon lists the structure of the selected table.

Tricks and Traps

As simple as this short command is, it nonetheless needs a couple of key points calling out.

- The desc command shows the field names as well as core information about the fields themselves. However, for the moment it is only the names of the fields that interest us. We will be looking at the other information in later chapters.
- You can only view the structure of one table at a time.

12. Modifying the Field Name in the Output

Many databases have cryptic—or frankly incomprehensible—field names. While as an analyst or data guru you might get used to this, it is not always a good idea to present information to users in a way that makes the data harder to understand than is really necessary. So, SQL allows you to output the data under a different field header to enhance readability. In this example, you will display the country field under another name. Start by taking a look at the code snippet and then at the output it returns in Figure 1.18:

```
SELECT CountryName, CountryISO3 AS IsoCode FROM country;
```

CountryName	IsoCode
Belgium	BEL
France	FRA
Germany	DEU
Italy	ITA
Spain	ESP
United Kingdom	GBR
United States	USA
China	CHN
India	IND
Switzerland	CHF

Figure 1.18: Changing a field name using an alias

How It Works

In the query output, the original field name is replaced by the name you have chosen—IsoCode in this example. This technique is called *aliasing*; you are giving the field another name in the query. Applying an alias has *no effect at all* on the underlying data and does not change the underlying field name. What it *does* do is apply a different (and ideally more comprehensible) name in the query output.

Tricks and Traps

Aliases have their own particular set of rules that must be adhered to if they are to work correctly. Essentially you need to remember the following points:

- You may have noticed that all the table and field names that have been used so far contain neither spaces nor special (that is, nonalphanumeric) characters. This is because SQL requires you to specify the names of what it calls *objects*—that is, fields and tables among other things—in a specific way. However, I do not want to make things appear over-complicated here, so as a starting point, let's just say you are better avoiding all nonalphanumeric characters when creating an alias for a field. Moreover, you should *never* use SQL keywords as aliases.

- If you want to add a space to an alias (suppose in the example used in this section you want to see "ISO Code" as the field heading), then you *must* place the alias inside single or double quotes—or inside back-facing quotes (`` ` ``), also known as *backticks*. That is, you can write any of the following— on most systemsto add a space to the alias ISOCode that you want to use instead of the real field name—on most systems:

```
SELECT CountryName, CountryISO3 AS 'Iso Code' FROM country;

SELECT CountryName, CountryISO3 AS "Iso Code" FROM country;

SELECT CountryName, CountryISO3 AS `Iso Code` FROM country;
```

In practice, many data people advise that you avoid spaces and nonstandard characters if you can, as once you have started down this route, you will have to add the backticks every time you refer to this alias (or table or field) in your code, which can get painful when writing complex queries. So, I will stick to names without spaces or nonalphanumeric characters in this book.

You may find that single or double quotes cannot be used to create table or field names containing spaces or non-standard characters. In this case—or if you are simply unsure—then use backticks, as these will work in all cases.

- In some queries you may find that you are faced with field names so cryptic that they are hard to read. In these cases, you could try using the underscore character instead of a space in a field name. This would give an alias that looks like Iso_Code in this example. While this is certainly a little "geeky," this is nonetheless easier to read than a name without any spaces while being much easier to use in more advanced (and complex) queries. An added advantage is that no quotes or backticks are required.

- An alias cannot be more than 256 characters long. However in most cases getting anywhere near this limit would make the alias longer than the field name and consequently make using an alias pointless—as well as harder to read.

13. Sorting Data

Now that you can select the fields that contain the data you want to see in the sequence that you want to see them, you probably also want to sort the data. For example, you might want to sort car sales by increasing sale price. To do this, just run the following snippet and take a look the numbers in the SalePrice field in Figure 1.19. They are now sorted from lowest to highest.

```
SELECT     *

FROM       SalesByCountry

ORDER BY SalePrice;
```

CountryName	MakeName	ModelName	Cost	RepairsCost	PartsCost	TransporUnCost	Color	SalePrice	LineItemDiscount	InvoiceNumber	SaleDate	CustomerName	SalesDetailsID
United Kingdom	Reliant	Robin	760.0000	500.0000	750.0000	150.0000	Black	950.00		GBPGB323	2018-12-31 00:00:00	Mrs. Ivana Telford	350
Belgium	Peugeot	205	760.0000	500.0000	750.0000	150.0000	British Racing Green	950.00	25.00	EURBE218	2018-01-10 00:00:00	Stefan Van Helsing	237
United Kingdom	Reliant	Robin	760.0000	500.0000	750.0000	150.0000	Black	950.00		GBPGB155	2017-05-20 14:17:00	London Executive Prestige Vehicles	168
United Kingdom	Peugeot	404	760.0000	500.0000	750.0000	150.0000	Black	950.00		GBPGB249	2018-04-23 00:00:00	Clubbing Cars	272
United Kingdom	Citroen	Rosalie	792.0000	500.0000	150.0000	150.0000	British Racing Green	990.00		GBPGB139	2017-03-31 14:09:00	Kieran O'Harris	152
United Kingdom	Austin	Princess	920.0000	500.0000	750.0000	150.0000	Black	1150.00		GBPGB212	2018-01-05 00:00:00	Mr. Evan Telford	231
United Kingdom	Trabant	500	920.0000	500.0000	750.0000	150.0000	Red	1150.00	1500.00	GBPGB303	2018-10-02 00:00:00	Marv Blackhouse	327
Italy	Peugeot	404	1000.0000	500.0000	750.0000	150.0000	Red	1250.00		EURIT281	2018-07-31 00:00:00	Smooth Rocking Chrome	304
United Kingdom	Trabant	600	1000.0000	500.0000	225.0000	150.0000	Red	1250.00		GBPGB259	2018-05-25 00:00:00	Bling Motors	282
France	Peugeot	203	1000.0000	500.0000	750.0000	150.0000	Silver	1250.00		EURFR113	2017-01-21 13:56:00	La Baonole de Luxe	126
United Kingdom	Citroen	Rosalie	1080.0000	500.0000	750.0000	150.0000	Black	1350.00		GBPGB252	2018-05-03 00:00:00	Birmingham Executive Prestige Ve...	275
United Kingdom	Trabant	600	1272.0000	500.0000	750.0000	150.0000	Black	1590.00		GBPGB319	2018-12-08 00:00:00	Boris Sorv	346
United Kingdom	Trabant	600	1560.0000	500.0000	750.0000	150.0000	Red	1950.00		GBPGB303	2018-10-02 00:00:00	Marv Blackhouse	328
France	Peugeot	203	1560.0000	500.0000	750.0000	150.0000	British Racing Green	1950.00		EURFR211	2018-01-05 00:00:00	Jean-Yves Truffaut	230
United Kingdom	Austin	Princess	1800.0000	500.0000	750.0000	150.0000	Canary Yellow	2250.00		GBPGB126	2017-02-14 14:03:00	Magic Motors	139
Switzerland	Citroen	Rosalie	1880.0000	500.0000	225.0000	150.0000	British Racing Green	2350.00		GBPCH161	2017-05-27 21:20:00	Matterhorn Motors	175
Switzerland	Peugeot	404	1880.0000	500.0000	750.0000	150.0000	British Racing Green	2350.00		GBPCH276	2018-07-30 00:00:00	Le Luxe en Motion	299
United Kingdom	Peugeot	404	1920.0000	500.0000	750.0000	150.0000	Canary Yellow	2400.00		GBPGB274	2018-07-30 00:00:00	Leslie Whittington	297
United Kingdom	Peugeot	404	1996.0000	500.0000	750.0000	150.0000	Canary Yellow	2495.00	45.00	GBPGB253	2018-05-03 00:00:00	Silver HubCaps	276
United Kingdom	Trabant	500	2000.0000	500.0000	750.0000	150.0000	Blue	2500.00		GBPGB303	2018-10-02 00:00:00	Marv Blackhouse	329

Figure 1.19: Sorting data in descending order

How it Works

To sort the data returned by a query, just add the ORDER BY keyword (it is considered to be a single keyword even if it is really two words) after the FROM clause of the SQL command. Then you add the field that you are sorting the data on. This creates an ORDER BY clause.

Equally important is the fact that, once again, writing SQL can be all about making simple extensions to the code that you have written so far. So, you do not have to produce instant reams of code that work the first time. You can start with a small snippet of code, test it, and then extend it until it does exactly what you want it to do.

Tricks and Traps

These are several key points to remember here:

- The ORDER BY keyword can also be used on text (in which case it sorts in alphabetical order), on numbers (where it sorts from lowest to highest), or on dates (in which case it places the dates in sequence from the earliest to the latest).

- If you want, you can add the ASC keyword after the sort field name to force an ORDER BY statement to sort the data in ascending order. However, MySQL sorts data in ascending order out of the box. So, the result would be the same even if you wrote this:

```
SELECT * FROM SalesByCountry ORDER BY SalePrice ASC;
```

  If you test this, you will see the same result that you saw when you added the ASC keyword to the ORDER BY clause in the SQL snippet at the start of this section. Techies refer to this as the *default sort order*.

- If you find that reiterating field names in the ORDER BY clause is somewhat laborious, then you can always apply a shortcut. Instead of using a field name, you can use a number to represent it. So, you could write the SQL query at the start of this section as follows:

```
SELECT    CountryISO3 AS IsoCode, CountryName
FROM      Country
ORDER BY  1;
```

  The number that you use in the ORDER BY clause stands for the position of the field in the SELECT clause of the SQL statement. So, in this example, 1 represents IsoCode, 2 means CountryName, and so on.

14. Sorting Data in Reverse Alphabetical Order

As you saw in the previous example, data can be sorted from lowest to highest really quickly and easily. You can also sort data from highest to lowest (or Z to A). Changing the sort order is as simple as replacing the ASC (short for *ascending*) keyword that you just met with the DESC (short for *descending*) keyword. You can see this in the output shown in Figure 1.20 which is the result of the following code snippet that sorts the country names in reverse alphabetical order of IsoCode:

```
SELECT     CountryISO3 AS IsoCode, CountryName

FROM       Country

ORDER BY   IsoCode DESC;
```

IsoCode	CountryName
USA	United States
ITA	Italy
IND	India
GBR	United Kingdom
FRA	France
ESP	Spain
DEU	Germany
CHN	China
CHF	Switzerland
BEL	Belgium

Figure 1.20: Sorting data in alphabetical order

How it Works

Switching the sort order is as easy as adding the DESC keyword at the end of the ORDER BY clause or replacing the DESC keyword with the ASC keyword at the end of the ORDER BY clause of a SQL command. Using DESC forces SQL to sort the results from highest to lowest (if they are numbers), Z to A (if they are text), or latest to earliest (if they are dates).

15. Applying Multiple Sort Criteria

Larger data sets can require that you sort data according to multiple criteria. Suppose, for instance, that you want to list all the cars sold first by country, then by make (per country), and finally by model if there are several makes sold for a specific country.

This is easy to do in SQL because it is a simple extension of the techniques that you have seen in the previous two sections. Take a look at the following code snippet:

```
SELECT    CountryName, MakeName, ModelName

FROM      SalesByCountry

ORDER BY  CountryName, MakeName, ModelName;
```

Executing this query will return a dataset similar to the one shown in Figure 1.21.

CountryName	MakeName	ModelName
Belgium	Alfa Romeo	Giulia
Belgium	Alfa Romeo	Spider
Belgium	Aston Martin	Rapide
Belgium	Aston Martin	Vantage
Belgium	Noble	M600
Belgium	Peugeot	205
Belgium	Peugeot	205
Belgium	Triumph	Roadster
Belgium	Triumph	TR4
Belgium	Triumph	TR6
France	Alfa Romeo	1750
France	Alfa Romeo	Giulia
France	Alfa Romeo	Spider
France	Aston Martin	DB4
France	Aston Martin	DB5
France	Aston Martin	DB6

Figure 1.21: Sorting sales using multiple fields

How it Works

Sometimes you will be faced with a table where some fields contain the same data elements repeated several times. A telephone directory is like this. You may have many pages of people named Smith, although nearly all may have different first names. Even if the last name and the first name are the same, they may have different middle initials. In these cases, you need to sort the data on successive fields so that (to continue the telephone directory analogy) you sort first by last name, then by first name, and finally by middle initial.

Entering several fields after the ORDER BY keyword tells SQL to sort the data progressively on the fields that you entered. In this example, it means the following:

- First by the country
- Then by the make (if there is more than one record with the same country)

- Finally by the model (if there is more than one record with the same country and make)

All you have to do is enter the field names separated by a comma in the ORDER BY clause.

Tricks and Traps

Applying a multiple sort order has its own specific set of core requirements. These include the following:

- While there may be technical limits to the number of fields you can sort on, in practice you do not need to worry and can extend the field list that you use in the ORDER BY statement to include many fields.

- In this example, you used the same fields in the SELECT statement that you used in the ORDER BY statement. This is not compulsory in SQL because there is no obligation in a basic SQL query to display the same fields that you use for ordering the data. However, when you are testing your SQL skills (or ensuring that the data looks like you think it should), it can be a good idea to use the same groups of fields in both clauses. This way you can see whether the output is what you expect.

- Sorting query results requires a lot of computing horsepower when you are dealing with large tables or small database servers. I recommend that you sort data only if it is really necessary.

- As was the case for SELECT clauses, you should not add a comma after the final field name in the ORDER BY clause.

16. Limiting the Number of Records Displayed

MySQL tables can contain millions—or even billions—of records. Each time that you run a query, all the records you see are sent from the server to the querying application. It follows that displaying *all* the rows in a huge table can place an unnecessary strain on the server that stores the data as well as on the network that connects the server to your workstation. So, in the real world, it is a good idea to display only a small number of records when examining a table. This is particularly true when looking at a table for the first time.

Fortunately, SQL has a way of limiting the number of rows returned by a query. This is nothing more than a simple extension to the command that you used in the previous section. Here you can see how to tweak a piece of SQL code to display only a few makes of vehicle:

1. Delete any SQL that might be in the query tab (or open a new query tab), and enter the following code snippet:

```
SELECT   *
FROM     make
         LIMIT 10;
```

2. Run the SQL code (by pressing [Command]-[Enter] on a Macintosh or [Shift]-[Control]-[Enter] on a Windows computer for instance). You will see the data displayed in Figure 1.22.

MakeID	MakeName	MakeCountry
1	Ferrari	ITA
2	Porsche	GER
3	Lamborghini	ITA
4	Aston Martin	GBR
5	Bentley	GBR
6	Rolls Royce	GBR
7	Maybach	GER
8	Mercedes	GER
9	Alfa Romeo	ITA
10	Austin	GBR

Figure 1.22: Limiting the number of records output from a query

How it Works

Executing this command will display all the columns in the table—but *only the first ten records.*

You may well be wondering *which* records you are seeing when you ask SQL to display only 10 rows (or indeed any other number or records). The answer is that you *might* not even see the same set of records when you run this command at different times. MySQL does not necessarily return the first (or last) ten records that were added to a table. Neither does it display the last ten to be updated, viewed, or printed.

This apparently minor question reveals an important fact about SQL databases. They can store records in *any order* (unless the database programmer instructed them to do otherwise). However, there is no immediate way of telling, when you look at a table, whether the data is stored in any sequence. You need to remember this when querying tables and never trust the data to be returned in any specific order *unless you have asked for this to happen using the ORDER BY keyword.*

Tricks and Traps

The following are a few points that I think are worth mentioning at this juncture:

- There are several ways to run the SQL code in a MySQL Workbench query window. Pressing [Shift]-[Control]-[Enter] is only one method. Another is to select Query⇨Execute (All or Selection) from the MySQL Workbench menu. Yet another alternative is to click the Execute button (the yellow lightning bolt) in the toolbar. Of course, other GUIs will have different options when it comes to executing queries.

- In most cases, you can enter the keywords as well as the table and column names in either uppercase or lowercase, or even a mixture of the two. This will depend on how your MySQL has been configured. In this book, however, I will always enter keywords in uppercase to help them stand out in the code snippet. Ideally, this will make them easier to learn.

- You do not have to write queries in a purely linear fashion, starting with the SELECT clause and continuing to the end of the query. You can start with any part of the query and build it up as you want. This could mean beginning with the FROM clause and then move on to the SELECT clause.

Conclusion

This chapter showed you how to perform elementary SQL queries. You saw how to open MySQL Workbench and connect to a specific database. Then you saw how to dig into some of the tables that make up a database and take a look at the data they contain.

You then learned how to be a little more selective when outputting data and consequently to choose which fields to display from a query. You also saw how to limit the number of records that a query returned as well as how to sort the data.

All in all, you have already made vast strides toward the basic analysis of MySQL data. With this knowledge safely acquired, it is time to move on to the next step: using data from multiple tables. This is what you will be looking at in the next chapter.

Core Knowledge Learned in This Chapter

SQL is a language that is built on a collection of core concepts and a set of clearly defined keywords. Using all of these correctly—and understanding exactly what they can and cannot do—is what learning to use SQL is all about. To help you build up your SQL vocabulary, I will always recapitulate any new concepts and keywords that you have met at the end of each chapter. The following are the fundamental keywords that you have learned to use in this chapter:

Concept	Description
Database	A database is a structured way of storing data following a clear set of rules.
Table	A table is a coherent unit of data storage.
Field	A field is a homogenous data definition for a column of data.
Record	A row of data elements made up of fields.
SELECT	This is one of the essential SQL keywords, and you will probably use it in just about every SQL command that you will ever write. It means "isolate and display."
FROM	This is another core keyword. It tells the database which tables you want to look at.
LIMIT	This keyword restricts the number of rows that a query displays. You can set either a precise number of records to show or a percentage of the total number of records in a table.
AS	This keyword lets you display a field under another name. It is called aliasing a field.
*	The star (or asterisk) keyword means "everything." Yes, this is a keyword too, even if it is only a single character. Using this avoids you having to know what the names of the fields in a table are.
ORDER BY	This keyword combination sorts the output from a query using the selected field or fields as the sort keys.
ASC	Adding this keyword to an ORDER BY clause sorts the data in ascending order.
DESC	Adding this keyword to an ORDER BY clause sorts the data in descending order.
use	This keyword, followed by the database name, tells the client interface which database to query.
desc	When used as a stand-alone keyword, and followed by a table name, this keyword
show tables	This keyword combination lists all the tables and views in a database.

CHAPTER 2

Using Multiple Tables When Querying Data

Now that you are at ease with the basics of querying, it is time to extend your SQL knowledge by looking at how to analyze data that is stored across multiple tables. All SQL databases are based on this simple principle: data is broken down into many separate tables that you then link together to deliver the results you are looking for. Indeed, querying data from several tables at once is so fundamental to SQL that you need to learn to master these techniques early in your SQL apprenticeship.

Storing Data in Multiple Tables

At this stage of your venture into the field of data analysis with SQL, you are probably wondering why data can be placed in several tables at once. It can seem peculiar to break data down into all these separate tables and then spend time joining them together again when you want to query the data.

Well, there are several reasons for taking this approach.

First, one of the main objectives of relational databases is to avoid the duplication of data. Put simply, if an element of data (an address, say) appears in two or more tables, then every time it needed to be updated, it would have to be modified in several places. This is complicated—and a big potential source for errors. One classic consequence is that you end up with multiple different addresses and no way of knowing which is the right one. Relational databases try to prevent this from happening by storing independent but homogeneous chunks of data in separate tables *once* only.

Another advantage of this approach is that avoiding duplication makes the data less voluminous. So, the cost of storing the data is reduced—often considerably in these days of explosive data growth.

Yet another reason to create multiple tables is to centralize reference data—like the table of countries you saw in the previous chapter. This is because certain data elements (such as country names) are likely to be reused frequently in multiple tables. In cases like this, it makes sense to store the country name—as well as any frequently used details—in lookup tables. You can then use a short code in one or more tables to refer to repetitive data in another single table. This way the reference data (such as the country name) will always appear the same way in all your analytical reports because it appears only once in the database.

A consequence of this architecture is that database designers often need to add fields that allow tables to be linked, as you will see throughout this chapter. These fields are called *key fields* and may contain numbers or alphanumeric codes. What really matters is that these keys allow data to be mapped across tables so that information can be reconstituted harmoniously and coherently from several tables.

Another (but not the final) reason for storing data in separate tables is that in most cases it allows data to be written to disk (and read from disk) more efficiently. This makes for faster response times. After all, do you want to wait longer than necessary for the answers to their questions?

To get you used to the concept of using multiple tables, this chapter will show you how to

- Join two or more tables.
- Select data from multiple tables.
- Remove duplicates from the output.
- Query *views*, instead of tables. These are, in essence, a way of reusing multiple table joins.

So that is the theory. Now it is time to move on to the practice of the real-world SQL that you will need to master. This chapter teaches you how you can use the links between tables to write more complex and powerful queries. This is an essential step in enabling you to deliver coherent analysis of the source data.

1. Joining Tables

As an initial step on your path to analyzing the data for Prestige Cars Ltd., you want to produce a complete list of every vehicle purchased and the amount paid to purchase it. After looking at the PrestigeCars database, you have found the Stock table that contains the purchase price of every car. However, it does not contain the model—only an internal ID number that means nothing to you. However, you have also found a table called Model, and this table contains the list of all the types of model that the company sells, as well as what appears to be the same ID number used in the Stock table. You can see this represented graphically in Figure 2.1.

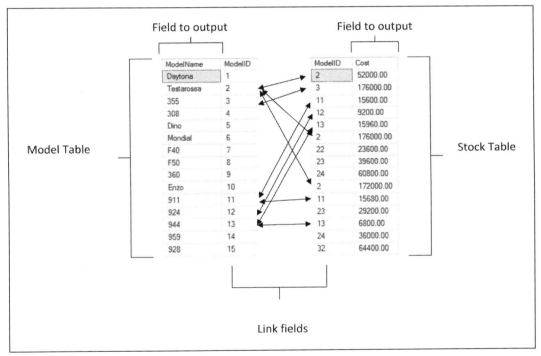

Figure 2.1: *Linking tables*

So, now you need to collate data from both of these tables so that you can see information from both of them in a single query. This will let you see both the model *and* the cost. Here is the SQL that will do exactly this for you:

```
SELECT      ModelName, Cost

FROM        model

JOIN        stock USING(modelID)

ORDER BY    ModelName;
```

Running this query gives the results shown in Figure 2.2 (assuming you have scrolled down the list a few rows).

ModelName	Cost
Arnage	68520.0000
Arnage	79960.0000
Arnage	45440.0000
Boxster	18000.0000
Brooklands	79600.0000
Brooklands	151600.0000
Cambridge	18000.0000
Continental	45560.0000
Continental	62000.0000
Continental	71600.0000
Continental	79600.0000
Corniche	71600.0000
Countach	98800.0000
Countach	2920.0000
Daytona	116000.0000

Figure 2.2: Using a join to output data from two tables

How it Works

The code you just wrote to join two tables is a little "dry" to say the least. It is probably easier to understand what you have just done if it is presented in a more visual way. Figure 2.3 illustrates what joining tables looks like.

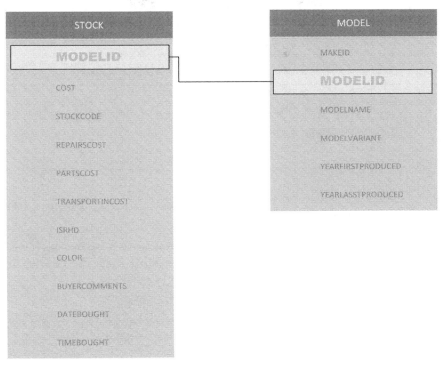

Figure 2.3: Representing table joins visually

Conceptually, joining pairs of tables means knowing which fields can be used to create the "bridge" between the two tables. Once again, this could mean talking to the people who designed the database or delving into any documentation that you may have been given. Sometimes you can easily guess which fields can be used as joins, such as when the two fields have the same name or when the data is clearly the same in both tables. At other times it can be really difficult to guess the join columns just by looking at the tables. For the moment, I will explain how the sample tables are joined each time to avoid you having to guess.

Practically, this code snippet takes three keywords that you already know well (SELECT, FROM, and ORDER BY) and extends the FROM clause with two new keywords: JOIN and USING. These keywords allow you to create links between tables so that you can display columns from both tables at once. Linking (or joining) two tables in SQL consists of the following steps:

First	Enter the name of the first table to join after the FROM keyword.
Second	Add the JOIN keyword after the table name.
Third	Enter the name of the second table to join to the first.
Then	Add the USING keyword and a left parenthesis.
Finally	Enter the name of the field that is the link between the two tables followed by a right parenthesis.

Tricks and Traps

As joining tables is a core concept, you should note these key points from the start:

- This particular join technique will only work when the two tables have a field with the same name in both tables that is used to join the tables. If this is not the case you will need to apply the technique described in the following section.

- The order in which you enter the tables in the FROM clause is unimportant. You could write the FROM clause in this example as follows without altering the result:

```
stock JOIN model
```

- The data in the tables that you are joining is probably not stored in both tables in the same order. However, this is irrelevant to SQL.

Note: I will use *keyword* to describe core SQL elements even when the "keyword" consists of several individual words used together.

2. Joining Tables With Different Link Field Names

Not all databases are designed so that the fields that are used to "link" tables in complex queries have the same name. So MySQL has an alternative technique to join tables when the field names are not the same in both tables. You can see this at work in the following query:

```
SELECT        CountryName

FROM          customer

JOIN          country

              ON customer.Country = country.CountryISO2;
```

This time you will see something like the result shown in Figure 2.4. As this piece of SQL does not contain an ORDER BY clause, you may not see data sorted in exactly the same way in your environment.

CountryName
United Kingdom
United Kingdom
United Kingdom
Germany
France
Switzerland
United Kingdom
France
United States
United Kingdom
United Kingdom
United Kingdom
France
United Kingdom
United Kingdom
France

Figure 2.4: Returning data from joined tables with an ON clause

This technique for joining tables extends the FROM clause with a new keyword: ON. This keyword allow you to create links between tables where the field that is used to join the tables has a different name in each of the two tables. In these circumstances, linking (or joining) two tables in SQL consists of the following steps:

First   Enter the name of the first table to join after the FROM keyword.

Second   Add the JOIN keyword after the table name.

Third   Enter the name of the second table to join.

Then   Add the ON keyword.

Finally   Enter the names of the two fields that are the link between the two tables, separated by the equal (=) sign.

Each of the fields used to link the tables can be preceded by the name of the table that contains the field followed by a period—as we did here. This makes the code easier to understand, especially if you are returning to it weeks or months later.

Tricks and Traps

Joining tables can become quite complex, so there are a few more important points to note:

- You can, if you prefer, apply this technique to join tables when the two tables are joined by a field that has the same name in both tables. If, however, the two fields have the *same* name, then you *must* precede each field name by the table name and a period. This is because MySQL gets confused if there is no way of uniquely identifying the field name—almost as if it doesn't know which field to take from which table to establish the join. Adding the table name and a period allows SQL to trace the field name back to its source table and consequently identify the correct field to use in the join.

- If the two field names in the two tables that you are joining are different, then you can just enter them "as is," separated by an equal sign without adding the table name. However, this will only work if neither of the field names appear anywhere else in the two tables.

  So you could write code like this (even if it is not best practice):

  ```
  ON Country = CountryISO2
  ```

- In practice, it is often best to identify uniquely the fields that are establishing the join by preceding each field with the name of the table it comes from and a period even if the field names are different in the two tables. Once again, this is a little like identifying a person by their last name and first name. In the world of SQL, it avoids confusion by making names uniquely identifiable. In more complex SQL, it allows you to see instantly which field in which table is being linked to which other field in another table. This will help you understand complex queries more easily.

- While taking this "table-period-field" approach in ON clauses is not strictly necessary, I will apply it as a best practice in the SQL examples in this book.

- Equally, the order of the fields in the ON clause is irrelevant; they do not have to be in the same order as the tables in the query.

3. Removing Duplicates from Query Output

As befits a company that sells its products across the globe, the CEO of Prestige Cars needs to know where its presence is felt the most. It follows that she wants you to produce a list of the countries where the company's customers can be found. A quick look at the database reveals a Customer table that contains a Country field—but it contains *only* the ISO two-character code for the country of the client. At first sight this is an issue because you want to display the full name for each country. Then you spot the Country table that contains not only the two-character ISO code but also the full name of the country. So, you are hoping that if you can join these two tables, you should be able to obtain the relevant data.

Fortunately, you are right. Here is the SQL that will produce the list you require:

```
SELECT DISTINCT   CountryName

FROM              customer

JOIN              country

                  ON customer.Country = country.CountryISO2

ORDER BY          CountryName;
```

This query returns the results shown in Figure 2.5.

CountryName
Belgium
France
Germany
Italy
Spain
Switzerland
United Kingdom
United States

Figure 2.5: Joining tables and returning data from one of the tables

How it Works

This query joins the Customer table to the Country table. It maps the Country field in the Customer table to the CountryISO2 field in the Country table. As I mentioned earlier, it really helps to know in practice which fields you can use to join tables. Once the two tables are joined, you can select fields from either of the tables. As all you want to display is the country for a customer, the CountryName field is all you need. SQL in effect goes through the Customer table and looks up the country name for each customer. Then it applies the DISTINCT keyword to remove any duplicates from the list of countries.

Before looking more deeply into the actual code, we need to make a fairly fundamental point about what this query is doing. A join like this one returns data *only when there is a common element in both tables*. In other words, the country reference (the Country field in the Customer table and the CountryISO2 field in the Country table) has to exist in *both* tables for data to be returned from either table. If there is *no corresponding element* in the two tables, then *no data is returned from either table*.

If you need to verify this, then look at the contents of the Country table. You will see that it contains two countries (India and China) that have no corresponding cross-reference in the Customer table. Consequently, these countries do *not* appear in the query output.

Another original aspect of this example is the DISTINCT keyword. This keyword is incredibly useful because it removes all duplicates from the query output before you even see the query results. To make this clearer, try running the same query without the DISTINCT keyword using SQL like this:

```
SELECT       CountryName

FROM         customer

JOIN         country

             ON customer.Country = country.CountryISO2;
```

This time you will see the result shown in Figure 2.6 (although the sort order may be different on your computer).

CountryName
United Kingdom
United Kingdom
United Kingdom
Germany
France
Switzerland
United Kingdom
France
United States
United Kingdom
United Kingdom
United Kingdom
France
United Kingdom
United Kingdom
France

Figure 2.6: *Returning data from a joined table without the DISTINCT keyword*

As you can see from Figure 2.5, the names of many countries appear several times. Without the DISTINCT keyword, you see several country names repeated as there are a good number of customers in the same country—and SQL would show the country for *each customer*, even if you did *not* ask for the customer to be displayed.

This happens because joining tables will cause SQL to return *all* the records that it can from *both* tables. This will happen whatever the fields that are in the SELECT clause, irrespective of which table they come from.

In the query without the DISTINCT keyword, SQL returns all the records from the Customer table (some 88 of them), even if *no* field from the Customer table was requested in the output. This has the effect of duplicating many of the country names because for each customer the query looks up the full country name and displays it in the query result.

Tricks and Traps

With a little practice, joining tables is not difficult. Nonetheless, it can have far-reaching consequences. So, you need to be mindful of the following:

- You may be wondering why you did not just use the Country table directly to produce this list. The reason is that the Country table is essentially a lookup table. It contains a list of country names, but you do not know if it contains all the countries in the world—or only those corresponding to countries where you have customers. So, it is best to use the Customer table as the basis for your query and use the Country table to look up the country name that corresponds to the country code for the actual customers.

- You could, theoretically, not add the table names before the fields in the ON clause. That is, the ON clause could look like this:

```
ON Country = CountryISO2
```

This will work because the field names are unique across the tables used. That is, they are not found more than once in two tables. However, this is far from usual in real-world data analysis, so, as I pointed out in the previous example, I prefer to add the table name to the field in the ON clause as a matter of good practice. This will leave you better prepared to deal with your own data sets.

- In the world of corporate databases, it can sometimes be really hard to find out which fields you need to use to join tables. In practice, nothing will save you quite as much time as acquiring some documentation on the database that you are using for your analysis.

4. Joining Multiple Tables

The CEO firmly believes that effective cost control is vital for the company's survival. So, she wants a list of all the cars that have ever been bought since Prestige Cars started trading. In fact, she wants a list of the purchase cost for every make and model ever held in stock.

This query reflects the fact that most databases consist of many tables. In certain queries you will have to join not just two tables—as you did in the previous section—but several tables at once. SQL lets you extend the technique you saw in the previous example to join multiple tables. As an example, suppose you want to list the cost of every make and model of car sold. However, a quick look at the database makes it clear that while the cost is in the Stock table, this contains only the ID for the model and does not contain the make at all. Equally, the Model table contains only an ID for the make and not the full name of the make—which is in the Make table. So, you need to "chain" all three tables (Stock to Model to Make) to return the data that you want to see.

This is probably easier to understand visually. Figure 2.7 shows you an image of three tables joined together using a different "bridge" field between each pair of tables. This approach allows you to select fields from any or all of the tables.

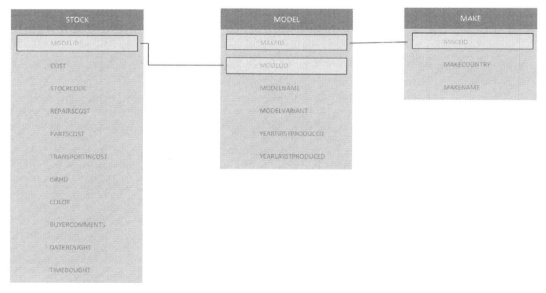

Figure 2.7: Chaining tables

The following piece of SQL shows you how this can be done:

```
SELECT      make.MakeName, Model.modelName, stock.Cost

FROM        stock

JOIN        model USING(ModelID)

JOIN        make USING(MakeID)

ORDER BY    make.MakeName, Model.modelName;
```

Running this query gives the results shown in Figure 2.8.

MakeName	modelName	Cost
Alfa Romeo	1750	2860.0000
Alfa Romeo	1750	7960.0000
Alfa Romeo	Giulia	20000.0000
Alfa Romeo	Giulia	14000.0000
Alfa Romeo	Giulia	5560.0000
Alfa Romeo	Giulia	8400.0000
Alfa Romeo	Giulia	2040.0000
Alfa Romeo	Giulia	10000.0000
Alfa Romeo	Giulia	4800.0000
Alfa Romeo	Giulia	6956.0000
Alfa Romeo	Giulietta	17200.0000
Alfa Romeo	Giulietta	4552.0000
Alfa Romeo	Giulietta	9240.0000
Alfa Romeo	Giulietta	8400.0000
Alfa Romeo	Giulietta	5200.0000
Alfa Romeo	Giulietta	14800.0000

Figure 2.8: *Data output from three tables*

How it Works

The real work done by this code is in the FROM clause. It works like this:

First: The Stock table is joined to the Model table (with the USING keyword and the shared ModelID field to link the two tables).

Second: The Make table is then added—with a second JOIN keyword—and linked to the Model table with the USING keyword and the shared MakeID field.

Finally: Any fields that you want to output are added to the SELECT clause.

The real point of this example is to demonstrate that you can chain together a sequence of virtually any number of tables to analyze data. What is essential is that any two tables share a field (or even several fields) common to both—and that the fields have been designed to be used to join the tables. Each time you want to add another table to the query, you introduce it with the JOIN keyword and then specify which column links it to which column in another table by entering the USING the ON keywords (as well as the relevant shared column or columns) to "bridge" the tables.

Tricks and Traps

Linking multiple tables in this way will take a little practice before it becomes second nature. To help you when using your SQL skills, here are a few practical considerations that you might want to bear in mind:

- You can begin by adding the fields to the SELECT clause *before* you complete the FROM clause, but it is often easier, conceptually, to concentrate on working out which tables need to be joined (and to join them) before adding the fields that you want to see in the output.

- You do not *always* have to indicate the table from which a field is drawn before the field name, as we have done here in specifying `Make.MakeName`, for instance. However, you can *only* use the field name on its own (without the table name to precede it) if the field name exists *only once* in *all* the selected tables. If there are several fields with the same name in the tables you are joining, MySQL will not know which field to use and will send back an error message rather than the result that you were expecting. So, once again, preceding each field name with the table name and a period is best practice when writing SQL.

- In this example, we are selecting a single field from each of the three tables that you have joined. In reality, you can select *any* of the fields from *any* of the joined tables—or even *all* the fields from all of the tables.

- You can use the keyword combination INNER JOIN instead of using JOIN if you prefer. The result will be the same. This keyword helps you (or another developer) to understand that this is a restrictive join that will only return data from records that contain the "link" field in both tables. We will continue, nonetheless, to use only the JOIN keyword to differentiate basic joins from the other join types that you will encounter throughout the course of this book.

5. Using Table Aliases

Analysis is often all about detail. So, it does not come as a surprise when the CEO comes to your desk and requests a list of all vehicles sold along with the selling price and any discounts that have been applied. To keep the CEO happy, you need to know that the PrestigeCars database contains two fairly essential tables called Sales and SalesDetails. These correspond roughly to an invoice header and the individual line items that make up a sale. These two tables contain all the information that you need to look at itemized sales. Let's suppose you need to analyze the discounts that have been applied to make the sales and see how they vary per car sold.

As an example, take a look at the following code snippet:

```
SELECT      S.InvoiceNumber, D.LineItemNumber, D.SalePrice

            ,D.LineItemDiscount

FROM        sales AS S

JOIN        salesdetails AS D USING (SalesID)

ORDER BY    S.InvoiceNumber, D.LineItemNumber;
```

Execute this query, and you should see the output in Figure 2.9. Be aware, however, that Figure 2.8 shows only the first few records and that you will have to scroll down the result set to see all the records returned by this query.

InvoiceNumber	LineItemNumber	SalePrice	LineItemDiscount
EURBE074	1	125000.00	1500.00
EURBE125	1	12500.00	750.00
EURBE132	1	86500.00	1250.00
EURBE171	1	3950.00	750.00
EURBE171	2	29500.00	750.00
EURBE171	3	12500.00	NULL
EURBE193	1	23500.00	NULL
EURBE193	2	10500.00	NULL
EURBE218	1	950.00	25.00
EURBE264	1	6950.00	NULL
EURDE004	1	11500.00	NULL
EURDE036	1	65890.00	750.00
EURDE036	2	6000.00	NULL
EURDE043	1	99500.00	500.00
EURDE066	1	61500.00	NULL
EURDE071	1	19500.00	NULL

Figure 2.9: Using aliases when joining tables

How it Works

This query joins the Sales and SalesDetails tables on the shared SalesID field. Then it outputs any required fields and sorts them by invoice number, followed by line number (this can be useful in cases where an invoice has more than one line item).

In the previous examples in this chapter, you saw that we added the table name to some field names when we built anything but the simplest query. Now, while this is not difficult, it can soon become extremely laborious because it can mean repeating the table name several times in different parts of the query. Fortunately, there is a way to make your coding easier, even if it has no effect on the final result.

The trick is to use *aliases* for tables—a bit like when you aliased field names in the previous chapter.

First: Add a space after the table name.

Then: Add the **AS** keyword.

Finally: Enter a short acronym that you will use instead of the table name elsewhere in the query.

Adding an alias to a table is used not to display the alias but to make the code more comprehensible. This is achieved by rendering the SQL less voluminous and consequently easier to understand.

In this example, the Sales table was given the alias S, and the SalesDetails table was given the alias D. Once you have aliased the tables, you use the alias instead of the table name everywhere in the code where you would otherwise have used the full table name. In other words, Aliases are applied in the FROM clause and then used everywhere else in the query where you would otherwise use the table name.

The alias is used in the same way as the table name would be used. So, when you have duplicate field names in separate tables, you can use the alias to distinguish them, rather than having to write out the full name of the table. This is particularly effective in the ON clause, which is consequently much shorter and easier to read.

Tricks and Traps

Table aliases, too, have their idiosyncrasies, so you need to be aware of the following:

- Once you have added an alias, you *have* to use it instead of the table name. That is, you *cannot* use the table name elsewhere in the query—in the SELECT or ON clauses, for instance. Once you have created an alias, you are stuck with it—in the current query at least.

- An alias can be as short as you like. A single character will suffice.

- You should not alias the field specified in a USING clause.

- An alias can be as long as you like (well, 256 characters anyway). However, the main aim of an alias is to make your life easier, so I suggest making aliases as short as possible while trying to balance this with the need for them to be comprehensible as well.

- It can help to try to make aliases memorable. This will help you understand which alias refers to which table when you write SQL queries—and when you revisit them many months later. As you can see in this example, I have tried to use short aliases that remind you of the table name.

- Conversely, while it is easier to alias tables using codes such as T1, T2, and so on, this can make the SQL much harder to understand.

- The AS keyword is optional when aliasing tables. You can simply add the table alias after the table name—and a space to separate the two—if you prefer. I will, nonetheless, stick to the practice of introducing aliases with the AS keyword in this book.

- If you need to visualize the joins between the tables, then you can always jump ahead to Figure 2.10 where you can see the core tables of the PrestigeCars database and how they are connected.

- Aliases can be applied to views exactly as they can be applied to tables.

6. Joining Many Tables

Ideally you are getting to know the PrestigeCars database better. To test your abilities, suppose you want to look at *all* the important fields from the database in a single query. Specifically, let's imagine you want to produce a list of cars sold that includes all vehicle data as well as all the essential customer data. This means joining virtually all the core tables in a single query. This SQL is quite voluminous compared to the code snippets you have been writing so far, but it is a practical example of the sort of code that you could be producing when analyzing your own data.

```
SELECT      CY.CountryName

            ,MK.MakeName

            ,MD.modelName

            ,ST.Cost

            ,ST.RepairsCost
```

```
              ,ST.PartsCost

              ,ST.TransportInCost

              ,ST.Color

              ,SD.SalePrice

              ,SD.LineItemDiscount

              ,SA.InvoiceNumber

              ,SA.SaleDate

              ,CS.CustomerName

FROM          stock ST

JOIN          model MD USING (modelID)

JOIN          make MK   USING (MakeID)

JOIN          salesdetails SD

              ON ST.StockCode = SD.StockID

JOIN          sales SA   USING (SalesID)

JOIN          customer CS   USING (CustomerID)

JOIN          country CY

              ON CS.country = CY.CountryISO2

ORDER BY      CY.CountryName

              ,MK.MakeName

              ,MD.ModelName;
```

If you run this query, you should see the output in Figure 2.10 (well, you will see all of it in MySQL Workbench; in this screenshot, the output has been truncated).

CountryName	MakeName	ModelName	Cost	RepairsCost	PartsCost	TransportInCost	Color	SalePrice	LineItemDiscount	InvoiceNumber	SaleDate	CustomerName
Belgium	Alfa Romeo	Giulia	8400.0000	500.0000	750.0000	150.0000	Black	10500.00	NULL	EURBE193	2017-11-06 21:36:00	Stefan Van Helsing
Belgium	Alfa Romeo	Spider	10000.0000	500.0000	750.0000	150.0000	Black	12500.00	NULL	EURBE171	2017-07-01 10:25:00	Stefan Van Helsing
Belgium	Aston Martin	Rapide	69200.0000	2000.0000	1500.0000	750.0000	Silver	86500.00	1250.00	EURBE132	2017-03-12 17:06:00	Diplomatic Cars
Belgium	Aston Martin	Vantage	100000.0000	500.0000	2200.0000	750.0000	Green	125000.00	1500.00	EURBE074	2016-08-23 00:00:00	Diplomatic Cars
Belgium	Noble	M600	23600.0000	1360.0000	750.0000	150.0000	Black	29500.00	750.00	EURBE171	2017-07-01 10:25:00	Stefan Van Helsing
Belgium	Peugeot	205	760.0000	500.0000	750.0000	150.0000	British Racing Green	950.00	25.00	EURBE218	2018-01-10 00:00:00	Stefan Van Helsing
Belgium	Peugeot	205	3160.0000	500.0000	750.0000	150.0000	Black	3950.00	750.00	EURBE171	2017-07-01 10:25:00	Stefan Van Helsing
Belgium	Triumph	Roadster	18800.0000	1360.0000	500.0000	150.0000	Black	23500.00	NULL	EURBE193	2017-11-06 21:36:00	Flash Voitures
Belgium	Triumph	TR4	5560.0000	500.0000	457.0000	150.0000	Red	6950.00	NULL	EURBE264	2018-06-03 00:00:00	Flash Voitures
Belgium	Triumph	TR6	10000.0000	500.0000	750.0000	150.0000	Red	12500.00	750.00	EURBE125	2017-02-12 16:02:00	Diplomatic Cars
France	Alfa Romeo	1750	7960.0000	500.0000	750.0000	150.0000	Blue	9950.00	NULL	EURFR241	2018-04-15 00:00:00	Vive La Vitesse
France	Alfa Romeo	Giulia	2040.0000	500.0000	750.0000	150.0000	British Racing Green	2550.00	50.00	EURFR031	2016-01-07 00:00:00	M. Pierre Dubois
France	Alfa Romeo	Spider	9200.0000	500.0000	150.0000	150.0000	Blue	11500.00	750.00	EURFR194	2017-11-12 11:37:00	Mme Anne Duport
France	Aston Martin	DB4	29200.0000	500.0000	500.0000	550.0000	Black	36500.00	NULL	EURFR160	2017-05-26 10:20:00	Laurent Saint Yves
France	Aston Martin	DB5	55600.0000	2000.0000	457.0000	750.0000	Blue	69500.00	NULL	EURFR304	2018-10-02 00:00:00	Jacques Mitterand
France	Aston Martin	DB6	36400.0000	500.0000	750.0000	550.0000	Red	45500.00	NULL	EURFR051	2016-06-15 00:00:00	Vive La Vitesse
France	Aston Martin	DB6	39664.0000	660.0000	500.0000	550.0000	Black	49580.00	NULL	EURFR047	2016-05-30 00:00:00	SuperSport S.A.R.L.
France	Aston Martin	DB6	44800.0000	1785.0000	500.0000	550.0000	Canary Yellow	56000.00	NULL	EURFR018	2015-07-25 00:00:00	SuperSport S.A.R.L.

Figure 2.10: Outputting all the key data from the database

How it Works

This query joins the Stock, Model, Make, SalesDetails, Sales, Customer, and Country tables. Then a list of fields from all the tables is added to the SELECT clause to return a list of detailed sales data from all the selected tables. It aliases each table to avoid repeating table names and also sorts the data by country, make, and model (in that order of precedence).

Tricks and Traps

Writing complex table joins comes with its own set of rules and constraints. They include the following:

- These seven tables make up the core Prestige Cars data set. You will occasionally use other tables in the queries in this book. However, the key data is contained in the tables that you joined in the query in this section.

- The order in which the tables are added to the FROM clause is unimportant. The only thing that matters is that each time a new table is added, you join it to a table that is already present in the list and correctly joined in the ON clause.

- The way we have written the fields in the SELECT clause is purely a formatting choice because I find that this makes the fields easier to handle in voluminous queries. You could just as easily run all the field names together on a single line if you prefer.

- I chose not to output the key fields (those that are used to link tables together) as they are largely meaningless from an analytical perspective because they are essentially codes for "internal" use only that have been created by the database designer to allow tables to be joined. You could extend the query to add them if you want.

- You can extend a query up to hundreds of fields in queries like this. Although I suspect that you won't need more than a dozen or so columns in the output, this is another way of saying that there are few practical limits to the number of fields that you can return from a query.

7. Visualizing Databases

Even after years of practice it is extremely difficult to visualize a database based on a piece of SQL. In databases—as in so many areas—a picture is worth a thousand words. Consequently, database designers have become proficient at creating drawings of how database tables can be combined to make up a database model.

These images of databases are called *entity-relationship diagrams* (or ERDs in "geek-speak"). They outline in a lucid and visual way these two key elements that make up a database:

- The tables that contain the data (known as *entities*)
- The joins that link these tables (known as *relationships*)

This is, inevitably, only a high-level definition of what an ERD is. Indeed, a complete ERD can contain much more information about a database than this. However, this definition is enough to get you started for the moment.

Now that you have the theory, it is time for a practical application. So, in Figure 2.11, you can see the ERD for the core tables in the PrestigeCars database.

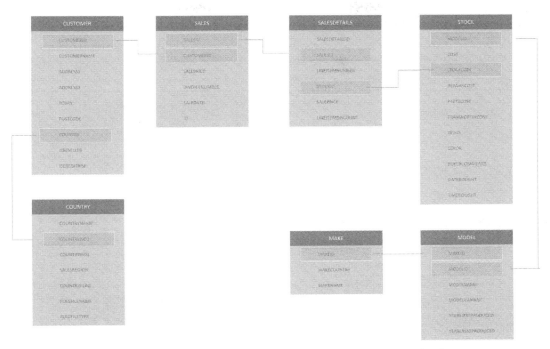

Figure 2.11: The ERD for the core tables in the PrestigeCars database

If ever you are unsure of how the tables used in the SQL samples in this book join together, you can flip back to this diagram to get a better idea of how the tables relate one to another. You can also use this image as a visual representation of the code you saw in the previous section to join all the core tables in the PrestigeCars database.

8. Using Views to Memorize Complex Table Joins

The code that you saw in section 2.6 was both long and complicated. Yet you could need to reuse complex code like this frequently. As it could become very wearing to rewrite or copy and paste intricate code like this time and again, MySQL has a solution that can make your life easier.

One solution that database developers apply is to memorize SELECT queries even, or indeed especially, if the queries contain multiple joins. This technique is called creating *views*. The outcome is that, instead of using multiple table names and complex joins, you simply use the view name in the FROM clause of the query.

The PrestigeCars database contains a view called SalesByCountry that contains all the tables you joined in section 6. So, if you wanted to use this view in the place of the seven tables and all the joins you used previously, the SQL would read as follows:

```
SELECT      CountryName
            ,MakeName
            ,modelName
            ,Cost
            ,RepairsCost
            ,PartsCost
            ,TransportInCost
            ,Color
            ,SalePrice
            ,LineItemDiscount
            ,InvoiceNumber
            ,SaleDate
            ,CustomerName
FROM        salesbycountry
ORDER BY    CountryName
            ,MakeName
            ,ModelName;
```

You will probably agree that this is a much simpler way of working. This is why, for the moment, I only wanted to explain what views are and how you can use them instead of tables in certain circumstances.

For the moment, the important point to remember is that a view can be used in a SQL query just like a table can. A view is a way of remembering how the joins were set up to deliver analysis from multiple tables at once.

Note: You need to be careful when using views instead of tables in SQL queries. This is because often you will often want to display only a *subset* of data. So, be careful that using a view does not mean you are filtering out essential data from a query without meaning to do so.

Conclusion

This chapter explained how you can use the multiple tables that you will probably find in most databases as the basis for your analytics.

You saw how to join tables using a shared field to look at data in one or both the tables that you queried. Then you saw how to extend this approach to join several tables and pick out any fields that interested you in the tables you joined. You also learned how to remove duplicates from a result set.

Although this chapter introduced you to the concept of table joins, it has not explained all that you will ever need to know to join tables in MySQL. There is more still to learn on this subject, and you will see more on this in the following chapter.

Core Knowledge Learned in This Chapter

The following are the keywords you learned in this chapter:

Concept	Description
Joins	This is the technique used to link tables so that you can return data from multiple tables coherently.
Intermediate tables	These are tables that are used in joins but do not send any data back to the query.
INNER JOIN	This keyword lets you add another table to a query.
ON	This keyword allows you to tell SQL how two tables are to be joined and, more specifically, which fields provide the link between the two tables
AS	Just as you can alias fields, you can alias tables with the AS keyword.
DISTINCT	This keyword removes duplicate records from a result set.

CHAPTER 3

Using Advanced Table Joins

Joining tables to produce the data you want to see is key to creating the analyses that drive your business. In this chapter, you will build on the knowledge that you acquired in the previous chapter and further develop your SQL skills so that you can create more complex and powerful queries. This means learning further variations of the JOIN clause to help you shape the data that is output from the SQL queries that you write.

The Many Types of Table Joins

In this chapter, you will learn to create the following:

- Outer joins that let you return all the data from one table and only some of the data in a second table that you join to it

- Intermediate joins where you join multiple tables in a query, but not all the tables are used as data sources

- Joins on multiple fields

- Joins on data ranges when you need to map a value in one table to a range of values in another table

- Self-joins where you join a table to itself to display hierarchical data

- Cross joins that allow you to return all the data from both tables in a join

I realize that these concepts may seem more than a little abstract when you read about them for the first time. But don't worry, you will see how all these ideas have a thoroughly practical application to SQL queries and can be used in your day-to-day data analysis. Indeed, applying these more advanced techniques is often the only way to obtain clear and accurate results from your SQL queries.

1. Using Left Joins to Return All the Data in One Table but Not from the Other Table

The IT director is convinced that the PrestigeCars database needs some polishing. He is certain that there are makes of vehicles stored in the Make table for which there are no corresponding models. Rather than manually looking through all the MakeIDs in the Make table and comparing them with the MakeIDs in the Model table, you write the following piece of code to use MySQL to find the missing values:

```
SELECT DISTINCT    MK.MakeName, MD.ModelName

FROM               make MK LEFT JOIN model MD USING(MakeID);
```

Running this query gives the result shown in Figure 3.1. You will need to scroll down the output to see all the data. Once again, as this query has no ORDER BY clause, the results that you see might not match the output in Figure 3.1 exactly. However, the NULL fields should, nonetheless, be at the bottom of the output.

MakeName	ModelName
Morgan	Plus 4
Morgan	Supersport
Noble	M14
Noble	M600
Triumph	TR4
Triumph	TR5
Triumph	TR6
Triumph	TR7
Triumph	GT6
Triumph	Roadster
Triumph	Stag
Triumph	TR3A
Trabant	500
Trabant	600
Peugeot	205
Peugeot	Type VA
Peugeot	404
Peugeot	203
Reliant	Robin
Riley	NULL
Cadillac	NULL

No Model

Figure 3.1: *The results of a query using a LEFT JOIN*

How it Works

This piece of SQL solves what at first sight appears to be a conundrum. How do you join two tables and show missing data given that joins only show data that is present in both tables?

The answer is to use a different type of join. This query did not use the JOIN keyword that you learned to apply in the previous chapter. Instead, you used the LEFT JOIN keyword to join the tables. This keyword will return *all* the records from one of the tables (the first table in the join) but *only* matching records from the second table. This lets you visualize any missing information across the two tables.

More precisely, the query is constructed like this:

First: Create a SELECT clause that returns the MakeName and ModelName fields. To make the results easier to read, you add the DISTINCT keyword to remove duplicates from the query result.

Second: Add a FROM clause and enter the table name from which you want to return *all* the data, the Make table in this example.

Third: Enter the LEFT JOIN keyword. This tells MySQL that you want to return all data from the first table (the Make table, the one to the left of the LEFT JOIN keyword).

Fourth: Add the second table from which you want to return information. This table will only return records where the join field contains identical values in the two tables.

Finally: Add a USING or an ON clause and specify which fields are used to "link" the two tables.

This query still joins the two tables on a specified field. However, *all the contents from the Make table are returned*, whether or not there are corresponding MakeIDs in the Model table.

To appreciate exactly what has happened here, you need to remind yourself that the join queries that you learned to use in the previous chapter returned data from tables that you joined *only* if there were corresponding values in the fields that were used in the USING or ON clause of the query in both tables. If this was not the case, then *no* records were returned from *either* table.

If you want to reassure yourself that this query really returns different results with a "simple" join, then try running the following code snippet:

```
SELECT DISTINCT    MK.MakeName, MD.ModelName

FROM               make MK

JOIN               model MD USING (MakeID)
```

I will not show the results here, but if you scroll down through the output, you will see that two makes are now "missing" from the result. These are Cadillac and Riley. This means that there are no NULL model names in this query output.

As this is a new and fairly powerful concept, let's imagine it in a more schematic way. Figure 3.2 shows you how a LEFT JOIN works.

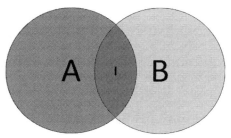

Figure 3.2: The concept of a LEFT JOIN

In this image:

- Circle A represents the table on the *left* of the LEFT JOIN keyword (the Make table in the code used previously). All data in this table (unless it is restricted in other ways that you will learn later in this book) is returned by the query.

- Circle B represents the table on the *right* of the LEFT JOIN keyword (the Model table in the code used previously). Only records that share values in the join fields provided in the ON or USING clause will be returned.

- I represents the data returned from table on the right of the join.

The result of using a LEFT JOIN is that *all* the data from the selected fields in table A is returned in the query output, but *only the matching records* from table B (shown as I in the image) are returned. Any records from table B where there is no corresponding data in the JOIN field are *not* present in the query result.

Tricks and Traps

I have a few comments to make about left joins.

- This kind of join that does not restrict the data returned from one table in a query is known as an *outer* join.

- We used table aliases when writing this SQL because this approach makes the code easier to understand. This is not strictly necessary but does help you to write shorter code than if you had used full table names.

- You can write LEFT OUTER JOIN instead of LEFT JOIN if you prefer. Indeed, you may see this in code that you inherit or in examples from other sources. The result is strictly the same. However, I prefer to use the "shorter" approach in this book and will always show you these kinds of queries written as LEFT JOIN because this is easier to write (and read) and you are nonetheless choosing *not* to restrict data in the output rather than aiming for a smaller result set.

- When actually writing LEFT JOINs, you may choose to adopt a style that places the first table *above* the second table (much as is the case with many of the query examples in this book). However, this still means that the first table (the one preceded by the FROM clause) is considered the *left*-hand table in the join.

- If there is no data in the table on the right of a left join, the data from the left-hand table will still be returned, even if nothing is returned from the right-hand table.

- If you are unsure whether applying an inner join or a left join will affect the result, then I suggest you run each type of query in turn and look at the number of records produced in each case.

2. Right Joins to Return All the Data in One Table but Not from the Other

There are several types of outer join in SQL. Fortunately, they all follow a similar principle. That is, the LEFT or RIGHT keywords (with, optionally the OUTER keyword as well) tell you that **all the data from one or more tables** will be returned by a query.

To show this, try running the following piece of SQL:

```
SELECT DISTINCT    MK.MakeName, MD.ModelName

FROM               model MD

RIGHT JOIN         make MK USING (MakeID);
```

I will not give the results of this query here because they are identical to those returned by the previous query. So, you can see the output in Figure 3.1.

How it Works

This query uses the Model table in the FROM clause and the Make table in the RIGHT JOIN. This means that the table order is now reversed compared to the previous query. However, using a right outer join tells MySQL to take all the data from the table on the *right* of the JOIN clause and only use the data from the tables on the *left* of the JOIN where there are matching values in both tables for the field used on the ON or USING clause.

You need to look closely at the FROM clause, however. This only works because the order of the two tables has been reversed compared to the previous query.

A right join is a mirror image of the left outer join that you saw previously. This applies the same principles to a join, in that it ensures that all the records on one "side" of a JOIN keyword (the right table) are returned by the query, but *only* matching records from the table on the *left* of the join.

To get a more visual idea of this, take a look at Figure 3.3.

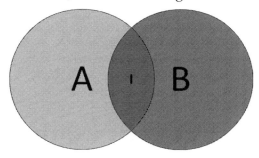

Figure 3.3: *The concept of a RIGHT JOIN*

This figure illustrates how a RIGHT JOIN takes all the data from the right-hand table and only records that share values in the "link" field from the left-hand table.

In this image:

- Circle A represents the table on the left of the RIGHT JOIN keyword (the Model table in the code used previously). Only records that share values in the join fields provided in the ON clause will be returned.
- Circle B represents the table on the right of the RIGHT JOIN keyword (the Make table in the code used previously). All data in this table (unless it is restricted in other ways that you will learn later in this book) is returned by the query.
- I represents the data returned from table A.

Finally, the choice between a RIGHT JOIN and a LEFT JOIN simply depends on the order in which you place the tables in the SQL you write.

Tricks and Traps

I have only a few comments to make about right outer joins.

- A RIGHT JOIN is a mirror image of a left join. Essentially it depends on which table you place before the LEFT or RIGHT JOIN keywords and which table you place after these keywords.

- You can write the SQL to place each table in a join on the same lines as the JOIN keywords or on separate lines; it is all the same to SQL.

- You can also use the keyword RIGHT OUTER JOIN if you prefer to achieve the same result.

3. Intermediate Table Joins

When you are analyzing data, there will almost certainly be times when you will need to join tables but *not use any data from them*. As an example, perhaps you want to look at the sales made in each separate country. Looking at the tables in the PrestigeCars database, you have discovered that the sales figures are in the Sales table, and the country names are in the Country table. However, these two tables have no common fields and so cannot be joined one to the other. However, these two tables both connect to the Customer table.

If this seems a little strange, then take a look at Figure 3.4.

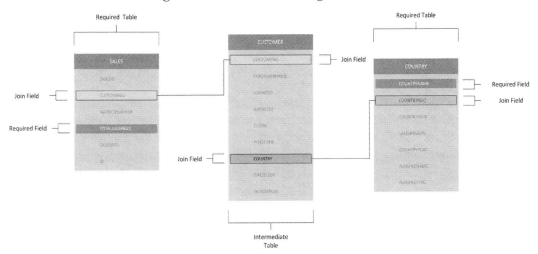

Figure 3.4: *Joining tables using an intermediate table*

So, you *can* join the Sales and Country tables if you add the Customer table as an intermediate (or link) table. The following SQL allows you to join these three tables:

```
SELECT     CO.CountryName, SA.TotalSalePrice

FROM       sales SA

JOIN       customer CS USING (CustomerID)

JOIN       country CO

           ON CS.Country = CO.CountryISO2

ORDER BY   CO.CountryName;
```

If you run this query, you should see the output in Figure 3.5.

CountryName	TotalSalePrice
Belgium	125000.00
Belgium	12500.00
Belgium	86500.00
Belgium	45950.00
Belgium	34000.00
Belgium	950.00
Belgium	6950.00
France	19900.00
France	66500.00
France	55600.00
France	59000.00
France	19600.00
France	8950.00
France	2550.00
France	5500.00
France	3575.00

Figure 3.5: The output when using intermediate tables to return data

How it Works

This query returns the country from the table on the right in the JOIN clause (the Country table) and the sales figure from the table on the left (the Sales table) but nothing at all from the middle table (the Customer table). Yet without the Customer table to provide the "bridge" between the two tables, it would not have been possible to link the two tables, which would have made it impossible to produce this data.

You can see that in the case of the Country table. The key field is *text*, not a numeric field, unlike the previous examples. This is perfectly normal in many databases. All that matters is that the database design allows you to specify the columns that join the tables.

Note: This query shows the full detail of each sale. You may want to see the aggregate result of all sales per country. This kind of query is explained in Chapter 7.

4. Using Multiple Fields in Joins

Not all tables can be successfully joined using a single field. Sometimes you may find that you need to use two or more fields to join two tables.

As an example of this, let's suppose that the marketing director of Prestige Cars has just spent a large amount of money on some external data about clients. You need to join this new table called MarketingInformation to the existing Customer table. However, this new table does not have a customer ID, only the customer name and country. Fortunately, as there are also customer name and country fields in the Customer table, SQL can join these tables on multiple fields, as the following SQL snippet shows:

```
SELECT      CS.CustomerName, MI.SpendCapacity

FROM        customer CS

JOIN        marketinginformation MI

            ON CS.CustomerName = MI.Cust

            AND CS.Country = MI.Country

ORDER BY    CS.CustomerName;
```

If you run this code, you will see the output shown in Figure 3.6.

CustomerName	SpendCapacity
Alex McWhirter	None
Alexei Tolstoi	Some
Alicia Almodovar	Some
Andrea Tarbuck	Some
Andy Cheshire	Lots
Antonio Maura	Immense
Autos Sportivos	Some
Beltway Prestige Driving	None
Birmingham Executive Prestige Vehicles	None
Bling Bling S.A.	None
Bling Motors	Immense
Boris Spry	Immense
Bravissima!	Immense
Capots Reluisants S.A.	Immense
Casseroles Chromes	Lots
Clubbing Cars	None

Figure 3.6: Output from a multiple field join

How it Works

In this example, you created a table join just as you did previously. However, once you have specified the first field you will be using to join the two tables, you extended the join by doing the following:

First: You added the AND keyword.

Second: You specified the second field from one of the tables that you need in the join.

Third: You entered the equal (=) sign.

Finally: You specified the second field from the other table that you need in the join.

You can imagine this kind of join more easily, perhaps, if you see it displayed graphically. Figure 3.7 illustrates a join using multiple fields.

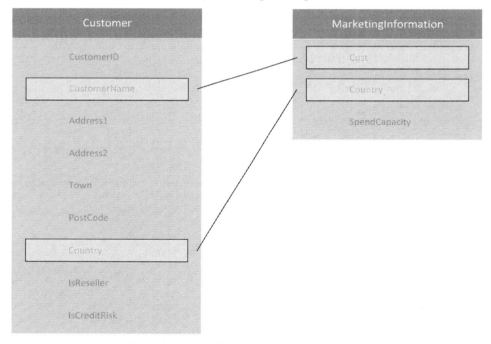

Figure 3.7: *A table join using multiple fields*

The reason for using multiple fields to join tables is that, sometimes, the data in a single column might not be sufficient to identify a record uniquely. Imagine that you are selling cars to a client with multiple sites in several countries. If each site has the same company name, the firm could exist several times in the table (the MarketingInformation table in this example). So, you need a further piece of information in the data that lets you *uniquely* identify each record. In this example, it is the Country field. The end result is that the *combination* of the elements in the fields used in the join defines a record without any risk of duplicate records being found.

Tricks and Traps

I have only a couple of comments to make here.

- You can extend this principle to join on three or more fields simply by introducing each pair of join fields with the AND keyword in the FROM clause of the SQL.

- If all the fields used to join the tables are identical in both tables you can apply the USING technique to link the tables. To take a hypothetical example, this would mean code like the following snippet:

```
Table1 JOIN Table2 USING (Field1, Field2)
```

- When more than one field is required to identify a record uniquely these fields make up a *composite key*.

5. Joining a Table to Itself

The CEO has requested a quick list of staff so that she can produce an organization chart for the next board meeting. She has even reminded you that there is a table in the database (the Staff table) that contains all the staff and their managers. You can see this in Figure 3.8.

StaffID	StaffName	ManagerID	Department
1	Amelia	NULL	NULL
2	Gerard	1	Finance
3	Chloe	1	Marketing
4	Susan	1	Sales
5	Andy	4	Sales
6	Steve	4	Sales
7	Stan	4	Sales
8	Nathan	4	Sales
9	Maggie	4	Sales
10	Jenny	2	Finance
11	Chris	2	Finance
12	Megan	3	Marketing

Figure 3.8: The Staff table

Using this table (whose existence you had forgotten about), you produce the following SQL to show which staff member reports to which manager:

```
SELECT        ST1.StaffName, ST1.Department, ST2.StaffName

              AS ManagerName

FROM          staff ST1

JOIN          staff ST2

              ON ST1.ManagerID = ST2.StaffID

ORDER BY      ST1.Department, ST1.StaffName;
```

Running this short piece of code gives the result shown in Figure 3.9.

StaffName	Department	ManagerName
Chris	Finance	Gerard
Gerard	Finance	Amelia
Jenny	Finance	Gerard
Sandy	Finance	Chris
Chloe	Marketing	Amelia
Megan	Marketing	Chloe
Andy	Sales	Susan
Maggie	Sales	Susan
Nathan	Sales	Susan
Stan	Sales	Susan
Steve	Sales	Susan
Susan	Sales	Amelia

Figure 3.9: *Joining the Staff table to itself to display manager names*

How it Works

The Staff table contains a field that contains the manager for each staff member. Unfortunately, however, this reference is in the form of the staff ID number of the manager and not the manager's actual name. So, you can use the data in the table twice (once to get the staff member's name and once to return their manager's name). However, this means using the table *twice* in the FROM clause of the SQL.

Then the SQL joins the table to itself. This is what allows the manager ID to be used to refer to the manager name using the second application of the table. It works like this:

First: You select the staff member's name from the Staff table. This is the standard and perfectly usual way of querying a table like this.

Second: You add the staff table a second time to the query with a JOIN. Each of the references to the Staff table uses a *different alias* (ST1 and ST2) so the SQL can differentiate between the two.

Third: You add an ON clause that tells the SQL that the StaffID field from the first reference to the Staff table (ST1) is linked to the ManagerID field in the second reference to the Staff table (ST2).

Finally: You use one of the table aliases in the SELECT clause for every field reference. This allows the SQL to know whether you are referring to *staff* details (those in the first table referenced as ST1) or to the *manager* details (those in the second table referenced as ST2). You also alias any fields that are used more than once.

This kind of table join is also called a *self-join*. You can see this more graphically in Figure 3.10.

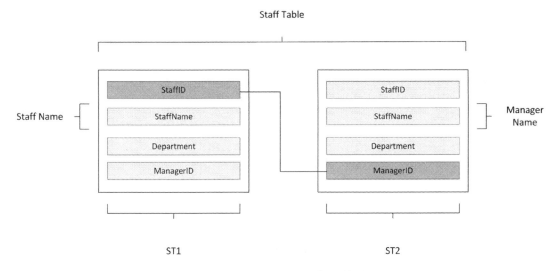

Figure 3.10: *Anatomy of a self-join*

Tricks and Traps

You need to be aware of the following key points when joining a table to itself:

- Be sure that you alias the two table references in the FROM clause so that you understand that you are using the information in the table *twice* to display *different elements* from the table. This means using a *different alias* each time that the same table is used in the join.

- It is vital to alias the fields that you use in the output that are used twice such as the StaffName field in this example. Otherwise, you will not know which piece of information is which.

- This approach is also known as a "Hierarchical Join".

6. Joining Tables on Ranges of Values

There are an infinite number of ways to store data, and you will probably encounter the need to analyze data in multiple tables where you cannot simply join one field in one table to another field in another table. An example of this is the SalesCategory table in the PrestigeCars database. This small table contains a company-specific set of reference information that allows the sales manager to categorize each car sold according to the sale price.

Now the sales manager wants you to use the data in the SalesCategory table to output the specific sales category of each vehicle sold. So, to begin with, you take a look at the table. You can see the data it contains in Figure 3.11.

LowerThreshold	UpperThreshold	CategoryDescription
10000	25000	Very Low
25001	50000	Low
50001	75000	Medium
75001	100000	High
100001	150000	Very High
150001	250000	Exceptional

Value
Thresholds

Figure 3.11: The SalesCategory table

The first thing you notice is that this table does not contain a unique value in a single column that you can link to a single value (the sale price) in another table. So, you need to find a way to map the *range* of values that are stored in two columns in the SalesCategory table to the SalePrice field in the SalesDetails table.

The following SQL shows you how this can be done:

```
SELECT
 MK.MakeName
,MD.ModelName
,SD.SalePrice
,CAT.CategoryDescription
FROM        stock ST
JOIN        model MD USING (ModelID)
JOIN        make MK  USING (MakeID)
JOIN        salesdetails SD
            ON ST.StockCode = SD.StockID
JOIN        salescategory CAT
            ON SD.SalePrice BETWEEN
                        CAT.LowerThreshold
                        AND CAT.UpperThreshold
ORDER BY    MK.MakeName, MD.ModelName;
```

Running this piece of SQL gives the result shown in Figure 3.12 (you will have to scroll down the output a little).

MakeName	ModelName	SalePrice	CategoryDescription
Bentley	Mulsanne	99500.00	High
BMW	Alpina	21500.00	Very Low
BMW	E30	33500.00	Low
Bugatti	Veyron	220500.00	Exceptional
Citroen	Torpedo	65890.00	Medium
Citroen	Traction Avant	25000.00	Very Low
Delahaye	135	25500.00	Low
Delahaye	145	29500.00	Low
Delahaye	145	39500.00	Low
Delahaye	175	12500.00	Very Low
Delorean	DMC 12	99500.00	High
Ferrari	355	205000.00	Exceptional
Ferrari	355	220000.00	Exceptional
Ferrari	355	125950.00	Very High
Ferrari	355	156500.00	Exceptional
Ferrari	355	155000.00	Exceptional

Figure 3.12: Joining tables on a range of values

How it Works

This query starts by joining the SalesDetails, Stock, Make, and Model tables using the techniques you have explored so far in this chapter and the previous one. You need to link these four tables so that you can return the following information:

Make name	From the Make table
Model name	From the Model table
Sale price	From the SalesDetails table

You are not actually returning any data from the Stock table. However, you need this table to act as a "link" table so that you can join the Model table to the SalesDetails table.

Once you have this core query in place, you can extend it by looking up the CategoryDescription value from the SalesCategory table. This is where you need to use the SalePrice field in the SalesDetails table and see into which category of the SalesCategory table each car falls.

This operation is carried out in the four lines of SQL in the query shown in bold. This join says, "Use the SalePrice field and compare it to the two fields (UpperThreshold and LowerThreshold) in the SalesCategory table—if the SalePrice field is between the upper threshold value and the lower threshold value, then join the tables."

This "range join" introduces a new keyword combination. This is the BETWEEN… AND operator. This keyword combination can be used to look up a value between a lower threshold and an upper threshold.

First:	Add the table to the FROM clause of the SQL query.
Second:	Add the ON keyword to introduce the fields that will be used to link the tables.
Third:	Add the BETWEEN keyword and the field name from the linked table that contains the *lower* threshold value.
Finally:	Add the AND keyword and the field name from the linked table that contains the *upper* threshold value.

Tricks and Traps

Joining tables on ranges of data is, admittedly, a fairly rare occurrence in practice. However, should you ever have to do this, it helps to be aware of the following points:

- Joining tables on a range of values is nearly always used—as was the case in this example—to look up data from a "reference" table. This kind of operation presumes that the ranges in the "lookup" table have been defined coherently and cannot overlap.

- When using the BETWEEN…AND operator you *must* always place the lower threshold value after the BETWEEN keyword and the upper threshold value after the AND keyword—or the query will not work.

- As an alternative to the BETWEEN…AND operator you can use the >= (greater than or equal) and <= (lesser than or equal) operators instead. Were you to do this, the SQL for the JOIN would look like this:

```
JOIN        SalesCategory CAT

    ON SD.SalePrice >=

            CAT.LowerThreshold

        AND SD.SalePrice <= CAT.UpperThreshold
```

- When using the >= (greater than or equal) and <= (lesser than or equal) operators you have to *repeat the field name* that you are using to join the tables. What is more, you can also place the threshold values in any order—that is, you can place the upper threshold first and the lower threshold second, if you want.

7. Cross Joins

The CEO wants a list of all countries that Prestige Cars sells to, with a list of all makes that the company has ever stocked. However, when you ask for more details, she says that she also wants to see *every make* appear for *every country* because this allows her to galvanize the sales teams to sell every make in every country. After a little thought, you produce the following piece of SQL:

```
SELECT        CountryName, MakeName

FROM          country

CROSS JOIN    make

ORDER BY      CountryName, MakeName;
```

Running this SQL produces the result shown in Figure 3.13. This query produces some 260 records, so I am not displaying the entire output. However, if you scroll through the output, you can see that the makes of car are repeated for each country.

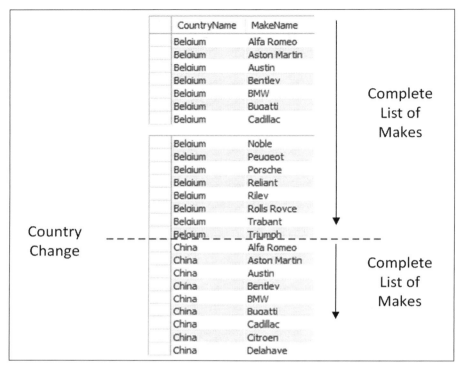

Figure 3.13: *The output from a CROSS JOIN*

How it Works

This query consists of four elements:

First: The SELECT clause, where you list the fields that you want returned from the two tables

Second: The first table that you want to return all the data from

Third: The CROSS JOIN keyword

Finally: The second table that you want to return all the data from

It really is that simple. A cross join query like this will return a collection of records where each record from each of the two tables will be paired up with each record in the other table.

Tricks and Traps

There is one vital point to be aware of if you ever start using cross joins in your queries—and a couple of minor points of interest—listed here:

- Cross joins can produce *huge* result sets. This is because they multiply all the rows in one table by the number of rows in the second table in the join. So, you should use them only when you need the specific kind of output that they deliver—and preferably only with small tables.

- A cross join does not have an ON clause because there is no link between any fields in the two tables.

- This kind of join is also known by SQL geeks as a *Cartesian join*.

8. Join Concepts

Learning about the various join types in MySQL can seem a little daunting at first sight. To make your learning curve smoother, take a look at Figure 3.14, where the main types of joins are explained graphically.

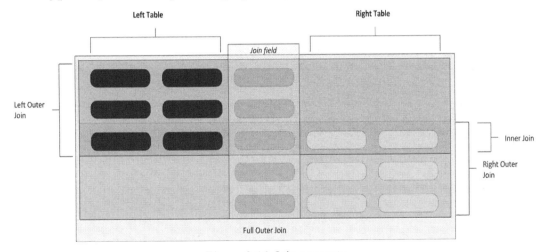

Figure 3.14: *Join concepts*

Conclusion

This chapter has extended the knowledge that you acquired in the previous chapter and has taken you further toward understanding some of the many techniques that you can apply when joining tables in MySQL.

You have seen the difference between inner and outer joins and how using the LEFT and RIGHT keywords in a join can completely change the data that is returned by a query. While looking at types of joins, you saw how an OUTER join can be used to return all the data from both tables in a join as well as how a CROSS JOIN can return a complete cross mapping of every field in the two tables. You also learned how to use multiple fields in a table join as well as how to join tables on a range of data and not just on a single value. As a final flourish, you even saw how to join a table to itself when querying hierarchies of data.

However, for the moment, it is appropriate to move on to another subject. So, in the next chapter, you will begin learning about some of the techniques you can apply in SQL queries to filter your data.

Core Knowledge Learned in This Chapter

The following are the keywords and concepts you learned in this chapter:

Concept	Description
LEFT JOIN	This type of join returns all the data from the first (left-hand) table in a join and only matching data from the second (right-hand) table.
RIGHT JOIN	This type of join returns all the data from the first (right-hand) table in a join and only matching data from the second (left-hand) table
Self Join	This technique consists of joining a table to itself.
BETWEEN...AND	This operator can be used to join tables on a range of values.
CROSS JOIN	This keyword multiplies all the rows in the first table by all the rows in the second table.

CHAPTER 4
Filtering Data

All over the world the amount of data that people and organizations create and store is growing at an ever-increasing rate. "Seeing the wood for the trees" is becoming more and more difficult—but ever more necessary. So, you need to be able to filter your data to deliver relevant and useful information from the multitude of facts and figures in the many tables that make up your database.

Using SQL to Filter Data

This chapter introduces the core techniques that you will need to learn to extend your queries so that you are delivering only the information you want. As you might expect, filtering data has been around as long as databases have existed. Consequently, a variety of methods exist that you can apply to restrict the data that is returned by a query. Sometimes there could be several ways to get the same result. This is why I will occasionally give you alternative solutions to a problem. However, our primary focus is to introduce you to the essential techniques that you can apply to your own queries to obtain a valid and reliable result.

To this end, you will take away the following key points from this chapter:

- Filtering data using table joins
- Finding records containing one or more pieces of text
- Finding records that do not contain a specific piece of text
- Using numbers as thresholds to filter output
- Using ranges of numbers to filter output
- Finding records that match a yes/no criterion

Data scientists often talk about the "logic" of data. This is because databases are (most often) the result of logical design, and consequently querying them requires a coherent and structured approach. This does not mean you need an advanced degree in philosophy or mathematics to analyze data with SQL. All you really need is a little rationality and some practice. This chapter will encourage you to use both of these as you take your first steps in filtering data.

1. Filtering Data Using Joins

I realize that you have spent the previous two chapters looking at ways of joining tables. Nonetheless, I have an extremely important point to make about joins in the context of filtering data.

First, you need to remember that a join (an inner join, that is, using only the JOIN keyword not an outer join using the LEFT or RIGHT join keywords) acts as a filter. An inner join guarantees that only the data in the records containing matching values in the fields that are used to join tables will be returned in the query result. This provides an initial filter on the underlying data.

Second, you need to be aware that *only a subset of data* from one of the tables in a LEFT or RIGHT join will be returned (more precisely, this affects the data in the table on the right of the join in a left outer join and the data in the table on the left of the join in a right outer join). So, these two join types also filter data, if only partially.

It might be that table joins have already filtered your data and provided the result that you are looking for. However, if this is not the case, then you can extend the filter effect of joins with a myriad of other options that are the subject of both this chapter and the next.

2. Filtering Data Using Multiple Table Joins

Selling classy cars may be great fun, but sooner or later the finance director will need to know which makes and models the company has bought and stocked. The following query lets you show him a list displaying all the makes and models ever held in stock:

```
SELECT DISTINCT     MK.MakeName, MD.ModelName

FROM                stock ST

JOIN                model MD USING(ModelID)

JOIN                make MK USING(MakeID)

ORDER BY            MK.MakeName, MD.ModelName;
```

Execute this query, and you should see the data in Figure 4.1.

MakeName	ModelName
Alfa Romeo	1750
Alfa Romeo	Giulia
Alfa Romeo	Giulietta
Alfa Romeo	Spider
Aston Martin	DB2
Aston Martin	DB4
Aston Martin	DB5
Aston Martin	DB6
Aston Martin	DB9
Aston Martin	Rapide
Aston Martin	Vanquish
Aston Martin	Vantage
Aston Martin	Virage
Austin	Cambridge
Austin	Lichfield
Austin	Princess

Figure 4.1: *Table joins acting as filters*

How it Works

This query joins the Make, Model, and Stock tables so that you can look up the make and model names for the vehicles in the Stock table.

However, this is not the really important thing about this query. This example emphasizes a really fundamental aspect of SQL—that joining tables actually *filters* data.

First: This query applies *two* filters—one for each join clause.

Then: It applies the DISTINCT keyword to filter out any duplicate records (that is, any makes and models that appear more than once in the output).

So, even a simple query like this one is filtering data "out of the box," even though you have not applied any specific criteria.

To appreciate the filter effect produced by a join, you need to know that the Make table contains an exhaustive list of makes of classic cars. However, *not all* of these have ever been bought by Prestige Cars Ltd.—no Cadillacs have been bought so far, for instance. Yet if you scroll down the list of makes and models returned by this query, you will not see any Cadillacs. Yet the make Cadillac appears in the Make table. Equally, the Model table contains a couple of models that do not appear in the results from this query (the Lagonda 3 liter is an example). This is because the query is filtering the output so that *only* data that is in *all* the tables that are joined in a query is displayed. All other records in the tables that are used are excluded from the result.

To make this concept easier to grasp, take a look at the simple Venn diagram in Figure 4.2.

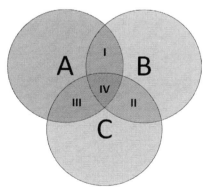

Figure 4.2: *Table filtering explained*

If you join tables A and B, you get the data outlined in I.

If you join tables B and C, you get the data outlined in II.

If you join tables A and C, you get the data outlined in III.

However, if you join tables A, B, and C, you get the data outlined in IV.

This aspect of database querying is so important that it needs to be repeated. When you join tables, *only the data that can be linked across all the tables will appear in the result.* If you take the principle explained in Figure 4.2 (the Venn diagram) and show this as a set of tables, you can see what really happens when you join tables.

To get a clearer idea of how this works, take a look at Figure 4.3. This image shows how only a common subset of data is returned from multiple tables. This is because the common elements that make up each table join filter the query results.

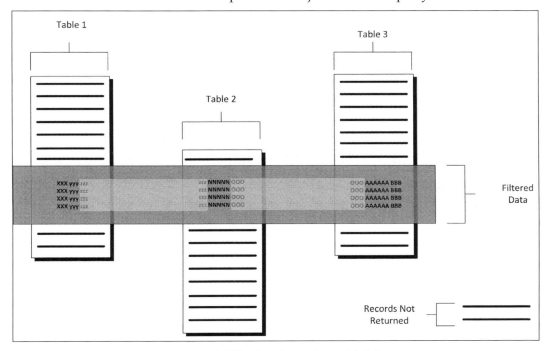

Figure 4.3: *Filtering data using table joins*

3. Filtering Data Output Using Intermediate Tables

Any business needs to see which products to sell. So, it is quite natural that the CEO should want to produce a list of all the models that Prestige Cars has ever sold and when they were sold.

The following SQL produces this list so that you can keep the CEO aware of the data that matters to her:

```
SELECT     MD.ModelName, SA.SaleDate, SA.InvoiceNumber

FROM       model AS MD

JOIN       stock ST USING (ModelID)

JOIN       salesdetails SD

           ON ST.StockCode = SD.StockID

JOIN       sales SA USING (SalesID)

ORDER BY   MD.ModelName;
```

Running this query gives the output shown in Figure 4.4.

ModelName	SaleDate	InvoiceNumber
135	2018-09-15 00:00:00	EURFR300
145	2017-04-05 20:10:00	EURES140
145	2018-09-15 00:00:00	GBPGB301
175	2018-09-15 00:00:00	EURIT302
1750	2018-06-03 00:00:00	GBPCH263
1750	2018-04-15 00:00:00	EURFR241
203	2018-01-05 00:00:00	EURFR211
203	2017-01-21 13:56:00	EURFR113
205	2018-01-10 00:00:00	EURBE218
205	2017-07-01 10:25:00	EURBE171
250SL	2018-04-09 00:00:00	GBPGB238
250SL	2017-08-04 11:29:00	USDUS179
280SL	2017-06-15 16:23:00	EURIT166
280SL	2018-09-04 00:00:00	GBPGB296
280SL	2018-07-25 00:00:00	GBPGB272
280SL	2017-06-01 20:21:00	GBPGB162

Figure 4.4: *Table joins acting as filters as well as simple joins*

How it Works

This short query joins the Model, Stock, SalesDetails, and Sales tables so that you can then select a detailed list of all the models that have been sold. As the SQL can seem a little dense, Figure 4.5 shows you in a more visual way exactly how the tables are linked.

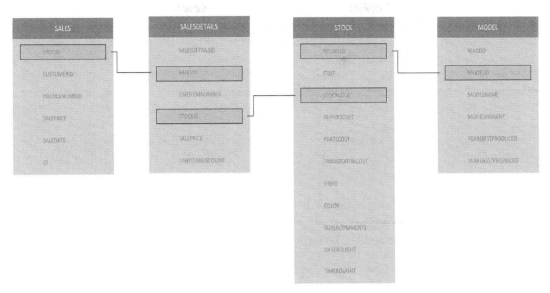

Figure 4.5: *A multi-table join*

These are the reasons you need these four tables:

SalesDetails Contains the stock number (the StockID field) of every car ever sold. However, it contains no details about the vehicle itself. To get these details, you need to join it to the Stock table.

Stock Contains all vehicles that are in stock—or have ever been in stock. It does not indicate whether they have been sold. Also, it contains only a code for the model and not the model name, which is what you need. To get the full name of the model, you need to join it to the Model table.

Model Contains the Model name.

Sales Contains the date of sale and the invoice number. You can join this to the SalesDetails table on the SalesID field.

Once these four tables have been joined, you can display the model name (and other sales details) for every vehicle that is in the SalesDetails table—in other words, every car ever *sold*. It is important to note that even if you are *not* extracting data from the Stock table, you need to include it in the query so that you can join the Model table to the SalesDetails table. As the SalesDetails and Model tables have no direct connection, the only way to write the query is to join them using the Stock table as an intermediate join table.

This query also applies filters to the data. As this concept is vital to understanding SQL, I prefer to show a couple of examples to make it really clear. In this query, the filters are applied like this:

First: The Model table contains one or two models that Prestige Cars has never had in stock. However, even if you are selecting the list of models from the Model table, as you are doing here, you will not see *all* the models that are in the Model table because *only* models that are in the Stock table will appear in the output. This is because any table join will act as a filter and limit the data that is returned to data that is in *both* tables.

Second: The Stock table contains all vehicles that have ever been in stock. Yet this query only displays models that have been *sold* (if you want confirmation of this, you can see a Ferrari Testarossa in the Stock table that has not yet been sold—so it does not appear in the output from this query). Once again, the table join will act as a filter and limit the data that is returned to data that is in *both* tables.

However, *no* data is excluded when the Sales table is joined to the SalesDetails table. This is because the Sales table (which contains the data used to print the invoice header) contains a link to every item in the SalesDetails table. Equally, the SalesDetails table contains no SalesIDs that are not in the Sales table. So, in this case you are looking at a simple join that returns data from two tables, without filtering data. This is because these two tables are in a hierarchical—or parent to child—relationship.

As you can see from Figure 4.1 (and as I explained in Chapter 2), the names of many models appear several times. This is because the filter effect of a table join will nonetheless return *all* the records from *both* tables (after any selective filtering has been applied) based on the fields that are in the SELECT clause, irrespective of which table the fields come from. In this case, MySQL returns the 351 records from the SalesDetails table—because the Model table does not contain any models that are absent from the Stock table, and the Stock table does not contain any vehicles that are not in the SalesDetails table. This is fortunate because otherwise Prestige Cars would be selling vehicles that it does not own.

Note: Be aware that not displaying data can lead to apparent anomalies. For instance, in this example, there are apparent duplicate records where the ModelName, SaleDate and InvoiceName are identical. This is because two cars of the same make and model are sold at the same time on the same invoice. If you want to avoid the impression of duplication you need to add the StockCode field as well. Alternatively, if all you want is the list of models and dates than you can add the DISTINCT keyword to the SELECT clause.

4. Filtering Text

Imagine that a new marketing director has just arrived at Prestige Cars. The first thing that she wants to know is how the color of cars varies by model purchased. More precisely, she wants a report displaying all the models Prestige Cars has had in stock in a specific color. This means you can get off to a good start by applying some more specific filters to your data. As the Stock table contains a Color field, you can quickly see which models of what color the company has ever had in stock. The following short piece of SQL delivers this:

```
SELECT DISTINCT MD.ModelName, ST.Color

FROM            stock ST

JOIN            model MD USING (ModelID)

WHERE           Color = 'Red'

ORDER BY        MD.ModelName;
```

Enter (or copy and paste) this query into the query window and run it. You should see a result something like in Figure 4.6.

ModelName	Color
280SL	Red
355	Red
404	Red
500	Red
57C	Red
600	Red
924	Red
944	Red
DB2	Red
DB5	Red
DB6	Red
DB9	Red
Flying Spur	Red
Ghost	Red
Giulia	Red
Mark X	Red

Figure 4.6: A simple equality filter

How it Works

This query introduces the WHERE clause, possibly the single most useful keyword in the SQL lexicon. A WHERE clause requires you to enter what data element you want to find in which column. Here that means saying that the Color field in the Stock table contains the element Red. This is done by specifying the following:

A field name	In this example, it is the Color column.
=	The equal operator tells SQL that you are looking for an exact match to an element.
The element to find in the field.	In this case, it is the color red.

Because you are looking for a text element (a color is not a number), you have to enclose the text that you are looking for in *single quotes*. This lets MySQL know you are looking for a string of characters (text if you prefer) and not a number.

Finally, you need to add the DISTINCT keyword that you first encountered in Chapter 2. Using this keyword ensures that you see only one example of each red model—and avoid repeating records for all the red models that have been sold.

Tricks and Traps

As this is the first time you applied a filter using the WHERE keyword, note the following important points:

- Any field contained in any of the tables that you have assembled in the FROM clause can be used to filter data. The field that appears in the WHERE clause does not have to be present in the SELECT clause.

- Although we humans can see instantly that a text is not a number, SQL does not find it so easy. So, you must remember always to enclose text in single quotes when writing SQL—and this is especially necessary when using a WHERE clause.

- On some MySQL systems you may be able to use double quotes as well to enclose a text. However this is not considered best practice.

5. Applying Multiple Text Filters

The new marketing director liked your initial analysis of sales for a specific color. So, she has returned with a second request. She wants you to extend the previous query so that she can get an idea of all models ever stocked in red, green, or blue. The following SQL will do this for you:

```
SELECT     MD.ModelName, ST.Color

FROM       stock ST

JOIN       model MD USING (ModelID)

WHERE      ST.Color IN ('Red', 'Green', 'Blue')

ORDER BY   MD.ModelName;
```

If you execute this query, you should see something like the output shown in Figure 4.7.

ModelName	Color
175	Blue
1750	Blue
250SL	Green
280SL	Green
280SL	Red
350SL	Green
355	Red
355	Blue
355	Red
360	Blue
404	Blue
404	Blue
404	Red
500	Blue
500	Red
500	Red

Figure 4.7: *Filtering on multiple criteria for a single column*

How it Works

This query extends the WHERE clause by adding the new keyword IN. This keyword lets you enter a list of elements that you want to filter on—colors in this example. Each element must—*if it is text*—be in single quotes and then separated by a comma from each other element in the list. *The entire list must then be enclosed in parentheses.* There is no real limit to the number of elements that you can add to a list like this when filtering data. In this example, however, you only see vehicles that are red, green, or blue.

Tricks and Traps

It is probably worth noting the following important points:

- You can enter multiple elements in an IN clause over many lines if you prefer. So, the IN clause could have been written like this:

```
IN (

    'Red'

    ,'Green'

    ,'Blue'

    )
```

6. Excluding an Element

The marketing director is on a roll. The more she digs into the data, the more ideas she comes up with. Her latest intuition is to look at all sales except Ferraris. Fortunately, SQL lets you exclude an element from the results when filtering data, so you can output a list of all makes ever stocked except for a specific make of car. The following SQL snippet does just that:

```
SELECT     DISTINCT MK.MakeName

           FROM make AS MK

JOIN       model AS MD USING(MakeID)

JOIN       stock AS ST USING(ModelID)

JOIN       salesdetails SD ON ST.StockCode = SD.StockID

WHERE      MK.MakeName <> 'Ferrari'

ORDER BY   MK.MakeName;
```

Running this code will return a list like the one in Figure 4.8.

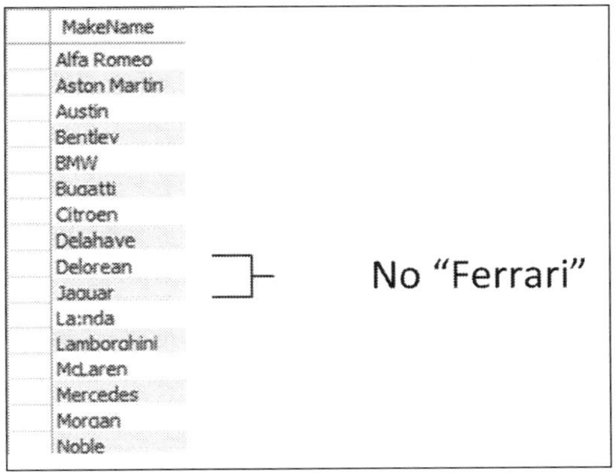

Figure 4.8: Applying an exclusion filter

How it Works

In this query, you started by finding all vehicles sold. This meant linking the four tables (Make, Model, Stock, and SalesDetails) that contain the fields that interest you. Then you applied a filter on a field (Make in this example). This time, however, you specified that the filter is used to *exclude*, rather than include, the element that you specify. This is done by using the <> (or "not equal") operator. This operator is the exact opposite of the equal operator that you saw in the previous section and effectively means "anything but." It will exclude from the results any single item you specify—Ferrari in this example. Here again, any field in the tables that you have assembled in the FROM clause can be used to filter data.

As you can see, sorting the list in alphabetical order has helped you to understand the output. Equally, showing each make only once thanks to the judicious use of the DISTINCT keyword makes the result clearer and more comprehensible.

It is probably worth remembering that an initial filter has already been applied through joining the tables, as I mentioned at the start of this chapter. Because, in effect, the SalesDetails table contains a subset of the vehicles in the Stock table (those whose StockID is present), you will not see *all* the cars in stock in this query, only those in the SalesDetails table (that is, those that have been sold). The WHERE clause then filters this data set further by excluding Ferrari from the output.

Tricks and Traps

When excluding a single element from a list, there is one variation that you might find interesting—and one important reminder.

- As an alternative to using <> in the WHERE clause, you can use != instead to signify "not equals"—and consequently exclude it from the output. Were you to use it in this example, the WHERE clause would look like this:

```
WHERE MakeName != 'Ferrari'
```

- Once again, any text that is used in a WHERE clause *must* be enclosed in single quotes. Numbers, however, should be entered without any quotes at all.

7. Using Multiple Exclusion Filters

An excited marketing director now wants even more data to power her research. This time she wants a list of all makes sold except Porsche, Aston Martin, and Bentley.

Luckily, it is also possible (and really not difficult) to exclude a selection of elements from a list in SQL. Take a look at the following code to see how to display a list of vehicles that excludes a specific list of makes:

```
SELECT     DISTINCT MK.MakeName

FROM       make AS MK

JOIN       model AS MD USING(MakeID)

JOIN       stock AS ST USING(ModelID)

JOIN       salesdetails SD ON ST.StockCode = SD.StockID

WHERE      MK.MakeName NOT IN ('Porsche', 'Aston Martin', 'Bentley')

ORDER BY   MK.MakeName;
```

If you run this code, you should see something like the output shown in Figure 4.9.

MakeName
Alfa Romeo
Austin
BMW
Bugatti
Citroen
Delahave
Delorean
Ferrari
Jaguar
La:nda
Lamborghini
McLaren
Mercedes
Morgan
Noble

Figure 4.9: Applying an exclusion filter using multiple criteria

How it Works

As you will see if you scroll through the query output, the cars that you specified in the NOT IN clause of this SQL are nowhere to be seen in the results.

This query is similar to the last one (and to some extent the one before that), so I will not explain the similarities, only the differences. In this query, the WHERE clause contains a list of elements (in parentheses, comma-separated and with each piece of text enclosed in single quotes), but the IN keyword has been extended to read NOT IN. The outcome is that any element in the list contained between the parentheses after NOT IN will *not* appear in the result set.

Tricks and Traps

I can think of only one main comment to make at this time.

- When you write queries to filter data, you will have to decide whether it is easier to include or exclude a specific list of elements in a dataset. In most cases, it is best to reduce coding to a minimum because this reduces the risk of error. So, if you have a shorter list of items to exclude than you have of items to include, then it is probably better to choose an exclusion list.

8. Filtering Numbers Over a Defined Threshold

Your reputation as an analytics guru is spreading through the company. Now it is the turn of the finance director to arrive at your desk with a request. He would like to get an idea of the higher-value cars that are in stock or have been sold; more specifically, he wants to see a list of all cars where the purchase price was over £50,000.00.

This request is a reminder that filtering data is not always a question of defining exact matches. This is especially true where numbers are concerned. The following query will do this:

```
SELECT     ModelName, Cost

FROM       model

JOIN       stock USING(ModelID)

WHERE      Cost > 50000;
```

If you run this code, you should see something like the output in Figure 4.10, where all vehicle costs are more than £50,000:

ModelName	Cost
Davtona	79600.0000
Davtona	116000.0000
Testarossa	132000.0000
Testarossa	172000.0000
Testarossa	156000.0000
Testarossa	52000.0000
Testarossa	156000.0000
Testarossa	200000.0000
Testarossa	176000.0000
355	124000.0000
355	164000.0000
355	100760.0000
355	135600.0000
355	176000.0000
355	127600.0000

Figure 4.10: Using a numeric comparison filter

How it Works

In this example, you queried the Stock and Model tables using a WHERE clause on the Cost field, which applied the greater-than operator (>) followed by a value used in the comparison. This, in effect, told SQL to "give me the costs greater than 50000." As you can see, the figure used for the comparison is not formatted in any way.

Tricks and Traps

There are three specific things to note here.

- The greater-than operator (>) means exactly what it says. This query will *not* return any records where the vehicle cost is *exactly* £50,000—only those where the cost is *at least* £50,000.01, that is, greater than 50,000.

- What is possibly the most important thing to remember when using numbers to filter data is that a figure does *not* need to be enclosed in single quotes like text does.

- You must *never* format a number that you are using in the WHERE clause to filter output. That is, you always enter the number without a thousands separators or currency symbols. The number must be entered "raw" for the filter to work.

9. Filtering Numbers Under a Defined Threshold

As a variation on the previous example, let's imagine you want to take a look at any cars that are or have been in stock where the cost of any spare parts was below a certain threshold. The following piece of SQL returns this information:

```
SELECT      ModelName, Cost

FROM        model

JOIN        stock USING(ModelID)

WHERE       PartsCost < 1000

ORDER BY    ModelName;
```

If you run this code, you should see something like the output in Figure 4.11, where the parts cost less than £1,000.

ModelName	Cost
135	20400.0000
145	23600.0000
145	31600.0000
175	10000.0000
175	18120.0000
1750	2860.0000
1750	7960.0000
203	1560.0000
203	1000.0000
205	760.0000
205	3160.0000
205	1800.0000
250SL	10360.0000
250SL	18080.0000

Figure 4.11: Using a less-than comparison filter

How it Works

This example tweaks the previous one to apply a slightly different filter. This time you are looking at vehicles where the cost of spare parts was *less* than £1000. All this was done by using the field that you want to use as a basis for the comparison, the less-than operator (the <symbol), and a value.

Tricks and Traps

There is one thing to remember when filtering using numbers.

- You do *not* need to include the parts cost in the output when filtering on this particular figure. However, it can be good practice to include the fields that you are using in a WHERE clause in the initial output as this enables you to "sanity check" the results of the query. Once you are satisfied that the results are accurate, you can always remove the field that you are filtering on from the SELECT clause.

10. Filtering on Values Up to and Including a Specific Number

Still looking at our stock of vehicles—past and present—let's imagine that the finance director wants to take a look at all cars where the repair cost was up to *and including*

£500.00. Writing the following SQL snippet will let you deliver the analysis that he wants to see:

```
SELECT      MD.ModelName, ST.RepairsCost

FROM        model MD

JOIN        stock ST USING(ModelID)

WHERE       ST.RepairsCost <= 500

ORDER BY    MD.ModelName;
```

Running this code will deliver something like the output in Figure 4.12, where all repair costs are less than or equal to £500. Note that I have scrolled to the bottom of the results in this query.

ModelName	RepairsCost
Vanquish	500.0000
Vantage	500.0000
Virage	500.0000
Virage	500.0000
Virage	500.0000
Virage	500.0000
XJ12	500.0000
XJ12	500.0000
XJS	500.0000
XJS	290.0000
XK120	500.0000
XK120	500.0000
XK120	500.0000
XK120	500.0000
XK150	390.0000
XK150	500.0000

Figure 4.12: Using a less-than-or-equal-to comparison filter

How it Works

This example is a variation on the last one and shows that both the less-than and greater-than operators can be amended to make them "or equal to" by adding the *equal sign*. This will start the comparison with the figure (or letters) used in the comparison. As you can see from the results of the query, records containing the figure that is used as the upper threshold in the WHERE clause (500) are included in the result set.

Tricks and Traps

You might want to note the following trick with the greater-than or lesser-than operators:

* You can add the equal sign to either the greater-than (>) or lesser-than (<) operator to convert it to, respectively, greater than or equal to and lesser than or equal to.

11. Filtering on a Range of Values

You can also filter results so that a range of data is returned. Let's take a look at an example of this by setting up a query to show all vehicles where the parts cost is between a lower and an upper threshold. This lets you answer a request from the CEO for a list of all makes of car that Prestige Cars has stocked where the parts cost is between £1,000 and £2,000. The following is the SQL to do this:

```
SELECT      DISTINCT MK.MakeName

FROM        make AS MK JOIN model AS MD USING(MakeID)

JOIN        stock AS ST USING(ModelID)

WHERE       ST.PartsCost BETWEEN 1000 AND 2000

ORDER BY    MK.MakeName;
```

If you run this query, you will see the output shown in Figure 4.13.

MakeName
Alfa Romeo
Aston Martin
Bentlev
Ferrari
Jaouar
La:nda
Lamborahini
Moraan
Noble
Porsche
Rolls Rovce

Figure 4.13: Using a range comparison filter

How it Works

This query starts by joining the Stock, Model, and Make tables. It then adds a WHERE clause. In this example, the WHERE clause is in two parts.

First: The BETWEEN operator followed by the figure for the *lower* threshold in your filter

Finally: The AND operator followed by the figure for the *upper* threshold in your filter

The overall result is that using the BETWEEN and AND operators in a WHERE clause lets you specify a range of data to filter on.

Tricks and Traps

The BETWEEN and AND operators are extremely powerful when applied to filters. However, there are several aspects of their use that require fairly close attention. These include the following:

- BETWEEN ... AND can also be used with text (in single quotes, of course). If you use letters rather than numbers, you can limit the output across an alphabetical range.

- You must begin a BETWEEN...AND filter with the lower threshold and end with the upper threshold. If you reverse the thresholds, then the query will likely return nothing at all.

- As you can see from this example (and, indeed, is the case in any other code using a WHERE clause), you do *not* have to place the field used in the WHERE clause in the SELECT statement. Of course, you can repeat the "filter" field in the SELECT clause if you want to be really sure that no data has been returned that does not meet the criteria you have entered. In fact, it can be advisable to do this when developing and testing queries—and then remove it once you are sure you have the correct result.

- If you prefer, you can write this kind of WHERE clause using the <= (less than or equal to) and >= (greater than or equal to) operators. The WHERE clause in this example, rewritten using these operators, would look like this:

```
WHERE       PartsCost >= 1000 AND PartsCost <= 2000
```

As you can see, this approach requires you to repeat the field name in the clause. However, when you write a filter that defines a range to exclude using greater than or equal to and lesser than or equal to, you do *not* have to enter the lowest threshold value first. In other words, this piece of SQL would work equally well:

```
WHERE      PartsCost <= 2000 AND PartsCost >= 1000
```

• You saw the BETWEEN…AND keyword combination in the previous chapter when applied to range joins. However, we are applying it here in a slightly different context—as part of a WHERE clause rather than in a table join. This is just one example of how SQL can use the same keywords in different situations to achieve different results.

12. Using Boolean Filters (True or False)

Sometimes a table may contain a simple yes or no value. Depending on the tool you are using to view the data, this might be displayed as Yes/No, True/False, or even 1/0. Filtering on fields like this is easy—but it requires you to know that data like this is, normally, stored as a one or a zero. In the Stock table, there is a field named IsRHD that is one of these fields. The following code snippet shows how you can use it to display all right-hand drive models that Prestige Cars has sold:

```
SELECT     DISTINCT MK.MakeName, MD.ModelName

FROM       make AS MK

JOIN       model AS MD USING(MakeID)

JOIN       stock AS ST USING(ModelID)

JOIN       salesdetails SD ON ST.StockCode = SD.StockID

WHERE      ST.IsRHD = 1

ORDER BY   MK.MakeName, MD.ModelName;
```

If you execute this query, you will see the output shown in Figure 4.14:

MakeName	ModelName
Alfa Romeo	1750
Alfa Romeo	Giulia
Alfa Romeo	Giulietta
Alfa Romeo	Spider
Aston Martin	DB2
Aston Martin	DB4
Aston Martin	DB5
Aston Martin	DB6
Aston Martin	DB9
Aston Martin	Rapide
Aston Martin	Vanquish
Aston Martin	Vantage
Aston Martin	Virage
Austin	Cambridge
Austin	Lichfield
Austin	Princess

Figure 4.14: Using a Boolean filter in a WHERE clause

How it Works

Here, again, we have joined the Stock and SalesDetails tables to get a list of vehicles sold. Then we have joined the Make and Model tables so that we can see the actual names of the make and model. To finish, we have added the DISTINCT keyword to ensure that no duplicates are returned—and the ORDER BY clause to output the result in alphabetical order to make it easier to read. The final tweak is to ensure that the WHERE clause only allows records that contain an IsRHD field with a value of 1—indicating that this vehicle is right-hand drive.

The really interesting aspect of this query is that it is adapted to a specific type of SQL data. The data type used in the IsRHD column is called a BIT data type. It will accept only a 1 or a 0 (true or false if you prefer).

It might, possibly, accept empty (or NULL) values as well. However, we will examine these subtleties in the following chapter.

Tricks and Traps

As I am introducing a new SQL concept, there are, inevitably, a few key points to retain.

- If you wanted to reverse this query to show only left-hand drive cars—which are stored in the SalesDetails table with the IsRHD column set to 0 (false)—you would tweak the WHERE clause to read as follows:

  ```
  WHERE     IsRHD = 0
  ```

- In MySQL, the value True is nearly always represented by a 1, and the value False is represented by a 0. So, when you are writing a SQL query on a true/false column, you *cannot* say =True or =False. You have to use a 1 or a 0.

- In geeky language, a yes/no filter like this is called a *Boolean condition*.

- You will always need to know how the concepts of true and false are stored in your database. They could—depending on the design of the database—be stored as:

- True/False (in a text field)

- Y/N (in a text field)

- Yes/No (in a text field)

- 1/0

  Indeed, there are many ways of representing this concept in data tables.

  It follows that you will need to use the appropriate value in your queries to represent "true". So, (in the Customer table—and depending on how the true or false value is actually represented) this *could* mean:

  ```
  WHERE     IsReseller = 'Yes'
  ```

  Or

  ```
  WHERE     IsCreditRisk = 'Y'
  ```

- When you are querying new data tables for the first time you are probably best advised to view the table data using a SELECT * query (adding LIMIT 100 to return only a sample of the available data) to see what the table actually contains and how true or false values are stored.

Conclusion

This chapter has taken you much further into the world of SQL querying. Where before you could select only tables and columns, now you can delve deep into the data itself and output only the parts that interest you.

First you saw how joining tables can filter the data that a query returns. Then you learned the importance of the WHERE clause and how to use the power of MySQL to choose to display only the contents—or even part of the contents—of certain fields. You saw how to select text and numbers, including ranges of numbers and figures above or below a specified value. Finally you learned how to filter on true or false values.

Core Knowledge Learned in This Chapter

This has been quite a full and fairly intense chapter. The following are the keywords you saw in this chapter:

Concept	Description
WHERE	This essential keyword starts every clause that allows you to filter data in a query.
IN	This keyword lets you enter a series of words or numbers that must exist in a column if the data for a record is to be displayed.
<>	This operator selects data that is not equal to a specified word, phrase, or number.
!=	This operator also selects data that is not equal to a specified word, phrase, or number.
NOT IN	This keyword combination excludes any records where a column does not contain one of a series of words or numbers.
>	This operator filters on numbers or letters that are less than a specified figure.
<	This operator filters on numbers or letters that are more than a specified figure.
>=	This operator filters on numbers or letters that are more than or equal to a specified figure.
<=	This operator filters on numbers t or letters hat are less than or equal to a specified figure.
BETWEEN...AND	This operator allows you to set a range (usually of figures) that you use to filter a data set.

CHAPTER 5
Applying Complex Filters to Queries

Filtering data is at the heart of SQL. In many cases you will have to apply multiple filters at the same time to extract exactly what you are looking for. This means learning how to apply a little logic to filter criteria to achieve the desired result. The logic you need may be quite simple—or possibly quite advanced. However, it will always be built using the same approach and similar methods.

Complex Filtering Techniques

In this chapter, you will extend the knowledge that you acquired in the previous chapter by learning how to use SQL filters to

- Search for data on alternative criteria
- Apply separate criteria simultaneously to narrow down a search
- Use simple logic to apply multiple criteria in more complex searches
- Use wildcard data searches, that is, finding a value that is only part of a field
- Filter data on a specific part of a field
- Find NULL (or empty) data

- Remove superfluous spaces from the start or end of a field
- Use regular expressions to find the contents of a field that match a pattern

1. Using Either/Or Filters

The CEO has just sent you an email. She needs to narrow down her analysis so that she can carry out an in-depth review of the sales of cars that are either red or Ferraris.

A request like this (however bizarre it may seem at first sight) makes the point that not all data searches are as simple as those you saw in Chapter 3. On many—if not most—occasions you will probably want to create more complex queries that require either one or another condition to be met. The following code snippet shows how to select data where either of two possible conditions is true:

```
SELECT      DISTINCT MK.MakeName, ST.Color

FROM        make AS MK

JOIN        model AS MD USING (MakeID)

JOIN        stock AS ST USING (ModelID)

JOIN        salesdetails SD ON ST.StockCode = SD.StockID

WHERE       ST.Color = 'Red' OR MakeName = 'Ferrari'

ORDER BY    MK.MakeName;
```

Executing this query will show something like the output in Figure 5.1.

MakeName	Color
Alfa Romeo	Red
Aston Martin	Red
Austin	Red
Bentley	Red
Bugatti	Red
Ferrari	Silver
Ferrari	Red
Ferrari	Green
Ferrari	Dark Purple
Ferrari	Night Blue
Ferrari	British Racing Green
Ferrari	Black
Ferrari	Blue
Jaguar	Red
Mercedes	Red
Peugeot	Red

Figure 5.1: *Filtering on alternative criteria*

How it Works

This example introduces a fundamental SQL keyword: OR. This keyword lets you apply alternative filter conditions. Here you have queried the SalesDetails, Stock, Make, Model and Colortables (so that you can see vehicles sold as well as the names—and not the codes—of the make and model) using a WHERE clause that filters on either a certain color *or* a specified make. This query shows you that when you are looking for elements in different columns, you need to use the OR keyword in the WHERE clause. You can see from the WHERE clause that you must always be extremely precise and indicate which column has which specific filter applied to it.

Tricks and Traps

When meeting a vital new concept for the first time, you need to take away a few key notions.

- By definition this kind of query will return more results than the more restrictive filters that you saw in Chapter 4 as it implies a wider search, given that it is an either/or selection.

- An OR query like this will return data when either of the two conditions is true or even when both of them are true. However, a record where both conditions are true (that is, where the make is Ferrari and the color is red) will *not* appear twice.

- Each part of the WHERE clause follows the logic you saw in Chapter 4. So, text is inside single quotes, as is normal when filtering on text data.

- The technical name for a filter like this is a *logical or*.

- You can add as many OR operators to a query as you want. However, you will have to repeat the column name for each different filter that you apply—even if the filters apply to the same column.

- You can use the OR operator as a substitute for the IN operator. However this means repeating the same filed name several times—as you can see in the following example:

```
WHERE ST.COLOR = 'Red' OR ST.COLOR = 'Blue'
```

2. Using Multiple Separate Criteria Concurrently

The CEO now wants to build on your query results and carry out a much narrower search—she wants to look for red Ferraris *only*. You can deliver the required result with only a small tweak to the code that you just wrote.

```
SELECT DISTINCT   MK.MakeName, ST.Color

FROM              make AS MK

JOIN              model AS MD USING (MakeID)

JOIN              stock AS ST USING (ModelID)

JOIN              salesdetails SD ON ST.StockCode = SD.StockID

WHERE             ST.Color = 'Red' AND MK.MakeName = 'Ferrari';
```

Running this query should show something like Figure 5.2.

MakeName	Color
Ferrari	Red

Figure 5.2: Searching on simultaneous criteria

How it Works

This query is similar to the previous one. So, let's just look at the differences. In this example, OR has been replaced by AND. This tells SQL that *both* criteria must be met for a record to pass the filter. So, only records where the vehicle is a red Ferrari will appear in the output.

Tricks and Traps

You are likely to use the AND keyword frequently in your SQL career. So, it is worth noting the following right from the start:

- The AND operator will narrow down the search considerably, as *both* filter conditions have to be met for a record to be allowed through to the output.

- A query can have multiple criteria that are applied to filter the data. This means in practice that you can add as many AND clauses to the WHERE clause that you like.

- The technical name for a filter like this is a *logical and*.

3. Using Multiple Filters and an Exclusion

Up until now, when using multiple selection criteria, you have looked at fairly limited selections using only two elements. Now, however, you have been asked to find all makes except Bentleys where the cars are red, green, or blue. You are lucky that SQL can help you to create much more complex filters that can apply these kinds of criteria really easily. To see how this kind of complex query is written, take a look at the following piece of SQL:

```
SELECT     DISTINCT MK.MakeName, ST.Color

FROM       make AS MK

JOIN       model AS MD USING (MakeID)

JOIN       stock AS ST USING (ModelID)

JOIN       salesdetails SD ON ST.StockCode = SD.StockID

WHERE      ST.Color IN ('Red', 'Green', 'Blue')

           AND MK.MakeName != 'Bentley'

ORDER BY   MK.MakeName, ST.Color;
```

Running this query will return the output in Figure 5.3.

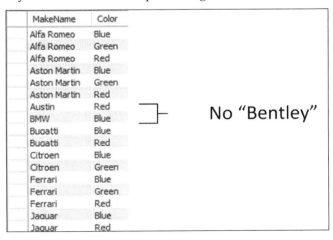

Figure 5.3: *Combining multiple selections with an exclusion*

How it Works

This query shows you that you can combine any of the filtering techniques that you have seen so far in this chapter and the previous one if they help you attain the required result. This filter mixes the IN operator to filter on a chosen selection of colors (red, green, or blue) but excludes all Bentleys from the result—whatever the color.

This query applies two conditions.

First: It itemizes a list of colors that the vehicle can be.

Second: It extends the criteria with an AND clause to add a second condition that excludes Bentley as the make.

The result is that you have a list of all makes except Bentley as long as the cars are red, green, or blue.

Tricks and Traps

I have only two points to make here.

- You can use either <> or != to exclude an element in a WHERE clause.
- We added the DISTINCT keyword to the SELECT clause to produce a list of makes that excludes duplicates.

4. Filtering on Both Text and Numbers Simultaneously

Sometimes you could want to filter data so that a certain condition is always met, and then a second criterion has to be met as well—only the second criterion can apply different, alternative criteria to other fields. Take, for example, the request from the finance director to see a report containing all the red cars ever bought where their repair cost or the cost of spare parts exceeds £1,000.00. The following SQL snippet shows this type of query in action:

```
SELECT     MD.ModelName, ST.Color, ST.PartsCost

           ,ST.RepairsCost

FROM       stock AS ST

JOIN       model AS MD
```

```
            USING (ModelID)

WHERE       ST.Color = 'Red' AND (ST.PartsCost > 1000

            OR ST.RepairsCost > 1000)

ORDER BY    MD.ModelName;
```

Executing this piece of SQL will return a list like that shown in Figure 5.4.

ModelName	Color	PartsCost	RepairsCost
355	Red	750.0000	2000.0000
355	Red	750.0000	9250.0000
57C	Red	457.0000	5500.0000
57C	Red	7500.0000	9250.0000
924	Red	750.0000	1360.0000
944	Red	500.0000	1360.0000
DB2	Red	750.0000	2000.0000
DB9	Red	750.0000	1490.0000
Mark X	Red	750.0000	2175.0000
Rapide	Red	750.0000	1360.0000
Testarossa	Red	1500.0000	2175.0000
Vevron	Red	2200.0000	9250.0000
Virage	Red	1500.0000	3950.0000
Wraith	Red	3150.0000	3950.0000
XK120	Red	500.0000	1100.0000

Figure 5.4: *Nested criteria*

How it Works

This query joins the Stock and Model tables and then specifies that only red cars must be output. Then it extends the filter with a second criterion to select data using another condition that must be met on *either* of two other columns.

The parentheses that are used to enclose the second part of the filter (after the AND operator) are an important part of the WHERE clause. Placing part of the WHERE clause inside parentheses like this means the following:

First: Any of the conditions inside the parentheses have to be true.

Second: The condition outside the parentheses must also be true.

So, the resulting filter is essentially in two parts.

Not only The Color field must contain the "Red" text.

As well as *Either* the parts cost must be over £1,000.00 *or* the repair cost must be over £1,000.00.

The filter is saying this: "For every red car, see whether either the parts cost or the repair cost is over 1,000." Only if both these criteria are met will the record containing this data appear in the result set.

Tricks and Traps

When writing queries that provide alternative filters, there are a couple of key points to take away.

- It is *vital* to place any alternative choices (in this example that means the cost of spares or the repair cost) inside parentheses. If you do *not* do this, then the query will be interpreted as "any red car or any repair cost over £1,000.00 or any parts cost over £1,000.00." This will return a completely different result set.

- If both the parts cost and the repair cost are over 1,000, then the filter will work, as it needs only one of them to match to function. Once one filter condition is met, SQL does not care if others are met or not. This does not, however, mean that a record that meets all the criteria will appear multiple times in the output. It just means that the minimal conditions for the row to be allowed through into the result set have been met.

- In this example we avoided using the DISTINCT keyword in the SELECT clause to ensure that the query delivered the complete list of vehicles matching the required selection criteria.

- Unless you have added an ORDER BY clause to the query there is no guarantee that the data will be returned in any specific sort order.

5. Applying Complex Alternative Filters at the Same Time

There could be days in your career as a data analyst when you will wonder why (and how) people can possibly dream up the requests that they send you. Take, for instance, this suggestion from the finance director: "I want to see all red, green, or blue Rolls-Royce Phantoms—or failing that any vehicle where both the parts cost and the repair cost are over £5,500.00."

You are, yet again, in luck because SQL queries can be tailored to filter data down to an extremely fine level of detail. This query supposes you need to see either of the following categories of sales:

- Red, Green, or Blue Rolls-Royce Phantoms
- Sales where both the parts and repair cost is over 5,500.00

I realize that this may seem to be a strange thing to ask—but believe me, I have seen more peculiar requirements in the past. In any case, here is the code that can satisfy the request:

```
SELECT DISTINCT  MD.ModelName, ST.Color, ST.PartsCost

                 ,ST.RepairsCost

FROM             stock AS ST

JOIN             model AS MD USING (ModelID)

WHERE            (ST.Color IN ('Red', 'Green', 'Blue')

                     AND

                 MD.ModelName = 'Phantom')

                 OR

                 (ST.PartsCost > 5500 AND ST.RepairsCost > 5500);
```

If you run this piece of SQL, you will see a data set like that shown in Figure 5.5. Be aware that the sort order might be slightly different on your system as the SQL does not include an ORDER BY clause.

ModelName	Color	PartsCost	RepairsCost
F50	Silver	7900.0000	9250.0000
Phantom	Green	1500.0000	5500.0000
Phantom	Green	2200.0000	1490.0000
Phantom	Red	750.0000	500.0000
57C	Red	7500.0000	9250.0000

Figure 5.5: Complex nested criteria

How it Works

This piece of SQL has two parts—each one on either side of the central OR keyword. What the filter does is to apply both parts of the WHERE clause independently and then return any records that match either (or both) conditions. It is as if there are two separate filters in action where each one is independent of the other.

To ensure that each side of the OR clause does exactly what you want it to, it is vital that you enclose each side of the clause in parentheses. This way, the filter consists of these three elements:

A first condition:	That defines the acceptable color and model.
The OR operator:	That tells SQL to apply either the first criterion or the second.
A second condition:	That sets a specific cost threshold for either of two fields.

As this WHERE clause is a little more complex, you might want to take a look at Figure 5.6, which explains how it works in a more visual way.

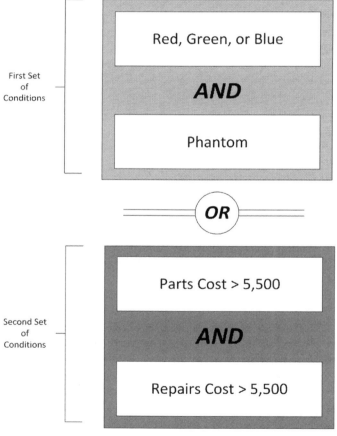

Figure 5.6: *The anatomy of a complex WHERE clause*

Tricks and Traps

These kinds of complex filters come with their own set of variations and caveats. You need to remember the following:

- You can write the WHERE clause as a single line or without indentation if you prefer so that it reads as follows:

```
WHERE (Color IN ('Red', 'Green', 'Blue') AND ModelName = 'Phantom')
OR (PartsCost > 1500 OR RepairsCost > 1500)
```

  This is purely a question of presentation. However, you may find that separating the WHERE clause over several lines makes it easier to read and to understand because a multi-line format enhances the fact that there are two separate aspects to the filter, each one on a separate side of the OR keyword.

- Once again, if both of the filter conditions are met, the filter will work because it needs only one of them to match to succeed. If one filter condition is met, SQL does not care if others are met or not.

6. Case-Sensitive Searches

When filtering text in a WHERE clause you can enter the text to look for in uppercase, lowercase or even a mixture of uppercase and lowercase characters. This will always be the case unless the MySQL server, the database or the specific field that you are using in a WHERE clause to filter data has been set to be case-sensitive.

Sometimes you may want to force MySQL to apply a case-sensitive search—that is, you only want to search for a text in the exact capitalization that you enter to the right of the equals sign. The following short piece of SQL shows how this can be done.

```
SELECT *
FROM    stock
WHERE   BINARY color = 'Dark purple';
```

Running this piece of code produces the result that you can see in Figure 5.7, where only a single record is returned out of all the many records for dark purple vehicles.

StockCode	ModelID	Cost	RepairsCost	PartsCost	TransportInCost	IsRHD	Color	BuyerComments	DateBought	TimeBought
01B087C6-00D1-40B2-808F-B4B5BC1E344D	54	17200.0000	500.0000	500.0000	150.0000	1	Dark purple	NULL	2017-02-04	12:55:00.000000
NULL	NULL	NULL	NULL	NULL	NULL	NULL	NULL	NULL	NULL	NULL

Figure 5.7: A WHERE clause that performs a case-sensitive search

How it Works

Making a filter element case sensitive simply means placing the BINARY keyword before the name of the field that you are using to filter in a WHERE clause. This keyword tells MySQL to compare characters using the internal system character codes used by the database and operating system and not just the letters. The effect in this example is to return the unique record where the word "purple" in the color field is spelled with a lowercase "p".

Running the same query without the BINARY keyword produces many more results, as you can see in Figure 5.8.

StockCode	ModelID	Cost	RepairsCost	PartsCost	TransportInCost	IsRHD	Color	BuyerComments	DateBought	TimeBought
01B087C6-00D1-40B2-808F-84B5BC1E34D	54	17200.0000	500.0000	500.0000	150.0000	1	Dark purple		2017-02-04	12:55:00.000000
13F9FBD7-9342-4A2D-A249-E3AD6AE9A9CB	74	54800.0000	500.0000	1500.0000	750.0000	1	Dark Purple		2018-07-25	12:55:00.000000
155E940E-7AA7-47EA-883F-83521F0B5718	11	55120.0000	500.0000	750.0000	750.0000	1	Dark Purple		2016-09-09	12:55:00.000000
18974E49-6B03-4C6E-BA0C-D564CFF868E0	31	62000.0000	2000.0000	1500.0000	750.0000	1	Dark Purple		2016-06-01	12:55:00.000000
23E43063-5402-4946-8830-0723F6B3CE1C	37	132000.0000	9250.0000	3150.0000	1950.0000	1	Dark Purple		2017-08-02	12:55:00.000000
356EE84B-F4FD-4923-9423-D58E2863E9A1	25	36480.0000	500.0000	500.0000	550.0000	1	Dark Purple		2016-07-31	12:55:00.000000
3CF2C0F8-21E1-4ADE-AE72-AB9DFE3790DD	35	79600.0000	1490.0000	750.0000	750.0000	1	Dark Purple		2016-12-01	12:55:00.000000
5F898C04-BDFB-437B-A640-AE520F14031E	91	23200.0000	500.0000	750.0000	150.0000	1	Dark Purple		2017-03-12	12:55:00.000000
61F8CF9A-F53C-4386-9BF8-578F54547CD2	7	215600.0000	5500.0000	1500.0000	1950.0000	1	Dark Purple		2018-05-01	12:55:00.000000

Figure 5.8: The same WHERE clause without applying case-sensitivity

Tricks and Traps

The following point is important when carrying out case-sensitive searches:

- You must add the BINARY keyword before *each individual field name* where you want to apply a case-sensitive search. So you may end up repeating the BINARY keyword several times in a WHERE clause.

7. Removing Case-Sensitivity in Filters

If you are working on a system where everything is case-sensitive there could be occasions when you want to search for an element regardless of capitalization.

The following SQL can do this:

```
SELECT    MD.ModelName, ST.Color, ST.PartsCost

          ,ST.RepairsCost

FROM      stock AS ST
```

```
JOIN       model AS MD

           USING (ModelID)

WHERE      UPPER(ST.Color) = 'DARK PURPLE'

ORDER BY   MD.ModelName;
```

Running this piece of SQL produces the result that you can see in Figure 5.9, where all the dark purple vehicles are returned—whatever the capitalization of the word "purple".

ModelName	Color	PartsCost	RepairsCost
135	Dark Purple	750.0000	1360.0000
350SL	Dark Purple	500.0000	660.0000
350SL	Dark Purple	457.0000	2000.0000
911	Dark Purple	750.0000	500.0000
Continental	Dark Purple	1500.0000	2000.0000
Continental	Dark Purple	750.0000	1490.0000
DB9	Dark Purple	500.0000	500.0000
Dino	Dark Purple	1500.0000	2175.0000
F40	Dark Purple	1500.0000	5500.0000
Giulietta	Dark purple	500.0000	500.0000
M600	Dark Purple	1500.0000	660.0000
Phantom	Dark Purple	750.0000	1490.0000
Roadster	Dark Purple	750.0000	500.0000
TR4	Dark Purple	750.0000	500.0000

Exception Record

Figure 5.9: A WHERE clause that performs a case-insensitive search

How it Works

This short query joins the Stock and Model tables and outputs the four fields that you can see in the SELECT clause. However, it is the WHERE clause that adds something new.

First: You Begin a WHERE clause.

Second: You wrap the field name that you are searching (Color in this example) inside the UPPER() function.

Finally: You add an equals operator and enter the text that you are looking for in *uppercase*—and in quotes.

What the UPPER() function does is to convert the contents of the field that it encloses to uppercase inside the filter action. As you are comparing the field that is, for the purposes of the query, now in uppercase to a text you entered in uppercase, you are effectively canceling out any case-sensitivity for this part of the filter. This is because you are comparing an uppercase text to uppercase field contents.

This query introduced a fundamental new concept—MySQL functions. As this is the first time that you are using a function in MySQL you need to know a little about MySQL functions and what they do.

- A function modifies the element that it is applied to. This element is often a field. This means that the function will be applied to every record in the table for the field that it is applied to.

- Simple functions—like the UPPER() function used here—are applied to a single field by placing the field name inside the parentheses that follow the function name.

- The field name (or other element that is enclosed inside the parentheses) is called a *parameter*.

- MySQL has a wealth of available functions built-in that help you to query data. You will be meeting many of them throughout the rest of this book.

Tricks and Traps

The following points are worth noting at this juncture:

- The UPPER() function will be explained in more detail in Chapter 9, where you can see other situations where this function can be used in queries.

- You have to apply the UPPER() function to *each field* where you want to remove case-sensitivity.

- Altering the case-sensitivity of the filter does *not alter the field contents*—as you can see in the query output shown in Figure 5.9, where all the colors are a mixture of uppercase and lowercase characters.

8. Using Wildcard Searches

Returning a list of data is nearly always easy when everything (including the data) is perfect. In the real world, however, this is not always the case. Maybe the data has not been entered correctly, or perhaps you cannot remember how it was spelled. Sometimes it could be a combination of both these circumstances. You are reminded of this when the receptionist comes to your desk with a request for some help. She knows that Prestige Cars has a customer with Peter (or was that Pete?) somewhere in their name, and you need to find this person in the database. Fortunately, SQL has a few solutions to help you filter a little more approximately. One example is given in the following piece of SQL:

```
SELECT      CustomerName

FROM        customer

WHERE       CustomerName LIKE '%pete%';
```

Running this query will return the output in Figure 5.10.

CustomerName
Peter McLuckie
Honest Pete Motors
Peter Smith
Pete Spring

Figure 5.10: Wildcard filtering

How it Works

This piece of code searched the Customer table for any element in the CustomerName field that contains the characters *pete*. Consequently, it found Pete and Peter and would also have found Peteer, Pete's Sake—well, you get the idea!

This kind of search is called a *wildcard* filter, and it requires you to adhere to a few basic principles.

- Wildcard searches require you to use the LIKE operator.
- As we are searching inside a text field, the text has to be enclosed in single quotes, as was the case in all queries that you saw previously that searched on text-based fields.
- The percentage symbol (%) really means "any character or characters." This symbol is called a *wildcard* in this context.
- You *must* place any percentage symbols *inside* the single quotes.

In other respects, a wildcard search is very much like a filter applied to any text-based column. The only real difference is the use of the % character to widen the range of elements that MySQL can return.

Tricks and Traps

Wildcard searches are powerful, but you do have to take care when using them. Here are some examples:

- When using these kinds of searches, it makes no difference if you enter the search text in uppercase or lowercase—or if the data in the table is in uppercase or lowercase. SQL will find all matching records no matter what the case of the search text or the data.

- If you want to locate a few characters anywhere inside a field, then you need to place the wildcard (the percentage symbol) on either side of the text that you are looking for.

- If you are certain the records you are looking for have a field that *begins* with the text that you are using to filter the result (*pete* in this example), then you can alter the WHERE clause so that it looks like this:

```
WHERE     CustomerName LIKE 'pete%'
```

As you can see, the wildcard is entered only *after* the search text. This, in effect, tells SQL that the field to look for begins with *pete*—and can have *any text* after this.

- If the records that you are looking for have a field that *ends* with the text that you are using to filter the result (*pete* in this example), then you can alter the WHERE clause so that it looks like this:

```
WHERE     CustomerName LIKE '%pete'
```

This code tells SQL to find records where the CustomerName field ends with *pete*—however many words or characters precede the text you are looking for.

- Wildcards will apply to letters, numbers, or even symbols; they are not limited to alphabetical letters. However, they are mostly used when filtering on text-based data.

9. Using Wildcards to Exclude Data

There could be occasions when you want to use wildcards to exclude data from the query output. Suppose, for instance, that you want to produce a list of all the customers *except* those with *pete* somewhere in their name. The following SQL extends the code from the previous example to do exactly this:

```
SELECT    CustomerName

FROM      customer

WHERE     CustomerName NOT LIKE '%pete%'

ORDER BY  CustomerName;
```

Running this query will show the kind of result that you can see in Figure 5.11 (note that not all the output is shown here).

CustomerName
Alex McWhirter
Alexei Tolstoi
Alicia Almodovar
Andrea Tarbuck
Andv Cheshire
Antonio Maura
Autos Sportivos
Beltwav Prestige Drivina
Birminaham Executive Prestige Vehicles
Blina Blina S.A.
Blina Motors
Boris Sorv
Bravissima!
Capots Reluisants S.A.
Casseroles Chromes
Clubbina Cars

Figure 5.11: Excluding data by applying a wildcard

How it Works

Preceding the LIKE operator with the NOT keyword reverses the filter logic. This means that—in this query at least—every customer will be displayed unless their name contains the characters *pete*. You can verify this by scrolling down through the result set. You will see that no customer with *pete* in their name is present.

10. Forcing Case-Sensitivity in Wildcard Filters

Sometimes you may want MySQL to apply a case-sensitive search when using wildcard filters. The following short piece of SQL shows that this is extremely easy to do.

```
SELECT *

FROM make

WHERE BINARY MakeName LIKE '%L%';
```

Running this piece of code produces the kind of result that you can see in Figure 5.12.

MakeID	MakeName	MakeCountry
3	Lamborghini	ITA
17	Lagonda	ITA
18	McLaren	GBR

Figure 5.12: A WHERE clause that performs a case-sensitive search when using a wildcard

How it Works

Making a wildcard search case sensitive simply means placing the BINARY keyword before the name of the field that you are using a wildcard filter on.

In this specific example you are only returning makes with a capital "L" in the name of the marque. As you are using the LIKE operator with wildcard symbols both before and after the character that you are looking for, the uppercase "L" can be *anywhere* in the name of the car. However, models with a lowercase l anywhere in the name are not returned—you do not see the makes Alfa Romeo or Bentley for instance.

Tricks and Traps

The following points are important when carrying out case-sensitive searches when using a wildcard:

- You must add the BINARY keyword before *each individual field name* where a case-sensitive search must be applied.

- If you want to exclude a character and retain case-sensitivity you can negate the filter using the NOT operator. So, for instance you could write code like the following to find makes *without* an uppercase L in the name:

```
SELECT * FROM Make WHERE BINARY MakeName NOT LIKE '%L%';
```

11. Using a Specific Part of Text to Filter Data

Just as you were glancing at the clock at the end of the day, the finance director appears beside your desk with an apparently strange demand. He informs you that the account number field is structured in such a way that you can identify the country of sale from certain characters at a specific point in the field. So, he wants you to use this to isolate all the sales made to French customers.

Put another way, what he means is "I have a field where each character—or certain characters—has a specific meaning and the field always has the same number of characters with the same subgroups of meaningful characters." A bank account or Social Security numbers (or other identity codes) in certain countries are examples of this kind of data. In these cases, you may well want to specify that a certain number of characters can be anything at all—but others (at a specific place in the field) have a meaning that you want to filter on.

The InvoiceNumber field of the Sales table is one of these fields. It is defined like this:

The left three characters	Indicate the currency of sale
Characters 4 and 5	Indicate the destination country
The last three characters	Provide a sequential invoice number

This approach is explained more graphically in Figure 5.13.

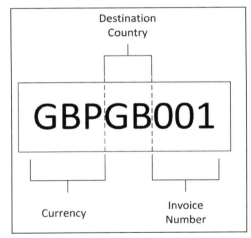

Figure 5.13: *Structured fields*

So, the invoice number GBPGB001 tells you that this sale was made in pounds sterling to a client in the United Kingdom—and is invoice No 001.

If you are faced with a structured field like this, you can search on *parts* of the field to isolate certain records. In this example, the following SQL returns only vehicles sold to *France*—whatever the currency and whatever the invoice number.

```
SELECT DISTINCT   MD.ModelName, SA. InvoiceNumber

FROM              make AS MK
```

```
JOIN            model AS MD

                USING (MakeID)

JOIN            stock ST

                USING (ModelID)

JOIN            salesdetails AS SD

                ON SD.StockID = ST.StockCode

JOIN            sales AS SA

                ON SA.SalesID = SD.SalesID

WHERE           SA.InvoiceNumber LIKE '___FR%'

ORDER BY        SA. InvoiceNumber;
```

Running this query (and specifically using three underscores in the WHERE clause before the FR%) will return the output in Figure 5.14.

ModelName	InvoiceNumber
944	EURFR005
911	EURFR009
944	EURFR013
280SL	EURFR015
DB6	EURFR018
XJS	EURFR018
Giulia	EURFR031
924	EURFR037
DB6	EURFR047
TR4	EURFR048
XK150	EURFR051
Flying Spur	EURFR051
DB6	EURFR051
XK120	EURFR064
911	EURFR069
Vanquish	EURFR075

Figure 5.14: Wildcard searches in structured fields

How it Works

This piece of SQL uses wildcards to filter a field. More precisely, it uses the underscore character as a single-character wildcard. So, the WHERE clause in this sample says this:

First: Find any *three* characters on the left of the field (*three underscores*).

Then: Filter on FR.

Finally: Don't filter on any other characters to the end of the text (let anything through, no matter how many characters). This is represented by the percentage symbol.

When faced with structured coded texts like this one, it is vital to know what each subset of characters means in the field. Providing that you know this, you can then filter on any part of the text, as you did here.

Tricks and Traps

While filtering on a specific part of a field is not difficult, it helps to remember the following points when you do this:

- Where there is a strict coding scheme, such as a bank account number, you can use the underscore wildcard to replace a *single* character, or a specified number of characters. However, there must be one character at least if you use an underscore. This is unlike the percentage wildcard that means *zero to any number* of characters.

- You can use the underscore wildcard anywhere in a search pattern—and even use it several times. For instance, you could also have written this WHERE clause as follows:

```
WHERE      InvoiceNumber LIKE '___FR___'
```

This pattern will find any initial three characters, FR, and then any three final characters.

- Be warned that wildcard searches (using % or _) can be slow on large data sets. If your work will entail carrying out lots of searches like these on massive tables, then it could be worth talking to your database administrator to see if he or she can implement a way of speeding up searches like these. If you have no one to help you, then you can find plenty of advice on the Web that explains how to accelerate text searches in MySQL.

- If you need to find the actual underscore or percentage characters in a field (and not use "_" and "%" as wildcards), then there is a solution. Simply place the wildcard character inside square brackets and SQL will treat it as a normal character. An example of this is:

```
WHERE name LIKE 'db[_]%
```

In this example the underscore is a standard character—and consequently this will be used as a filter. The percentage symbol is still used as a wildcard. The result is that this filter will return all records that begin with db_.

12. Using NULLs, or Nonexistent Data

Finding data is fairly easy if the data is present. However, real-world databases can contain missing data elements. Indeed, the marketing director has noticed that the corporate database is missing postcodes (ZIP codes) for some clients. So, she has asked for a list of all customers without this vital piece of information.

Fortunately, SQL can handle empty data fields easily. So, you use the following short piece of SQL to deliver the report that will make the man from the marketing department very happy:

```
SELECT    CustomerName, PostCode

FROM      customer

WHERE     PostCode IS NULL

ORDER BY CustomerName;
```

Running this query will return the output shown in Figure 5.15.

CustomerName	PostCode
Antonio Maura	NULL
Autos Sportivos	NULL
Bling Bling S.A.	NULL
Capots Reluisants S.A.	NULL
Casseroles Chromes	NULL
Diplomatic Cars	NULL
El Sport	NULL
Flash Voitures	NULL
Francois Chirac	NULL
Francoise LeBrun	NULL
Glitz	NULL
Jacques Mitterand	NULL
Jason B. Wight	NULL
Jayden Jones	NULL
Jean-Yves Truffaut	NULL
Khader El Ghannam	NULL

Figure 5.15: Finding NULL fields

How it Works

Nonexistent data is handled in specific ways in SQL because "empty" fields are considered special. Indeed, any missing or empty data element is even given a particular name; it is called a *NULL* value by SQL.

I have to be up-front with you and admit that dealing with NULL values can get tricky. So, rather than explain everything that you need to know about them in one fell swoop, I prefer to introduce the various techniques that you will need to know as required during the course of this book.

For now, you need to know that you can filter on NULL values using the IS keyword followed by the word NULL. This will allow you to isolate data on nonexistent elements.

Tricks and Traps

To begin your acquaintance with NULLs, you should take note of the following points:

- Although MySQL Workbench displays the word NULL in output from queries, this is only a way of indicating that the field is blank. The field itself contains nothing at all—and certainly not the word NULL.

- If you need to filter on records where there actually *is* data, you can use SQL like the following:

```
SELECT    CustomerName
FROM      customer
WHERE     PostCode IS NOT NULL
```

Here, as you can see, any nonempty elements can be displayed by negating the IS NULL command and instead writing IS NOT NULL.

You *cannot* look for non-null fields by writing <> NULL.

- An alternative method of telling MySQL to return data when a column contains no information is to write SQL like this :

```
SELECT    CustomerName
FROM      customer
WHERE     NOT PostCode  <=> NULL;
```

However, this approach is rarely used, and so I prefer to use the IS NOT NULL technique. As, however, you might come across the alternative method if you are reviewing other people's SQL code, it is best to be aware that it exists.

- As SQL uses the equal operator for other filters, you could be tempted to write code like this:

```
WHERE     PostCode = NULL
```

However, you need to be aware that this will *not* work correctly. In fact, it will always return a blank record set. So, you could be lured into a false sense of security and end up believing that there are no empty items in a dataset when this is far from the case.

- Be warned, however, that NULL means a field that is empty. If users have entered spaces or even a couple of single quotes (which are invisible to the eye but mean that the field is not strictly empty), then these fields will not be caught by IS NULL.

- To find fields containing a space, you can use SQL like this:

```
WHERE     PostCode = ' '
```

- To find fields containing a blank, you can use SQL like this:

```
WHERE     PostCode = ''
```

13. Searching Using Regular Expressions

The marketing director has come up with a final challenge for you. She wants to look for all customers whose name begins with "Pe" and ends with "g".

Fortunately you know that MySQL can apply regular expressions when filtering data, and you write the following piece of SQL to produce the result shown in Figure 5.16.

```
SELECT    CustomerName

FROM      customer

WHERE     CustomerName REGEXP '^Pe.*g$';
```

CustomerName
Pete Spring

Figure 5.16: Using regular expressions to filter data

How it Works

Sometimes you may need to apply quite complex filters to the data in a table. You could be looking for emails that do not match a valid email format, or social security numbers that are not correct, for instance.

In cases like these MySQL can help you by using regular expressions in the WHERE clause of an SQL query. Regular expressions are a text filtering and verification technique that has been around for a very long time, and is used in many different programming languages, databases and applications.

I have to be clear about one thing at this juncture. Regular expressions are a vast subject and can be extremely complex. So all I will be doing here is to introduce you to one of the ways that you can use regular expressions in MySQL. If you need to study regular expressions in depth then I suggest that you look at one of the many excellent resources available either on the web or in print that can explain this technique in detail.

Anyway, in this particular example I use the following approach:

First: In the WHERE clause, enter the field that you want to apply a regular expression to

Second: Enter the REGEXP keyword

Finally: Enter the regular expression pattern in quotes

Tricks and Traps

You need to be aware of the following points when using regular expressions in MySQL.

- Regular expressions can be combined with other filtering techniques in the WHERE clause.
- You can enclose the regular expression pattern in either single or (on many systems) double quotes.
- If you prefer you can use RLIKE instead of REGEXP.
- Regular expression patterns can be fiendishly complex. As even a cursory overview of regular expressions could take several chapters, I will not be explaining the pattern used here.

Conclusion

This chapter took you much further into the world of SQL filtering. You saw how to apply either/or filters as well as define multiple cumulative conditions using the data from different fields in a SQL query. Moreover, you also saw how to apply more complex logic to force MySQL to apply certain conditions but not others—or to combine conditions—to deliver the result you wanted. Then, you learned that you can apply filter conditions to certain parts of a field—and that you can even filter on nonexistent (or NULL) data. Finally, after carrying out "fuzzy" searches using wildcards you saw how to use regular expressions to apply sophisticated filters to text fields.

Core Knowledge Learned in This Chapter

These are the keywords that you saw in this chapter:

Concept	Description
AND	This logical operator forces a filter to meet two conditions if a record is to be displayed in the output.
OR	This logical operator allows a filter to let data through to the result if either of two filter conditions is met.
NOT	This logical operator reverses the logic of a filter.
LIKE	This keyword lets you look for the partial contents of a column when filtering records.
%	This operator is used with the LIKE keyword to filter on the partial contents of a column and can represent any characters—or none.
REGEXP	This keyword lets you look for a complex pattern of text in the contents of a column when filtering records.
IS NULL	This operator is used to filter on empty fields.
IS NOT NULL	This operator is used to filter on non-empty fields.
<=>	This operator is used to filter on non-empty fields.
RLIKE	This keyword lets you look for a complex pattern of text in the contents of a column when filtering records.
_	This operator is used with the LIKE keyword to filter on the partial contents of a column. It represents any single character.
<>	This operator excludes an element from a query.
!=	This operator excludes an element from a query.

CHAPTER 6
Making Simple Calculations

SQL is not limited to merely finding, filtering, and eventually aggregating data. It can also carry out calculations that range from elementary math to relatively advanced statistical operations. It follows that an essential aspect of writing SQL queries consists of learning how to apply math to the core data to deliver increased insight and analysis.

Performing Calculations in SQL

In this chapter, I will show you how to perform simple math on the numeric data contained in MySQL data tables. One you have mastered the basics, you should be able to build on this knowledge to enhance your own SQL queries to deliver all kinds of numerical analysis.

More specifically, you will see how to

- Perform basic arithmetic
- Create formulas that force MySQL to perform calculations in the right order
- Identify numeric fields in tables
- Handle missing (or NULL) numeric data
- Use calculations to filter data

None of this is at all difficult, so now is the time to start learning to use SQL to practice your math.

1. Doing Simple Math

The finance director is fuming. He cannot find a spreadsheet that tells him what the exact cost of every car sold is, including the purchase cost along with any repairs, parts, and transport costs. Inevitably this becomes something that you have to deal with. So, let's see how to calculate the total cost of each vehicle sold. A quick look at the SalesByCountry view shows that there are four columns that itemize the cost elements, which are the purchase cost of the vehicle and the cost of repairs, parts, and transport. The following code snippet shows how you can add them together to produce the cost of sales on the fly in SQL:

```
SELECT    MakeName, ModelName

          ,Cost + RepairsCost + PartsCost  + TransportInCost

          AS TotalCost

FROM      salesbycountry

ORDER BY MakeName, ModelName;
```

Executing this code returns the output shown in Figure 6.1.

MakeName	ModelName	TotalCost
Alfa Romeo	1750	4260.0000
Alfa Romeo	1750	9360.0000
Alfa Romeo	Giulia	22260.0000
Alfa Romeo	Giulia	15735.0000
Alfa Romeo	Giulia	7260.0000
Alfa Romeo	Giulia	9800.0000
Alfa Romeo	Giulia	3440.0000
Alfa Romeo	Giulia	11400.0000
Alfa Romeo	Giulia	6200.0000
Alfa Romeo	Giulia	8256.0000
Alfa Romeo	Giulietta	18350.0000
Alfa Romeo	Giulietta	5952.0000
Alfa Romeo	Giulietta	10640.0000
Alfa Romeo	Giulietta	9800.0000
Alfa Romeo	Giulietta	6600.0000
Alfa Romeo	Giulietta	16200.0000
Alfa Romeo	Giulietta	17560.0000
Alfa Romeo	Spider	11400.0000

Figure 6.1: Adding up the data from several columns

How it Works

This code snippet takes a view rather than a joined set of tables as the basis for the calculation. If you cast your mind back to Chapter 2, you will remember that a view is a way of memorizing a set of tables and all the joins required to link them. You could have replaced the single view in the FROM clause with several lines of SQL, but I am trying to keep things simpler for the moment so that you can concentrate on the math. In any case, using this view lets you access all the fields that you need to analyze the sales data.

As you can see, adding up the data in a set of columns is as simple as entering the columns as part of a SELECT clause with a plus (+) operator between each column name. The key element is that all the columns must contain numeric data.

So, although MySQL is a database, it can perform a wide variety of calculations. These range from the elementary to the complex. While the math that you used to work out the cost of sales is not particularly demanding, it is a useful introduction to basic calculations that you can apply to your data using SQL.

Tricks and Traps

As I am introducing a new concept in SQL, there are—perhaps inevitably—a few key points to retain when carrying out elementary calculations.

- As a matter of principle, I have added an alias to the calculated column that is returned to avoid it being called "Cost + RepairsCost + PartsCost + TransportInCost"—as it would if you did not give it an alias.

- All in all, carrying out calculations in MySQL is similar to carrying out arithmetical operations in Excel (or any other spreadsheet). Only in SQL you define the calculation *once* for a column or a set of columns rather than for a cell reference, and it will be applied to *every row* in the query output without you having to copy the formula down over hundreds—or even tens of thousands—of rows as you would have to in a spreadsheet.

- Remember that you *must* place commas between fields when laying out your SQL. You can add them to the end of lines or the start of lines—it is all the same to SQL. This is why the second line of this example begins with a comma (and this is also why there is no comma at the end of the first line).

- You should *not*, however, place commas between the fields used in calculations like the one in this section. This is because the output of the calculation is considered as a single field.

- You can try and calculate data using the contents of a non-numeric column if you really have to. This can be necessary when a database has been designed with a field that has been set to a character data type—but has been filled with numbers. MySQL will attempt to convert the numbers stored as text to numeric values when carrying out the calculation. However, it only takes a single text element to appear instead of a number in one record out of tens (or hundreds) of thousands for the query to return a wrong result—without you suspecting that the output is incorrect.

2. Examining Data Types in MySQL Views

When using SQL to carry out calculations, it is *fundamental* that the columns you reference contain *numbers* and not strings of characters. It takes only a single column in a calculation to contain some text for calculations to be inaccurate. This is because MySQL will simply ignore text values that cannot be interpreted as numbers, without warning you that there are potential errors.

It follows that you need to learn to be careful when choosing the columns that you can—and cannot—use when performing calculations in SQL. Fortunately, data tables do contain some reliable indications of which columns can be used to store only numbers. Columns like this are known as having *numeric data types*. Generally, database designers will have used them to contain numeric data that you can use in your calculations.

In Chapter 1, you saw how to expand a table in MySQL Workbench to look at the columns in the table. This technique has the added advantage of letting you see what the data type of each column is so that you can build your calculations safely and reliably. You can also apply this approach to views, which is what you will learn how to do now:

1. In MySQL Workbench, expand the contents of the database containing the view that interests you (the PrestigeCars database in this example).

2. Expand the Views folder.

3. Click on the view whose data types you want to examine (we will use the SalesByCountry view in this example).

4. Take a close look at the Information panel at the left of the screen below the Navigator. You should see something like Figure 6.2.

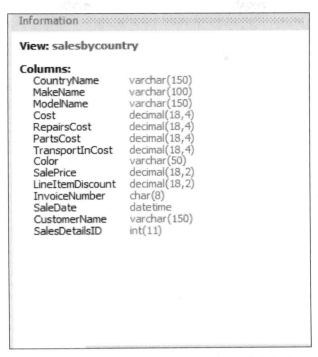

Figure 6.2: *Displaying the columns in a view and their data types*

You can see that the columns you used in the query in the previous section (Cost, RepairsCost, PartsCost, TransportInCost) and also, SalePrice, and LineItemDiscount are all the following data type:

- Decimal

This is good news because this is one of MySQL's numeric data types. The following are other numeric data types:

- Float
- Double
- Numeric
- Int
- Integer
- Tinyint
- Mediumint
- Bigint
- Smallint

As long as the columns you want to use in a calculation are any of these data types, then your calculation should not give you an error.

There are, inevitably, many other MySQL data types, but I prefer to introduce them as the need arises rather than overwhelm you with technical details this early in your SQL querying career.

Tricks and Traps

Life in SQL is not always GUI-based. So you also need to know how to obtain data type information from the command line.

- To display the details about a view from the command line client (and assuming that you have connected to the prestigecars database), enter the following command and press [Enter].

  ```
  desc salesbycountry;
  ```

You should see the results shown in Figure 6.3.

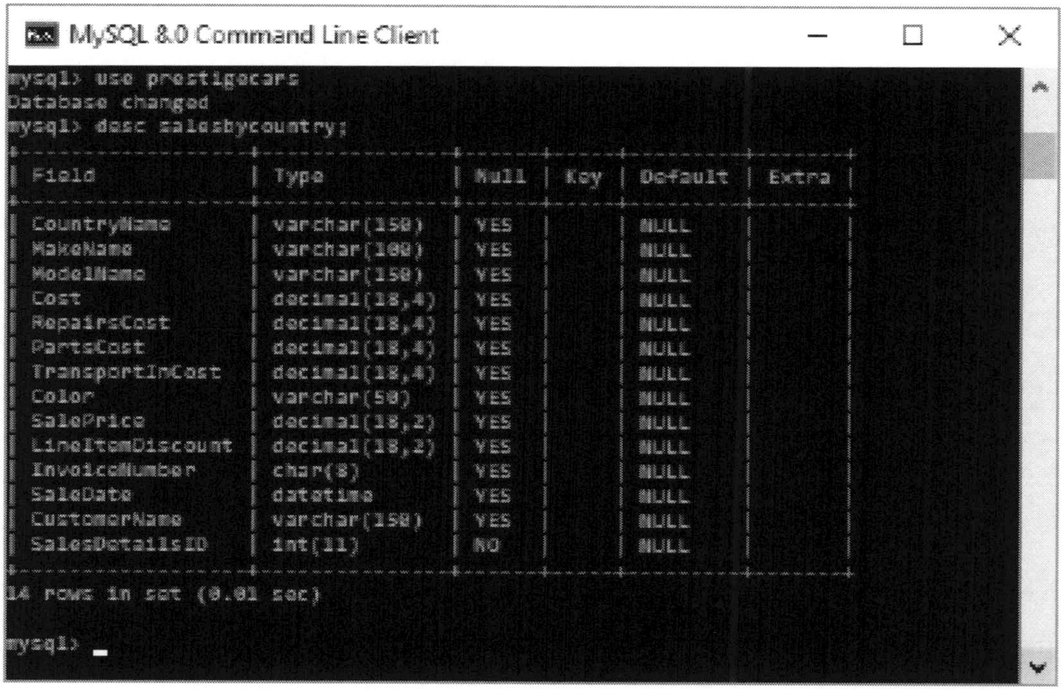

Figure 6.3: *Using the desc command to display the datatypes in a view from the command line*

3. Isolating Sections of Formulas When Applying Math

Now let's return to the finance director's analysis of costs. He was pleased with your cost of sales calculation. However, he wants you to subtract this from the sale price to give the net margin. The piece of code that follows delivers exactly what he is looking for. As you can see, it groups certain elements inside parentheses to isolate parts of the formula so that they are calculated independently of the rest.

```
SELECT    MakeName, ModelName

          ,SalePrice - (Cost + RepairsCost + PartsCost + TransportInCost)

          AS GrossMargin

FROM      SalesByCountry;
```

If you run this code, you should get the output in Figure 6.4.

MakeName	ModelName	TotalCost
Alfa Romeo	1750	10820.0000
Alfa Romeo	Giulia	71756.0000
Alfa Romeo	Giulietta	73752.0000
Alfa Romeo	Spider	50920.0000
Aston Martin	DB2	469072.0000
Aston Martin	DB4	269352.0000
Aston Martin	DB5	271872.0000
Aston Martin	DB6	896556.0000
Aston Martin	DB9	832760.0000
Aston Martin	Rapide	242000.0000
Aston Martin	Vanquish	351632.0000
Aston Martin	Vantage	274800.0000
Aston Martin	Virage	862912.0000
Austin	Cambridge	18000.0000

Figure 6.4: Nesting calculations to guarantee precedence in SQL math

How it Works

Even simple arithmetic may require that certain elements of the calculation have to be worked out before others. Adding parentheses around the cost elements guarantees that the fields containing the vehicle costs will be added together *before* the resulting figure is subtracted from the sale price. I realize that this may seem obvious and that you are probably used to creating calculations like this in Excel. However, I prefer to make it clear from the start that all calculations in MySQL can be "nested" in parentheses like this to force an order of precedence in your arithmetic. This way, certain parts of the calculation are carried out before others.

Tricks and Traps

As simple as the math is, here are a couple of key points to note:

- It is always safer to nest fields inside parentheses rather than to trust a computer to get things right every time. Not only that, but adding parentheses to "nest" calculation elements can help you to make your logic clearer, especially when you return to it weeks or even months later.

- Any calculated field really should have a meaningful alias. This, too, can help you better understand the logic when you look at it again in days to come.

4. Calculating Ratios

The finance director is getting more and more excited at the thought that SQL can apply the math he needs for his analyses. So, now he wants you to give him a list containing the ratio of cost to sales (this is also known as the *cost of goods sold ratio* or the *cost of sales to revenue ratio*). As this is quite simply the gross profit (that you calculated in the previous section) divided by the sale price, the SQL for this is as follows:

```
SELECT    (SalePrice -

          (Cost + RepairsCost + PartsCost + TransportInCost))

          / SalePrice AS RatioOfCostsToSales

FROM      SalesByCountry;
```

When you run this code, MySQL gives you the output shown in Figure 6.5.

RatioOfCostsToSales
0.17240000
0.08800000
0.15086705
-0.15443038
0.12338983
0.08800000
0.11446809
0.06666667
-1.27368421
0.04071942
0.13000000
0.16238994
-0.00253165
0.13777778
0.04180791
0.03529412
0.10700280
0.17115292

Figure 6.5: *Calculating a ratio*

How it Works

As you have already seen addition and subtraction, now is a good time to move on to simple division in SQL. This formula is a three-step process.

First: It adds up the total costs per vehicle (the field names nested inside the inner parentheses).

Second: It subtracts the cost of sales from the sale price. This calculation is contained in the outer parentheses and is the gross margin.

Finally: It divides the gross margin by the sale price to return the cost of goods sold ratio per vehicle. The forward slash operator is the divide operator—exactly as it is in a spreadsheet.

The result is that you see the ratio of costs to sale for every vehicle sold. For the moment, the result has no formatting applied, and consequently it looks much as it probably would in a spreadsheet. I fully realize that raw data can be hard to read. However, we will look at formatting output in Chapter 10 so that you can concentrate on the calculation techniques for the moment.

Tricks and Traps

I only have one point to note here:

- Instead of the forward slash character to divide numbers you can use the DIV operator. However this is only suited to integer division and will only return an integer value—never a decimal value. This makes it unsuitable for calculating percentages. If you wanted to use the DIV function, this is how you would apply it.

```
(Cost + RepairsCost + PartsCost + TransportInCost)) DIV SalePrice
```

5. Avoiding Divide by Zero Errors

Fortunately, your calculation of the ratio of cost to sales worked first time. However, as an experienced spreadsheet user you are all too aware that dividing a figure by zero can produce an error. So it is important to know that divide by zero errors in a query will return NULLs for a record. Consequently, you have researched how to prevent this kind of problem in MySQL, and come up with the following code snippet to handle these kind of errors.

```
SELECT    (SalePrice - (Cost + RepairsCost + PartsCost + TransportInCost))

          / NULLIF(SalePrice, 0) AS RatioOfCostsToSales

FROM      SalesByCountry;
```

Running this piece of code gives the output that you have already seen in Figure 6.4.

How it Works

This piece of SQL wraps the divisor (the field containing the values that will divide the result of the sales cost calculation) in the NULLIF() function.

The NULLIF() function works like this:

First:	You enter the two parameters that you are comparing.
Then:	The function compares them, and returns the first value if they are different—and NULL if they are the same.

So, to test division by zero the function requires the following two parameters.

First:	The field whose contents you are testing to see if it contains a zero
Second:	The figure 0.

As the NULLIF() function detects that two values are identical and returns NULL if this is the case, it will prevent a division by zero by replacing the divide by zero error with NULL as, fortunately, dividing by NULL returns a NULL rather than an error. So if the field by which you are dividing a value contains 0 (zero) the NULLIF() function will work out that this is equal to the zero in the second parameter and will return NULL for the specific record only—and leave other records unaffected. This, in turn, prevents a divide by zero error affecting the entire query.

Tricks and Traps

As simple as this function is, there are a few very important points to note:

- A divide by zero error can prevent an entire query working. That is, the error does not just affect the row(s) containing the error—it affects the entire query and prevents any results being displayed.

- Adding a NULLIF() function when dividing one figure by another cannot cause any harm, and can be a valid way of preventing errors in the future.

- There are other potential applications of the NULLIF() function, but I will not be looking at them here.

6. Increasing Values by a Defined Percentage

To finish your tour of elementary math in SQL, let's imagine that the sales director wants to test the improvement in margins if you increased the sale prices by 5 percent but kept costs the same. The SQL formula that does this is shown here:

```
SELECT    MakeName, ModelName

          ,(SalePrice * 1.05)

          - (Cost + RepairsCost + PartsCost + TransportInCost)

             AS ImprovedSalesMargins

FROM      salesbycountry

ORDER BY  MakeName, ModelName;
```

When you execute this code, you should get something like the result shown Figure 6.6.

MakeName	ModelName	ImprovedSalesMargins
Alfa Romeo	1750	1087.5000
Alfa Romeo	1750	-506.2500
Alfa Romeo	Giulia	873.7500
Alfa Romeo	Giulia	3990.0000
Alfa Romeo	Giulia	37.5000
Alfa Romeo	Giulia	2640.0000
Alfa Romeo	Giulia	1725.0000
Alfa Romeo	Giulia	-762.5000
Alfa Romeo	Giulia	1225.0000
Alfa Romeo	Giulia	100.0000
Alfa Romeo	Giulietta	1225.0000
Alfa Romeo	Giulietta	225.0000
Alfa Romeo	Giulietta	4225.0000
Alfa Romeo	Giulietta	3225.0000
Alfa Romeo	Giulietta	1287.5000
Alfa Romeo	Giulietta	1487.5000
Alfa Romeo	Giulietta	22.5000
Alfa Romeo	Spider	612.5000

Figure 6.6: "What if" calculations in SQL

How it Works

This formula extends the gross margin calculation you created earlier and multiplies the sale price by 5 percent. It is, to all intents and purposes, a "what if" projection. In practice (and just as you would in a spreadsheet), this means the following:

First: Take the existing formula and add the asterisk (*) as the multiplication operator after the SalePrice field.

Second: Type in **1.05** to "hard-code" the 5 percent increase (100 and 5 percent, literally).

Third: Nest this projected sale price calculation in parentheses to ensure that it is calculated correctly—and separately—from the rest of the formula.

Finally: The cost elements are added together. These fields are also enclosed in parentheses to guarantee that this calculation is carried out independently of the remainder of the formula. Then the total cost is subtracted from the increased sale price to give the new, improved, margin.

One other thing that this formula teaches you is that you can mix static values and fields in SQL formulas. To extend the spreadsheet analogy that I have been using so far in this chapter, you can mix references and values in a formula in SQL just as you can in Excel.

7. Sorting Output by the Result of a Calculation

Knowing even the most basic math in SQL can help you unlock real insights. As an example, let's see how using the knowledge—and SQL techniques—that you have seen so far in this chapter can be used to produce the list of the 50 most profitable sales in percentage terms. Here is the SQL to deliver this:

```
SELECT      MK.MakeName

            ,(SD.SalePrice - (ST.Cost + ST.RepairsCost

                            + ST.PartsCost + ST.TransportInCost))

            / NULLIF(SD.SalePrice, 0) AS Profitability

FROM        make AS MK

JOIN        model AS MD ON MK.MakeID = MD.MakeID

JOIN        stock AS ST ON ST.ModelID = MD.ModelID

JOIN        salesdetails SD ON ST.StockCode = SD.StockID

ORDER BY    Profitability DESC

            LIMIT 50;
```

Executing this code should return the data shown in Figure 6.7 (and if you scroll through the output, you will see that it contains only 50 records).

MakeName	Profitability
Aston Martin	0.18701470
Lamborghini	0.18392157
Lamborghini	0.18319149
Ferrari	0.18178082
Bugatti	0.18164179
Ferrari	0.18140000
Aston Martin	0.18000000
Ferrari	0.17989950
Mercedes	0.17960000
Bentley	0.17915567
Aston Martin	0.17818182
Aston Martin	0.17800000
Rolls Royce	0.17765363
Bentley	0.17718665
Lamborghini	0.17714286
Bugatti	0.17708116

Figure 6.7: Sorting on a calculated column

How it Works

This formula combines many of the techniques you have seen in this chapter as far as calculations are concerned.

First: It calculates the ratio of costs to sales as described previously. This time, however, we are using the base tables rather than a view.

Second: It orders the output by this ratio (which you have aliased, which means that you can now use the alias to sort the results).

Third: The ORDER BY keyword—with DESC to specify that the sort is from greatest to smallest figure—presents the data in descending order.

Finally: It finishes by limiting the number of rows returned to 50 using the LIMIT keyword.

The useful trick here is to mix the LIMIT and ORDER BY keywords. As you are requesting that the data is output from the most profitable through to the least profitable sale, the first 50 will—by definition—be the 50 most profitable sales.

In Figure 6.7, I have deliberately chosen not to display all the 50 records that the query returns. However, you can scroll through the result set in the query tab if you want to check that only 50 records are displayed.

Tricks and Traps

There is one major point to note when you are sorting on the result of a calculation.

- When sorting the output in a query, you can—fortunately—*sort on the column alias* that you have applied to a calculation. If you do not apply an alias, you will have to repeat the *entire* calculation in the ORDER BY clause to sort on the calculation. In other words, if you had not specified that the calculated column was named Profitability, then you would have had to create an ORDER BY clause like this:

```
ORDER BY (SalePrice - (Cost + RepairsCost + PartsCost
            + TransportInCost)) / NULLIF(SalePrice, 0) DESC
```

8. Handling Missing Data

The sales director has lost her sunny optimism. She has stormed over to your desk and asked how it can be possible that a top-of-the-range sports car can cost nothing. To prove her point, she scrolls down the output from the query that you wrote to calculate gross margin (in section 3) and points at the records shown in Figure 6.8.

Ferrari	355	175950.0000
Ferrari	355	114160.0000
Ferrari	355	145250.0000
Ferrari	355	185650.0000
Ferrari	355	134700.0000
Ferrari	355	132500.0000
Ferrari	360	110900.0000
Ferrari	360	81600.0000
Ferrari	360	121050.0000
Ferrari	Davtona	82350.0000
Ferrari	Davtona	NULL
Ferrari	Dino	167950.0000
Ferrari	Dino	103225.0000
Ferrari	Enzo	216700.0000
Ferrari	Enzo	329400.0000
Ferrari	Enzo	298650.0000
Ferrari	F40	224550.0000
Ferrari	F40	209050.0000
Ferrari	F50	267100.0000

Missing Value

Figure 6.8: The effect of NULLs on a calculation

Unfortunately, this is the effect that a NULL has produced in a calculation. One car does not have a repairs cost. However, instead of ignoring this—or treating it as a zero—SQL invalidates the *whole calculation* for that record.

There is a safeguard that you can apply to your calculations to prevent NULLs from distorting the results you were expecting. The solution involves wrapping numeric fields inside the SQL IFNULL()function to convert any NULL values in a field to another value that you specify. When handling NULLs in calculations, this nearly always means replacing the NULL with a zero.

To show you how this can be done, here is the SQL from the previous section using the IFNULL() function to prevent errors from creeping into the calculation this time:

```
SELECT   MK.MakeName, MD.ModelName

         ,ST.Cost + ST.RepairsCost

         + IFNULL(ST.PartsCost, 0) + ST.TransportInCost

         AS TotalCost

FROM     make AS MK

JOIN     model AS MD USING(MakeID)

JOIN     stock AS ST USING(ModelID)

JOIN     SalesDetails SD ON ST.StockCode = SD.StockID;
```

This code returns the records shown in Figure 6.9—However, where previously the value was a NULL it now shows the correct result of the calculation.

| Ferrari | Daytona | 121900.0000 |

Figure 6.9: Applying the IFNULL() function to a calculation

How it Works

This query uses the Make, Model, SalesDetails and Stock tables that you used previously. The SELECT clause is almost identical to the query from the previous section; the only difference is that the PartsCost field (that contains NULL values) is wrapped in the IFNULL() function so that any NULLs will be converted to zeros—thus ensuring that the calculation will work correctly for every record (as a zero has no effect on an arithmetical calculation).

You have seen a few functions in previous chapters. The IFNULL() function works like the functions you have already met. However, the IFNULL() function needs you to place *two* elements inside the parentheses.

A field or value   In this case, it is the numeric field that can contain NULLs.

A replacement value   In this case, it is a 0 (zero).

When you enclose the PartsCost field inside the IFNULL() function, you are saying "If the PartsCost field contains a NULL, then use a zero instead." This way the calculation will add a zero to the costs that you are adding up instead of making the calculation fail for any record with a NULL in the PartsCost field.

Tricks and Traps

As you will be using more and more SQL functions as you continue through this book, you need to be aware of a few core principles that underlie their use.

- The elements that are inside the parentheses of any function are called *parameters* that you pass in to the function. When using the IFNULL() function the first parameter that the function requires is the field that it must be applied to, and the second parameter (after the comma) is the number to apply if the field is NULL.

- You can, of course, wrap any numeric field used in a calculation in the IFNULL() function as a simple precaution against MySQL returning a NULL value rather than the result that you were expecting.

- In most cases, the parameters you use in functions are compulsory. That is, if you do not add a parameter, all you will get is an error message.

- IFNULL() can also be used to replace NULLs with text values (when applied to columns that contain text data). In this case the second parameter—the replacement value—must be enclosed in quotes.

- Do not confuse IFNULL()which replaces a NULL value with a designated value—and NULLIF() which compares two values and returns NULL if the two parameters are identical.

- Geeks call using a parameter in a function like this *parameter passing*.

- You can obtain the same result by using the COALESCE() function instead of the IFNULL() function. If you were to do this, the SELECT clause from the beginning of this section would look like the following snippet:

```
SELECT   MK.MakeName, MD.ModelName
         ,ST.Cost + ST.RepairsCost
         + COALESCE(ST.PartsCost, 0) + ST.TransportInCost
         AS TotalCost
```

9. Filtering on a Calculation

It is hard to argue with the idea that there is no more fundamental business metric than profitability. So, it will come as no surprise to learn that the CEO of Prestige Cars Ltd. wants to know what the net profit is on sales. She particularly wants to see a list of sales for all vehicles making a profit of more than £5,000.00. This SQL snippet shows you how to keep her happy:

```
SELECT    DISTINCT MK.MakeName, MD.ModelName, SD.SalePrice

FROM      make AS MK

JOIN      model AS MD USING(MakeID)

JOIN      stock AS ST USING(ModelID)

JOIN      salesdetails SD ON ST.StockCode = SD.StockID

WHERE     SD.SalePrice -

          (ST.Cost + ST.RepairsCost + IFNULL(ST.PartsCost, 0)

          + ST.TransportInCost) > 5000

ORDER BY  MK.MakeName, MD.ModelName, SD.SalePrice DESC;
```

If you execute this piece of SQL, you will see data similar to the output shown in Figure 6.10.

MakeName	ModelName	SalePrice
Aston Martin	DB2	99990.00
Aston Martin	DB2	62500.00
Aston Martin	DB2	61500.00
Aston Martin	DB2	52500.00
Aston Martin	DB2	49500.00
Aston Martin	DB2	45950.00
Aston Martin	DB2	45000.00
Aston Martin	DB2	39500.00
Aston Martin	DB4	56950.00
Aston Martin	DB4	56850.00
Aston Martin	DB4	46900.00
Aston Martin	DB4	42500.00
Aston Martin	DB4	36500.00
Aston Martin	DB5	69500.00
Aston Martin	DB5	56890.00
Aston Martin	DB5	49500.00
Aston Martin	DB5	45000.00

Figure 6.10: *Filtering on a calculation*

How it Works

SQL can also use calculations in WHERE clauses to filter data. As our data does not contain the figure for the net profit, we must calculate this metric "on the fly" if we want to use it as a filter criterion.

This query shows how you can use calculated data to filter the data that is returned by a SQL query. The SQL calculates the net profit by adding up all the costs and then deducting this figure from the sale price. If the result exceeds 5000, then the record is displayed. As we want to show the make and model, we need to join the Make and Model tables, and as we want to see actual sales (and not stock), we need to join the SalesDetails table to the Stock table and join the Stock table to the Model table as well.

Tricks and Traps

The one point you need to take away from this example is this:

- You do not have to add the calculation used in a WHERE clause to a SELECT clause. However, it can be useful to start out by adding the calculation to the output so that you can verify the result.

10. Using Complex Calculated Filters

It is late in the day, and you are thinking of heading home. Just as your eyes drift toward the door, in rushes the sales director with a seemingly interminable request for data. She wants a list of all car makes and models sold where the profit exceeds £5,000.00 and the car is red and the discount greater than or equal to £1,000.00— or both the parts cost and the repairs cost are greater than £500.00.

This query is an extension of the code used in the previous example. So, you can build on your previous experience and discover that even seemingly complex requests often require nothing more than a well-thought-out WHERE clause to deliver the required result. The code you need is given here:

```
SELECT     DISTINCT MK.MakeName, MD.ModelName

FROM       make AS MK

JOIN       model AS MD USING(MakeID)

JOIN       stock AS ST USING(ModelID)

JOIN       salesdetails SD ON ST.StockCode = SD.StockID
```

```
WHERE      (ST.Color = 'Red' AND SD.LineItemDiscount >= 1000

           AND (SD.SalePrice - (ST.Cost + ST.RepairsCost

                               + IFNULL(ST.PartsCost, 0)

                               + ST.TransportInCost)) > 5000)

           OR (ST.PartsCost > 500 AND ST.RepairsCost > 500)
ORDER BY   MK.MakeName, MD.ModelName;
```

Running this query should show something like Figure 6.11.

MakeName	ModelName
Alfa Romeo	Giulia
Alfa Romeo	Giulietta
Aston Martin	DB2
Aston Martin	DB5
Aston Martin	DB6
Aston Martin	DB9
Aston Martin	Rapide
Aston Martin	Vanquish
Aston Martin	Vantage
Aston Martin	Virage
Austin	Cambridge
Austin	Lichfield
Bentley	Arnage
Bentley	Brooklands
Bentley	Continental
Bentley	Flying Spur
Bentley	Mulsanne
Bugatti	57C

Figure 6.11: A complex query filtering on several fields and a calculation

How it Works

This query starts by joining all the tables that we need either to display output (Make and Model) or to use in a filter (SalesDetails and Stock)—or both. It then applies the WHERE clause to filter records where

Either The color of the vehicle is red, the discount greater than £1,000.00, and the net profit over £5,000.00

Or The parts and repair cost are greater than £500.00

As you can see, the focus of this query is on the WHERE clause. Inside this clause it is worth paying particular attention to the parentheses that are used. The filters on either side of the OR operator are enclosed in parentheses. This means all the conditions inside the parentheses must be true for the filter to be successful. Consequently, the parts cost must be more than 500 as must the repair cost for a sale to make the grade. Alternatively, all the three conditions for the other filter (red; discount of 1,000 or more; and profit of at least 5,000) must be met for the record to make it through to the final output.

The only potentially tricky aspect of this query is the way you have to "nest" criteria inside parentheses to obtain the result you are looking for. This can take a little practice, but the effort is well worth it. Of course, if you have any experience writing formulas using Microsoft Excel or Access, then you are probably used to this concept already. In any case, breaking down filter requirements into logical, isolated steps is a key part of learning to write efficient SQL.

Tricks and Traps

Complex WHERE clauses can become easier to understand and simpler to write if you remember the following points:

- When you have to produce complex WHERE clauses, it may help to begin by isolating the "levels" of the logic over several lines, as you can see in Figure 6.12.

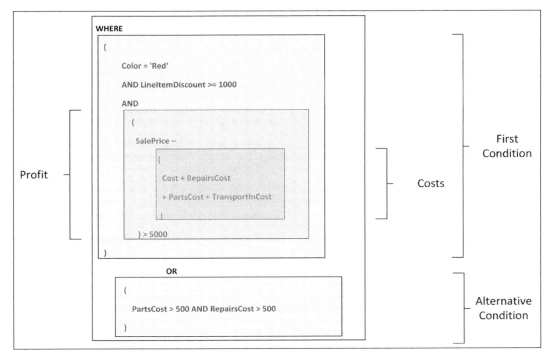

Figure 6.12: Nesting parentheses

- Even a complicated query is nothing more than a series of component parts that you assemble to apply a filter based on a set of criteria. Our advice when faced with complex queries is to try to break them down into their constituent elements and to try to understand what is required *before* you start writing SQL code.

- It can help if you first try to write out the filter as "pseudo-code"—that is, more as a description of the required logic than an exact and accurate piece of SQL. This can help you to understand the underlying requirements of the filter and how to

- Create all the individual comparison elements that make up the whole

- Group the filter elements so that they respect the final logic that is required

- In this query, I chose not to add the fields that were used in the WHERE clause to the query output. You can, of course, add them to check that the filter is working if you so desire.

11. Writing Accurate SQL Code Faster

Producing good SQL requires a certain attention to detail. As you have probably noticed already, the slightest error will make your code not only refuse to deliver the results that you were expecting but also return extremely irritating error messages.

Fortunately, MySQL Workbench, and indeed, most graphical interfaces that work with MySQL, can help you face up to the challenge of avoiding basic coding errors. It can do this by letting you drag and drop table and field names from the database in the Navigator (left-hand) window into a query tab

Suppose you want to show the country names from the Country table. One way to do this with very little typing is as follows:

1. Expand the PrestigeCars database in the Object Explorer window and then expand the Tables folder.

2. Expand the Country table and then expand the Columns folder.

3. Open a new query tab.

4. Enter **SELECT** and a space.

5. Drag the CountryName field from the Object Explorer window and drop it after the SELECT keyword. The field name will appear at the cursor position.

6. Press the Return key to begin a new line and enter **FROM**.

7. Drag the Country table from the Object Explorer window and drop it after the FROM keyword. The query should look like it does in Figure 6.13.

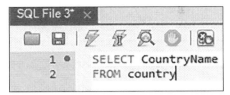

Figure 6.13: Using drag and drop to create queries

8. Execute the query.

Tricks and Traps

I have one final trick and one comment to add in conclusion to this chapter.

- Instead of dragging and dropping a field from the Navigator to the query window you can simply double-click on a field name in the Navigator. This will make the field appear at the cursor position in the query window.

- Certain Graphical User Interfaces will help you to write SQL by suggesting table and field names as well as keywords when you enter your SQL.

Conclusion

In this chapter, you saw some of the ways that SQL can be used to carry out simple arithmetic. You learned how to perform basic math using the data in fields as well as values that you add to your code to perform calculations across multiple rows and columns in a few lines of code.

You also saw how to pre-empt errors when the source data contains NULLs or when attempt to divide a value by zero.

All in all, you have already made vast strides toward the basic analysis of MySQL data. With this knowledge safely acquired, it is time to move on to the next step—aggregating data to deliver totals, subtotals, and other simple calculations. This is what you will be looking at in the next chapter.

Core Knowledge Learned in This Chapter

These are the fundamental keywords you have learned to use in this chapter:

Concept	Description
+	This is the arithmetical addition symbol; it adds two elements (fields or values).
-	This is the arithmetical subtraction symbol; it subtracts two elements (fields or values).
*	This is the arithmetical multiplication symbol; it multiplies two elements (fields or values).
/	This is the arithmetical division symbol; it divides two elements (fields or values).
NULLIF()	This function compares two values and returns NULL if the two parameters are identical.
ISNULL()	This function converts NULL (or empty) values into a value that can be used in your calculations.
Parentheses	Parentheses are used in calculations to force certain parts of a formula to be calculated before others.

CHAPTER 7
Aggregating Output

Analyzing data consists of much more than just selecting records from a database. There is no denying that you have to start by choosing the right columns from the right tables, joining the tables correctly, and of course filtering the data accurately. However, SQL really starts to deliver true insights when you begin to aggregate data so that you can see the high-level figures that drive your business.

Aggregating Data in SQL

It is well worth looking at how SQL can aggregate metrics. This is because it is particularly good at returning totals, averages, and a multitude of analytical insights with little effort—and often in a short time. In this chapter, you will start to explore the basic techniques that you can use to apply aggregations to your data and to deliver real insight straight from the database. More specifically, you will learn how to

- Generate grand totals
- Group elements with aggregate totals
- Count categories of elements
- Find maximum and minimum values

- Calculate averages
- Filter data on aggregate values

So, without further ado, it is time to discover how SQL can aggregate data in many different ways at multiple levels to deliver the analysis you need.

1. Calculating Table Totals

To begin with (and, you guessed it, following a call from the finance director), let's suppose that you want to calculate the total cost of all the vehicles that have ever been stocked by Prestige Cars Ltd. The SQL looks like this:

```
SELECT        SUM(Cost) AS TotalCost

FROM          stock;
```

Running this query gives the results shown in Figure 7.1.

TotalCost
19759164.0000

Figure 7.1: Using the SUM() function to calculate the total for a field

How it Works

Adding up a column of figures is easy to do in SQL. You can use the SUM() function on any numeric field in a table to get the total of the values in the column. In this example, the SUM() function was applied to the Cost field of the Stock table. The result is simply the total—the sum—of all the available figures in the Cost field (or *column* if you prefer) of the Stock table. What you did is to wrap up the name of the field that you wanted to add inside the parentheses that are part of the SUM function. This simple modification was all that MySQL needed to return the *total*, rather than the detail for each record.

Tricks and Traps

As this is the first time you have used a function to aggregate data, you need to be aware of the following essential points:

- SUM() is what is known as an *aggregation function*—it returns a single value for a calculation across a set of values (a field in this case). This makes it different from the functions you have seen so far in this book. Up until now, any function was applied to each record in a table. Functions like SUM()

do not work at such a detailed level and cannot show the detail of each individual row. They exist only to provide a high-level aggregation of values.

- The SUM() function requires numeric values to work. If you try to calculate the total of a field containing text, then MySQL will only return a zero (unless there are unformatted numbers in certain fields, in which case these will be added up).

- It is always a good idea to provide an alias for aggregation functions because otherwise MySQL will add the column heading "SUM(Cost)."

2. Using Calculated Aggregations

Muttering that he is too busy to copy formulas down over hundreds of records in a spreadsheet, the finance director has tasked you with extending the previous example to calculate the aggregate sales, cost, and gross profit for all vehicles sold. Fortunately, you can use multiple aggregate expressions in the same query. Here is the SQL to do this:

```
SELECT      SUM(ST.Cost) AS TotalCost
            ,SUM(SD.SalePrice) AS TotalSales
            ,SUM(SD.SalePrice) - SUM(ST.Cost) AS GrossProfit
FROM        stock ST
JOIN        salesdetails SD
            ON ST.StockCode = SD.StockID;
```

Executing this query gives the results displayed in Figure 7.2.

TotalCost	TotalSales	GrossProfit
17629960.0000	22047450.00	4417490.0000

Figure 7.2: Calculating the total for several fields using SUM()

How it Works

This code snippet shows you that you can return the total for *any* numeric field from any table in a query. This piece of SQL is also a reminder that joining tables acts as a filter (as you saw in Chapter 3). In this example, the filter effect means you only see result where vehicles appear in both the Stock and SalesDetails tables—that is, you only see the totals for cars that have actually been sold. As a final touch, this piece of code calculates aggregations by subtracting the total purchase cost from the total sale price.

As the SQL makes clear, you can apply aggregation functions such as SUM() to several columns and then apply calculations to the aggregated value just as you did to nonaggregated fields in the previous chapter.

Tricks and Traps

Aggregation functions have a couple of cool features. So, be aware of the following:

- One helpful feature of the SUM() function (and this applies to all the aggregation functions that you will meet in this chapter) is that it handles NULL values without affecting the result. If you remember, a NULL in a calculation at row level will make the result of the calculation into NULL too. However, any number of NULLs in a column that you aggregate using SUM() will not cause any difficulties at all.

- It is important to wrap each numeric column inside its own SUM function when carrying out calculations on aggregated values. In theory, you could have expressed the calculation as follows:

```
SUM(SD.SalePrice - ST.Cost)
```

This code may appear to work at first sight if you try it. However, it is *not* guaranteed to work in all circumstances. This is because NULL values in a column are handled without difficulty by the SUM() function only if *each* column is wrapped inside its own SUM(). If you use a single SUM() function for several fields, NULLs could cause the wrong results to be displayed.

3. Using Grouped Aggregations

The sales manager has just emailed you an apparently simple request for data. She wants the aggregate cost for each model of car. The next piece of SQL shows you just how easy it is to segment your data this way with SQL:

```
SELECT    MD.ModelName, SUM(ST.Cost) AS TotalCost

FROM      stock ST

JOIN      model MD USING(ModelID)

GROUP BY  MD.ModelName

ORDER BY  MD.ModelName;
```

If you run this query, you should see the results shown in Figure 7.3.

ModelName	TotalCost
135	20400.0000
145	55200.0000
175	28120.0000
1750	10820.0000
203	2560.0000
205	5720.0000
250SL	28440.0000
280SL	236232.0000
308	156000.0000
350SL	109380.0000
355	1078720.0000
360	415600.0000
400GT	116000.0000
404	25956.0000
500	4196.0000
500SL	60400.0000

Figure 7.3: Grouping aggregated results using GROUP BY

How it Works

The previous two examples showed you that SQL can calculate the grand total for a column in one or more tables easily and quickly. In practice, however, you will probably want to analyze results broken down into separate categories. In this query, you joined the Model and Stock tables (so that you could see the model name, and not just a code) and output the model name and the total cost. Then you added a new keyword—GROUP BY—to the end of the SQL statement. Simply adding another field that is *not* being aggregated (usually a text field) to the GROUP BY clause is enough for MySQL to calculate the total for each individual element in the field that is *not* wrapped in an aggregate function.

While not strictly necessary, it is normal—most of the time—to add the field that you are grouping on to the SELECT statement so that you can see which figure corresponds to which aggregated element.

Tricks and Traps

There are a couple of potential traps for the unwary in code that groups data.

- It is *vital* that any nonaggregated fields in the SELECT clause (the ones that are not enclosed in aggregation functions such as SUM) are repeated in the GROUP BY clause. If you do not do this, then MySQL will display only *one* of the nonaggregated fields along with the aggregated value. This could lead to erroneous analysis at worst and confusing output at the very least.

- Adding a GROUP BY clause can sort the data—but to be completely certain you are best adding an ORDER BY clause to the SQL. The ORDER BY clause always follows the GROUP BY clause.

4. Using Multiple Levels of Grouping

Fired up by the analysis you have provided so far, the finance director wants you to dig deeper into the data and compare the total purchase cost for every make and model of vehicle bought. This is easier than you might think, as the following code illustrates:

```
SELECT      MK.MakeName, MD.ModelName, SUM(ST.Cost) AS TotalCost

FROM        stock ST

JOIN        model MD USING(ModelID)

JOIN        make AS MK USING(MakeID)

GROUP BY    MK.MakeName, MD.ModelName

ORDER BY    MK.MakeName, MD.ModelName;
```

Executing this query should return the results in Figure 7.4.

MakeName	ModelName	TotalCost
Alfa Romeo	1750	10820.0000
Alfa Romeo	Giulia	71756.0000
Alfa Romeo	Giulietta	73752.0000
Alfa Romeo	Spider	50920.0000
Aston Martin	DB2	469072.0000
Aston Martin	DB4	269352.0000
Aston Martin	DB5	271872.0000
Aston Martin	DB6	896556.0000
Aston Martin	DB9	832760.0000
Aston Martin	Rapide	242000.0000
Aston Martin	Vanquish	351632.0000
Aston Martin	Vantage	274800.0000
Aston Martin	Virage	862912.0000
Austin	Cambridge	18000.0000
Austin	Lichfield	24080.0000
Austin	Princess	9520.0000
Bentley	Arnage	255120.0000
Bentley	Brooklands	231200.0000

Figure 7.4: Grouping on multiple fields

How it Works

This SQL snippet shows you that you can extend the grouping principle by adding as many nonaggregated fields as you want to a query. Each field that you add to the SELECT clause (and also to the GROUP BY clause) will entail a deeper level of detail in the output—giving you a hierarchical analysis of your data.

As you can see in the results from the query, the total sales appear for each make by model. So, grouping data on multiple fields in effect creates a hierarchy in the output. This hierarchy corresponds to the order in which the fields are entered in the GROUP BY clause. In other words, the first field (MakeName) is the topmost level in the hierarchy, and then ModelName is the second level.

Finally the output is sorted by the same fields that are in the SELECT and GROUP BY clauses.

Tricks and Traps

Grouping on multiple fields comes easily with a little practice. Nonetheless, it can help to remember the following:

- It is important to add the fields you are aggregating in a coherent order in both the SELECT clause and the GROUP BY clause. This is because the output will be perceived as a logical hierarchy by your users. In practice, this means starting with the highest level on the left and working down through successive lower levels of data. This is because users probably expect a model to be a subdivision of a make of car—and not the reverse.

- Although you do not have to apply the same sort order for the fields you are using to segment data in the SELECT and GROUP BY clauses, it is generally best to keep them identical—for the sake of the person viewing the data. This is because it can become extremely confusing if you sort the data using one kind of sequence and then display the fields in another. In any case, the actual hierarchy is defined by the fields in the GROUP BY clause, whatever the sequence of the fields in the SELECT clause.

- Once again, it is usually best to add an alias to any field that is the result of an aggregation.

5. Calculating Averages

An essential business metric is the average cost of goods bought. So, it was inevitable that the finance director would want to see the average purchase price of every make and model of car ever bought. Fortunately, SQL makes this kind of calculation easy—as the following piece of code illustrates:

```
SELECT      MK.MakeName, MD.ModelName

            ,AVG(ST.Cost) AS AverageCost

FROM        make AS MK

JOIN        model AS MD USING(MakeID)

JOIN        stock AS ST USING(ModelID)

GROUP BY    MK.MakeName, MD.ModelName

ORDER BY    MK.MakeName, MD.ModelName;
```

Running this query should return the results shown in Figure 7.5.

MakeName	ModelName	AverageCost
Alfa Romeo	1750	5410.00000000
Alfa Romeo	Giulia	8969.50000000
Alfa Romeo	Giulietta	10536.00000000
Alfa Romeo	Spider	8486.66666667
Aston Martin	DB2	42642.90909091
Aston Martin	DB4	33669.00000000
Aston Martin	DB5	38838.85714286
Aston Martin	DB6	56034.75000000
Aston Martin	DB9	48985.88235294
Aston Martin	Rapide	60500.00000000
Aston Martin	Vanquish	43954.00000000
Aston Martin	Vantage	68700.00000000
Aston Martin	Virage	71909.33333333
Austin	Cambridge	18000.00000000
Austin	Lichfield	12040.00000000
Austin	Princess	2380.00000000
Bentley	Arnage	63780.00000000
Bentley	Brooklands	115600.00000000

Figure 7.5: *Calculating the average purchase price using the AVG() function*

How it Works

This code snippet introduces another aggregation function: AVG(). As its name implies, the AVG() function calculates the average of the values in a column.

Once again, all the required tables are joined in the FROM clause of the query. Then any required fields that will be used to aggregate the data added to the SELECT and GROUP BY clauses. Finally, the AVG() function is "wrapped" around the Cost field from the Stock table to calculate the average purchase price of every make and model.

Tricks and Traps

There is one point that I need to make here.

- Without the ORDER BY clause there is no guarantee that an SQL statement with a GROUP BY clause will always output the results in the same order.

6. Counting Grouped Elements

The CEO has stated categorically that any business must be able to see at a glance how many items have been sold per product category. In the case of Prestige Cars Ltd., this means visualizing the number of cars sold by make and model. SQL can answer these kinds of questions with consummate ease, as the following SQL snippet shows:

```
SELECT      MK.MakeName, MD.ModelName

            ,COUNT(SD.SalesDetailsID) AS NumberofCarsSold

FROM        make AS MK

JOIN        model AS MD USING(MakeID)

JOIN        stock AS ST USING(ModelID)

JOIN        salesdetails SD ON ST.StockCode = SD.StockID

GROUP BY    MK.MakeName, MD.ModelName

ORDER BY    MK.MakeName, MD.ModelName;
```

Running this query should return the results in Figure 7.6.

	MakeName	ModelName	NumberofCarsSold
▶	Alfa Romeo	1750	2
	Alfa Romeo	Giulia	8
	Alfa Romeo	Giulietta	7
	Alfa Romeo	Spider	5
	Aston Martin	DB2	8
	Aston Martin	DB4	7
	Aston Martin	DB5	6
	Aston Martin	DB6	14
	Aston Martin	DB9	15
	Aston Martin	Rapide	4
	Aston Martin	Vanquish	7
	Aston Martin	Vantage	4
	Aston Martin	Virage	12
	Austin	Cambridge	1
	Austin	Lichfield	2
	Austin	Princess	4
	Bentley	Arnage	4
	Bentley	Brooklands	2

Figure 7.6: Counting cars by model using the COUNT() function

How it Works

The SQL aggregation functions are not limited to just adding up columns of numbers. You can also *count* the number of records that make up a subset of data. So, this piece of SQL introduces the COUNT() aggregation function. As its name implies, it counts the number of rows in a group of records, rather than adding up any figures.

The trick in this piece of SQL is to use exactly the same grouping element in the GROUP BY clause as in the SELECT clause. So, as we have concatenated the make and model in the SELECT clause, we have to do the same in the GROUP BY clause.

Tricks and Traps

Although the COUNT() function works in a virtually identical way to the SUM() and AVG() functions you have already seen, there are nonetheless a few things to be aware of.

- Sometimes all you want to do is to find the total number of rows in a table. Perhaps you are looking at a large table and want an idea of its size. Should this be the case, then the SQL is extremely simple. Just use the following:

```
SELECT COUNT(*) FROM Stock
```

This will return the total number of records in a table.

You could be tempted to use COUNT(*) when analyzing data, but I advise that you always add the name of the field that you are interested in between the parentheses when using the COUNT() function. This is because COUNT(*) will count all rows—*whether they contain data or not*. COUNT(Cost) will count only the records where there *is* a cost figure (and not a NULL), and the two results could be different.

- The trick in any SQL that counts the number of elements is to use *exactly the same grouping elements* in the GROUP BY clause as in the SELECT clause. So, as we have used the make and model in the SELECT clause, we have to use them in the GROUP BY clause as well.

- You can apply the COUNT() function to text fields as well as to numeric fields.

7. Counting Unique Elements

There could be occasions when you need to analyze a dataset and deduce the number of specific and individual elements that it contains, as opposed to the total number of rows. You discovered this when the sales director appeared at your desk and asked for the number of different countries that Prestige Cars has ever sold vehicles to.

Fortunately, SQL makes this kind of high-level investigation really easy; it can be done in a couple of lines of code like in the following snippet:

```
SELECT   COUNT(DISTINCT CountryName) AS CountriesWithSales

FROM     SalesByCountry;
```

Running this query will show the results in Figure 7.7.

CountriesWithSales
8

Figure 7.7: Counting unique values in a list

How it Works

In this query you are using the SalesByCountry view that you met earlier as the source of the data. Once again you are using the COUNT() function to return a number of records, and you are specifying that you want to see the number of records where the CountryName field contains data.

However, you have also added the DISTINCT keyword inside the parentheses for the COUNT() function, and this changes everything. Because now, instead of getting the total number of records where there is a country, you are returning the *number of unique countries* in the CountryName field.

8. Displaying Upper and Lower Numeric Thresholds

Data analysis is frequently about identifying limits and thresholds. At least, this is what the sales manager seems to think because she wants you to identify the largest and smallest sale prices for each model of car sold. SQL makes it easy to perform analyses of the threshold values in datasets, as you can see from the following piece of SQL:

```
SELECT        MD.ModelName
              ,MAX(SD.SalePrice) AS TopSalePrice
              ,MIN(SD.SalePrice) AS BottomSalePrice
FROM          model AS MD
JOIN          stock AS ST USING(ModelID)
JOIN          salesdetails SD ON ST.StockCode = SD.StockID
GROUP BY      MD.ModelName
ORDER BY      MD.ModelName;
```

If you execute this query, you will see the results in Figure 7.8.

ModelName	TopSalePrice	BottomSalePrice
135	25500.00	25500.00
145	39500.00	29500.00
175	12500.00	12500.00
1750	9950.00	3575.00
203	1950.00	1250.00
205	3950.00	950.00
250SL	22600.00	12950.00
280SL	62500.00	22500.00
350SL	33600.00	23500.00
355	220000.00	125950.00
360	135000.00	99500.00
400GT	145000.00	145000.00
404	19500.00	950.00
500	2500.00	1150.00
500SL	45000.00	30500.00
57C	365000.00	295000.00
600	1950.00	1250.00
911	68900.00	17500.00

Figure 7.8: Using the MAX() and MIN() functions to show the maximum and minimum values for a data group

How it Works

The FROM clause in this query ensures that you are looking at sales data (and not just stock) and that you can access the model names. It does this by joining the SalesDetails, Stock and Model tables. Then you use SELECT to specify the model name and the sale price (twice—once for each aggregation function). However, you have applied the MAX() and MIN() functions on the SalePrice field to calculate the maximum and minimum, respectively. Finally—and once again—any nonaggregated fields that you have placed in the SELECT clause are added to the GROUP BY clause.

Tricks and Traps

As simple as they are, the MAX() and MIN() functions necessitate a couple of comments.

- You can extend the principle by adding further fields to the SELECT and GROUP BY clauses to drill down into a finer level of analytical detail, as you saw previously in section 4.

- If you are applying a series of aggregation functions to the same field, you will have to repeat the field name for each function used.

9. Filtering Groups

The sales director was pleased with your ability to aggregate results using all the available data in a database. So, she wants you to push the envelope and filter the data so that she can see how many red cars have been sold. Of course, SQL will let you do this—and you can build on the knowledge that you have acquired so far in this book by applying any of the filtering techniques you saw in previous chapters.

As an example, here is how to count the cars sold in a specific color:

```
SELECT    MK.MakeName, COUNT(SD.SalePrice) AS RedCarsSold
FROM      make AS MK
JOIN      model AS MD USING(MakeID)
JOIN      stock AS ST USING(ModelID)
JOIN      salesdetails SD ON ST.StockCode = SD.StockID
WHERE     ST.Color = 'Red'
GROUP BY  MK.MakeName
ORDER BY  MK.MakeName;
```

This code returns the output shown in Figure 7.9.

MakeName	RedCarsSold
Alfa Romeo	1
Aston Martin	6
Austin	1
Bentley	2
Bugatti	3
Ferrari	2
Jaguar	5
Mercedes	1
Peugeot	1
Porsche	3
Rolls Royce	2
Trabant	3
Triumph	3

Figure 7.9: *A calculated aggregation with a filter applied*

How it Works

This code snippet returns the number of cars sold, using the technique you saw in section 7 of this chapter. What is new is the WHERE clause, which is applied just as you would use it in a "normal" (that is nonaggregated) query. What you have to remember is that the WHERE clause *must* be placed before the GROUP BY clause, or you will get an error message.

Tricks and Traps

I have only one point to make (again) here; it is an important one, so it bears repetition.

- Although I said it in a previous chapter, it is worth repeating that if you want to filter on a field, then the table containing the filtered field *must* be present in one of the tables in the FROM clause. As this query shows, this does not mean you have to add this field to the SELECT clause.

10. Filtering on Aggregated Results

As part of the company's worldwide sales drive, the sales director wants to focus Prestige Cars' marketing energies on the countries where you are making the most sales. This section shows you how to show the data only for countries where more than 50 cars have been sold. To start with, take a look at the following SQL snippet:

```
SELECT      CountryName, COUNT(SalesDetailsID) AS NumberofCarsSold

FROM        salesbycountry

GROUP BY    CountryName

HAVING      COUNT(SalesDetailsID) > 50;
```

Running this code gives the output in Figure 7.10.

CountryName	NumberofCarsSold
France	69
United Kingdom	165

Figure 7.10: Applying a filter to an aggregation

How it Works

There will be occasions when you will need to use an aggregation to filter data. That is, you want to calculate an aggregated value and use this metric to filter a dataset. In cases like these, you need to apply a filter that is not a straight comparison with a value stored in a table, as was the case in the preceding example.

This query uses the SalesByCountry view that joins all the main tables in the database. This is first to remind you that you can also query views and second to avoid swamping the query in a seven-table join clause. This way you can use all the fields from the Country, Make, Model, Sales, Stock, SalesDetails, and Customer tables without having to pay too much attention to a complex JOIN.

What is interesting in this query is the HAVING clause. It is here that the aggregate filter is applied. What this clause says is this: "Allow aggregated output into the result set only where there are more than 50 source records (that is, sales) in the aggregate source set." Put another way, it counts the number of sales (identified by the SalesDetailsID value of each individual sale) for each element in the GROUP BY clause (the country)—and then *only* returns rows where the *country* that you have grouped on has more than 50 sales.

The end result is that the HAVING clause acts like a filter. Only whereas a WHERE clause operates at the level of each individual record, the HAVING clause filters data on an aggregated value—the number of sales made for each aggregated element. If you want to see the number of sales for all countries then you can select this piece of SQL without the HAVING clause and execute it.

11. Selecting Data Based on Aggregated Results as Well as Specific Filter Criteria

The sales director has surpassed herself. This time she has left a note with what looks like a complicated request. She wants to know who are the clients who have not only bought at least three cars but where each of the three vehicles generated a profit of at least £5,000.00. So, before getting anxious about it, let's consider what question is really being asked. Her demand could be translated as follows: "Find all car sales making more than £5,000 in profit. Now group them by customer. Finally, display only those customers who have at least three cars making at least this much profit."

Believe us, this sounds more complicated than it really is. So, before your eyes glaze over, take a look at the following SQL:

```
SELECT      CU.CustomerName, COUNT(SD.SalesDetailsID)

                AS NumberofCarsSold

FROM        make AS MK

JOIN        model AS MD USING(MakeID)

JOIN        stock AS ST USING(ModelID)

JOIN        salesdetails SD ON ST.StockCode = SD.StockID

JOIN        sales AS SA ON SA.SalesID = SD.SalesID

JOIN        customer CU ON SA.CustomerID = CU.CustomerID

WHERE       (SD.SalePrice

              - (

                  ST.Cost + IFNULL(ST.RepairsCost,0) + ST.PartsCost

                  + ST.TransportInCost)

              ) > 5000

GROUP BY    CU.CustomerName

HAVING      COUNT(SD.SalesDetailsID) >= 3

ORDER BY    CU.CustomerName;
```

Running this code gives the output shown in Figure 7.11.

CustomerName	NumberofCarsSold
Alexei Tolstoi	4
Alicia Almodovar	3
Antonio Maura	6
Birmingham Executive Prestige Vehicles	3
Casseroles Chromes	3
Convertible Dreams	4
Eat My Exhaust Ltd	3
Glittering Prize Cars Ltd	4
Glitz	4
Honest Pete Motors	7
King Leer Cars	6
Laurent Saint Yves	8
Le Luxe en Motion	4
Liverpool Executive Prestige Vehicles	3
M. Pierre Dubois	3
Magic Motors	5

Figure 7.11: *A calculated aggregation with both a HAVING clause and a WHERE clause*

How it Works

Once again, the FROM clause merely guarantees that you can access all the fields that are needed to answer the query. The SELECT clause merely says that you want to list the customer name and the number of vehicles sold to that customer. As this is an aggregation query, the field you are using to break down the data (customer name) must also appear in the GROUP BY clause.

The power of this query resides in using two types of filter that are applied in sequence.

- A classic WHERE clause for a nonaggregated filter
- An aggregate filter in a HAVING clause

Each of these performs a separate and distinct function in the query in a specific order.

First: The WHERE clause calculates the individual margin for each sale and allows only those records that match this criterion through to the next (grouping) stage.

Finally: The HAVING clause takes the resulting filtered records that have been grouped and aggregated and applies a second level of filter. This time only groups that have at least three elements (that is, three cars making more than £5,000.00 profit) are let through into the query output.

The main thing to remember with queries like this one is that there is a strict filter priority that is applied by SQL. It will apply a WHERE clause before it will apply a HAVING clause.

Tricks and Traps

As you are meeting a new concept—and a new keyword—for the first time, you need to be wary of a few potential issues that have to be managed carefully when you are using the HAVING clause.

- Note that we used the IFNULL() function that was described in the previous chapter when calculating the profit for each car sold. Had we not used this function, MySQL would have returned a NULL rather than the profit for any car with a NULL value in the RepairsCost field.

- The order of the clauses in the SQL statement is extremely important when you are applying a HAVING clause to the code. You must always place the HAVING clause after the GROUP BY clause—and before the ORDER BY clause (if there is one).

12. Sorting by Aggregated Results

The CEO wants to see what drives the company's bottom line. More specifically, she wants to isolate the three most lucrative models sold so that she can focus sales efforts around those brands. Aggregation queries can, of course, be used to help you to analyze and prioritize your data. A classic example is when you want to see what brings in the most money. The following short piece of SQL illustrates this:

```
SELECT      MK.MakeName

FROM        make AS MK

JOIN        model AS MD USING(MakeID)

JOIN        stock AS ST USING(ModelID)

JOIN        salesdetails SD ON ST.StockCode = SD.StockID

GROUP BY    MK.MakeName

ORDER BY    SUM(SD.SalePrice) DESC

            LIMIT 3;
```

Executing this code snippet gives something like the output shown in Figure 7.12.

MakeName
Ferrari
Aston Martin
Bugatti

Figure 7.12: Using LIMIT, ORDER BY, and GROUP BY to segment data

How it Works

This query groups the output data by make and shows you that you can also add an ORDER BY clause to sort the output. What is interesting is that you can sort by an aggregated field—whether it is present in the SELECT clause or not. What is more, the LIMIT keyword can be used in aggregation queries too.

To encourage you to persevere with SQL, just consider the potential value of the information returned by such a concise and efficient query. You can see where your company is really making money. This, after all, is worth a little effort on the SQL learning curve.

Conclusion

This chapter has introduced you to the vast potential of SQL to calculate aggregations. You saw how to group data into separate segments and return totals, counts, maxima, and minima for these segments in a few lines of code.

Then you learned how to use calculations alongside aggregations to perform deeper analyses. You also saw how to filter data using aggregation functions to isolate certain data elements.

Finally, you saw how to combine aggregation functions with some of the filter techniques that you saw in previous chapters to deliver in-depth analysis.

Core Knowledge Learned in This Chapter

The following are the keywords you learned in this chapter:

Concept	Description
SUM()	This function returns the total for a column of numbers. It will also calculate the total for or for each segment of data where grouping is applied.
GROUP BY	This phrase tells MySQL that you want to segment results into groups of elements.
COUNT()	This function tells you how many records there are in a table or for each segment of data.
COUNT(DISTINCT)	Adding the DISTINCT operator to the COUNT() function returns the number of unique elements.
MAX()	This function returns the largest value in a column of numbers for each segment of data.
MIN()	This function returns the lowest value in a column of numbers for each segment of data.
HAVING	This clause filters the data on aggregate values (unlike the WHERE clause, which filters individual records).

CHAPTER 8

Working with Dates in MySQL

Most data analysis has a time-based component. You could want to look at sales for a certain day, month, or year. Perhaps you need to compare margins with the previous year or the preceding month. Indeed, the list of possible questions that need answering when it comes to analyzing data over time is virtually infinite. It follows from this that it can be really important to understand how MySQL handles dates. Indeed, it can rapidly become essential to master the techniques that you need to apply when adding a time element to your analyses.

Analyzing Data over Time

Fortunately, MySQL delivers a range of solutions when it comes to analyzing data over time. The possibilities are as far reaching as the analytical requirements that you could face. This chapter introduces how to deal with dates in data analysis because this will prepare you for the real-world challenges you may face when analyzing data over time.

Handling time analysis (or querying dates in databases if you prefer) is a vast subject. As you are still taking your first steps with SQL, I will not attempt to provide answers to every imaginable question on this subject in one chapter. I will, however, try to provide you with a basic understanding of how MySQL databases can be used as the basis for deep insights into how data evolves over time.

This involves learning how to

- Filter by a specific date
- Filter by a range of dates
- Isolate data by year, month, week, and day
- Aggregate values over time
- Handle SQL date data types and avoid common pitfalls

I would like to make clear from the start that—for the moment at least—I am using date and time as interchangeable concepts for the most part in this chapter. For the moment, we will be dealing only with dates as you learn to analyze data over time. Later in this book you will see how to deal with the hours and minutes that make up the time element of certain data elements. For the moment, however, what matters is bringing the date element to the fore when analyzing data.

1. Filtering Records by Date

Suppose that the sales director wants to see the list of cars bought on July 25, 2015. The following SQL does just that:

```
SELECT      MK.MakeName, MD.ModelName, ST.DateBought

FROM        make AS MK

JOIN        model AS MD USING(MakeID)

JOIN        stock AS ST USING(ModelID)

WHERE       ST.DateBought = 20150725;
```

Run this code and you will see something like the output in Figure 8.1.

MakeName	ModelName	DateBought
Porsche	944	2015-07-25
Aston Martin	DB6	2015-07-25
Jaguar	XJS	2015-07-25

Figure 8.1: Using dates in a WHERE clause

How it Works

Once you have joined the necessary tables (Make, Model, and Stock) to output all the details of vehicles that have been bought, you can filter on the field that shows when a car was bought. You do this by applying a WHERE clause—just as you would do for text or numbers. The interesting thing is how you represent the data to filter on in the WHERE clause.

The way that you enter a date in MySQL is called the *date specification*. The date is best specified as YYYYMMDD—that is, four digits for the year, then two digits for the month (including a leading zero for months 1–9), and then two digits for the day (including a leading zero for days 1–9). No separator elements are required (that is, no hyphens or slashes are needed to separate the year from the month or the day).

Otherwise, this is a pretty standard WHERE clause. It uses the equal operator to specify that you are looking to filter data on a specific date.

Tricks and Traps

As you are just beginning to learn how to handle dates in SQL queries, there are inevitably key elements that you have to retain. The following are the major starting points:

- The date can be enclosed in single or (possibly) double quotes as if it were text, or kept as a figure.

- There are many other ways of representing dates in SQL. However, some of them depend on the date format matching the local settings of your MySQL server. To avoid complications, I therefore prefer to use dates in the YYYYMMDD format when querying, as this is independent of the MySQL configuration. In practical terms, it means that queries that use this method of specifying a date should work in nearly all circumstances. I will be showing you some other ways of entering dates later in this chapter. However, you need to be aware that some of the other date formats that you can use to specify a date will depend on the local language settings of your MySQL. Consequently, other ways of entering dates cannot be guaranteed to work in all situations and contexts.

- You can use other operators besides the equal operator (=) when entering dates. For instance, you can use >= (greater than or equal to) to list all records from—and including—a specific date. To list data up to and including a specific date, you can use the <= (less than or equal to) operator. For dates before or after a given date, you can use the < (less than) or > (greater than) operator.

2. Using a Range of Dates to Filter Data

Pleased with your initial answer to her request, the sales director now wants a list of all the cars bought between July 15, 2018, and August 31, 2018. The following SQL shows how to do this:

```
SELECT     MK.MakeName, MD.ModelName
FROM       make AS MK JOIN model AS MD
           USING(MakeID)
JOIN       stock AS ST ON ST.ModelID = MD.ModelID
WHERE      ST.DateBought BETWEEN '2018-07-15' AND '2018-08-31'
ORDER BY   MK.MakeName;
```

Figure 8.2 shows the output from this piece of SQL.

MakeName	ModelName
Aston Martin	DB2
Aston Martin	DB2
Aston Martin	DB6
Aston Martin	DB6
Aston Martin	DB9
Aston Martin	DB9
Aston Martin	DB9
Aston Martin	Virage
Aston Martin	Virage
Aston Martin	Virage
Aston Martin	Vantage
Aston Martin	Vanquish
Bentley	Mulsanne
Bentley	Arnage
Bugatti	57C
Ferrari	360
Jaguar	XK120
Morgan	Plus 4
Noble	M14
Peugeot	404
Peugeot	404
Peugeot	404

Figure 8.2: Filtering on a range of dates using the BETWEEN operator

How it Works

Once again (with the FROM clause duly configured to include all the required tables), you can apply a WHERE clause to filter on dates, this time outputting *all* the records where the sale date was in the range specified in the WHERE clause. In this example, I chose to enter the dates in the YYYY-MM-DD format (in single quotes) as it is easier to read. This format works with *most* language versions of MySQL too and so will avoid nearly all potential errors when entering dates. In any case, if a date filter does not work when you use the YYYY-MM-DD format, you can always adjust the query so that the date is in the YYYYMMDD format.

Tricks and Traps

Dealing with date ranges means you have to be precise, specifically as far as the following are concerned:

- When you use the BETWEEN and AND keywords, SQL will include the start and end dates in the range that you define. In the case of this particular query, that means from June 30, 2015, through July 31, 2015, inclusive.

- In a date range query using the BETWEEN...AND operators it is really important that you place the start date *before* the end date and *not* vice versa. If you reverse these elements and write the filter as follows:

  ```
  WHERE DateBought BETWEEN '2018-08-31' AND '2018-07-15'
  ```

  It will return no results, even if you are certain that there are records for the date range you have specified.

- You can also enter date ranges using the <= and >= operators if you prefer. Using these, the WHERE clause for the query in this example would be as follows:

  ```
  WHERE DateBought >= '2018-07-15 AND DateBought <= '2018-08-31'
  ```

  If you are using the <= and >= operators, you can enter the upper and lower threshold values in any order.

- As you saw in this query, dates can also be specified as 'YYYY-MM-DD'— that is, year-month-day. However if you do this you *must* place the date in single (or possibly double) quotes and use a punctuation character such as a dash, slash or period as the separator. You do not, however, have to add the leading zero for months and days if these are in the range of 1 through 9.

3. How to Specify Dates in MySQL Queries

Getting dates right in MySQL can be perplexing for beginners. So, apart from the ways that you can enter dates that you have already seen in previous sections, there is a slightly more laborious—but utterly reliable—way to define a date.

If you want another way to enter a date that will work under any circumstances—that is, whatever the language settings of your database—you can use the STR_TO_DATE() function. It is a little more long-winded than a simple date as a text or as a number, but the following code will also let you enter July 31, 2015, wherever you need to specify a date:

```
SELECT STR_TO_DATE('2018-07-25','%Y-%m-%d')
```

The STR_TO_DATE() function takes two parameters.

First: The date—entered as a combination of day, month and year. The date parameter should really be enclosed in single quotes (although many MySQL implementations will accept a date without quotes).

Second: The date format—which tells MySQL exactly how your date is constructed. What the date format does is to specify the order of the constituent parts of the date (day, month and year) plus any separator characters that are used in the date itself. The format code *must* be enclosed in single quotes (or double quotes if your system allows this).

The date format is composed of three elements (the day, the month and the year) that you can enter:

* In any order
* Using any separator character

What the date format does is allow you to specify how the date that you are entering is actually defined. You can see examples of this in Table 8-1, that also shows how you can mix separator characters.

Table 8-1. Date formats for STR_TO_DATE()

Date Structure	Date Format	Example
Year Month Day	'%Y-%m-%d'	STR_TO_DATE('2018-07-25','%Y-%m-%d')
Day Month Year	'%d-%m-%Y'	SELECT STR_TO_DATE('25-7-2018','%d-%m-%Y')
Month Day Year	'%m/%d/%Y'	SELECT STR_TO_DATE('7/25/2018, '%m/%d/%Y')

Date Structure	Date Format	Example
Year Day Month	'%Y %d%m'	SELECT STR_TO_DATE('2018 2507', '%Y %d%m')

All that you have to remember is that you *must* make the date format that you enter map to the way that the date is constructed.

A fundamental use for the STR_TO_DATE() function is when you have dates entered as *text* in a column. Using the STR_TO_DATE() function allows you to specify exactly how MySQL should interpret the date—and consequently ensure that the date is handled correctly in any filters.

Tricks and Traps

Dealing with dates can be tricky at first sight. So it can be worth remembering the following points:

- Instead of using four figures for the year (2018 for instance) you can just use the last two figures (18). Just be aware that year values in the range 70-99 are converted to 1970-1999, whereas year values in the range 00-69 are converted to 2000-2069.

- Fortunately, you do not need to add a leading zero to the figure for the month or the day if either of these is less than 10.

- You can use *any* separator character between the three elements that make up a date and date format. You can even have two different separator characters inside the date and format code. However these characters *must be used in an identical fashion* for both the date and the date format.

- There are other date format codes that you can apply. These are explained in greater detail in Chapter 10.

- If you are using the STR_TO_DATE() function on a text field that contains dates you must be sure that all the data in the column adheres to the same format. Although MySQL will always attempt to convert the source text to a date if the mapping is not accurate you risk the date being interpreted incorrectly.

- As an alternative to the STR_TO_DATE() function you can also use the CAST() function. Indeed, if you inherit MySQL queries from other people you may see this function applied to convert columns containing texts to dates. While the CAST() function is extremely useful, it is more limited than the STR_TO_DATE() function in our opinion. In the interests of completeness, here are a few examples:

  ○ `SELECT CAST('18-7-25' AS DATE);`

```
o   SELECT CAST('2018-07-25' AS DATE);
o   SELECT CAST('2018/07/25' AS DATE);
o   SELECT CAST('2021-7-25' AS DATE);
o   SELECT CAST(20180731 AS DATE);
```

Be aware, however, that the CAST() function is more limited than the STR_TO_DATE() function, and might not convert certain date strings to valid dates correctly.

4. Finding the Number of Days Between Two Dates

The finance director is keen to make sure that cars do not stay on the firm's books too long—he says that they tie up expensive capital. So, he wants a list of the makes and models and the number of days that each vehicle remained, unsold, on the lot until they were bought by a customer. After a few minutes you deliver the following piece of code:

```
SELECT

            MK.MakeName

            ,MD.ModelName

            ,ST.DateBought

            ,SA.SaleDate

            ,DATEDIFF(SA.SaleDate, ST.DateBought)

                AS DaysInStockBeforeSale

FROM        make AS MK

JOIN        model AS MD USING(MakeID)

JOIN        stock AS ST USING(ModelID)

JOIN        salesdetails AS SD ON ST.StockCode = SD.StockID

JOIN        sales AS SA USING(SalesID)

ORDER BY    DaysInStockBeforeSale DESC;
```

Executing this code snippet gives the output shown in Figure 8.3.

MakeName	ModelName	DateBought	SaleDate	DaysInStockBeforeSale
Bentley	Flying Spur	2015-09-30	2018-02-17 00:00:00	871
Aston Martin	DB6	2015-04-30	2017-03-31 13:08:00	701
Bentley	Brooklands	2016-10-03	2018-02-17 00:00:00	502
Porsche	911	2016-07-03	2017-11-01 17:36:00	486
Ferrari	355	2015-09-11	2016-09-19 00:00:00	374
Trabant	600	2017-06-01	2018-05-25 00:00:00	358
Triumph	TR4	2017-06-08	2018-05-25 00:00:00	351
Porsche	944	2015-07-25	2016-04-30 00:00:00	280
Aston Martin	DB6	2016-07-25	2017-03-31 16:08:00	249
Alfa Romeo	1750	2017-11-11	2018-04-15 00:00:00	155
Triumph	TR6	2016-10-01	2017-02-12 16:02:00	134
Aston Martin	DB2	2018-04-01	2018-04-29 00:00:00	28
Porsche	959	2018-05-01	2018-05-25 00:00:00	24
Ferrari	360	2018-05-01	2018-05-25 00:00:00	24
Mercedes	280SL	2018-07-01	2018-07-25 00:00:00	24
Alfa Romeo	Giulietta	2018-05-01	2018-05-25 00:00:00	24

Figure 8.3: *Using the DATEDIFF() function to calculate the difference in days between two dates*

How it Works

This SQL introduces the DATEDIFF() function. This function allows you to calculate the number of days between two dates. The DATEDIFF() function needs *two* elements (or *parameters*—to give them their technical name) to work properly.

First: The end (or later) date for the calculation. This means defining the initial date in the calculation, which is the SaleDate field from the Sales table in this example. This must be in a format that MySQL can recognize as a date.

Second: The start (or lower) date for the calculation. In this example, you want to end the period with the date that the vehicle is sold. This means using the DateBought field from the Stock table. This parameter, too, has to be in a format that MySQL can recognize as a date.

Naturally, if you are using these fields, you need the tables that contain them (SalesDetails, Sales and Stock) in the FROM clause. Indeed, as the SELECT clause also requires the make and model, the FROM clause has to join the Make and Model tables as well.

As you can see in Figure 8.3, the DateBought field contains only a date, whereas the SaleDate field contains both a date and the time of day. This is because the DateBought field has been defined as being a DATE data type and the SaleDate field is defined as a DATETIME data type. You will be looking at how these data types can affect date queries a little later in this chapter.

Tricks and Traps

The DATEDIFF() function is not difficult to apply to SQL queries. However, you do need to be aware of a few key aspects of its use.

- The dates you use in the DATEDIFF() function must also be entered in a way that lets MySQL recognize them as being dates. In other words, they must be entered as a valid date data type. This can be YYYYMMDD, YYYY-MM-DD, or indeed any date that your version of MySQL recognizes.

- You need to add an alias to the function as MySQL will never try to guess a column name when a function is used. If you do not add an alias, the column will be entitled "DATEDIFF(SA.SaleDate, ST.DateBought)".

- You can test the DATEDIFF() function independently of the rest of the query in a code snippet or use a fixed date as one or both of the date parameters that you apply to the function like this:

```
SELECT DATEDIFF('20150815', '20150701')
```

This code will return the number of days between the two dates you specify.

- This particular query only shows the vehicles that have actually been sold. If you wish to include cars that are *not yet sold* you need to alter the FROM clause so it looks like this:

```
FROM       make AS MK
JOIN       model AS MD USING(MakeID)
JOIN       stock AS ST USING(ModelID)
LEFT JOIN  salesdetails AS SD ON ST.StockCode = SD.StockID
LEFT JOIN  sales AS SA USING(SalesID)
```

Running the query using LEFT JOINs to link the SalesDetails and Sales tables will return the kind of output that you can see in Figure 8.4 (where I have scrolled down to show the NULL output for unsold cars).

MakeName	ModelName	DateBought	SaleDate	DaysInStockBeforeSale
Ferrari	360	2017-02-02	NULL	NULL
Aston Martin	DB6	2015-10-29	NULL	NULL
Aston Martin	DB6	2016-02-11	NULL	NULL
Aston Martin	DB9	2018-04-01	NULL	NULL
Porsche	944	2018-05-01	NULL	NULL
Aston Martin	DB9	2018-07-25	NULL	NULL
Porsche	944	2016-08-11	NULL	NULL

Figure 8.4: Displaying NULL output when date data is missing

5. Aggregating Data over a Date Range

Suppose the CFO wants to know the average daily purchase spend on cars over a six-month period. After a few minutes of thought, you come up with the following code snippet:

```
SELECT    SUM(ST.Cost)

          / DATEDIFF('20151231', '20150701')

             AS AverageDailyPurchase

FROM      make AS MK

JOIN      model AS MD USING(MakeID)

JOIN      stock AS ST USING(ModelID)

WHERE     ST.DateBought BETWEEN '20150701' AND '20151231';
```

You can see how this code works in Figure 8.5.

AverageDailyPurchase
4191.36612022

Figure 8.5: Calculating an average using the number of days between two dates with the DATEDIFF() function

How it Works

You just saw that SQL can determine the number of days between two dates—and this can be extended to calculate the average purchase price over a period of days. To achieve this objective, this query begins by defining all the tables that are required to provide the necessary data in the FROM clause. This means the Make, Model and Stock tables.

Then the SQL used here filters the date range used for the calculation to the period from July 1, 2016, to December 31, 2016. This date range is defined in the WHERE clause.

Then the SQL applies the SUM() function to the SELECT clause to calculate the total cost of all vehicles. This will apply only to vehicles bought between the two dates specified in the WHERE clause. Next, the DATEDIFF() function is used again in the SELECT clause to calculate the number of days between the two dates. Finally, the SQL divides the total purchase price by the number of days. The result is then displayed as the single figure that the query returns.

Once again, the DATEDIFF() function is used to calculate the number of days between two dates. The two dates, this time, are "hard-coded" into the DATEDIFF() function.

The start date: is entered as 20150701 because in this example you want to start the evaluation period on July 1, 2015.

The end date: is entered as 20161231 because you want to end the evaluation period on December 31, 2015.

Tricks and Traps

There are two vital points to make here.

- Make sure that the date period used in the WHERE clause matches the dates specified in the DATEDIFF() function or the result will not be correct because you will, in effect, have not calculated the same number of months in the WHERE clause as are used in the SELECT clause to find the average value.

- The DATEDIFF() function requires you to enter the *later* date parameter *first*. This is the opposite of how BETWEEN...AND works in the WHERE clause—where the *earlier* date is placed first.

6. Eliminating the Time Element in a Date Filter

Some databases are designed to store dates and times of certain events in case the time element is important too. If you need to remind yourself of this, then take another look at Figure 8.3, where you can see a field with only a date element (the DateBought field) as well as a field with a date and time element (the SaleDate field). While undeniably useful in certain cases, this can cause potential issues when filtering on dates alone. This is because when you enter just a date (as you did in the previous sections), SQL presumes you mean that the event took place a fraction of a second after midnight on the date you entered. No other time of day will count when filtering the data. The consequence of this is that if a sale is made during normal office hours for a single date (or for the final date in a range), SQL will *not* find the sale because the exact time was not specified when filtering on the date. This is because the hours until midnight (when the next day begins) are excluded from the output by the filter\.

As mishandling the time element of a date can seriously distort the results, it follows that there will be occasions when you will need to strip out the time part of any fields that contain both date *and* time elements. Doing this will guarantee that *only the date part* is used in the filter and that the time part will not skew the results. The following SQL gives an example of this:

```
SELECT     MK.MakeName, MD.ModelName

FROM       make AS MK

JOIN       model AS MD USING(MakeID)

JOIN       stock AS ST USING(ModelID)

JOIN       salesdetails SD ON ST.StockCode = SD.StockID

JOIN       sales AS SA ON SA.SalesID = SD.SalesID

WHERE      DATE(SA.SaleDate) = '20160228';
```

You can see this code in action in Figure 8.6.

MakeName	ModelName
Lamborghini	Countach

Figure 8.6: Filtering on the date in a DATETIME field using the DATE() function

How it Works

In this query you apply the DATE() function to a DATETIME or TIMESTAMP field (one that contains both the date and time elements for an event) to remove the time part. This, in effect, means that you are comparing a date (June 30 in this example) to the *date part only* of the field. So, whatever the time of the sale, only the *date* is used in the filter. This makes the time irrelevant and prevents the query from returning erroneous results.

The DATE() function simply wraps around a field containing DATETIME data. This will remove the time element from the field contents. This way, the SaleDate field—

that is defined in the database to use the DATETIME data type—will be converted to a Date data type. This conversion removes the time element from the field and prevents possible errors in the query.

Tricks and Traps

Understanding the difference between date and datetime fields can be a little daunting when you start writing time-based queries. To help you in this, try remembering the following:

- When beginning to use SQL—and when dealing with a database that you do not yet know inside out—you may well wonder exactly how you can be sure that you have a field that contains both date and time parts. The simple solution is to carry out a simple SELECT on the field in question. If you see only the date (whatever the format), then you have a date field. If you see time elements after the date, then the field is one of the datetime data types.

  You can see in the PrestigeCars database that the DateBought field contains only the date, whereas the SaleDate field contains both date and time elements.

- When filtering on date data—and if you are not sure whether a field is a date or a date and time—then you can always apply the DATE() function to the field that you are not sure about. Doing this cannot cause any harm and will not cause a filter on a date field (that is, one without a time element) to go wrong.

- As an alternative to applying the DATE() function you can use the CAST() function instead. Indeed, you might see this used in SQL that you inherit in your day job. You can see an example of this in the following code snippet:

```
WHERE      CAST(SA.SaleDate AS DATE) = '20160228'
```

7. Filtering by Year

As Prestige Cars has been selling cars for several years, the finance director wants to isolate the records for a specific year. SQL makes this easy, as the following code shows:

```
SELECT     MK.MakeName, MD.ModelName

           ,YEAR(SA.SaleDate) AS YearOfSale

FROM       make AS MK

JOIN       model AS MD USING(MakeID)
```

```
JOIN        stock AS ST USING(ModelID)

JOIN        salesdetails AS SD ON ST.StockCode = SD.StockID

JOIN        sales AS SA USING(SalesID)

WHERE       YEAR(SA.SaleDate) = 2015

ORDER BY    MK.MakeName, MD.ModelName;
```

Running this SQL delivers the output shown in Figure 8.7.

	MakeName	ModelName	YearOfSale
	Alfa Romeo	Giulia	2015
	Aston Martin	DB4	2015
	Aston Martin	DB5	2015
	Aston Martin	DB5	2015
	Aston Martin	DB6	2015
	Aston Martin	DB6	2015
	Aston Martin	DB6	2015
	Aston Martin	Virage	2015
	Bentley	Flving Spur	2015
	Ferrari	355	2015
	Ferrari	355	2015
	Ferrari	Testarossa	2015
	Ferrari	Testarossa	2015
	Jaguar	XJS	2015
	Jaguar	XJS	2015
	Jaguar	XK120	2015
	Jaguar	XK150	2015
	Mercedes	280SL	2015

Figure 8.7: Using the YEAR() function on a date field

How it Works

This query uses the YEAR() function to extract the year from the date in the WHERE clause so that you can then specify which year to filter on. Although it is perhaps not strictly necessary, we have added this same function to the SELECT clause as well so that you can then confirm, visually, that the year that interests you is being returned by the query. As you can observe, the YEAR() function extracts the year element from a date field, irrespective of the month and day of the month. As is the case with all SQL functions, you can use this function in any part of the query. Applying it to the WHERE clause means that it is used to filter on the year.

We also added an ORDER BY clause to this piece of SQL merely to add some structure to the output—and to remind you that this can be done whatever the type of query that you are writing.

Tricks and Traps

There are a few interesting points to make here.

- The YEAR function outputs (or *returns* in geek-speak) the year as a number. This means that when using YEAR in a query, you do not need to enter the year in single quotes. Fortunately, however, MySQL is very tolerant, and will still recognize the year if you do enclose it in quotes.

- You can always begin by adding any fields that you are using in the WHERE clause to the SELECT clause when you are writing and testing the query. Once you are satisfied that the SQL is working correctly, you can then remove these fields from the SELECT clause unless you really need to display the data.

- Instead of using the YEAR() function, you may prefer to apply (or sometimes see) the EXTRACT function. In this case the WHERE clause of this query would look like the following piece of SQL:

```
WHERE       EXTRACT(YEAR FROM SA.SaleDate) = 2015
```

8. Filtering Records over a Series of Years

Now that he has the sales lists for 2015, the finance director wants to compare the list of makes and models sold in both 2015 and 2016. Fortunately, SQL does not limit you to analyzing data for a single year, as the following query makes clear:

```
SELECT DISTINCT MK.MakeName, MD.ModelName, YEAR(SA.SaleDate)

            AS YearOfSale

FROM        make AS MK

JOIN        model AS MD USING(MakeID)

JOIN        stock AS ST USING(ModelID)

JOIN        salesdetails SD ON ST.StockCode = SD.StockID

JOIN        sales AS SA USING(SalesID)

WHERE       YEAR(SA.SaleDate) IN (2015, 2016)

ORDER BY    YEAR(SA.SaleDate), MakeName, ModelName;
```

Run this query and you will get the output shown in Figure 8.8. You will have to scroll down the output to see the change in the year of sale.

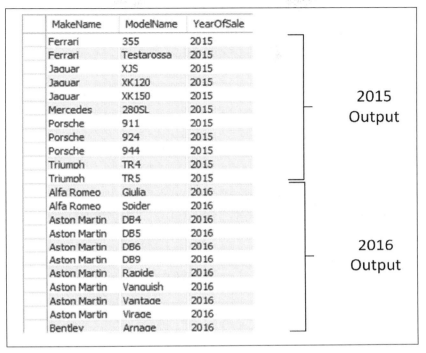

Figure 8.8: Filtering on a series of years using the IN keyword

How it Works

Once you have defined the FROM clause to join all the tables that are needed to access the Make, Model, and SaleDate columns, you only have to add a WHERE clause that tells MySQL to filter the results so that only data for 2015 to 2016 is returned. This is done using an IN keyword—just as you did in Chapter 4. As was the case with the previous queries that used the IN keyword, each separate filter element is separated by a comma from the other elements, and the complete list is enclosed in parentheses.

Finally, the results are sorted by year, make, and model. However, to sort by the year, you need, once again, to apply the YEAR() function to the SaleDate field in the ORDER BY clause.

Tricks and Traps

I hope that you did not find this kind of query difficult. To make things easier when you are writing your own queries to isolate data over time, you may want to pay attention to the following key points:

- You can enter as many years as you like in an IN function—just remember to separate each year with a comma (,). As was the case when filtering on a single year, the YEAR() function uses figures, so no single quotes are needed. However, MySQL is very tolerant and will let you place the year in quotes if you want.

- You can enter the years in an IN function in any order.

- For a wide range of years you might prefer to avoid entering each year individually and use the BETWEEN…AND syntax in the WHERE clause to specify a range of years, like this:

```
WHERE YEAR(SaleDate) BETWEEN 2013 AND 2016
```

Note that in this case you need to place the earlier date after the BETWEEN operator.

- You need to repeat the YEAR() function in a SQL query *every time* you need to extract the year from a date or datetime field. This kind of function can be applied to most parts of SQL queries.

- Instead of using the YEAR() function, you may prefer to apply the EXTRACT function. In this case the WHERE clause of this query would look like this:

```
WHERE    EXTRACT(YEAR FROM SA.SaleDate) IN (2015, 2016)
```

9. Isolating Data for a Specific Year and Month

The CEO is convinced that some months are better for sales than others. She has asked for the sales for July 2015 to check out her hunch. Fortunately, SQL lets you be as precise as you like when querying for data. If you want to list the vehicle sales for a certain month in a given year, you could use code like the following:

```
SELECT     MK.MakeName, MD.ModelName, SA.SaleDate

FROM       make AS MK

JOIN       model AS MD USING(MakeID)

JOIN       stock AS ST USING(ModelID)

JOIN       salesdetails SD ON ST.StockCode = SD.StockID

JOIN       sales AS SA USING(SalesID)

WHERE      YEAR(SA.SaleDate) = 2015

           AND MONTH(SA.SaleDate) = 7;
```

Execute this code snippet, and you will see the cars that are displayed in Figure 8.9.

MakeName	ModelName	SaleDate
Aston Martin	DB6	2015-07-25 00:00:00
Alfa Romeo	Giulia	2015-07-12 10:00:00
Jaguar	XK150	2015-07-15 00:00:00
Jaguar	XJS	2015-07-25 00:00:00

Figure 8.9: Using the YEAR() and MONTH() functions to filter output

How it Works

The MONTH() function isolates the month part of a date. More precisely, it returns— or, in this example, *filters on*—the number of the month in the year. So, January is 1, February is 2, and so on, until 12 (December). As you can combine both the YEAR() and MONTH() functions in a WHERE clause, limiting the output data to a specific month and year is not difficult. However, you do have to filter on the year and the month separately. This is why the query required you to say "I want the year 2015 *and* the month of July."

Tricks and Traps

There is one variation on a theme that you need to be aware of when using the MONTH() function.

- Instead of using the MONTH() function, you may prefer to apply the EXTRACT function. In this case the second part of the WHERE clause of this query would look like this:

```
AND EXTRACT(MONTH FROM SA.SaleDate) = 7
```

- You can mix the use of the EXTRACT(MONTH FROM …) and MONTH() functions inside the same SQL query—one in the SELECT clause and the other in the GROUP BY clause for instance. This is because they are synonymous and deliver exactly the same output.

10. Finding Data for a Given Quarter

The CEO was disappointed about the sales in July 2015, so now she wants to see sales for the entire third quarter of 2015. SQL can recognize calendar quarters (or trimesters) too, as the following code snippet makes clear:

```
SELECT    MK.MakeName, MD.ModelName

FROM      make AS MK
```

```
JOIN        model AS MD USING(MakeID)

JOIN        stock AS ST USING(ModelID)

JOIN        salesdetails SD ON ST.StockCode = SD.StockID

JOIN        sales AS SA USING(SalesID)

WHERE       QUARTER(SA.SaleDate) = 3

            AND YEAR(SA.SaleDate) = 2015;
```

Figure 8.10 shows you what happens when you run this code (although not necessarily sorted the same way).

MakeName	ModelName
Porsche	924
Aston Martin	DB6
Alfa Romeo	Giulia
Jaguar	XK120
Jaguar	XK150
Jaguar	XJS
Triumph	TR4
Triumph	TR5

Figure 8.10: Filtering on the calendar quarter with the QUARTER() function

How it Works

The QUARTER() function can isolate the calendar quarter of the year. Consequently, the months of January through March are quarter 1, the months of April through June are quarter 2, the months of July through September are quarter 3, and the months of October through December are quarter 4. The number of the quarter can then be used in a WHERE clause. In this example, the result is that only sales for the third quarter of 2015 are returned.

The QUARTER() function needs only a single parameter to be applied—The field containing the date.

In this query, the QUARTER() function is applied to the SaleDate field. Consequently, it returns the calendar quarter for each sale. This will inevitably be a number between 1 and 4. Then the WHERE clause looks for the *third* quarter of the date of sale, or, more precisely, says this: "The quarter of the SaleDate field equals three." So, you will see sales for the third quarter only. As you want to limit the result to the third quarter of a specific year (and not just any third quarter of every year for which there is data), you have to extend the WHERE clause by specifying the year to filter on as well.

Tricks and Traps

The QUARTER() function is really simple to use. The following are the only things to remember:

- The QUARTER() function will work only if the field that you apply to the QUARTER() function is either one of the date (or datetime) data types or a text or number that can be interpreted as a date.

- You do not have to specify a year, of course, but it is probably rare not to want to narrow down the search to sales for a specific year.

- Instead of using the QUARTER() function, you may prefer to apply the EXTRACT function. In this case the first part of the WHERE clause of this query would look like the following piece of SQL:

```
EXTRACT(QUARTER FROM SA.SaleDate) = 3
```

11. Filtering Data by Weekday

When analyzing sales, you may well want to isolate all purchases for a given weekday to find the most profitable day of the week for your business. SQL can do this using code like this:

```
SELECT     MK.MakeName, MD.ModelName

FROM       make AS MK

JOIN       model AS MD USING(MakeID)

JOIN       stock AS ST USING(ModelID)

JOIN       salesdetails SD ON ST.StockCode = SD.StockID

JOIN       sales AS SA USING(SalesID)

WHERE      DAYOFWEEK(SA.SaleDate) = 6

           AND YEAR(SA.SaleDate) = 2016

ORDER BY   MK.MakeName, MD.ModelName;
```

Running this code snippet produces output similar to that in Figure 8.11.

MakeName	ModelName
Aston Martin	DB5
Aston Martin	DB6
Aston Martin	DB9
Aston Martin	Rapide
Aston Martin	Virage
Bentley	Continental
Ferrari	355
Ferrari	Testarossa
Jaguar	XK120
Jaguar	XK120
Porsche	911
Porsche	944
Porsche	944
Porsche	944
Triumph	TR4
Triumph	TR6
Triumph	TR7

Figure 8.11: Finding all the vehicles sold on a specific day of the week

How it Works

The DAYOFWEEK() function lets you isolate the weekday for a date. It returns the weekday as a number, where 1 is Monday, 2 is Tuesday, 3 is Wednesday, 4 is Thursday, 5 is Friday, 6 is Saturday, and 7 is Sunday. Knowing this allows you to use DAYOFWEEK() in a WHERE clause to filter by day of the week.

Once again, you have narrowed down the search to a specific year as a separate part of the WHERE clause.

In this example the day of the week is set to 6, which is a Friday. So MySQL is showing the sales on Fridays per model.

12. Finding Records for a Specific Week of the Year

The sales director has announced that she would like to look at the sales for a specific week. SQL helps you to do this by filtering data by week. You can see an example of this in the following SQL, which finds sales for the 26th week of 2017:

```
SELECT     MK.MakeName, MD.ModelName

FROM       make AS MK
```

```
JOIN       model AS MD USING(MakeID)
JOIN       stock AS ST USING(ModelID)
JOIN       salesdetails SD ON ST.StockCode = SD.StockID
JOIN       sales AS SA USING(SalesID)
WHERE      WEEKOFYEAR(SA.SaleDate) = 26
           AND YEAR(SA.SaleDate) = 2017;
```

Execute this code, and you will get results similar to those shown in Figure 8.12.

MakeName	ModelName
Rolls Royce	Silver Seraph
Alfa Romeo	Spider
Noble	M600
Peugeot	205

Figure 8.12: Using the WEEKOFYEAR() function to isolate the week of the year

How it Works

This code sample selects all records where the sale took place in the 26th week of the year in 2017. Here, you used the WEEKOFYEAR() function to extract the week of the year from the date. As this function is used in a WHERE clause, you are filtering the data so that only sales records for week 26 are returned. As the WEEKOFYEAR() function only specifies the week you need to extend the WHERE clause to include the year to filter on as well.

Tricks and Traps

When using the WEEKOFYEAR() function you only really have to remember the following points:

- The WEEKOFYEAR() function can be used virtually anywhere in a SQL query. This means you can apply it in the SELECT clause, for instance, if you want to see the weeks when sales took place.

- Instead of using the WEEKOFYEAR() function, you may prefer to apply the EXTRACT function. In this case the first part of the WHERE clause of this query would look like this:

```
EXTRACT(WEEK FROM SA.SaleDate) = 26
```

- The week of the year can, actually, be quite an advanced concept This is because there can be up to 53 weeks in a year in some calendars—such as those used in the retail sector. I will not be looking at these complexities here.

13. Aggregating Data by the Day of Week in a Given Year

The HR manager needs to see how sales vary across days of the week. He has explained that he needs to forecast staff requirements for busy days. So, let's suppose he wants to see, overall, which were the weekdays where Prestige Cars made the most sales in 2015. This piece of SQL does just that:

```
SELECT      DAYOFWEEK(SA.SaleDate) AS DayOfWeek

            ,SUM(SD.SalePrice) AS Sales

FROM        make AS MK

JOIN        model AS MD USING(MakeID)

JOIN        stock AS ST USING(ModelID)

JOIN        salesDetails SD ON ST.StockCode = SD.StockID

JOIN        sales AS SA USING(SalesID)

WHERE       YEAR(SA.SaleDate) = 2015

GROUP BY    DAYOFWEEK(SA.SaleDate)

ORDER BY    Sales DESC;
```

If you run this code, you will get the table shown in Figure 8.13.

DayOfWeek	Sales
1	403695.00
5	306950.00
6	231140.00
3	186000.00
7	154150.00
2	107100.00
4	31940.00

Figure 8.13: Grouping output by day of week using the DAYOFWEEK() function

How it Works

MySQL numbers the days of the week from 1 to 7, where 1 is Monday and 7 is Sunday. It can output the number of the day of the week from any date or datetime field type (or a number or text that MySQL can interpret as a date) using the DAYOFWEEK() function.

This code returns the seven days of the week and the aggregate sales per weekday. It uses the DAYOFWEEK() function in two ways in this query.

First: The DAYOFWEEK() function is used in the SELECT query. This lets you see the weekday in the output.

Second: The DAYOFWEEK() function is used again in the GROUP BY clause. This ensures that the data is aggregated at the level of the day of the week.

The WHERE clause filters on a specific year (2015 in this example). Finally, for good measure, the query sorts the aggregated output by sales value from highest to lowest. This way it is clear which days have the greatest sales over a specific year.

Tricks and Traps

Analyzing data over time does have its traps, as well as a few things that you might need to know.

- You can group output on a function—such as DAYOFWEEK—just as you would on any field. You could also sort on a function like this if you needed.

- MySQL can sort on an alias even if the alias is the same as a table name. However, in practice, I advise you to avoid aliases that are the same as table names.

14. Grouping Data by the Full Weekday Name

The HR manager liked the information that you just gave him. However, he would prefer to see the days of the week written out in full and not just have them appear as numbers in the output. After a couple of simple modifications, your SQL now looks like this:

```
SELECT      DAYNAME(SA.SaleDate) AS DayOfWeek

            ,SUM(SD.SalePrice) AS sales

FROM        make AS MK

JOIN        model AS MD USING(MakeID)

JOIN        stock AS ST USING(ModelID)

JOIN        salesdetails SD ON ST.StockCode = SD.StockID

JOIN        sales AS SA USING(SalesID)
```

```
WHERE      YEAR(SA.SaleDate) = 2015
GROUP BY   DAYNAME(SA.SaleDate)
ORDER BY   WEEKDAY(SA.SaleDate);
```

If you execute this code, you will get the table shown in Figure 8.14.

	DayOfWeek	sales
►	Monday	107100.00
	Tuesday	186000.00
	Wednesday	31940.00
	Thursday	306950.00
	Friday	231140.00
	Saturday	154150.00
	Sunday	403695.00

Figure 8.14: Grouping output by day of week using the DAYNAME() function

How it Works

Displaying the day of the week as a number can be a little brutal. So, SQL has a function that can "humanize" the output if you want. So, to display the actual weekday, you can tweak the first line of the query so that it looks like this:

```
SELECT     DAYNAME(SA.SaleDate) AS DayOfWeek
```

Applying the DAYNAME() function makes the weekday appear as the text (not the number) of the weekday extracted from the date or datetime field (SaleDate in this example).

Although the WEEKDAY() function does not appear in the SELECT clause you are able to use it to sort the data because it is essentially similar to the DAYNAME() function. This means that as the DAYNAME() function is used in the SELECT clause you can sort the output using either of these two functions.

Tricks and Traps

There is only one key point to make here.

- Sorting on the WEEKDAY() function makes the days of the week appear in the traditional order of the days of the week. If you were to sort on the DAYNAME() function, the weekdays would appear in *alphabetical* order.

15. Aggregated Totals and Averages by Day of Year

The sales manager has had another of her ideas. You can tell this by her smile as she walks over to you at lunch in the Prestige Cars restaurant. Her idea, fortunately, is unlikely to spoil your meal. What she wants is the total and average sales for each day of the year since Prestige Cars started trading.

Once back at your desk you produce the following piece of SQL:

```
SELECT      DAYOFYEAR(SA.SaleDate) AS DayOfYear

            ,SUM(SD.SalePrice) AS TotalSales

            ,AVG(SD.SalePrice) AS AverageSales

FROM        salesdetails SD

JOIN        sales AS SA USING(SalesID)

GROUP BY    DAYOFYEAR(SA.SaleDate)

ORDER BY    DAYOFYEAR(SA.SaleDate);
```

Running this query produces the results that you can see in Figure 8.15.

DayOfYear	TotalSales	AverageSales
1	372000.00	74400.000000
2	369200.00	52742.857143
5	162110.00	27018.333333
7	32050.00	16025.000000
9	12650.00	12650.000000
10	210400.00	42080.000000
11	22500.00	22500.000000
12	125950.00	125950.000000
13	8850.00	8850.000000
14	9950.00	9950.000000
15	370950.00	185475.000000
21	1250.00	1250.000000
22	56950.00	56950.000000
25	220000.00	220000.000000
30	56500.00	56500.000000
31	111950.00	55975.000000
34	19500.00	19500.000000
38	365000.00	365000.000000

Figure 8.15: Grouping output by day of year using the DAYOFYEAR() function

How it Works

MySQL can isolate the day of the year (even in leap years) from any field that contains either a date or a date and time. It does this by wrapping the date or datetime field inside the DAYOFYEAR() function. This function only takes a single parameter (a date) and outputs the day of the year that it contains. This will be between 1 and 365 in any normal year and between 1 and 366 in a leap year.

The SQL in this example joins the SalesDetails and Sales tables to access the required fields and then adds the following three elements to the SELECT clause:

- The DAYOFYEAR() function—applied to the sale date field
- The SUM() function—applied to the sale price field
- The AVG() function—applied to the sale price field

Finally the SQL adds a GROUP BY clause on the DAYOFYEAR() function applied to the sale date field, so that this non-aggregated value is used to group the output—and sorts the output by the same function to deliver the days of the year in ascending order. As is best practice, all the fields that appear in the SELECT clause are given aliases.

16. Aggregated Totals and Averages by Day of the Month

The CEO wants you to give her the total and average sales for each day of the month for all sales, ever. Fortunately your mastery of MySQL date functions makes this easy. After a few minutes work you produce the following piece of SQL:

```
SELECT      DAY(SA.SaleDate) AS DayOfMonth

            ,SUM(SD.SalePrice) AS TotalSales

            ,AVG(SD.SalePrice) AS AverageSales

FROM        salesdetails SD

JOIN        sales AS SA USING(SalesID)

GROUP BY    DAY(SA.SaleDate)

ORDER BY    DAY(SA.SaleDate);
```

Running this query produces the results that you can see in Figure 8.16.

DayOfMonth	TotalSales	AverageSales
1	1886740.00	67383.571429
2	878490.00	38195.217391
3	425760.00	60822.857143
4	449840.00	44984.000000
5	864320.00	41158.095238
6	529275.00	52927.500000
7	1063550.00	132943.750000
8	1064590.00	96780.909091
9	546990.00	78141.428571
10	1485650.00	67529.545455
11	331950.00	47421.428571
12	874785.00	79525.909091
13	477450.00	68207.142857
14	102025.00	17004.166667
15	2203730.00	66779.696970

Figure 8.16: Grouping output by day of month using the DAY() function

How it Works

MySQL can isolate the day of the month, too from any field that contains either a date or a date and time. It does this by wrapping the date or datetime field inside the DAY() function. This function only takes a single parameter (a date) and outputs the day of the month that it contains.

The SQL in this example joins the SalesDetails and Sales tables to access the required fields and then adds the following three elements to the SELECT clause:

- The DAY() function—applied to the sale date field to return the day of the month
- The SUM() function—applied to the sale price field
- The AVG() function—applied to the sale price field

Then the SQL adds a GROUP BY clause on the DAY() function applied to the sale date field, so that this non-aggregated value is used to group the output.

Finally an ORDER BY clause is added to make quite sure that the output will appear in a rational sequence of days of the month. Consequently the ORDER BY clause also wraps the SaleDate field in the DAY() function.

Tricks and Traps

There are three points that are well worth noting when grouping output using the DAY() function.

- • Instead of using the DAY() function, you may prefer to apply the EXTRACT function. In this case the GROUP BY clause of this query would look like the following piece of SQL:

```
GROUP BY  EXTRACT(DAY FROM SA.SaleDate)
```

- • You can, if you remember, group on an alias (if you have used one in the SELECT clause) rather than repeating a function in the GROUP BY clause. So, for instance, you could write the GROUP BY clause for this example as:

```
GROUP BY  DayOfMonth;
```

- • You can write DAYOFMONTH() instead of DAY() if you prefer, as the two functions produce identical results and are synonyms.

17. Displaying Aggregated Values per Month

Just as you are about to leave for home, the CEO flags you down on your way out of the office and insists that she needs the number of vehicles sold per month in 2018. Fortunately you have already prepared a piece of SQL to provide this. So you are able to both impress her and get home in time thanks to the following code snippet:

```
SELECT      MONTHNAME(SA.SaleDate) AS Month

            ,COUNT(*) AS sales

FROM        salesdetails SD

JOIN        sales AS SA USING(SalesID)

WHERE       YEAR(SA.SaleDate) = 2018

GROUP BY    MONTH(SA.SaleDate)

ORDER BY    MONTH(SA.SaleDate);
```

If you run this code you will obtain the results that you can see in Figure 8.17.

Month	Sales
January	16
February	10
March	8
April	16
May	11
June	6
July	15
August	9
September	11
October	12
November	3
December	10

Figure 8.17: Returning the number of sales per month using the MONTH() and MONTHNAME() functions

How it Works

This query first joins the Sales and SalesDetails tables. You need the Sales table for the date of sale and the SalesDetails table to calculate numbers of sales.

Then the query adds two elements to the SELECT clause.

First: The MONTHNAME() function is wrapped around the SaleDate field to isolate the actual text for the month (rather than the number of the month).

Second: The COUNT() aggregation function is used to calculate the number of records for each grouped element.

Then you added a WHERE clause to filter on a specific year—2018 in this example.

Then the query adds a GROUP BY clause using the MONTH() function enclosing the SaleDate field. This way the query groups and counts records for each of the months in the output data set.

The query finishes by adding an ORDER BY clause using the MONTH() function applied to the SaleDate field. However, the output is ordered not by the MONTHNAME() function but by the MONTH() function. This because the months will now be ordered by number, from 1 to 12, and not in alphabetical order (as would be the case if you sorted the output by the name of the month).

Tricks and Traps

You might want to take away an interesting point about how the data is grouped here.

- You can group and sort using either the MONTHNAME() or MONTH() functions as both will isolate the underlying month—whether it is a text or a number.

18. Displaying Cumulative Data over 75 Days Up to a Specific Date

The HR manager has emailed another request. He needs to calculate the final bonus of a salesperson who is leaving the company and consequently needs to see the accumulated sales made by this staff member for a 75 day period up to July 25, 2015. SQL can do this (and I will imagine here that it is for the salesperson who sells Jaguars for Prestige Cars). So, to see her sales for the 75 days up to the specified date, you would write SQL like this:

```
SELECT      SUM(SD.SalePrice) AS CumulativeJaguarSales

FROM        make AS MK

JOIN        model AS MD USING(MakeID)

JOIN        stock AS ST USING(ModelID)

JOIN        salesdetails SD ON ST.StockCode = SD.StockID

JOIN        sales AS SA USING(SalesID)

WHERE       SA.SaleDate BETWEEN DATE_SUB('20170725', INTERVAL 75 DAY)

            AND '20170725'

            AND MK.MakeName = 'Jaguar';
```

Run this piece of SQL, and you will see the output shown in Figure 8.18.

CumulativeJaguarSales
29500.00

Figure 8.18: *Using the DATE_SUB() function to specify a time period relative to a date*

How it Works

As you can see, this piece of SQL returns the total sales for Jaguars. However, what is new is the way that a time period is defined in the WHERE clause. There is no need to reach for a calendar and work out exactly what was the exact date 75 days previously; SQL can do this for you using the DATE_SUB() function.

The DATE_SUB() function needs *four* elements—or *parameters*—to work.

First:	The date for the number of days to be added to—or subtracted from. Once again, it is more reliable to enter this in the YYYYMMDD format—in quotes if you prefer—and a comma.
Second:	The keyword *INTERVAL*.
Third:	The number of time periods—75 in this example.
Finally:	The time interval that you want—days, months, quarters, years, and so on. In this case, you want to see a number of days, so the DAY keyword is used.

Using the DATE_SUB() function in the WHERE clause means that you are saying this: "Filter on a date range between a specified date (July 25, 2015) and 75 days previous to the date that I specify."

Tricks and Traps

There are a few interesting points here.

- You need to ensure that you use the same dates in both the DATE_SUB() function and the BETWEEN...AND operator. Otherwise the calculated number of days will likely be wrong.

- You can also use the DATE_ADD() function to specify a date range that projects a number of days into the future from the data that you specify.

- The DATE_SUB() function can use a negative interval. In this case the date that it calculates will be the specified number of days beyond the given date.

- The DATE_ADD() function can use a negative interval. In this case the date that it calculates will be the specified number of days in the past compared to the given date.

19. Displaying the Data for the Previous Three Months

Now suppose you want to see the rolling sum of car sales for each make sold during the previous three months up to and including the current date. This piece of SQL can do it for you:

```
SELECT      MK.MakeName, SUM(SD.SalePrice) AS CumulativeSales

FROM        Make AS MK

JOIN        Model AS MD USING(MakeID)

JOIN        Stock AS ST USING(ModelID)

JOIN        SalesDetails AS SD ON ST.StockCode = SD.StockID

JOIN        Sales AS SA USING(SalesID)

WHERE       CAST(SA.SaleDate AS DATE)

            BETWEEN DATE_SUB(CURDATE(), INTERVAL 3 MONTH)

            AND CURDATE()

GROUP BY    MK.MakeName

ORDER BY    MK.MakeName ASC;
```

Run this code, and you will see output something like that shown in Figure 8.19. Be aware, however, that this output will vary depending on the date that the query is run.

MakeName	CumulativeSales
Alfa Romeo	39525.00
Aston Martin	668270.00
Bentley	99500.00
Bugatti	345000.00
Ferrari	728000.00
Jaguar	153000.00
Mercedes	33450.00
Morgan	18500.00
Noble	31450.00
Peugeot	6000.00
Porsche	89500.00
Trabant	1250.00
Triumph	23530.00

Figure 8.19: Returning sales for a time period up to a specific date

How it Works

This code snippet introduces another new date function, the CURDATE() function. All this function means in SQL is "today." So, this query will always display data relative to the day that it is run. If you run it today, you will see data up to today's date. Run it tomorrow and the data will be different because the rolling total now ends on a different date.

This query does the following:

First: It aggregates the total sales for each make, using a SUM on the SalePrice field and a GROUP BY on the MakeName field so that you see the total sales by make. This requires joining five tables so that the necessary fields can be used in the query.

Second: It limits the data to the last three months using the DATE_SUB() function that was introduced in the previous section and specifies that the period covers "now until three months subtracted from now"—using the BETWEEN...AND function. This time, however, the time interval is defined as MONTH.

Finally: It presents the results in alphabetical order of make using the MakeName field in the ORDER BY clause.

The principal available interval types that you can use with the DATE_SUB() and DATE_ADD() functions are shown in Table 8-2.

Table 8-2: *The available Interval Types For The DATE_SUB() AND DATE_ADD() Functions*

Interval Code	Interval Type
DAY	A number of days
WEEK	A number of weeks
MONTH	A number of months
QUARTER	A number of quarters
YEAR	A number of years
YEAR_MONTH	Years and Months

Tricks and Traps

There is one important point that I have to make about this approach.

- What can make this WHERE clause seem a little complex at first is the fact that it also applies the CAST() function. If you remember from earlier in this chapter, some dates also have time elements, which can make results go awry on certain occasions. So, you have to remove the time element to ensure that everything will work cleanly. The CAST() function is one of the ways to strip the time element from a DATETIME field type.

20. Finding the Current System Date

If all you want to do is to check the current date, then a single line of SQL can do this for you.

```
SELECT CURDATE()
```

Running this code will return the date that your MySQL server assumes to be the current date.

How it Works

This short piece of code simply returns the current date for the database server. You do not need to add a FROM clause to this short piece of code.

Tricks and Traps

I have just four final points to make here.

- It can be useful to check the system date before carrying out date calculations. After all, you should never trust a computer!

- You can use CURRENT_DATE instead of CURDATE() if you prefer as the two functions are identical.

- You can also use the NOW() function. This will return the date and time. So you must wrap this function inside the DATE() or CAST() functions to remove the time element if all you want is the date part.

- The CURTIME() or NOW() functions will show the time according to the MySQL server.

Conclusion

This chapter has taken you on a whirlwind tour of the core date functions that you will need to analyze how data evolves over time. You have discovered how to query data for a specific date or a range of dates. You have seen, too, that you can look at data over years, quarters, weeks, months, or days. Indeed, you learned how to analyze data "to date" and how to compare data with previous time periods, as well as aggregating data across different time periods.

Analyzing data over time is such a vast subject that we have been able only to scratch the surface in a single chapter of all that you can do. However, you can rest assured that you will be seeing many more ways of handling date and time data in Chapter 20.

Core Knowledge Learned in This Chapter

These are the keywords that you learned in this chapter:

Concept	Description
DATEDIFF()	This function finds the number of days between two given dates.
CAST()	This function converts a datetime data type to a date.
YEAR()	This function isolates the year part of a date.
MONTH()	This function isolates the month part of a date.
DAY()	This function isolates the day part of a date.
DATE_SUB()	This function subtracts a number of days, months, years, and so on, to or from a given data and finds the date in the future or the past.
DATE_ADD()	This function adds a number of days, months, years, and so on, to or from a given data and finds the date in the future or the past.
MONTHNAME()	This function returns the full name of the month from a date.
DAYOFYEAR()	This function returns the day of the year from a date
DAYNAME()	This function returns the full name of the weekday from a date.
WEEKDAY()	This function returns the number of the day of the week from a date.

Concept	Description
WEEKOFYEAR()	This function returns the week of the year from a date.
QUARTER()	This function returns the quarter from a date.
INTERVAL()	This keyword—used with the DATE_ADD() or DATE_SUB() functions defines the time period to calculate.
EXTRACT()	This function extracts part of a date from a date field.
NOW()	This function finds the current date and time.
CURRENT_DATE	This function finds the current date.
CURDATE ()	This function finds the current date.

CHAPTER 9

Formatting Text in Query Output

A large part of SQL code is written purely to delve into mounds of data and return carefully chosen and filtered output. However, this is not the whole picture. Sometimes you will need your SQL skills to tweak the presentation of the data you are delivering. This chapter explains how to take the text that is returned by a query and make the output easier to read as well as more meaningful.

Enhancing the Output from SQL Queries

So, after the logical and technical focus of the previous chapters, it is time to learn some presentation techniques. You may not need these approaches on all occasions, but there are bound to be times when you will need to select not just a column of data but part of a field. Perhaps you will need to amalgamate two or more columns into one. Maybe you will need to convert the contents of a field to lowercase. Alternatively, it could be as simple as adding some additional text to the contents of a field.

Presenting your data is, then, the subject of this chapter. After all, delivering clear and comprehensible analysis is your aim. It follows that knowing how to polish the final delivery is every bit as fundamental as the initial analysis.

1. Adding Text to the Output

On some occasions you may want not just to list some data but to add repetitive text to the output. Suppose, for instance, that you want to add the word Customer: before each customer name in a query. You can do this using the following code:

```
SELECT CONCAT('Customer: ', CustomerName) AS Customer

FROM    customer;
```

Executing this piece of code will give you a result similar to that shown in Figure 9.1.

Customer
Customer: Magic Motors
Customer: Snazzy Roadsters
Customer: Birmingham Executive Prestige Vehicles
Customer: WunderKar
Customer: Casseroles Chromes
Customer: Le Luxe en Motion
Customer: Eat My Exhaust Ltd
Customer: M. Pierre Dubois
Customer: Sondra Horowitz
Customer: Wonderland Wheels
Customer: London Executive Prestige Vehicles
Customer: Glittering Prize Cars Ltd
Customer: La Bagnole de Luxe
Customer: Convertible Dreams

Figure 9.1: *Adding text to the output from a column*

How it Works

Any text that you like can be added to the data in an output column. Mixing added text with the contents of a field works like this:

First: Enter the **CONCAT** keyword, followed by a left parenthesis.

Second: Add the first element to join to the output. This can be a field or a descriptive text.

Finally: Enter the second element to join to the output. This can be a field or a descriptive text, followed by a right parenthesis.

Of course, you can start with the column name and then add some fixed text afterward if you prefer. Indeed, the CONCAT() function is immensely flexible in that it does not limit you to only one or two parameters. You can enter a whole series of field names or text elements one after the other inside the parentheses as long as each individual element is separated from the others by a comma. Any additional text must be enclosed in single quotes.

Tricks and Traps

Although this technique is relatively simple, there are nonetheless a good few things you should know.

- You can use most printable characters (such as spaces) in the text that you add to a column name. Just ensure that any text is inside the single quotes.

- You can use either single or double quotes (on most systems) to enclose a text that you want to add to the output. So the code that you entered could look like this:

  ```
  CONCAT("Customer: ", CustomerName)
  ```

- The CONCAT() function automatically converts the contents of numeric or date fields to text.

- If you do not provide an alias, MySQL will use the formula as the column header. In this example this would be: "CONCAT('Customer: ' CustomerName)".

- The alias can be the same as the original field name.

- If you want to add a single quote to the complementary text in the CONCAT() function, then you will need to double up on any quotes used. So, to add the text *Yesterday's Sales for*, the SQL will look like this:

  ```
  SELECT CONCAT('Yesterday''s Sales for ', CustomerName)
  FROM    SalesByCountry;
  ```

2. Adding Multiple Pieces of Text to Numbers

Occasionally you may want to output data from text and numeric fields joined together in a single element. You could, for instance, want to add the word *Sales* before the sale price and a currency indicator afterward. The following SQL shows you how this can be done:

```
SELECT     CONCAT('Sales: ', TotalSalePrice ,' GBP')
               AS SalePriceInPounds
FROM       sales
```

Running this code gives the results shown in Figure 9.2.

	SalePriceInPounds
1	Sales: 65000.00 GBP
2	Sales: 220000.10 GBP
3	Sales: 19500.00 GBP
4	Sales: 11500.00 GBP
5	Sales: 19900.00 GBP
6	Sales: 29500.00 GBP
7	Sales: 49500.20 GBP
8	Sales: 76000.90 GBP
9	Sales: 19600.00 GBP
10	Sales: 36500.00 GBP
11	Sales: 89000.00 GBP
12	Sales: 169500.00 GBP
13	Sales: 8950.00 GBP
14	Sales: 195000.00 GBP
15	Sales: 22950.00 GBP

Figure 9.2: Adding text to the output from a numeric field using the CONCAT() function

How it Works

Using the CONCAT() function is one way to format numeric output in MySQL. After all, formatting consists of adding custom text to output in many cases.

In this example the CONCAT() function is used to:

First: Add descriptive text before a field.

Second: Add the contents of a field.

Finally: Add a second text after the field.

Once again, the principle is to add each required element inside the CONCAT() function, separated by a comma and enclosed in quotes where necessary.

Tricks and Traps

The CONCAT() function can really be incredibly useful. You can really take advantage of it if you bear the following points in mind:

- Normally you don't worry about formatting numbers in SQL like you do in Excel or reporting software. Indeed, you nearly always have to leave numbers unformatted because otherwise they will be considered text by MySQL. However, there could be cases where you need to format numbers (albeit to a limited extent). One way to do this is to append text to a number.

- Note that you can include spaces inside the single quotes around the text you are appending to the figures (the GBP) to enhance the final appearance of the output.

- This example shows only three elements inside the CONCAT() function, but there you can add several more fields and text if you want.

- The CONCAT() function will also handle date data types and convert them to strings.

- Formatting numbers can make it difficult—or impossible—to use them in calculations.

3. Amalgamating Columns Using Different Separators

The CEO was pleased with your last piece of work. However, she wants the addresses formatted in a particular way, with a dash before each zip code (or postcode if you prefer).

Take a look at the following code snippet that delivers what she is looking for:

```
SELECT CustomerName, CONCAT(Address1, ' ', Town, ' - ', PostCode)

                AS FullAddress

FROM    customer;
```

Executing this code returns the output in Figure 9.3.

CustomerName	FullAddress
Magic Motors	27. Handsworth Road Birmingham - B1 7AZ
Snazzy Roadsters	102. Bleak Street Birmingham - B3 5ST
Birmingham Executive Prestige Vehicles	96. Aardvark Avenue Birmingham - B2 8UH
WunderKar	NULL
Casseroles Chromes	NULL
Le Luxe en Motion	Avenue des Indes. 26 Geneva - CH-1201
Eat My Exhaust Ltd	29. Kop Hill Liverpool - L1 8UY
M. Pierre Dubois	NULL
Sondra Horowitz	NULL
Wonderland Wheels	57. Grosvenor Estate Avenue London - E7 4BR
London Executive Prestige Vehicles	199. Park Lane London - NW1 0AK
Glittering Prize Cars Ltd	46. :lders Green Road London - E17 9IK
La Bagnole de Luxe	NULL
Convertible Dreams	31. Archbishop Ave London - SW2 6PL
Alexei Tolstoi	83. Abbey Road London - N4 2CV
SuperSport S.A.R.L.	NULL
Theo Kowalski	NULL
Peter McLuckie	73. Entwhistle Street London - W10 BN

Figure 9.3: Concatenating data from several columns using different separators

How it Works

Using the CONCAT() function is the fundamental way to assemble the contents of various fields by stringing them together—or even to add descriptive text—with a little tweaking. Moreover, the CONCAT() function allows you to "hand-craft" the output using different separator elements or descriptive text anywhere in the concatenated output. This lets you join together multiple fields and/or text to produce the output that you want.

In this example the CONCAT() function works just as it did in the first example in this chapter. Here, however, you are joining several fields together to create a single output column. All you have to do is to:

First: Enter **CONCAT(**.

Second: Add a series of fields and separator elements with a comma between each one. Each separator element must be in single quotes (or, possibly, double quotes—depending on your system).

Finally: Add the closing parenthesis.

The CONCAT() function is not limited to joining text from only one column to another piece of text. You can join many different elements to create a single output column. These elements can be:

- Fields
- Custom text
- Symbols
- Numbers

The guiding principles are:

- Separate each element that you want to output from other elements by a comma.
- Enclose any custom text (including spaces) inside single or double quotes.
- Enter as many elements as you want to join in a single output column.
- Add an alias to the column that you are creating using the CONCAT() function.

Tricks and Traps

Here are some of the tricks and traps you need to know:

- As you are, by definition, using data from several fields, SQL cannot know what name to give to the resulting column. So, you should probably add an alias when concatenating data.
- If any of the fields that you are concatenating contains a NULL then the *entire concatenated output for that field will be NULL.* You can see how to get round this in the next section.
- Make sure you separate each text or field with a comma and that you place all added text in single or double quotes.
- To avoid the contents of columns running into each other without any spacing you should add spaces—or some other separator character— manually to separate the fields inside the CONCAT() function. This can mean adding
- A comma
- An opening double quote
- A space
- A closing double quote

Any separator character must be enclosed in single or double quotes.

4. Avoiding NULLs in Concatenated Output

If you take a closer look at the output shown in Figure 9.3, you will see a large number of records that only show NULL as the result of joining the Address, Town, and PostCode fields. Yet if you look at the data in these fields in the Customer table, you will notice that there is data for at least one of these fields for clients—and yet when the fields are concatenated, they show nothing at all.

Fortunately, SQL has a solution to this problem. Take a look at the following SQL snippet that is adapted from the initial code in the previous example:

```
SELECT CustomerName, CONCAT(IFNULL(Address1, '')

                    , ' ', IFNULL(Town, '')

                    , ' - '

                    , IFNULL(PostCode, ''))

                    AS FullAddress

FROM    customer;
```

The result will now look like the record set shown in Figure 9.4.

CustomerName	FullAddress
Magic Motors	27. Handsworth Road Birmingham - B1 7AZ
Snazzy Roadsters	102. Bleak Street Birmingham - B3 5ST
Birmingham Executive Prestige Vehicles	96. Aardvark Avenue Birmingham - B2 8UH
WunderKar	AlexanderPlatz 205 Berlin -
Casseroles Chromes	29. Rue Gi:ndas Lyon -
Le Luxe en Motion	Avenue des Indes. 26 Geneva - CH-1201
Eat My Exhaust Ltd	29. Koo Hill Liverpool - L1 8UY
M. Pierre Dubois	14. Rue De La Hutte Marseille -
Sondra Horowitz	10040 Great Western Road Los Angeles -
Wonderland Wheels	57. Grosvenor Estate Avenue London - E7 4BR
London Executive Prestige Vehicles	199. Park Lane London - NW1 0AK
Glittering Prize Cars Ltd	46. :lders Green Road London - E17 9IK
La Bagnole de Luxe	890 Place de la Concorde Paris -
Convertible Dreams	31. Archbishop Ave London - SW2 6PL
Alexei Tolstoi	83. Abbey Road London - N4 2CV
SuperSport S.A.R.L.	210 Place de la Republique Paris -
Theo Kowalski	1000 East 51st Street New York -
Peter McLuckie	73. Entwhistle Street London - W10 BN

Figure 9.4: Adding the IFNULL() function to avoid NULL propagation

How it Works

A NULL value in any field—even if it is a text field—will "propagate" a NULL value into all the other fields you concatenate it with. This will result in a NULL being output. This is to all intents and purposes the same effect as you saw for numbers in Chapter 3. However, I imagine that this is not what you expected—and certainly not what you want to see in the result.

The solution is the same for both letters and numbers. If you suspect that a column contains NULLs, then you are best advised to enclose the field name in the IFNULL() function. This function requires the following:

First: The field containing possible NULL values you want to trap and replace with another character.

Second: The replacement character: That can be a blank space or an empty character (as it is in this example) in which case two single quotes will do the trick.

5. Concatenating and Grouping

The sales manager now wants a list of all the different make and model combinations that have ever been sold with the total sale price for each combination. However, this time she wants the make and model output as a single column. As she is hovering near your desk, you quickly produce the following piece of SQL to deliver what she wants:

```
SELECT     CONCAT(MakeName, ', ', ModelName) AS MakeAndModel

           ,SUM(SalePrice) As TotalSold

FROM       stock ST

JOIN       model MD USING(ModelID)

JOIN       make MK USING(MakeID)

JOIN       salesdetails SD

           ON ST.StockCode = SD.StockID

JOIN       sales SA USING(SalesID)

GROUP BY   CONCAT(MakeName, ', ', ModelName);
```

Running this query produces the output in Figure 9.5.

MakeAndModel	TotalSold
Alfa Romeo. 1750	13525.00
Alfa Romeo. Giulia	89695.00
Alfa Romeo. Giulietta	92190.00
Alfa Romeo. Spider	48100.00
Aston Martin. DB2	456440.00
Aston Martin. DB4	281700.00
Aston Martin. DB5	300340.00
Aston Martin. DB6	1019095.00
Aston Martin. DB9	959500.00
Aston Martin. Rapide	302500.00
Aston Martin. Vanqu	361040.00
Aston Martin. Vantage	343500.00
Aston Martin. Virage	1078640.00
Austin. Cambridge	22500.00
Austin. Lichfield	30100.00
Austin. Princess	11900.00

Figure 9.5: *Grouping on concatenated fields*

How it Works

You can use a concatenated field to group data simply by reproducing the full CONCAT() function used in the SELECT clause in the GROUP BY clause.

Tricks and Traps

There is one variation on a theme you can use when grouping on aggregated fields, noted here:

- It is vital when you are using a GROUP BY clause to include *all the fields that are in the SELECT clause in the GROUP BY clause*—if these fields are not part of an aggregation function such as SUM(). This means you generally have to copy the fields from the SELECT clause to the GROUP BY clause, as we did in this example.

- In most case you do not need to add the functions to the fields that are used in the SELECT clause. That is, you could write the GROUP BY clause like this:

```
GROUP BY   MakeName, ModelName
```

- Alternatively, MySQL will let you repeat, in the GROUP BY clause, the alias that you added to the CONCAT() function in the SELECT clause. This prevents you having to copy the entire piece of code—and allows you to keep the two clauses in 'sync as you develop your SQL. In this particular example this would mean a GROUP BY clause like the following:

```
GROUP BY MakeAndModel
```

6. Amalgamating Columns

The CEO wants a list of all the customers' addresses. As the various elements that make up a complete address are spread across several columns, you have put together the following SQL to satisfy this particular request:

```
SELECT CustomerName, CONCAT_WS(' ', Address1,  Town, PostCode)

            AS FullAddress

FROM    customer;
```

Executing this code returns the output in Figure 9.6.

CustomerName	FullAddress
Magic Motors	27. Handsworth Road Birmingham B1 7AZ
Snazzy Roadsters	102. Bleak Street Birmingham B3 5ST
Birmingham Executive Prestige Vehicles	96. Aardvark Avenue Birmingham B2 8UH
WunderKar	AlexanderPlatz 205 Berlin
Casseroles Chromes	29. Rue Gi:ndas Lyon
Le Luxe en Motion	Avenue des Indes. 26 Geneva CH-1201
Eat My Exhaust Ltd	29. Kop Hill Liverpool L1 8UY
M. Pierre Dubois	14. Rue De La Hutte Marseille
Sondra Horowitz	10040 Great Western Road Los Angeles
Wonderland Wheels	57. Grosvenor Estate Avenue London E7 4BR
London Executive Prestige Vehicles	199. Park Lane London NW1 0AK
Glittering Prize Cars Ltd	46. :lders Green Road London E17 9IK
La Bagnole de Luxe	890 Place de la Concorde Paris
Convertible Dreams	31. Archbishop Ave London SW2 6PL
Alexei Tolstoi	83. Abbey Road London N4 2CV
SuperSport S.A.R.L.	210 Place de la Republique Paris

Figure 9.6: *Concatenating data from several columns*

How it Works

Relational databases—by definition—fragment data into small, independent pieces. That is a key factor in their success and the way they work. Yet when you want to output data, you frequently need to join data from two or more columns into one piece of information. This technique is called *concatenation* and can be applied to any column containing any type of data.

Joining several columns of data into a single output column means using the CONCAT_WS() function. You apply it in this way.

First: Enter **CONCAT_WS** and a left parenthesis.

Second: Add (in quotes) the character that you want to use to separate each element in the output. In this example it is a space.

Next: Add a comma.

Then: Add each column that you want to use in the output, each one separated from the others by a comma.

Finally: Add a right parenthesis (to end the CONCAT_WS function) and add an alias to the column.

Tricks and Traps

Here are some of the tricks and traps you need to know about the CONCAT_WS() function:

- The separator can be made up of multiple characters if you need this.

- There is virtually no practical limit to the number of columns that you can join together in this way.

- The CONCAT_WS() function converts all numbers and dates to text.

- The CONCAT_WS() function is not affected by NULL values in any of the records that are concatenated. This means that it does not return blank output for the entire field if it ever meets a NULL in any of the fields used in the function.

7. Converting Text to Uppercase

MySQL can store alphabetical data in either uppercase or lowercase characters. However, the sales director wants a list of all the customer names in uppercase for a mail-merge operation. This reflects the fact that there will inevitably be times when you want to standardize the output without having to worry about how the data itself is stored, SQL can, of course, do this for you:

```
SELECT     UPPER(CustomerName) AS Customer

FROM       customer;
```

Running this query gives the results shown in Figure 9.7.

Customer
MAGIC MOTORS
SNAZZY ROADSTERS
BIRMINGHAM EXECUTIVE PRESTIGE VEHICLES
WUNDERKAR
CASSEROLES CHROMES
LE LUXE EN MOTION
EAT MY EXHAUST LTD
M. PIERRE DUBOIS
SONDRA HOROWITZ
WONDERLAND WHEELS
LONDON EXECUTIVE PRESTIGE VEHICLES
GLITTERING PRIZE CARS LTD
LA BAGNOLE DE LUXE
CONVERTIBLE DREAMS
ALEXEI TOLSTOI
SUPERSPORT S.A.R.L.
THEO KOWALSKI

Figure 9.7: Converting the text in a field to uppercase using the UPPER() function

How it Works

Applying the UPPER() function to the CustomerName field ensures that every customer name that is output by the query will appear in uppercase. The UPPER() function requires one field as its parameter.

Tricks and Traps

These are a few suggestions of things you might need to be aware of when using the UPPER() function:

- Using a function—any function—means that SQL will not deduce the column name (even if it seems obvious). So, you will have to add an alias if you want the query output not to say "UPPER(FieldName)" for any columns you are converting to uppercase.

- This function will have no effect on any non-alphabetic characters in a field. So, numbers and punctuation will not change.

- This function is purely "decorative" and has no effect whatsoever on the underlying data. If the customer name is stored in lowercase in the database, it will stay that way.

- You can apply the UPPER() function to multiple fields at once if you need to do so. So, you could write SQL like this:

```
SELECT      UPPER(CONCAT(CustomerID, ' ', InvoiceNumber))
FROM        sales
```

- There is also an UCASE() function that is a synonym for UPPER(). As they both do exactly the same thing you can use either.

8. Converting Text to Lowercase

Just as you can convert text (or *strings*, to give them their technical definition) to uppercase, you can convert them to lowercase. Take a look at the following code:

```
SELECT      LOWER(ModelName) AS Model
FROM        model;
```

Executing this query gives the output shown in Figure 9.8.

Model
davtona
testarossa
355
308
dino
mondial
f40
f50
360
enzo
911
924
944
959

Figure 9.8: Converting strings to lowercase using the LOWER() function

How it Works

Applying the LOWER() function to the ModelName field ensures that every vehicle model that is output by the query will appear in lowercase. This will not affect the way that the original data is stored and will produce the same result whether the original data in the source table is in lowercase, uppercase, or a mixture of the two. As you can see, numbers are not affected by this function.

Tricks and Traps

I have one comment to note when using the LOWER() function:

- There is also an LCASE() function that is a synonym for LOWER(). Given that they both do exactly the same thing you can use either.

9. Extracting the First Few Characters from a Field

Sometimes text can be just too long. At least this is what the marketing director thinks, as she wants to show the make names as acronyms using the first three letters of each make in a catalog of products. Fortunately, SQL lets you choose to output only a few characters of longer text—as you can see in the next code excerpt:

```
SELECT     CONCAT(ModelName, ' (', LEFT(MakeName, 3), ')')

           AS MakeAndModel

FROM       make

JOIN       model USING(MakeID);
```

Running this query gives the results in Figure 9.9.

MakeAndModel
Davtona (Fer)
Testarossa (Fer)
355 (Fer)
308 (Fer)
Dino (Fer)
Mondial (Fer)
F40 (Fer)
F50 (Fer)
360 (Fer)
Enzo (Fer)
911 (Por)
924 (Por)
944 (Por)
959 (Por)
928 (Por)
Boxster (Por)

Figure 9.9: Using the LEFT() function to extract a specific number of characters from the left of a string

How it Works

Not only does this SELECT clause concatenate strings from two fields (ModelName and Make), it adds brackets to the result. The LEFT() function ensures that only the three leftmost characters from the Make field are used when creating the make and model composite name.

The LEFT() function works like this:

First:	Enter **LEFT** and a left parenthesis.
Second:	Enter the field name containing the data you want to extract a few characters from, followed by a comma.
Third:	Enter the number of characters to extract from the field as the second parameter of the LEFT() function.
Finally:	Add a right parenthesis to end the LEFT() function.

Tricks and Traps

When using functions like this one, you need to be mindful of the following:

- Functions like LEFT() that require more than one parameter require that each parameter inside the parentheses is separated by a comma.

- The LEFT() function requires you first to specify the *field* you are extracting characters from and then the *number* of characters you want to display. It is important to respect the order of these two elements (field first and then number of characters) when you use the LEFT() function.

- Text functions are frequently used as part of a more complex formatting requirement. As you go through this chapter, remember that you can combine multiple text functions in many ways to get the output you are looking for.

- As is the case when using most functions, LEFT() really requires you to add an alias because it will not deduce the column name in the output header row.

10. Displaying the Three Characters at the Right of Text

On some occasions you may have to isolate a series of characters from the right of a field. In Prestige Cars' system, for instance, the finance director wants you to select only the three characters at the right of the invoice number as these indicate the sequential number for the invoice. The SQL to do this is as follows:

```
SELECT     RIGHT(InvoiceNumber, 3) AS InvoiceSequenceNumber

FROM       sales

ORDER BY   InvoiceSequenceNumber;
```

Running this query returns results similar to Figure 9.10.

InvoiceSequenceNumber
001
002
003
004
005
006
007
008
009
010
011
012
013
014
015

Figure 9.10: Extracting characters from the right of a string using RIGHT()

How it Works

The RIGHT() function ensures that only a specified number of characters from the right of the InvoiceNumber field are displayed. Any characters to the left of these characters (however many there may be) are discarded. The RIGHT() function is pretty much like the LEFT() function—only it operates at the other end of the text in a field. You specify the field that you are using as the base data and then give the number of characters to extract from the right of the field.

One other thing that you did here is to sort the data on the output from the RIGHT() function. There are two ways of doing this.

Either: Specify the same function—RIGHT(InvoiceNumber, 3)—that you used in the SELECT statement in the ORDER BY statement.

Or: Use the alias from the SELECT clause in the ORDER BY clause as we did here.

Tricks and Traps

The trick to using functions like RIGHT()—or LEFT() for that matter—largely concern sorting the data.

- Using the alias to sort data is often a lot simpler than rewriting the function that produced the output data.

- If you are sorting the data by a *subset* of the contents of a field, then you *must* either use the alias from the SELECT clause or copy the function in the ORDER BY clause. If you use the field name, you will probably not get the output you are expecting.

11. Displaying a Given Number of Characters at a Specific Place in Text

In the Prestige Cars IT system, the fourth and fifth characters of the invoice number indicate the country where the vehicles were shipped. Knowing this, the sales director wants to extract only these characters from the invoice number field in order to analyze destination countries. Here is the SQL to do this:

```
SELECT      SUBSTRING(InvoiceNumber, 4, 2) AS DestinationCountry

FROM        sales;
```

If you execute this query, you will see the data that is shown in Figure 9.11.

DestinationCountry
GB
GB
GB
DE
FR
GB
GB
GB
FR
US
GB
GB
FR
GB

Figure 9.11: *Extracting a fixed number of characters from inside a field using SUBSTRING()*

How it Works

If you are always extracting a fixed number of characters from the same starting point in the text of a field, then SUBSTRING() is the function to use. However, this function takes three parameters (or needs three pieces of information) to work correctly.

First: Indicate the field you are working on.

Second: Give the number of characters in from the left where you want to start extracting text.

Finally: Provide the number of characters to extract commencing at the starting point defined in the preceding parameter.

As with all functions, each parameter is separated from the others by a comma.

As this function can seem unwieldy at first glance, Figure 9.12 explains it more visually.

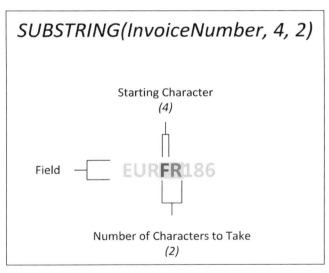

Figure 9.12: *The anatomy of a SUBSTRING() function*

Tricks and Traps

There are a couple of important points to retain here.

- It is vital to respect the order that you enter the parameters (starting point and number of characters) when using the SUBSTRING function, or you are likely to get only gibberish returned.

- Only a few functions require more than one or two parameters to be supplied, so SUBSTRING is fortunately more an exception than a rule.

- There are two synonyms for SUBSTRING() that you can use instead, if you prefer. They are SUBSTR() and MID(). You can use whichever you want, as all three produce identical results.

12. Filtering Records Based on Part of a Field

In the Prestige Cars database, the invoice number field always begins with three characters that indicate the currency of payment (even if all the invoices are in pounds sterling). This allows you to produce a list of sales in a specified currency—which is great as the sales director has requested a list of sales where the invoice was paid in Euros. The SQL that can do this is mercifully simple.

```
SELECT      InvoiceNumber, TotalSalePrice

FROM        sales

WHERE       LEFT(InvoiceNumber, 3) = 'EUR';
```

Executing this query gives the results in Figure 9.13.

InvoiceNumber	TotalSalePrice
EURDE004	11500.00
EURFR005	19900.00
EURFR009	19600.00
EURFR013	8950.00
EURFR015	22950.00
EURFR018	75500.00
EURFR031	2550.00
EURDE036	71890.00
EURFR037	39500.00
EURDE043	99500.00
EURFR047	49580.00
EURFR048	5500.00
EURFR051	174650.00
EURES058	79500.00

Figure 9.13: Using a string function in a WHERE clause

How it Works

This approach allows you to filter the InvoiceNumber field and output only those records where the three leftmost characters are EUR.

Here you are using a string function in the WHERE clause of a SQL query. This function is applied just as it would be in a SELECT clause. In this particular case, the LEFT() function is used. The first parameter is the field from which you want to extract part of the data (the InvoiceNumber field). The second parameter is the number of characters to extract (three in this case). The value that is returned from the function is then used to filter the data.

Tricks and Traps

Note the following:

- You can use a function in a WHERE clause without using it in the SELECT clause.

- You can use the "full" field that you are filtering on in the SELECT clause without affecting the WHERE clause in any way.

- You might want to add the function that you are using in the WHERE clause to the SELECT clause initially (with or without the filter) so that you can see whether the function is giving the result you expect.

13. Filtering Data Using Specific Characters at a Given Position Inside a Field

The sales director now wants to see all the cars shipped to France but made in Italy. Fortunately, the invoice number definition used by Prestige Cars guarantees that the fourth and fifth characters of the invoice number contain the two-character code of the country where the car was shipped. So, you can use this information to extract a list of vehicles delivered to one country—and use another field to restrict the country of manufacture. The SQL to do this is as follows:

```
SELECT    SA.InvoiceNumber, SA.TotalSalePrice

FROM      make AS MK JOIN model AS MD

          ON MK.MakeID = MD.MakeID

          JOIN stock AS ST ON ST.ModelID = MD.ModelID

          JOIN salesdetails SD ON ST.StockCode = SD.StockID

          JOIN sales AS SA ON SA.SalesID = SD.SalesID

WHERE     SUBSTRING(SA.InvoiceNumber, 4, 2)  = 'FR'

          AND MK.MakeCountry = 'ITA';
```

Running this query gives the results that you can see in Figure 9.14.

InvoiceNumber	TotalSalePrice
EURFR186	155000.00
EURFR254	269500.00
EURFR235	310000.00
EURFR151	255950.00
EURFR122	395000.00
EURFR121	365000.00
EURFR107	169500.00
EURFR189	235000.00
EURFR031	2550.00
EURFR194	62700.00
EURFR241	9950.00

Figure 9.14: Using SUBSTRING() and a standard comparison operator in a WHERE clause

How it Works

The point of this example is to make it clear that a WHERE clause can contain multiple criteria—both straight comparisons and more complex filters using functions. Here you are using a WHERE clause to filter the InvoiceNumber field where the fourth and fifth characters are FR (to isolate cars delivered to France), as well as using a different field (country of make) to specify that the car was built in Italy.

The WHERE clause of this query is where the action takes place. Its anatomy is as follows:

First: The SUBSTRING() function is applied. The first parameter (the field name) is InvoiceNumber in this example. The second parameter—the number of characters from the left where the extraction will begin—is set to four. Then the number of characters to extract at this point in the text is set to two. The filter is then defined as being the two characters FR (for France).

Second: An AND operator is added to the WHERE clause to add a second filter element to the query.

Finally: The MakeCountry field is filtered on ITA (for Italy). Of course, this means knowing that the MakeCountry field uses ISO three-character acronyms to represent countries—but this is part and parcel of the need to know your data before you can use it.

Tricks and Traps

I suggest that you note the following:

* Here, again, you can use SUBSTR() or MID() instead of SUBSTRING() if you prefer.

14. Joining on Part of a Field

The sales director wants a "quick list" (in her words) of all vehicles sold and the destination country. She has specified that she wants to see the complete country name in the output. Now that you know how to isolate part of a field, it only takes you a few minutes to satisfy her request. Th following SQL snippet shows you how this can be done:

```
SELECT      SA.CustomerID, SA.TotalSalePrice, CO.CountryName

FROM        sales AS SA

JOIN        country CO

            ON CO.CountryISO2 = SUBSTRING(SA.InvoiceNumber, 4, 2)

ORDER BY    CO.CountryName, SA.CustomerID;
```

Running this query gives the results that you can see in Figure 9.15.

	CustomerID	TotalSalePrice	CountryName
▶	0034	12500.00	Belgium
	0034	86500.00	Belgium
	0034	125000.00	Belgium
	0049	45950.00	Belgium
	0049	950.00	Belgium
	0049	34000.00	Belgium
	0067	6950.00	Belgium
	0005	59000.00	France
	0005	55600.00	France
	0005	66500.00	France
	0005	19900.00	France
	0008	2550.00	France
	0008	120000.00	France
	0008	56500.00	France

Figure 9.15: Using SUBSTRING() to join tables on part of a field

How it Works

The ability to extract part of a field is not only useful when displaying or filtering data. You can use this technique when joining tables, too. In this particular example the challenge is to display the full country name (from the Country table) when there is no field in the Sales table that maps "out of the box" to a field in the Country table.

However, the Country table does have a two character field named CountryISO2 that displays the two character ISO country code—the same code that appears inside the InvoiceNumber field of the Sales table. So, in this example, the SUBSTRING() function is used in the ON clause to isolate the two character code from the InvoiceNumber field so that it can map to the CountryISO2 field from the Country table.

Otherwise this is a fairly simple query. You select the fields that you want to output from the two source tables (and specifically the CountryName field) and sort the output.

Conclusion

This chapter gave you an overview of some of the core techniques you can apply to your code to adjust the presentation of text-based data. You saw how to extract part of a column of text and convert text from uppercase to lowercase, and vice versa. You also learned how to mix text and numbers in a single column and add extra fixed text to the output.

These techniques enable you to use and shape the data so that you can go beyond merely listing columns of data. Armed with the knowledge you have acquired in this chapter, not only can you query MySQL data but you can present it in a more meaningful and comprehensible way to your users.

Core Knowledge Learned in This Chapter

These are the keywords and concepts you learned in this chapter:

Concept	Description
UPPER()	This function converts any text into uppercase characters. Numbers and symbols are not affected by this function.
LOWER()	This function converts any text into lowercase characters. Numbers and symbols are not affected by this function.
CONCAT()	This function amalgamates custom text and the contents of one or more fields.

Concept	Description
WS_CONCAT()	This function amalgamates the contents of several fields all separated by the same character
LEFT()	This function extracts a defined number of characters from the left of a string.
MID()	This function extracts a defined number of characters from a string, beginning at a specified number of characters from the left of the string.
RIGHT()	This function extracts a defined number of characters from the right of a string.
SUBSTR()	This function extracts a defined number of characters from a string, beginning at a specified number of characters from the left of the string.
SUBSTRING()	This function extracts a defined number of characters from a string, beginning at a specified number of characters from the left of the string.
UCASE()	This function converts any text into uppercase characters. Numbers and symbols are not affected by this function.
LCASE()	This function converts any text into lowercase characters. Numbers and symbols are not affected by this function.
Concatenation	This technique joins the output from two or more columns into a single output field.

CHAPTER 10

Formatting Numbers and Dates

SQL will always attempt to present numbers at the most detailed level possible. This could mean displaying more decimals than you actually need. Equally it may display dates in a way that you (or the users you deliver the output to) find a little clunky. So, you need to be able to format both numbers and dates in ways that make the data more readable and intuitively comprehensible. This chapter covers a range of techniques that will help you achieve these objectives.

Presenting Numbers and Dates

While learning to query data so that you always return the exact output you need is a science, presenting the results in a way that both you and your users understand is an art. You may want to remove the decimals from the output or apply a specific number format, for instance. Alternatively, you could need to display a date in a certain way—much as you would in Excel.

This chapter introduces the basic formatting techniques you should find essential when you are enhancing the presentation of your query results. So, while these techniques do not alter the accuracy of the output, they can make it considerably easier to understand.

Note: Formatting dates and numbers converts them into text. This means SQL may no longer be able to carry out any calculations on a formatted date. It will almost certainly not be able to calculate a formatted number. So, you should always format numbers and dates once you are sure that this is the final result of a query.

1. Removing the Decimals from the Output

In some reports you just don't need decimals. So, SQL lets you remove them from output data really easily. Just take a look at the following snippet, which applies this technique to the Sale Price field:

```
SELECT      TotalSalePrice, FLOOR(TotalSalePrice) AS SalePriceRoundedDown

FROM        sales

ORDER BY    SalesID;
```

Applying this query gives the results in Figure 10.1. I have kept the original "untouched" data as well as the output from the FLOOR() function so that you can see the difference when the function is applied.

Figure 10.1: Truncating decimals from a number using the FLOOR() function

How it Works

The FLOOR() function can be used to round down the decimals from a column of figures. No rounding is applied—the numbers are simply stripped of the decimal part. If the number does not contain any decimals, then it simply stays the same.

Tricks and Traps

You must remember one main factor when applying the FLOOR() function.

* The FLOOR() function can be applied only to numeric data types.

2. Rounding a Field Up to the Nearest Whole Number

Just as you can round numbers down, you can also round them up in SQL. The following code snippet shows you how to do this to the TotalSalePrice field:

```
SELECT      TotalSalePrice, CEILING(TotalSalePrice) AS SalePriceRoundedUp

FROM        sales

ORDER BY    SalesID;
```

Running this query gives the results in Figure 10.2.

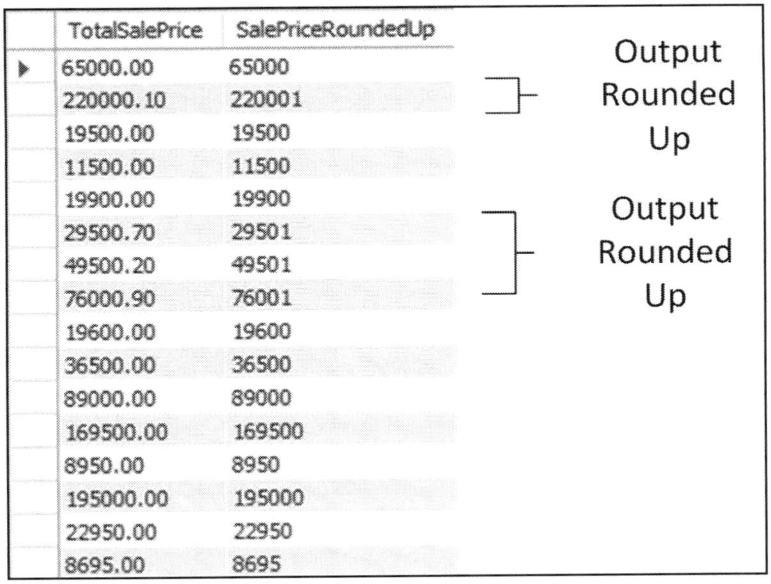

TotalSalePrice	SalePriceRoundedUp
65000.00	65000
220000.10	220001
19500.00	19500
11500.00	11500
19900.00	19900
29500.70	29501
49500.20	49501
76000.90	76001
19600.00	19600
36500.00	36500
89000.00	89000
169500.00	169500
8950.00	8950
195000.00	195000
22950.00	22950
8695.00	8695

Output Rounded Up

Output Rounded Up

Figure 10.2: Rounding up a decimal number to the next highest whole number using the CEILING() function

How it Works

The CEILING() function removes the decimals from the figures that you are outputting but rounds the number up to the next highest whole number (or integer if you prefer the term). I have included the original data in the output so that you can compare the two versions of the numbers. In the real world, you would probably display only one version of the data in the output.

Tricks and Traps

As was the case with the FLOOR() function, the following is true when using the CEILING() function:

- The CEILING() function can be applied only to numeric data types.

3. Rounding a Value to the Nearest Whole Number

If you want to round decimals up or down to the nearest whole number, MySQL has the ROUND() function to do this, as the following SQL snippet makes clear:

```
SELECT      TotalSalePrice, ROUND(TotalSalePrice, 0) AS SalePriceRounded
FROM        sales
ORDER BY    SalesID;
```

Running this query shows you both the original and rounded values, as you can see in Figure 10.3.

TotalSalePrice	SalePriceRounded	
65000.00	65000	Output Rounded
220000.10	220000	
19500.00	19500	
11500.00	11500	
19900.00	19900	
29500.70	29501	Output Rounded
49500.20	49500	
76000.90	76001	
19600.00	19600	
36500.00	36500	
89000.00	89000	
169500.00	169500	
8950.00	8950	
195000.00	195000	
22950.00	22950	
8695.00	8695	

Figure 10.3: Applying the Round function to numeric output

How it Works

When used in this way, the ROUND() function finds the nearest whole number—be it higher or lower than the numeric value that you want to output. As you can see from Figure 10.12 (where you can compare the sale price to the rounded sale price), this can mean rounding down, just like it can mean rounding up.

The ROUND() function needs you to add a parameter that indicates how many decimal places the number is rounded to. Using a 0 as the second parameter means no decimals—effectively removing the decimals from the field that is used as the first parameter.

Tricks and Traps

I have only couple of comments to make here.

- Exporting a rounded output to a spreadsheet (or any other application) and then calculating the total for the column can produce rounding errors (compared to calculating the total for a column where no rounding has been applied), as the decimals have been limited or removed definitively.

- You can treat the second parameter in the ROUND() function as optional. That is, if you simply apply a ROUND() function to a field it will round to the nearest integer as if you had added a zero as the second parameter.

- To round to a specific number of decimals you use a positive number as the second parameter of the ROUND() function.

4. Rounding a Value Up or Down to the Nearest Thousand

When you are dealing with really large figures, you may want to round up or down to hundreds or even tens of thousands. SQL can do this easily, as the following code snippet shows:

```
SELECT     TotalSalePrice, ROUND(TotalSalePrice, -3)

           AS SalePriceRoundedToThousand

FROM       sales;
```

Executing this query gives you the original data and the rounded output, as you can see in Figure 10.4.

TotalSalePrice	SalePriceRoundedToThousand
65000.00	65000
220000.10	220000
19500.00	20000
11500.00	12000
19900.00	20000
29500.00	30000
49500.20	50000
76000.90	76000
19600.00	20000
36500.00	37000
89000.00	89000
169500.00	170000
8950.00	9000
195000.00	195000
22950.00	23000
8695.00	9000

Figure 10.4: *Rounding to the nearest thousand*

How it Works

Used like this, the ROUND() function takes two compulsory parameters.

First: The numeric field whose output you want to modify.

Second: The type of rounding to be applied. This can be a positive or negative number. A positive number affects the number of decimals, and a negative number affects the integer values (the whole number).

In this example, the SalesDate field is rounded to the nearest thousand. This happens because the second parameter used in the ROUND() function is *negative*. Consequently, the rounding is applied to the nearest thousands in this particular case. You can even set this to be tens, hundreds, thousands, millions or billions if you want.

The negative number you use as the second parameter indicates how the number is rounded. Table 10-1 shows how you apply the number shown in the left column as the second parameter of the ROUND() function to obtain the result described in the right column.

Table 10-1: Rounding Up Numbers

Parameter	Effect
-1	Rounds to the nearest 10
-2	Rounds to the nearest 100
-3	Rounds to the nearest 1,000
-4	Rounds to the nearest 10,000
-5	Rounds to the nearest 100,000

You can continue and round to millions or billions if you really want, but hopefully you get the idea—the parameter represents the number of zeros that you will get in the rounded result. If you are looking only at rounding to a decimal value, then you simply make the second parameter of the ROUND() function a positive number.

Tricks and Traps

There is only one point to be aware of when using the ROUND() function.

- If you leave out the second parameter (and the comma that precedes it) then the ROUND() function simply removes the decimals from the field.

5. Displaying a Value in a Specific Numeric Format

The sales director wants you to make some of the reports that you send directly from MySQL to appear looking slightly easier to read (as she puts it). So she wants you to present data with a thousands separator and two decimals. Fortunately MySQL makes this kind of presentation really easy as the following code snippet shows:

```
SELECT     FORMAT(cost, 2) AS UKSalePrice

FROM       stock

ORDER BY   stockcode;
```

Executing this query gives you the original data and the formatted output, as you can see in Figure 10.5.

UKSalePrice
20.000.00
15.600.00
6.040.00
17.200.00
66.072.00
146.000.00
47.600.00
4.400.00
34.360.00
130.000.00
40.960.00
2.860.00
7.400.00
124.000.00
14.000.00
176.400.00

Figure 10.5: Formatting numbers for readability

How it Works

This query introduces the FORMAT() function. This function requires two parameters. They are:

First: The numeric field to format.

Second: The number of decimals to display.

In this specific case the Cost field from the Stock table is stored as a number without any thousands separator or specific number of decimals (there could be between 0 and 4 decimals for this field). So, in order to make the output more palatable to the eye, the FORMAT() function is used. This function does two things:

First: It adds a thousands separator every three figures to the left of the decimal point.

Second: It limits the number of decimals to display to the figure specified as the second parameter of the FORMAT() function.

Tricks and Traps

I have only a couple of comments to make here.

*   As is the case with virtually all columns that involve using a function, it is generally a good idea to add a column alias.

- You can also format the output from a calculation using the FORMAT() function.

6. Displaying a Value in a Specific Currency

The sales director is in a hurry and says that she will not have the time to format the data you send her. As a consequence, she wants you to output a list of vehicle sales that can be immediately presented to the CEO. She wants the output to include thousands separators, two decimals and a British pound symbol.

You can do this, too, as the following short SQL example shows:

```
SELECT      MakeName, ModelName

            ,CONCAT("£ ", FORMAT(SalePrice, 2)) AS SterlingSalePrice

FROM        salesbycountry

ORDER BY    MakeName, ModelName, SterlingSalePrice DESC;
```

Running this query gives the results in Figure 10.6, where the result appears in pounds sterling.

MakeName	ModelName	SterlingSalePrice
Alfa Romeo	1750	£ 9.950.00
Alfa Romeo	1750	£ 3.575.00
Alfa Romeo	Giulia	£ 8.695.00
Alfa Romeo	Giulia	£ 6.950.00
Alfa Romeo	Giulia	£ 6.000.00
Alfa Romeo	Giulia	£ 25.000.00
Alfa Romeo	Giulia	£ 2.550.00
Alfa Romeo	Giulia	£ 17.500.00
Alfa Romeo	Giulia	£ 12.500.00
Alfa Romeo	Giulia	£ 10.500.00
Alfa Romeo	Giulietta	£ 6.500.00
Alfa Romeo	Giulietta	£ 5.690.00
Alfa Romeo	Giulietta	£ 21.500.00
Alfa Romeo	Giulietta	£ 18.500.00
Alfa Romeo	Giulietta	£ 17.950.00
Alfa Romeo	Giulietta	£ 11.550.00
Alfa Romeo	Giulietta	£ 10.500.00
Alfa Romeo	Spider	£ 5.950.00
Alfa Romeo	Spider	£ 5.650.00
Alfa Romeo	Spider	£ 12.500.00

Figure 10.6: Formatting numbers as British pounds

How it Works

It is worth noting that if you are using SQL output directly—that is, not as a source for another program like Excel for instance—then you may want to produce formatted output that is easier for your public to understand. However, databases are not naturally presentation tools. Consequently a little work can be necessary to produce polished output directly from a SQL query.

Formatting numbers generally implies a two-pronged approach.

First: Use the FORMAT() function to display the number with the required number of decimals and the thousands separator.

Second: Use the CONCAT() function to add a currency unit before or after the formatted figure.

In practice this means nesting the FORMAT() function inside the CONCAT() function. You can see this illustrated in Figure 10.7.

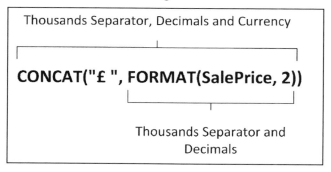

Figure 10.7: *Combining the CONCAT() and FORMAT() functions to format numbers*

Tricks and Traps

It is important to remember that SQL is at its heart a query language and not a presentation tool. So, you need to take the following into consideration when delivering formatted output:

- You need to be careful if you are formatting numbers in SQL. This is because using the FORMAT() function will convert the number to a string. This can make it difficult (if not impossible) to use the formatted number in a further calculation.

- It is probably obvious, but I prefer to mention anyway that there is no exchange rate conversion taking place here. All that happens is that the figures are formatted in pounds—just as you would in Excel, for instance.

- You can add any text before or after the formatted numbers. So you can use ISO currency specifications or units of distance or weight if you need to.

7. Specifying the National Number Format to Use

If the built-in number formats that MySQL provides "out of the box" do not let you display a column as you would like, then you can alter number formats to display figures in the way that is traditional for certain countries. The following SQL snippet gives you an example of how you can do this to give the CEO a list of "Excel-style" sales figures with decimals and thousands separators in the German style—that is with a period as the thousands separator and a comma as the decimal:

```
SELECT      FORMAT(TotalSalePrice, 2, 'de_DE') AS GermanSalePrice

FROM        sales

ORDER BY    TotalSalePrice DESC;
```

Running this piece of SQL will produce the output in Figure 10.8.

SterlingSalePrice
395.000,00
368.000,00
365.000,00
355.000,00
355.000,00
345.000,00
335.000,00
310.000,00
305.000,00
295.000,00
295.000,00
269.500,00
267.950,00
255.950,00

Figure 10.8: Applying a custom number format

How it Works

In this example, the "raw" output from the SalePrice field is made more presentable using the FORMAT() function. This function takes *three* parameters.

First: The field to format.

Second: The number of decimals to display.

Finally: The code that specifies the locale. This is a code that must be enclosed in single quotes. As there are several dozen of these "locale" codes I suggest that you search on-line for the one that interests you.

What is interesting here is that you have seen that the FORMAT() function can take either two or three parameters. The first two are compulsory. The third—that specifies the formatting style—is optional.

Tricks and Traps

I have two major points to make here.

- Formatting codes *must* be applied to date fields. They will have no effect on text fields.

- The localization codes are case-sensitive. So you have to use the *exact capitalization* shown in the MySQL documentation for them to work correctly.

8. Outputting a Date in a Specific Date Format

Suppose you need to send a list of data to the CEO that contains a date, and you need that date to be in the specific format that she has requested (first the day, then the abbreviation for the month, and finally the year in four figures in this occurrence). The following SQL will do that for you:

```
SELECT      InvoiceNumber

            ,DATE_FORMAT(SaleDate, '%c %b %Y') AS SaleDate
FROM        sales
```

Running this query gives the results shown in Figure 10.9.

InvoiceNumber	SaleDate
GBPGB001	1 Jan 2015
GBPGB002	1 Jan 2015
GBPGB003	2 Feb 2015
EURDE004	2 Feb 2015
EURFR005	1 Jan 2015
GBPGB006	3 Mar 2015
GBPGB007	3 Mar 2015
GBPGB008	3 Mar 2015
EURFR009	4 Apr 2015
USDUS010	4 Apr 2015
GBPGB011	4 Apr 2015
GBPGB012	5 May 2015
EURFR013	5 May 2015
GBPGB014	5 May 2015

Figure 10.9: Outputting a date in a specific format using the DATE_FORMAT() function

How it Works

If you want to display a date in a wide range of possible formats you can use the DATE_FORMAT() function to display dates in the precise format you require.

The DATE_FORMAT() function takes a date, time or datetime field and forces the result to be output in one of the multitude of date and time formats that MySQL can deliver.

The DATE_FORMAT() function takes two input parameters.

First: The field you want to convert. This must be a date or datetime field—or a field that MySQL can convert to a datetime data type. The SaleDate field suits the purpose here.

Second: The internal code that indicates the output format. This *must* be enclosed in quotes.

As with all functions, you just need to make sure you enter the parameters (or elements if you prefer) in the correct order, from left to right.

The code format that you apply will always consist of one or more placeholder codes and possibly separator characters enclosed in single quotes. Each code starts with a percentage sign (%) followed by a single letter.

Table 10-2 lists the possible date format codes that you can use and combine to present dates.

Table 10-2: Date Formats

Format Code	Description	Example
%e	Number of day in month	1
%d	Number of day in month with a leading zero, if a single figure	01
%D	Number of day in month expressed as an ordinal number	1st
%j	Day of year	365
%c	Numeric month	1
%m	Numeric month with a leading zero, if a single figure	01
%M	Full name of month	January
%b	Abbreviated name of month	Jan
%y	Year as two digits	18
%Y	Year as four digits	2018
%a	Abbreviated day of week name	Mon
%W	Full day of week name	Monday
%w	Number of day of week	0 (Sunday) … 6 (Saturday)
%U	Week (00..53), where Sunday is the first day of the week	24
%u	Week (00..53), where Monday is the first day of the week	25
%V	Week (1..53), where Sunday is the first day of the week	24
%v	Week (1..53), where Monday is the first day of the week	25

Don't worry about ever trying to learn these codes. In all probability you will only ever need a few of them, and you will almost certainly end up by remembering the ones you use most often. If you need a complete list of all the possible codes, then they are available on the MySQL website.

As creating date format codes can appear to be a little daunting at first sight, Table 10-3 contains a set of sample date formats to give you a few ideas as to how to create your own date formats.

Table 10-3: Sample Date Formats

Format Code	Example
DATE_FORMAT(SaleDate, '%d %b %Y')	25 Jul 2018
DATE_FORMAT(SaleDate, '%W, %D of %M %Y')	Saturday, 25th of July 2015
DATE_FORMAT(SaleDate, '%Y%m%d')	20180725
DATE_FORMAT(SaleDate, '%d/%m/%y')	25/07/18

Tricks and Traps

There are a few things to note when formatting dates.

* This approach will work only if the field is—or can be converted to—a date. If this is not the case SQL will return a NULL.

* If you use the DATE_FORMAT() function, you are, in effect, converting the date to text. Consequently, you may no longer be able to carry out date calculations once the field has been formatted.

* It is vital that you respect the capitalization of the format codes when you write your own output formats for dates. For instance, using a lowercase *y* for the year displays two figures whereas an uppercase Y displays four figures.

* On most systems you can use either single or double quotes to enclose the format codes that you apply. In case of doubt it is best to use single quotes.

* The format codes in their entirety must be placed inside single quotes. You should not enclose each individual element inside separate quotes.

* You can add any separators you want between the format codes—hyphens, slashes, spaces etc—or even additional text.

9. Outputting a Date in the ISO Date Format

Suppose that you need to send a list of data to the CEO that contains a date, and you need that date to be in the specific format that she has requested (year, month and day in figures in this occurrence). The following SQL will do that for you, without having to juggle with date format codes:

```
SELECT      InvoiceNumber

            ,DATE_FORMAT(SaleDate, GET_FORMAT(DATE, 'ISO'))

                AS SaleDate

FROM        Sales;
```

Running this query gives the results that you can see in Figure 10.10.

InvoiceNumber	SaleDate
GBPGB001	2015-01-02
GBPGB002	2015-01-25
GBPGB003	2015-02-03
EURDE004	2015-02-16
EURFR005	2015-01-02
GBPGB006	2015-03-14
GBPGB007	2015-03-24
GBPGB008	2015-03-30
EURFR009	2015-04-06
USDUS010	2015-04-04
GBPGB011	2015-04-30
GBPGB012	2015-05-10
EURFR013	2015-05-20
GBPGB014	2015-05-28
EURFR015	2015-06-04
GBPGB016	2015-07-12
GBPGB017	2015-07-15
EURFR018	2015-07-25

Figure 10.10: Outputting a date using the DATE_FORMAT() and GET_FORMAT() functions

How it Works

As assembling date formats from codes can get a little fastidious, MySQL can help you to output dates in a few set ways both quickly and easily. You do this by specifying that the format codes used in a DATE_FORMAT() function are, themselves, *created automatically* by the GET_FORMAT() function.

First:	Enter the **DATE_FORMAT** keyword and a left parenthesis.
Second:	Add the date or datetime field whose output you want to present in a preset way followed by a comma.
Third:	Enter the GET_FORMAT keyword and a left parenthesis.
Fourth:	Enter the DATE keyword as the first parameter of the GET_FORMAT() function followed by a comma.

Fifth: Add, in quotes, the definition of the predefined date format that you want to apply. In this example it is ISO.

Finally: Close the two functions with two right parentheses.

The GET_FORMAT() function takes two parameters.

First: The word DATE (if you want to deliver only the date element) or DATETIME (if you want to output both date and time elements).

Second: A predefined data format specification code (ISO in this example).

In effect, the GET_FORMAT() function becomes the second parameter of the DATE_FORMAT() function. This means that instead of entering a set of codes, you simply specify which of the predefined date or datetime formats you want to apply in the query output.

A list of some of the possible date formats available when applying the GET_FORMAT() function is given in Table 10-4.

Table 10-4: Date Formats

Format Code	Description	Example
'USA'	*US date format with four digit year*	*10.31.2012*
'EUR'	*European date format with four digit year*	*25.07.1995*
'INTERNAL'	*Internal date format*	*20120725*
'ISO'	*ISO date format*	*2015-07-25*

If you want MySQL to display the *time* as well as the date then you need to alter the first parameter of the GET_FORMAT() function to DATETIME—as you can see in the following code snippet:

```
GET_FORMAT(DATETIME, "INTERNAL")
```

MySQL also comes equipped with predefined formats for dates and times. A list of some of the possible datetime formats is given in Table 10-5.

Table 10-5: Date and Time Formats

Format Code	Description	Example
'USA'	*US date and time format*	*10.31.2012 08.10.59*
'EUR'	*European date and time format*	*25.07.1995 08.10.59*

Format Code	Description	Example
'INTERNAL'	*Internal date and time format*	*20120725081059*
'ISO'	*ISO date and time format*	*2015-07-25 08:10:59*

As I mentioned earlier, don't worry about ever trying to learn these codes. In all probability you will only ever need a couple of them, and you will almost certainly end up by remembering the ones you use most often.

Tricks and Traps

There are a few things to note here:

- The format code that you add as the second parameter to the GET_FORMAT() function must be in quotes. However, these can be single or (on most systems) double quotes.

- You can enter the format code in uppercase or lowercase characters (or even a mixture of the two if you prefer).

- You can enter DATE or DATETIME as the first parameter of the GET_FORMAT() function in uppercase or lowercase characters.

10. Presenting the Time in a Specific Format

You can decide how to present time elements just as you can format dates in MySQL. Indeed, you do this using the same function (but with different formatting codes) that you learned in the previous section, as the following SQL snippet shows.

```
SELECT      InvoiceNumber

            ,DATE_FORMAT(SaleDate, '%r') AS SaleTime

FROM        Sales;
```

Running this query gives the results shown in Figure 10.11.

InvoiceNumber	SaleTime
GBPGB001	08:00:00 AM
GBPGB002	12:00:00 AM
GBPGB003	10:00:00 AM
EURDE004	08:00:00 AM
EURFR005	10:33:00 AM
GBPGB006	12:00:00 AM
GBPGB007	12:00:00 AM
GBPGB008	12:00:00 AM
EURFR009	12:00:00 AM
USDUS010	12:00:00 AM
GBPGB011	12:00:00 AM
GBPGB012	12:00:00 AM
EURFR013	12:00:00 AM
GBPGB014	12:00:00 AM

Figure 10.11: *Outputting a date in a specific format using the DATE_FORMAT() function*

You apply a time format to a datetime or time field exactly as you applied it to a date field in the previous section:

First: Enter **DATE_FORMAT** and a left parenthesis

Second: Enter the field you want to convert and a comma

Finally: Enter the internal code that indicates the time format that you want to apply (in quotes) and a right parenthesis

Table 10-6 lists the possible time format codes that you can use to present dates and times.

Table 10-6: *Time Formats*

Format Code	Description	Example
%k	*Hour*	*0…23*
%l	*Hour*	*1..12*
%i	*Minutes*	*00..59*
%S	*Seconds*	*00..59*
%p	*AM or PM*	*PM*
%f	*Microseconds*	*000000..999999*
%r	*Time*	*hh:mm:ss followed by AM or PM*

Tricks and Traps

The same comments apply to time formatting as applied to formatting dates.

- You can use either single or double quotes to enclose the format codes that you apply.

- The format codes in their entirety must be placed inside quotes—not each individual element.

- You can add any separators you want between the format codes—hyphens, slashes, spaces, colons, text etc.

- You can combine date and time formatting, of course. To display the date and time, you could combine formatting codes like this, for instance:

```
DATE_FORMAT(SaleDate, '%d %b %Y : %r')
```

Conclusion

This chapter showed you some of the core techniques you can use to alter the way that numbers and dates are output from a SQL query. You learned how to round numbers both up and down—as well as rounding by tens, hundreds, and even thousands. Then you saw how to apply thousand separators and apply locale-specific formatting. Finally, you saw how to present both dates and numbers in a variety of ways using both predefined and custom formats.

Core Knowledge Learned in This Chapter

The following are the keywords and concepts you learned in this chapter:

Concept	Description
CAST()	This function converts one data type to another data type, where possible.
CONVERT()	This function converts one data type to another data type, where possible, and can format numbers and dates in predefined ways.
FLOOR()	This function rounds numbers down to the nearest integer.
CEILING()	This function rounds numbers up to the nearest integer.

Concept	Description
ROUND()	This function rounds numbers to integers—and factors of 10.
DATE_ FORMAT()	This function alters the way a date (and time, if available) is presented in the output.
GET_FORMAT()	This function is used with the DATE_FORMAT() function to specify a predefined date or date and time format.
FORMAT()	This function applies an output format to numbers and dates either from a predefined list or according to a user-defined format.

CHAPTER 11
Using Basic Logic to Enhance Analysis

Accurate data selection is a good first step in effective analysis. However, there may be times when you are faced with so much data that it is difficult to detect the nuggets of truly valuable information hidden in all the columns and rows of facts and figures. To prevent you from missing key details, MySQL can highlight the records that stand out from the rest—and give you greater control over your data.

Applying SQL Logic

Applying logic in a SQL query generally involves testing data for the characteristics that interest you and either flagging any records that need to be investigated further or handling the output in specific ways depending on the result of a logical process. This can mean applying different scenarios depending on the values in a field or excluding data based on a logical test.

Logic tests are, essentially, limited only by your requirements and imagination. So, in this chapter, I will introduce you to some of the techniques you can apply to use SQL to do some of the heavy lifting when it comes to analyzing data.

1. Generating an Alert When a Value Is Too High

Keeping track of costs is an essential part of any business. Let's suppose that the finance director of Prestige Cars Ltd. wants a report that flags any car ever bought where the parts cost was greater than the cost of repairs. The following code does this by adding an extra column to the list of parts and repairs costs that draws your attention to any potential anomalies:

```
SELECT      Cost, RepairsCost, PartsCost

            ,IF(PartsCost > RepairsCost, 'Cost Alert!', NULL)

            AS CostAnalysis

FROM        Stock;
```

Running this query gives the results in Figure 11.1.

Cost	RepairsCost	PartsCost	CostAnalysis
20000.0000	1360.0000	750.0000	NULL
15600.0000	2000.0000	750.0000	NULL
6040.0000	500.0000	750.0000	Cost Alert!
17200.0000	500.0000	500.0000	NULL
66072.0000	1490.0000	457.0000	NULL
146000.0000	5500.0000	1500.0000	NULL
47600.0000	500.0000	500.0000	NULL
4400.0000	500.0000	750.0000	Cost Alert!
34360.0000	970.0000	750.0000	NULL
130000.0000	3950.0000	3150.0000	NULL
40960.0000	1360.0000	500.0000	NULL
2860.0000	500.0000	750.0000	Cost Alert!
7400.0000	500.0000	750.0000	Cost Alert!
124000.0000	3950.0000	3150.0000	NULL
14000.0000	1360.0000	225.0000	NULL
176400.0000	9250.0000	2200.0000	NULL
100000.0000	500.0000	1500.0000	Cost Alert!

Figure 11.1: Using conditional logic and the IF() function to test output

How it Works

This short piece of SQL introduces the IF() function. This function is another of the "three-parameter" functions in SQL, and it requires the following:

First: A test to be carried out. Normally this consists of comparing the data in a column with either a fixed value or the data in another column—or even in a calculation. In this example, the test examines whether the data in the PartsCost column is of a higher value than the data in the RepairsCost column for each record.

Second: A result that is displayed if the test proves *true* (in this example that means a parts cost greater than the repair cost). This can be text, a number, a calculation, or nothing at all. In this example, you are displaying the text "Cost Alert!" Because the result is a text in this case, it has to be in single quotes.

Finally: A result that appears if the test proves *false* (in this example, that means a parts cost less than or equal to the repair cost). This part of the function can also be text, a number, a calculation, or indeed nothing at all. In this example, you want to show nothing, so the NULL keyword is used because that means "nothing" in this context.

Figure 11.2 shows you how this works in a more graphic way.

Figure 11.2: *The anatomy of an IF() expression*

Tricks and Traps

IF() expressions can be a powerful addition to your SQL armory. However, when using them, you will always have to bear these key points in mind:

- If you wanted to show something other than a blank cell in the output (the word *OK*, for instance), you could use the IF() function in the following way instead:

```
IF(PartsCost > RepairsCost, 'Alert', 'OK')
```

- You can consider the "test" that is the first parameter of an IF() function as being a mini WHERE clause to some extent. This is because you apply the same sort of comparative logic in the test parameter as you would in a WHERE clause. Only in this case the result must return an outcome that can be interpreted by SQL as *true* or *false*.

- An IF() function is not limited to just displaying text. It can also carry out calculations in the second and third parts of the function.

- You can add virtually anything as the "true" or "false" output to an IF() function. It can be a text, a number, a field a NULL or even the result of another function.

- You may already have seen the IIF() function in Microsoft Access or even the IF() function in Excel. If this is the case, then you can breathe easily because the MySQL IF() function works in virtually the same way as the corresponding functions in these two other applications.

2. Shortening Text and Adding Ellipses to Indicate Truncation

The sales director wants some customer feedback. She knows that the sales database has comments from clients in it, but she does not need—or want—to display all the text. All she wants is to show only the first few characters and then use ellipses to indicate that the text has been shortened. This way she can always extract the full comment at a later date. Applying SQL logic to your output can do just this, as the following code snippet shows:

```
SELECT    Cost, RepairsCost, PartsCost
          ,IF(
              LENGTH(BuyerComments) < 25
              ,BuyerComments
              ,CONCAT(LEFT(BuyerComments, 20), ' ...')
          ) AS Comments
FROM      Stock
WHERE     BuyerComments IS NOT NULL;
```

Running this query gives the results in Figure 11.3.

Cost	RepairsCost	PartsCost	Comments
15600.0000	660.0000	0.0000	An absolute example ...
52000.0000	2175.0000	1500.0000	Superb Car! Wish I c ...
39600.0000	2500.0000	1500.0000	FAbulous motor!

Figure 11.3: Applying conditional logic to alter output using the IF() function

How it Works

Here an IF() function tests the contents of a column. However, instead of comparing one value with another, it calculates the number of characters in the column for each record, using the LENGTH() function. This function quite simply calculates the number of letters or numbers in a string. In this example, if there are less than 25 characters in the field, then it is output in full. If not, then only the first 20 characters are allowed through into the result, but with three dots (an ellipsis) appended to them. This way, you can be certain that you will never see more than 25 characters when displaying the buyer comments.

The point of this example is to make it clear that the output from an IF() function need not just be hard-coded text as you saw previously. An IF() function will let you use database fields as the output for both the true and false parameters.

3. Designing Complex Calculated Alerts

This time the sales director has left you astounded. She wants you to look at the profit on each car sold and flag any sale where the profit figure is less than 10 percent of the purchase cost—while at the same time the repair cost is at least twice the parts cost! However abstruse at first sight, this request illustrates the fact that you will frequently need to isolate specific cases from the rest of the data when analyzing datasets.

In practice, this often means that any tests that you apply to your data can be more complex than those that you have seen so far in this chapter. It is possible to use functions—like IF()—to carry out quite complex logical tests and to return a value depending on the outcome of those tests. The following SQL is an example of this:

```
SELECT     ST.Cost, ST.RepairsCost, ST.PartsCost

    ,IF(

        (SD.SalePrice -

        (ST.Cost + SD.LineItemDiscount

            + ST.PartsCost

            + IFNULL(ST.RepairsCost, 0)

            + ST.TransportInCost

        )
```

```
             )

             < (SD.SalePrice * 0.1)

             AND (ST.RepairsCost * 2) > ST.PartsCost

        ,'Warning!!'

        ,'OK'

        ) AS CostAlert

FROM         stock ST

        JOIN salesdetails SD ON ST.StockCode

        = SD.StockID;
```

Executing this SQL gives the results in Figure 11.4.

Cost	RepairsCost	PartsCost	CostAlert
52000.0000	2175.0000	1500.0000	Warning!!
176000.0000	5500.0000	2200.0000	Warning!!
15600.0000	660.0000	0.0000	OK
9200.0000	500.0000	750.0000	OK
15960.0000	1360.0000	500.0000	OK
23600.0000	500.0000	750.0000	OK
39600.0000	2500.0000	1500.0000	Warning!!
60800.0000	3250.0000	750.0000	Warning!!
15680.0000	890.0000	500.0000	OK
29200.0000	1950.0000	500.0000	Warning!!
6800.0000	250.0000	225.0000	OK
64400.0000	500.0000	750.0000	OK
135600.0000	5500.0000	2200.0000	OK
7160.0000	500.0000	750.0000	Warning!!
156000.0000	6000.0000	1500.0000	OK
18360.0000	550.0000	500.0000	OK

Figure 11.4: More complex logical tests using IF()

How it Works

Here, the IF() function tests the sales and costs for every vehicle sold and flags any sales where the profit is less than 10 percent of the purchase price and *also* where the repair costs are at least double the parts cost. All this is done in the first part of the IF() function.

If anything, this example shows you that an IF() function can be as complex as you need it to be and that it can include nested parentheses just like a WHERE clause.

In a complex IF() function, it is the first parameter—the test—that is usually complex. The actual output can be quite simple. In this example, the test is in two parts.

First: The net profit is calculated (as you have done previously in this book) by subtracting the total of all the cost elements from the sale price.

Second: Ten percent of the sale price is calculated. This, too, is enclosed inside its own set of parentheses.

Third: The SQL then compares the net profit to 10 percent of the sale price.

Finally: The code then multiplies repair costs by a factor of two (which is isolated from the rest of the test through being placed in parentheses) and compares this to the parts cost.

Only if both these tests are true will the IF() function display "Warning" as its output.

Tricks and Traps

When designing complex tests using the IF() function, it can help to remember the following:

- If you want to try a complex IF() function, you can always start by using the "test" part of the IF() statement (the first parameter) in the WHERE clause. This will allow you to see the filter effect of the test code. Then, once you are sure the code does exactly what you want, you can place it inside an IF() function in the SELECT statement.

- Using parentheses efficiently can be a real boon when building complex tests (that is, the first parameter of an IF() function) in SQL. More specifically, they can help you to isolate separate aspects of the test so that you can concentrate on each "unit" separately.

- Because the test acts like a small WHERE clause, it can use the same logical operators—AND, OR, and NOT—that you first saw in Chapter 4.

- As the final output does not show the profit figure you may prefer to add this to the SELECT clause initially in order to verify the logic and reassure yourself that the query is working as you expect.

4. Creating Key Performance Indicators

As a final flourish for the dashboard that she wants to present to the board of directors, the sales manager wants to create a set of key performance indicators (KPIs). This involves defining the output from the analysis as Good, Bad, or Acceptable.

This kind of request illustrates the fact that not all tests on your data can give simple "black or white" results. Sometimes you may require a more nuanced answer. You may well have to output three or more states that categorize the output. The following piece of SQL is designed for precisely this kind of eventuality:

```
SELECT      ST.Cost, ST.RepairsCost, ST.PartsCost
            ,IF(
                (SD.SalePrice -
                  (ST.Cost + SD.LineItemDiscount
                        + ST.PartsCost
                        + IFNULL(ST.RepairsCost, 0)
                        + ST.TransportInCost
                  )
                )
                < (SD.SalePrice * 0.1)
                AND (ST.RepairsCost * 2) > ST.PartsCost
            ,'Warning!!'
            ,IF(
                (SD.SalePrice -
                    (ST.Cost + SD.LineItemDiscount
                        - IFNULL(ST.PartsCost, 0)
                      + ST.RepairsCost + ST.TransportInCost)
                  ) < SD.SalePrice * 0.5, 'Acceptable', 'OK'
                )
            ) AS CostAlert
FROM        stock ST
            JOIN salesdetails SD ON ST.StockCode = SD.StockID;
```

Running this query gives the results in Figure 11.5.

Cost	RepairsCost	PartsCost	CostAlert
52000.0000	2175.0000	1500.0000	Acceptable
176000.0000	5500.0000	2200.0000	Warning!!
15600.0000	660.0000	0.0000	OK
9200.0000	500.0000	750.0000	OK
15960.0000	1360.0000	500.0000	OK
23600.0000	500.0000	750.0000	Acceptable
39600.0000	2500.0000	1500.0000	Acceptable
60800.0000	3250.0000	750.0000	Warning!!
15680.0000	890.0000	500.0000	OK
29200.0000	1950.0000	500.0000	Warning!!
6800.0000	250.0000	225.0000	Acceptable
64400.0000	500.0000	750.0000	Acceptable
135600.0000	5500.0000	2200.0000	OK
7160.0000	500.0000	750.0000	Acceptable

Figure 11.5: *Nested logic tests using IF()*

How it Works

This type of query probably looks more complicated than it really is. It is called a *nested* IF() statement because you are placing one IF() function inside another. What it does is this:

First: It calculates the sale price minus all the associated costs (the net margin) and then compares the result to the sale price multiplied by 10 percent. If the margin is *lower* than the 10 percent of the sale price, the function displays "Warning" and goes no further.

Then: If the net margin is greater than 10 percent, but less than 50 percent of the sale price the function displays "Acceptable." If not (which means that we have a net margin of more than 50 percent), it displays "OK."

A nested IF() function like this is extremely logical and will try to stop the tests as fast as possible. So, when writing them, you want to ensure that you have defined a clear progression through the various parts of the test. This nearly always means beginning with the lowest value for the comparison (10 percent in this example) and then progressing to the next level in the comparison (50 percent here), and so on. If you make the succession of tests coherent and progressive, they will probably be easier to write as well as both simpler to understand and easier to correct if there are errors. It will also make it easier to update the test if you come back to it weeks—or even months—later.

Figure 11.6 makes this concept clearer. This shows the progression through the tests from the lowest to the highest values.

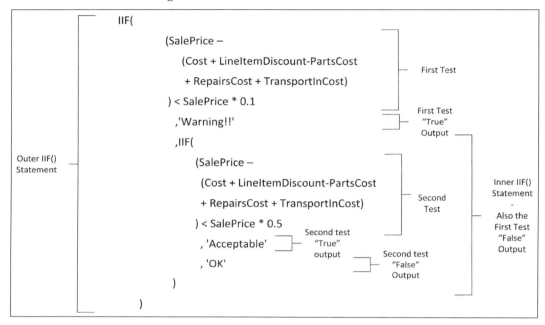

Figure 11.6: *The anatomy of a nested IF() expression*

Tricks and Traps

Designing successive nested tests in SQL is both an art and a science. With this in mind, you might want to consider the following points:

- The really hard part to writing nested IF statements is getting the parentheses right. This can take a little practice, so be patient if you are starting out down this particular route.

- If you have spent any time writing nested IF statements in Excel—or nested IIF statements in Access for that matter—then you are probably used to this particular technique because it is similar in MySQL.

- If you nest too many IF statements it can become hard to write the SQL correctly, so I advise you to move on to using CASE statements (described in the following sections) if your requirements become so challenging that they require multiple levels of nesting.

5. Classifying a Series of Elements Without the Necessary Categories Present in Your Data

The finance director needs to manage exchange rate risk. So, he wants you to add each client's currency area to a printout. Unfortunately, the database does not have a field that holds the currency area. Moreover, you are not able to modify the data structures to add a new category to the database. The following SQL shows how you can carry out this kind of operation to extend your analysis by superposing an ad hoc categorization on an existing dataset:

```sql
SELECT      CountryName
            ,CASE CountryName
                WHEN 'Belgium' THEN 'Eurozone'
                WHEN 'France' THEN 'Eurozone'
                WHEN 'Italy' THEN 'Eurozone'
                WHEN 'Spain' THEN 'Eurozone'
                WHEN 'United Kingdom' THEN 'Pound Sterling'
                WHEN 'United States' THEN 'Dollar'
                ELSE 'Other'
            END AS CurrencyRegion
FROM        country;
```

Running this query gives the results in Figure 11.7.

CountryName	CurrencyRegion
Belgium	Eurozone
Switzerland	Other
China	Other
Germany	Other
Spain	Eurozone
France	Eurozone
United Kingdom	Pound Sterling
India	Other
Italy	Eurozone
United States	Dollar

Figure 11.7: Using a CASE statement to add categories

How it Works

The PrestigeCars database may not contain currency areas, but it does contain the countries for each client. Fortunately, there are not too many of them. This means you can write some SQL to check the country name and then, depending on the country, output one of the following:

- Eurozone
- Pound sterling
- Dollar

You do this with a CASE statement. This statement does the following:

First: Define the field to test by adding it after the word CASE. In this example, the test is extremely succinct—it is simply CASE CountryName. That is all that is required.

Second: List all the possible outcomes, by saying "If the country is [whatever the country], then output the following...." This is done by entering the THEN keyword followed by the output you want to see. In this example, the output is text, so it is enclosed in single quotes. What is more, you can add up to 255 WHEN clauses to a CASE statement.

Third: Say what is to happen if none of the tests is true—in other words, what must be output if the database contains a country not in your list? This is done by entering the ELSE keyword, followed by the output you want to see in this case.

Finally: Add the END keyword—and provide a column alias if you want.

This example is carrying out a simple equality test. All you are doing is comparing the contents of a field with a list you enter and telling SQL what to do when a match is found.

To make this a little clearer, take a look at Figure 11.8.

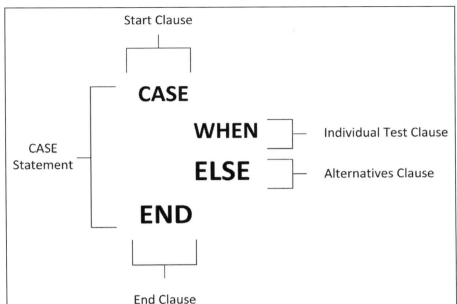

Figure 11.8: The anatomy of a CASE expression

Put another way, the test says "WHEN (if the country is), followed by THEN—and the output that you want to see".

Tricks and Traps

You need to bear the following in mind when using CASE statements:

- A CASE statement (a bit like a nested IF() statement) will "exit" (that is, return an output value) at the first possible opportunity. So, if there are several elements in your list that can cause the statement to match a value, it will take *only the first one* that it comes to when going down through the list. Any others will *not* count and will not be applied to the data.

- If you are using a CASE statement to test multiple numeric thresholds be sure to place the statements in order of increasing value with no gaps in the sequence of values.

- The ELSE clause is not an absolute requirement in a CASE statement. However, without it, you could be excluding data from the output that has not been "caught" by the WHEN clauses.

6. Creating Ad Hoc Category Groupings

The finance director is overjoyed that you solved his previous conundrum and were able to add currency areas to the output. So, now he wants to take this one step further and has asked you for a report that counts the makes of car according to the geographical zone where they were built.

Fortunately, you can extend the use of CASE statements to group and aggregate data even when you are adding categories that do not exist in the underlying database— as the following piece of SQL illustrates:

```sql
SELECT    CASE

                WHEN MK.MakeCountry IN ('ITA', 'GER', 'FRA')

                    THEN 'European'

                WHEN MK.MakeCountry = 'GBR' THEN 'British'

                WHEN MK.MakeCountry = 'USA' THEN 'American'

                ELSE 'Other'

            END AS SalesRegion

            ,COUNT(SD.SalesDetailsID) AS NumberOfSales

FROM      make AS MK

JOIN      model AS MD USING(MakeID)

JOIN      stock AS ST USING(ModelID)

JOIN      salesdetails SD

            ON ST.StockCode = SD.StockID

GROUP BY  CASE

                WHEN MK.MakeCountry IN ('ITA', 'GER', 'FRA')

                    THEN 'European'

                WHEN MK.MakeCountry = 'GBR' THEN 'British'

                WHEN MK.MakeCountry = 'USA' THEN 'American'

                ELSE 'Other'

            END;
```

Executing this query gives the output that you can see in Figure 11.9.

SalesRegion	NumberOfSales
American	1
British	189
European	161

Figure 11.9: Using a CASE function to group data

How it Works

This code snippet lets you add a custom grouping element that is not contained in the source data. However, at its heart it uses the same, identical CASE statement twice.

First: In the SELECT clause to output the new grouping element (European, British, American, or Other)

Second: In the GROUP BY clause to group and aggregate the output using the same categorization

The way that the CASE statement is structured is nonetheless slightly different from how it is used in the previous example. This time the field that is being tested appears in *each* WHEN clause and not once only after the CASE keyword. Although this may seem a little more long-winded, it is actually much simpler to apply. As you can see, you no longer have to detail every possible individual comparison separately as you can now use the IN function to enter lists of alternatives. This makes for shorter code that is easier to understand and maintain—even if you have to repeat the name of the field that you are testing.

Otherwise, this SQL is quite normal—it uses a COUNT() function to give the total number of sales using the Make, Model, Stock, and Sales tables as the data source. A standard FROM clause joins the Make, Stock, Model, and SalesDetails tables so that you can access all the fields that you need in the rest of the query.

Tricks and Traps

There a couple of key points to note when using CASE statements (in either the SELECT or GROUP BY clause).

- As in the previous example, the CASE statement ends with an ELSE clause (to handle any categorizations that you have not thought of) and with the END keyword (to tell SQL that the CASE statement is finished).

- You can, instead, use the alias from the SELECT clause in the GROUP BY statement rather than copying the entire CASE statement. If you were to do this the GROUP BY clause would be:

```
GROUP BY SalesRegion
```

7. Applying Multiple Ad Hoc Categories

Applying categories that no one thought of when the database was being built is pretty normal in the world of SQL. However, there are times when users request quite complex analyses that can require you to provide some clever SQL. As a case in point, the sales director wants you to create a category that is built on two complementary analyses, categorizing purchasers by both type and geography. The following SQL does exactly this, if you want to take a look:

```
SELECT    CustomerName
          ,CASE
          WHEN IsReseller = 0 AND country IN ('IT', 'DE', 'FR'
                                                ,'ES', 'BE')
                THEN 'Eurozone Retail Client'
          WHEN IsReseller = 0 AND country IN ('GB')
                THEN 'British Retail Client'
          WHEN IsReseller = 0 AND country IN ('US')
                THEN 'American Retail Client'
          WHEN IsReseller = 0 AND country IN ('CH')
                THEN 'Swiss Retail Client'
          WHEN IsReseller = 1 AND country IN ('IT', 'DE', 'FR'
                                                ,'ES', 'BE')
                THEN 'Eurozone Reseller'
          WHEN IsReseller = 1 AND country IN ('GB')
                THEN 'British Reseller'
          WHEN IsReseller = 1 AND country IN ('US')
                THEN 'American Reseller'
          WHEN IsReseller = 1 AND country IN ('CH')
```

```
        THEN 'Swiss Reseller'

END AS CustomerType

FROM    customer;
```

If you run this query, you should see the output in Figure 11.10.

CustomerName	CustomerType
Magic Motors	British Reseller
Snazzy Roadsters	British Reseller
Birmingham Executive Prestige Vehicles	British Reseller
WunderKar	Eurozone Reseller
Casseroles Chromes	Eurozone Reseller
Le Luxe en Motion	Swiss Reseller
Eat My Exhaust Ltd	British Reseller
M. Pierre Dubois	Eurozone Retail Client
Sondra Horowitz	American Retail Client
Wonderland Wheels	British Reseller
London Executive Prestige Vehicles	British Reseller
Glittering Prize Cars Ltd	British Reseller
La Bagnole de Luxe	Eurozone Reseller
Convertible Dreams	British Reseller

Figure 11.10: *Complex evaluation using CASE statements*

How it Works

This code analyzes two separate fields to decide whether a client is a reseller and if so (or if not) which geographical area they belong to. It does this using a CASE statement, but this *must* be structured in the "second" way that you saw in this chapter—that is, you have to specify *each* of the fields that you are using to test data every time in *each* WHEN clause. This approach may seem a little laborious, but its key advantage is that *every* individual WHEN clause can contain its *own specific logic* that is completely separate from the other WHEN clauses. In this example, the combinations of reseller status and country are used to define a series of overall categories: Eurozone Retail Client, British Retail Client, American Retail Client, Swiss Retail Client, Eurozone Reseller, British Reseller, American Reseller, and Swiss Reseller.

Tricks and Traps

Complex case statements like this one entail being aware of the following key points:

- If tracking all these variations on a theme becomes difficult, then you can organize CASE statements into nested subgroups, as you can see in the following section.

- MySQL limits you to 255 WHEN elements in a CASE statement.

- You can format the WHEN clause as you see fit. We placed the WHEN… THEN clauses on separate lines to make the code easier to understand. However, there is nothing to stop you writing the following, for instance, with all the SQL on a single line:

  ```
  WHEN IsReseller = 1 AND Country IN ('US') THEN 'American Reseller'
  ```

- When there is only a single element to test in the WHEN clause, you can use equal (=) rather than IN.

8. Categorizing Data Using Multiple Nested Classifications

The sales director wants you to flag various customers by their credit status and geographical region. The following piece of SQL explains how to do that, but in a slightly different way from the one you saw in the previous example. In fact, to make custom categorizations easier to understand, you can nest the elements you are examining into structured hierarchies to make the concept—and the code—easier to comprehend.

```
SELECT      CustomerName
        ,CASE
            WHEN IsCreditRisk = 0 THEN
                    CASE
                        WHEN country IN ('IT', 'DE', 'FR'
                                            ,'ES', 'BE')
                            THEN 'Eurozone No Risk'
                        WHEN country IN ('GB')
                            THEN 'British No Risk'
                        WHEN country IN ('US')
                            THEN 'American No Risk'
                        WHEN country IN ('CH')
                            THEN 'Swiss No Risk'
                    END
```

```
            WHEN IsCreditRisk = 1 THEN

                 CASE

                     WHEN country IN ('IT', 'DE', 'FR'
                                        ,'ES', 'BE')
                         THEN 'Eurozone Credit Risk'
                     WHEN country IN ('GB')
                         THEN 'British Credit Risk'
                     WHEN country IN ('US')
                         THEN 'American Credit Risk'
                     WHEN country IN ('CH')
                         THEN 'Swiss Credit Risk'

                 END

            END AS RiskType

FROM        Customer;
```

Running this query gives the results in Figure 11.11.

CustomerName	RiskType
Magic Motors	British No Risk
Snazzy Roadsters	British Credit Risk
Birmingham Executive Prestige Vehicles	British No Risk
WunderKar	Eurozone No Risk
Casseroles Chromes	Eurozone No Risk
Le Luxe en Motion	Swiss Credit Risk
Eat My Exhaust Ltd	British No Risk
M. Pierre Dubois	Eurozone No Risk
Sondra Horowitz	American No Risk
Wonderland Wheels	British No Risk
London Executive Prestige Vehicles	British Credit Risk
Glittering Prize Cars Ltd	British No Risk
La Bagnole de Luxe	Eurozone No Risk
Convertible Dreams	British No Risk
Alexei Tolstoi	British No Risk
SuperSport S.A.R.L.	Eurozone Credit Risk

Figure 11.11: Nested CASE statements

How it Works

This SQL query has an outer and an inner group of CASE statements.

First: The outer statement looks at the IsCreditRisk field. It begins by saying the following: "When the credit risk is absent, move on to the inner CASE statement (and carry out further tests on the country). Then, if the customer poses a credit risk (that is, the field is true or contains a 1 for this kind of field), continue processing with another, separate CASE statement and test the country."

Then: The inner statement in either case looks at the country and applies separate tests. Only if the outer and inner tests give a positive result (for instance, if a customer is not a credit risk and the country is Britain) will one of the outcomes be returned—"British No Risk" in the event of a British risk-free customer.

Tricks and Traps

I have only a couple of comments to make about nested CASE statements.

* It is best to avoid too many levels of nested CASE statements.
* In this example, the two "inner" CASE statements were nearly identical—they both contained the same tests on the country. This approach is specific to this particular example and will not always be the case in practice.

9. Aggregating Ad-Hoc Categories

The sales director clearly adores MySQL's ability to deliver custom categorizations on the fly. Now she wants you to produce a report that breaks down total sales values into a set of custom bandings by value and show how many vehicles have been sold in each category.

After a few minutes thought, you are able to produce the following SQL:

```
SELECT      'Sales By Category'

            ,SUM(CASE WHEN SD.SalePrice < 5000 THEN 1 ELSE 0 END)

                AS 'Under 5000'

            ,SUM(CASE WHEN SD.SalePrice BETWEEN 5000 AND 50000

                    THEN 1 ELSE 0 END) AS '5000-50000'
```

```
           ,SUM(CASE WHEN SD.SalePrice BETWEEN 50001 AND 100000

                  THEN 1 ELSE 0 END) AS '50001-100000'

           ,SUM(CASE WHEN SD.SalePrice BETWEEN 100001 AND 200000

                  THEN 1 ELSE 0 END) AS '100001-200000'

           ,SUM(CASE WHEN SD.SalePrice > 200000 THEN 1 ELSE 0 END)

                  AS 'Over 200000'

FROM       make AS MK

JOIN       model AS MD USING(MakeID)

JOIN       stock AS ST USING(ModelID)

JOIN       salesdetails SD

           ON ST.StockCode = SD.StockID;
```

Executing this piece of SQL produces the output that you can see in Figure 11.12.

Sales By Category	Under 5000	5000-50000	50001-100000	100001-200000	Over 200000
Sales By Category	29	174	88	37	23

Figure 11.12: Using multiple CASE statements to aggregate custom classifications

How it Works

The aim of this piece of SQL is to evaluate the sale price of each car sold and see which of the following bands it fits into:

- Less than 5,000
- Between 5,000 and 50,000
- Between 50,001 and 100,000
- Between 100,001 and 200,000
- Over 200,000

As the source data has no table that contains these bandings, you have to create the segmentation "on the fly". So you take the following approach for each range of values that you are testing. Here is how this is done for the first (under 5,000) category.

First: Create a CASE statement that tests the SalePrice field of the SalesDetails table to see if it is under 5,000.

Second: If the value is less than 5,000 return a 1—otherwise, return a 0.

Third: Wrap this CASE function in a SUM() function. This means that the 1 or 0 returned for each record will be aggregated. So each time there is a 1 returned (because the vehicle is in the desired range) MySQL will include this row in the total for this category.

Finally: Add an alias to describe the output.

You then repeat this process for each of the sale price segments that you are evaluating. You must take care to apply the precise selection criteria for each set of threshold values. This way each segment appears as a separate column in the output because each element is separated from the others by a comma just like any other field would be.

As a final flourish you can add a text as the first column to make the output more readable.

Tricks and Traps

I have only a few comments to make about these kind of aggregated CASE statements.

- Each field output is a distinct CASE statement. So each must finish with an END keyword and contain a valid WHEN clause.

- Take care that you do not leave any gaps when defining the successive ranges of values in each WHEN clause.

- Rather than using the BETWEEN...AND operators you can, if you so wish, use the >= and <= operators instead. An example would be:

```
CASE WHEN SD.SalePrice >= 5000 AND SD.SalePrice <= 50000 THEN 1
ELSE 0 END
```

- The WHEN clause is very much like a WHERE clause, and can be used to apply similar logic.

- You can extend code like this to provide the segmentation by Make, for instance, simply by adding a GROUP BY clause like the following:

```
GROUP BY MakeName
```

Assuming that you also replace 'Sales By Category' with MakeName as the first field in the SELECT clause, the output will look like Figure 11.13.

MakeName	Under 5000	5000-50000	50001-100000	100001-200000	Over 200000
Alfa Romeo	2	20	0	0	0
Aston Martin	0	25	42	9	1
Austin	3	4	0	0	0
Bentley	0	0	19	1	0
BMW	0	3	0	0	0
Bugatti	0	0	0	0	6
Citroen	3	2	1	0	0
Delahaye	0	4	0	0	0
Delorean	0	0	1	0	0
Ferrari	0	0	3	16	10
Jaguar	1	19	5	0	0
Lagonda	0	0	1	1	0
Lamborghini	1	1	0	3	5
McLaren	0	0	0	0	1
Mercedes	0	13	2	0	0
Morgan	0	1	0	0	0
Noble	0	5	1	0	0
Peugeot	10	1	0	0	0
Porsche	0	40	6	0	0
Reliant	2	0	0	0	0
Rolls Royce	0	0	7	7	0
Trabant	5	0	0	0	0
Triumph	2	36	0	0	0

Figure 11.13: Using multiple CASE statements to group and aggregate custom classifications

10. Placing NULLs at the Start or End of a List

The sales director has presented you with a quandary. She requested a list of sales by increasing value of discounts, which you duly delivered. However, as there were a large quantity of sales where no discount was applied, MySQL began the list with the NULL values for the LineItemDiscount field because NULLs are considered to be smaller than any numerical value.

However, this is not what the sales director wants. She wants a list that begins with the smallest values and places any empty (non-discounted) sales at the bottom of the list.

This is where a little SQL logic can assist you, as the following code snippet shows:

```
SELECT      *
FROM        salesbycountry
ORDER BY    CASE WHEN LineItemDiscount IS NULL THEN 1 ELSE 0 END ASC
            ,LineItemDiscount;
```

Running this code will return the output in Figure 11.14.

CountryName	MakeName	ModelName	Cost	RepairsCost	PartsCost	TransportInCost	Color	SalePrice	LineItemDiscount	InvoiceNumber	SaleDate	CustomerName	SalesDetailsID
Belgium	Peugeot	205	760.0000	500.0000	750.0000	150.0000	British Racing Green	950.00	25.00	EURBE218	2018-01-10 00:00:00	Stefan Van Helsing	237
France	Porsche	944	7160.0000	500.0000	750.0000	150.0000	Green	8950.00	25.00	EURFR013	2015-05-20 00:00:00	M. Pierre Dubois	14
United Kingdom	Porsche	944	7840.0000	500.0000	750.0000	150.0000	Canary Yellow	9800.00	35.00	GBPGB236	2018-03-19 00:00:00	Pierre Blanc	258
United Kingdom	Peugeot	404	1996.0000	500.0000	750.0000	150.0000	Canary Yellow	2495.00	45.00	GBPGB253	2018-05-03 00:00:00	Silver HubCaps	276
United Kingdom	Porsche	911	18360.0000	500.0000	750.0000	150.0000	Black	22950.00	50.00	GBPGB025	2015-11-10 00:00:00	Convertible Dreams	27
United Kingdom	Porsche	944	6800.0000	250.0000	225.0000	150.0000	Blue	8500.00	50.00	GBPGB011	2015-04-30 00:00:00	Wonderland Wheels	11
France	Alfa Romeo	Giulia	2040.0000	500.0000	750.0000	150.0000	British Racing Green	2550.00	50.00	EURFR031	2016-01-07 00:00:00	M. Pierre Dubois	33
United Kingdom	Porsche	944	6000.0000	500.0000	750.0000	150.0000	British Racing Green	7500.00	75.00	GBPGB084	2016-09-05 00:00:00	Birmingham Executive Prestige Vehicles	91
United Kingdom	Alfa Romeo	Giulia	6956.0000	400.0000	500.0000	150.0000	Red	8695.00	95.00	GBPGB016	2015-07-12 10:00:00	Convertible Dreams	17
United States	Triumph	TR4	4400.0000	500.0000	750.0000	150.0000	Night Blue	5500.00	500.00	USDUS019	2015-08-02 08:00:00	Theo Kowalski	21
United Kingdom	Triumph	TR5	10056.0000	2000.0000	500.0000	150.0000	Black	12570.00	500.00	GBPGB214	2018-01-05 00:00:00	Pierre Blanc	233
United States	Aston Martin	DB9	45520.0000	1360.0000	500.0000	550.0000	Silver	56900.00	500.00	USDUS233	2018-03-08 00:00:00	Theo Kowalski	253
United Kingdom	Triumph	TR6	5200.0000	500.0000	750.0000	150.0000	Black	6500.00	500.00	GBPGB062	2016-08-02 00:00:00	Silver HubCaps	68
United Kingdom	Triumph	TR5	4544.0000	500.0000	150.0000	150.0000	Canary Yellow	5680.00	500.00	GBPGB079	2016-08-29 00:00:00	King Lear Cars	86
United Kingdom	Porsche	911	17720.0000	1360.0000	750.0000	150.0000	Night Blue	22150.00	500.00	GBPGB049	2016-06-15 00:00:00	Honest Pete Motors	53
United Kingdom	Bentley	Flying Spur	64400.0000	500.0000	750.0000	750.0000	British Racing Green	80500.00	500.00	GBPGB011	2015-04-30 00:00:00	Wonderland Wheels	12

Figure 11.14: Using a CASE statement to place NULL values at the end of a list

How it Works

The trick to handling NULL values in a sort order is to add an initial sort key that deals with the NULL values and then sorts the non-NULL values afterward.

This is what the ORDER BY clause has done here:

First: An initial sort element is applied using a CASE statement. In this example, this piece of logic says, "If the LineItemDiscount field contains a NULL, consider it to contain a 1; otherwise, consider any value as a 0." So, the first sort key is, effectively, a 1 or a 0, meaning that NULLs are 1s and so appear after all the 0s.

Second: The ORDER BY clause sorts on the LineItemDiscount field once the sort on the NULL fields (that have now been converted to ones and zeros for the sort operation) has been applied.

Tricks and Traps

I have only two comments to make about these kind of CASE statements.

- You can place the NULL values at the top or bottom of the output simply by switching the 1 and 0 values in the CASE statement. So, to place the NULLs at the top of the list, you would write the following:

  ```
  ORDER BY   CASE WHEN LineItemDiscount IS NULL THEN 0 ELSE 1 END
  ```

- Although the ASC keyword is, technically, superfluous (as an ascending sort order is the default) stating the sort order explicitly can help you to understand how the code works. This is particularly true when you return to the SQL many months later.

11. Classifying Data by Impromptu Categories

Sometimes, just sometimes, you may have to categorize data from a custom list. Suppose the sales director wants to make it clear in which season a vehicle is sold. None of the SQL built-in functions can do this. So, you need to tell SQL to map the month to a specific list that you have defined. The following code does this:

```
SELECT

MONTH(SaleDate) AS MonthNumber

,SaleDate

,ELT(MONTH(SaleDate), 'Winter', 'Winter', 'Spring', 'Spring', 'Summer'

            , 'Summer','Summer','Summer','Autumn','Autumn'

            , 'Winter','Winter')

        AS SalesSeason

FROM      Sales;
```

Running this query gives the results in Figure 11.15.

	MonthNumber	SaleDate	SalesSeason
▶	1	2015-01-02 08:00:00	Winter
	1	2015-01-25 00:00:00	Winter
	2	2015-02-03 10:00:00	Winter
	2	2015-02-16 08:00:00	Winter
	1	2015-01-02 10:33:00	Winter
	3	2015-03-14 00:00:00	Spring
	3	2015-03-24 00:00:00	Spring
	3	2015-03-30 00:00:00	Spring
	4	2015-04-06 00:00:00	Spring
	4	2015-04-04 00:00:00	Spring
	4	2015-04-30 00:00:00	Spring
	5	2015-05-10 00:00:00	Summer
	5	2015-05-20 00:00:00	Summer
	5	2015-05-28 00:00:00	Summer
	6	2015-06-04 16:37:00	Summer
	7	2015-07-12 10:00:00	Summer

Figure 11.15: Using ELT() to return elements from a custom list

How it Works

This code finds the number of the month using the MONTH() function that you saw in Chapter 8. It then uses the number to select the "Nth" element in the list of seasons. This list contains 12 elements, so month 1 (January) maps to the first element in the list Winter. Month 2 (February) maps to Winter too. However, the third month—March—maps to the third element, which is Spring. The process then continues for all the elements in the list.

To achieve these ends the SQL applies the ELT() function. This function consists of:

First: A number followed by a comma. This number can be the contents of a field—or, as is the case here, a number extracted from a field.

Second: A list of elements, each separated from the previous one by a comma.

What the ELT() function does is to look for (and return) the "Nth" element in the comma-delimited list.

Tricks and Traps

You need to be aware that the ELT() function comes with a few minor restrictions.

- If the list contains fewer elements than the figure that is used to select an element, then MySQL just returns NULL—that is, nothing. It does not warn you that something might not be working as you would expect.

- More generically, the ELT() function can be used to map any number to the corresponding element in a list. However, the first parameter in the ELT() function *must* be a number—it cannot be text.

Conclusion

This chapter showed you some of the techniques that you can apply with MySQL to extend your queries with some elementary logic. First you saw how to use IF and CASE statements to detect data elements and vary the output depending on the tests that the SQL carried out. Then you learned how to make logical tests more complex by nesting IF functions and CASE statements. This chapter showed you how to test data for exceeding thresholds that you define or for showing unexpected characteristics. You discovered several ways to apply impromptu classifications to existing data. Then you saw that a little logic applied to a query can help you to see through a mountain of data and focus your attention on the outliers and anomalies that can be of real interest.

You are now at a staging post in your journey into the world of SQL. It is now time to take stock and to prepare for the next phase of your SQL apprenticeship.

Core Knowledge Learned in This Chapter

You learned the following keywords in this chapter:

Concept	Description
IF()	This function allows you to test output and apply one or another outcome.
CASE	This function can test multiple data states and apply a choice of outcomes.
WHEN	This keyword is used with a CASE statement where it lets you apply a test to data.
ELSE	This keyword is used with a CASE statement where it lets you apply an outcome for any untested cases.
ELT()	This selects an element from a comma-separated list based on an initial number.
LENGTH()	This function detects the length of a string of text.

CHAPTER 12
Subqueries

Now that you have mastered the basics of SQL, it is time to move on and start resolving some more complex analytical challenges. The first step on this path is to learn how you can use independent SQL queries inside other queries. This technique is called using subqueries. It is particularly useful in data analysis as it allows you (among other things) to include aggregated data in detailed rowsets, for instance, or to compare a whole dataset with subsets of data.

What Are Subqueries?

Subqueries are more of a new technique than a new set of SQL keywords. In fact, you can write subqueries using only the SQL knowledge that you have acquired so far. Nonetheless, learning to use subqueries to solve data challenges is a key part of your SQL apprenticeship. Once you master the art of the subquery, you are able to produce clear, concise, and in-depth analytics quickly and efficiently.

I want to convince you that subqueries are not an abstract database concept but an analytical skill that helps you dig deep into your data and unearth the insights that keep you ahead of the competition. In this chapter you learn how to

- Compare categories of data to the whole dataset and calculate percentages
- Isolate top and bottom elements in a dataset and use them as a basis for filtering records
- Filter data by comparing records to averages and overall thresholds

These—and many more analytical solutions—are made possible through the application of subqueries in your SQL. Let's now move on to some real-world examples that illustrate how subqueries can turn raw data into meaningful information.

1. Adding Aggregated Fields to Detailed Data Sets

Data analysis often means comparing individual elements to either all or a part of a dataset. As a first step, suppose that you want to count the number of cars sold per country and that you also want to see the total car sales for all vehicles, whatever their country, in the same query. Here is the SQL that lets you do this:

```
SELECT      CO.CountryName
            ,COUNT(SD.SalesDetailsID) AS CarsSold
            ,(SELECT COUNT(SalesDetailsID)
              FROM salesdetails) AS SalesTotal
FROM        salesdetails SD
JOIN        sales AS SA USING (SalesID)
JOIN        customer CU USING (CustomerID)
JOIN        country CO ON CU.country = CO.CountryISO2
GROUP BY    CO.CountryName;
```

Running this query gives the results that you can see in Figure 12.1.

CountryName	CarsSold	SalesTotal
Belgium	10	351
France	69	351
Germany	13	351
Italy	18	351
Spain	27	351
Switzerland	18	351
United Kingdom	165	351
United States	31	351

Figure 12.1: Using a subquery

How it Works

Inevitably there are occasions in your analytical career when you want to see how a part of a set of data relates to a whole dataset. This approach frequently allows you to relativize values and to put them in a wider context.

This query exists to help you add perspective to the data. At its heart, it is a simple aggregation of sales by country. Once the Sales, SalesDetails, Customer, and Country tables have been joined, the SQL groups the data on the Country field and uses the COUNT() function to return the total number of sales for each country. Then— and this is where you are moving on to new territory—it adds a subquery to the SELECT clause to return the total number of sales *without any grouping*. In effect, this returns the total for all sales as a separate column alongside the number of cars sold. However, the SQL is carrying out this calculation for every row in the query output so that you can see—and possibly use—the total in every row.

To get a more visual idea of how a subquery works, take a look at Figure 12.2. The outer query "hosts" the separate inner query, yet both queries run at the same time and output their results together.

Figure 12.2: A conceptual view of subqueries

The code shows you how MySQL lets you mix separate queries in a single output using a *subquery*. The principle characteristics of a subquery are

- It is included in the SELECT, WHERE, or HAVING clause of the "main" (outer) query, just as a normal field name would be. When used in a SELECT query the output from the subquery is considered to be a field—so it is separated from the other fields by a comma.

- It is enclosed in parentheses.

- It is a *complete, separate query* with—at a minimum—its own SELECT and FROM clauses.

- If used in a SELECT clause it can only return *one* value (that is, you cannot output more than one field from the subquery).

Tricks and Traps

Inevitably a new concept implies a few key points that you need to remember:

- You do not have to use an alias for the name of the field returned by a subquery—but it *is* easier to understand the results if you do use aliases. You may also find that using a meaningful alias helps you understand the query better when you return to it at a later date.

- Any subquery can be executed independently of the main/outer query. This means that you can select the text that makes up the subquery (but not including the parentheses that contain it) and run it by pressing [SHIFT]-[CONTROL]-[ENTER] on Windows or [Command]-[Enter] on a Macintosh or by clicking the toolbar Execute button (the lightning flash) at any time (assuming that you are using MySQL Workbench as the query tool). In this example, you select the following code:

```
SELECT COUNT(SalesDetailsID) FROM salesdetails
```

Running this code returns a dataset like the one shown in Figure 12.3.

COUNT(SalesDetailsID)
351

Figure 12.3: Executing a subquery independently

- Although you can only output a single value from a subquery, you can make the value that is returned the result of a calculation in the subquery if you need to. You will see this in the next section.

- The subquery can be as simple or as complex as your requirements demand and can contain its own independent WHERE or GROUP BY clauses.

2. Displaying a Value as the Percentage of a Total

Calculating *ratios*—or percentages of a whole—is a core requirement in data analysis. Let's imagine that the sales director has put in a request for a list of sales by make of car sold that also displays the percentage of the total sales that the value for each make represents. Subqueries can help you do this easily and simply, as the following SQL snippet shows:

```
SELECT      MK.MakeName

            ,SUM(SD.SalePrice) AS SalePrice

            ,SUM(SD.SalePrice) / (SELECT SUM(SalePrice)

                        FROM SalesDetails) AS SalesRatio

FROM        make AS MK

JOIN        model AS MD USING(MakeID)

JOIN        stock AS ST USING(ModelID)

JOIN        salesdetails SD ON ST.StockCode = SD.StockID

GROUP BY    MK.MakeName;
```

Running this query gives the results that you can see in Figure 12.4.

MakeName	SalePrice	SalesRatio
Alfa Romeo	243510.00	0.011045
Aston Martin	5102755.00	0.231444
Austin	64500.00	0.002926
Bentley	1689240.00	0.076618
BMW	60500.00	0.002744
Bugatti	1915500.00	0.086881
Citroen	101080.00	0.004585
Delahaye	107000.00	0.004853
Delorean	99500.00	0.004513
Ferrari	5540850.00	0.251315
Jaguar	882955.00	0.040048
Lagonda	218000.00	0.009888
Lamborghini	1727150.00	0.078338
McLaren	295000.00	0.013380
Mercedes	496115.00	0.022502
Morgan	18500.00	0.000839
Noble	206900.00	0.009384
Peugeot	40545.00	0.001839
Porsche	1169240.00	0.053033
Reliant	1900.00	0.000086
Rolls Royce	1637000.00	0.074249
Trabant	8440.00	0.000383
Triumph	421270.00	0.019107

Figure 12.4: Using a subquery to calculate a ratio

How it Works

This query works like this:

First: It joins the tables (Make, Model, Stock, and SalesDetails) that are required to return the make as well as the selling price for each vehicle sold.

Second: It groups on the MakeName field and selects this field as well as the SUM() of the sale price to aggregate the selling price per make.

Finally: It adds a new calculated field that divides the sum of the sale price by the total sale price of all vehicles sold. The "grand total" for all sales is defined using a subquery. In effect, this field (SalesRatio) divides the aggregate total for each make by the overall total and so calculates the percentage of total sales that each make represents.

Tricks and Traps

I am pushing the concept of subqueries quite a bit further in this example. Note that

- SQL frequently forces you to repeat a calculation if you need its output more than once. In this example, you can see that you need the total of vehicles sold *twice* to calculate the percentage of total sales: once for each make and once to calculate the overall total. Consequently, you have to repeat the formula

  ```
  SUM(SalePrice)
  ```

  This means that SQL is not like a spreadsheet where you can "chain" cells using cell references to produce ripple-through calculations. It follows that it is perfectly normal to repeat a calculation several times in a piece of SQL each time you need it.

- Percentages are expressed as a decimal value when they are calculated, just as they are in a spreadsheet. You may prefer to multiply the result by 100 to obtain a more visually comprehensible result:

  ```
  (SUM(SD.SalePrice) / (SELECT SUM(SalePrice)
                        FROM salesdetails)) * 100 AS SalesRatio
  ```

If you use SQL like this in the lines that appear in bold earlier, you get the output in Figure 12.5.

MakeName	SalePrice	SalesRatio
Alfa Romeo	243510.00	1.104481
Aston Martin	5102755.00	23.144423
Austin	64500.00	0.292551
Bentley	1689240.00	7.661838
BMW	60500.00	0.274408
Bugatti	1915500.00	8.688080
Citroen	101080.00	0.458466
Delahaye	107000.00	0.485317
Delorean	99500.00	0.451299

Figure 12.5: Multiplying a percentage calculation to deliver a more comprehensible result

- If you want to format the result as a percentage, you can use the following SQL in the third line of the code snippet:

```
CONCAT(FORMAT(SUM(SD.SalePrice) / (SELECT SUM(SalePrice)
                       FROM salesdetails) * 100 , 2), ' %')
                AS SalesRatio
```

Doing so gives you the kind of output that you can see in Figure 12.6.

MakeName	SalePrice	SalesRatio
Alfa Romeo	243510.00	1.10 %
Aston Martin	5102755.00	23.14 %
Austin	64500.00	0.29 %
Bentley	1689240.00	7.66 %
BMW	60500.00	0.27 %
Bugatti	1915500.00	8.69 %
Citroen	101080.00	0.46 %
Delahaye	107000.00	0.49 %
Delorean	99500.00	0.45 %
Ferrari	5540850.00	25.13 %

Figure 12.6: Formatting a percentage output

You need to be aware that the calculation is nested inside both the CONCAT() and FORMAT() functions (as well as being multiplied by 100). This is purely to present the output as a percentage. These techniques are explained in Chapter *21*.

- The main query in both this example and the previous one is an aggregate query. In practice the outer and inner queries can apply different levels of aggregation. This means that you can use aggregated subqueries inside simple list queries as well as in list-style subqueries inside aggregate outer queries.

- It is vital to remember that the two queries are completely independent of each other. This means that the SUM() used in the outer query is calculated for each grouped element—whereas the SUM() in the subquery applies to the entire table. This is also why the SalePrice field has an alias in the "main" query but does not need an alias in the subquery.

3. Using a Subquery to Filter Data

Prestige Cars' new marketing director is convinced that some colors of car sell better than others. She wants you to find the color—or colors—of the most expensive vehicles sold. Here is the SQL that can do this:

```
SELECT      ST.Color

FROM        stock AS ST

JOIN        salesdetails SD ON ST.StockCode = SD.StockID

WHERE       SD.SalePrice = (SELECT MAX(SalePrice) FROM salesdetails);
```

Running this query gives the results you can see in Figure 12.7.

Color
British Racing Green

Figure 12.7: Using a subquery in the WHERE clause of a query

How it Works

This query is really in two parts.

A subquery	This short piece of code finds the sale price for the most expensive vehicles sold.
The main query	The main query itself simply selects the Color field from the Stock table and joins this table to the SalesDetails table so that the sale price can be used in the WHERE clause as a filter criterion. It uses the figure calculated by the subquery as the criterion for returning the color (or colors) of any vehicles sold at this price from the main query.

What this example shows is that subqueries are not restricted to being used in a SELECT clause. As you can see here, you can also use them in a WHERE clause to restrict the results returned from the main/outer query.

Tricks and Traps

I only have one comment to make about this kind of subquery:

* Technically this piece of SQL is a single query. However, I prefer to describe it as a main query and a subquery purely because I feel that this helps you understand the code more easily.

Selecting the subquery and running it gives you the result you can see in Figure 12.8.

MAX(SalePrice)
395000.00

Figure 12.8: The output from a subquery

This is the value that is used by the main query to filter the query output.

4. Using a Subquery as Part of a Calculation to Filter Data

As part of a company cost containment exercise, you have been asked to take a closer look at any vehicles whose repair cost is significantly over the average for all the vehicles in stock. Specifically, the finance director wants to see a list of all vehicles whose repair cost is more than three times the average repair cost. The following SQL snippet does just this:

```
SELECT     MK.MakeName, MD.ModelName, ST.RepairsCost

FROM       make AS MK

JOIN       model AS MD USING(MakeID)

JOIN       stock AS ST USING(ModelID)

WHERE      ST.RepairsCost > 3 * (SELECT AVG(RepairsCost) FROM Stock);
```

Running this query gives the results that you can see in Figure 12.9.

MakeName	ModelName	RepairsCost
Ferrari	Testarossa	6000.0000
Ferrari	355	9250.0000
Ferrari	355	9250.0000
Ferrari	355	9250.0000
Ferrari	355	5500.0000
Ferrari	355	5500.0000
Ferrari	Dino	9250.0000
Ferrari	Dino	5500.0000
Ferrari	F40	5500.0000
Ferrari	F50	9250.0000
Ferrari	F50	5500.0000
Ferrari	360	5500.0000
Ferrari	360	9250.0000
Ferrari	Enzo	9250.0000
Ferrari	Enzo	9250.0000
Lamborghini	Diabolo	9250.0000
Lamborghini	Diabolo	5500.0000
Lamborghini	400GT	9250.0000

Figure 12.9: Applying a calculation and a subquery in the WHERE clause

How it Works

This query shows how you can use a subquery in a calculation to highlight certain records in a dataset. The main/outer query simply selects the cost of repairs for all makes and models of vehicle in the database using the Make, Model, and Stock tables. The clever part is placing a subquery in the WHERE clause. What this subquery does is

First: It calculates the average repair cost. This is £1533.14 for the Prestige Cars dataset. You can verify this by selecting and running only the SQL for the subquery.

Second: It multiplies this average repair cost by a factor of three.

Finally: It compares this to the repair cost for each vehicle and *only* displays those where the repair cost is greater than three times the average repair cost—that is, over £4,599.42.

You may be thinking that it is a little strange to refer to the same table—the Stock table, in this example—twice in the same query. After all, it is already used in the outer query, so why would you need it in the subquery, too?

The reason is that you are looking at the data in two different ways:

The outer query	Looks at the data at a *detailed level,* where each record is processed individually.
The subquery	Looks at the *whole table* to calculate the average repair cost for all records in the table.

Because each query is *completely independent* of the other, both have separate SELECT clauses no matter which tables and fields are used.

The technical term for these two ways of looking at data is *granularity*. In effect, a SQL query can look at either the detail (that is, at a granular level) or groups of records (a higher level of granularity) or even the whole dataset—but it cannot combine multiple levels of focus at the same time in the same query. So, if you need to mix the whole with the parts, you need to use more than one query, even if the queries combine their results in a single output.

To see this more clearly, take a look at Figure 12.10. This is a visual representation of how granularity works in datasets.

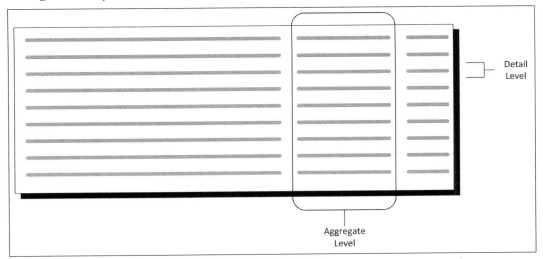

Figure 12.10: Data granularity

Using subqueries enables you to look at data at two or more separate levels of detail. Indeed, you *need* subqueries to return data at different levels of granularity in a single query.

Tricks and Traps

Here are a couple of useful points that you may need to remember when applying this kind of query:

- If you want to check that the calculation of the average cost of repairs really is the figure that we quoted, all you have to do is *select the SQL in the subquery* and execute it. This means running the following short piece of code that you can see in the WHERE clause of the SQL at the start of this section:

```
SELECT AVG(RepairsCost) FROM stock
```

You should see the result shown in Figure 12.11. This is the average repair cost for all vehicles in the Stock table.

AVG(RepairsCost)
1533.14720812

Figure 12.11: The output from a subquery

- It is perfectly normal to query the same table or tables in both a main query and a subquery. This only proves that the two queries are strictly independent of each other.

- Unfortunately, MySQL cannot apply the LIMIT operator to return only the top "n" records from a subquery. However, you can work around this using table joins—as you will see in the following chapter.

5. Filtering on an Aggregated Range of Data Using Multiple Subqueries

A further aspect of the finance director's corporate cost control project is to analyze all sales in which repair costs are within 10 percent of the average repair cost for all stock. The following SQL does this for you:

```
SELECT     MK.MakeName, MD.ModelName, ST.Cost, ST.RepairsCost

FROM       make AS MK

JOIN       model AS MD USING(MakeID)

JOIN       stock AS ST USING(ModelID)

WHERE      ST.RepairsCost BETWEEN

                      (SELECT AVG(RepairsCost) FROM stock) * 0.9
```

AND

```
(SELECT AVG(RepairsCost) FROM stock) * 1.1
```

ORDER BY   MK.MakeName, MD.ModelName, ST.Cost;

Running this query gives the results that you can see in Figure 12.12.

MakeName	ModelName	Cost	RepairsCost
Aston Martin	DB6	55600.0000	1490.0000
Aston Martin	DB6	66072.0000	1490.0000
Aston Martin	DB9	62000.0000	1490.0000
Aston Martin	DB9	63600.0000	1490.0000
Aston Martin	DB9	79600.0000	1490.0000
Aston Martin	Virage	82920.0000	1490.0000
Bentley	Arnage	79960.0000	1490.0000
Bentley	Continental	71600.0000	1490.0000
Bentley	Flying Spur	52712.0000	1490.0000
Bentley	Flying Spur	58000.0000	1490.0000
Delorean	DMC 12	79600.0000	1490.0000
Porsche	959	53200.0000	1490.0000
Porsche	959	71600.0000	1490.0000
Rolls Royce	Ghost	79160.0000	1490.0000
Rolls Royce	Phantom	79600.0000	1490.0000
Rolls Royce	Phantom	95680.0000	1490.0000
Rolls Royce	Silver Seraph	79960.0000	1490.0000
Rolls Royce	Silver Sha	68000.0000	1490.0000

Figure 12.12: Using multiple subqueries in the WHERE clause

How it Works

You can use as many subqueries as you need in a SQL query. A practical use for this is when you need to isolate a dataset that falls between a range of values—such as when you are using a BETWEEN…AND operator in the WHERE clause.

This query selects the make, model, cost, and repair cost for all vehicles. It then filters the data in the WHERE clause. However, since the WHERE clause uses the BETWEEN…AND technique to select a range of values—and this approach requires a lower and an upper limit to the range—it needs *two* subclauses to calculate the average repair cost.

The range boundaries are defined like this:

The lower limit   Takes the overall average repair cost and multiplies by 0.9 to get the figure for 90 percent of the average value (£1,379.83).

The upper limit   Takes the overall average repair cost and multiplies by 1.1 to get the figure for 110 percent of the average value (£1,686.46).

These two range limits are then used by the BETWEEN…AND elements of the WHERE clause to filter the rows that are returned by the main query. This way only vehicles whose repair cost is plus or minus 10 percent of the average repair cost are displayed.

So, once again, you need to write a separate and independent subquery to return a specific result. You can even include multiple subqueries to apply multiple calculations across many different data tables.

Tricks and Traps

I need to make a couple of points here:

- In cases like these, you have to repeat the subquery and make sure that you have ensured that both subqueries do exactly what is required of them in their respective contexts.

- Remember that when using the BETWEEN … AND technique, you *must* always begin with the lower threshold (90 percent in this example) and end with the higher threshold (110 percent in this example).

6. Filtering on Aggregated Output Using a Second Aggregation

On certain occasions your analysis may lead you to compare an aggregate from one dataset with a completely separate aggregate. This can happen, for instance, when salespeople request a list of the average sale price of all makes whose average sale price is over twice the average sale price. SQL allows you to compare data in this way, too, as the following SQL snippet shows:

```
SELECT     MK.MakeName, AVG(SD.SalePrice) AS AverageUpperSalePrice

FROM       make AS MK

JOIN       model AS MD USING(MakeID)

JOIN       stock AS ST USING(ModelID)

JOIN       salesdetails SD ON ST.StockCode = SD.StockID

GROUP BY   MK.MakeName

HAVING     AVG(SD.SalePrice) > 2 * (SELECT AVG(SalePrice)

                        FROM   salesdetails);
```

Running this query gives the results that you can see in Figure 12.13.

	MakeName	AverageUpperSalePrice
	Bugatti	319250.000000
	Ferrari	191063.793103
	Lamborghini	172715.000000
	McLaren	295000.000000

AVG(SalePrice)
62813.247863

Query Result

Subquery Output

Figure 12.13: Applying a calculation and a subquery in the HAVING clause

How it Works

You can also use a subquery in the HAVING clause of an SQL query. As you might remember from Chapter 7, the HAVING clause operates at the level of the aggregation that has been applied to a dataset rather than at the level of individual records. So, when you apply a subquery to an aggregate query's HAVING clause, you are filtering the data on a total, an average, or any other aggregated value.

In this example

First: The outer query calculates the average sale price for each make.

Second: The subquery calculates the overall average sale price for all vehicles sold.

Finally: The subquery then multiplies this average by two and compares it to the average sale price by make for all the makes of car sold.

The result is that any make with an average sale price over twice the overall average sale price is then listed in the query output.

Tricks and Traps

When using calculations to filter data, you need to be aware that

- There are several ways of carrying out the calculation used in the query. If you prefer, you can use arithmetic like this:

```
HAVING AVG(SD.SalePrice) / 2 > (SELECT AVG(SalePrice)
                                    FROM    salesdetails)
```

This code gives exactly the same result as the SQL at the start of this example. It is a simple choice between two arithmetical approaches.

7. Nested Subqueries

The CEO is sure that the luxury car market is changing. She is convinced that unusual colors are now in vogue. So she wants a list of all the cars ever sold where the color of the car figures in sales for 2015.

After shrugging your shoulders at such a strange request, you write the following piece of SQL to satisfy the boss.

```
SELECT      MK.MakeName, MD.ModelName, SD.SalePrice

            ,ST.Color, YEAR(SA.SaleDate) AS YearOfSale

FROM        make AS MK

JOIN        model AS MD USING(MakeID)

JOIN        stock AS ST USING(ModelID)

JOIN        salesdetails SD ON ST.StockCode = SD.StockID

JOIN        sales AS SA USING(SalesID)

WHERE       Color IN (SELECT      DISTINCT STX.Color

                      FROM        stock AS STX

                      JOIN        salesdetails AS SDX

                                  ON STX.StockCode = SDX.StockID

                      JOIN        sales AS SAX USING(SalesID)

                      WHERE       YEAR(SAX.SaleDate) = 2015

                      )

ORDER BY    YearOfSale DESC, MK.MakeName, MD.ModelName, SD.SalePrice

            DESC;
```

Running this SQL gives the output that you can see in Figure 12.14:

	MakeName	ModelName	SalePrice	Color	YearOfSale
▶	Alfa Romeo	1750	9950.00	Blue	2018
	Alfa Romeo	1750	3575.00	Black	2018
	Alfa Romeo	Giulia	6950.00	Black	2018
	Alfa Romeo	Giulietta	18500.00	Blue	2018
	Alfa Romeo	Giulietta	17950.00	Night Blue	2018
	Alfa Romeo	Giulietta	11550.00	Night Blue	2018
	Alfa Romeo	Giulietta	10500.00	Black	2018
	Alfa Romeo	Giulietta	5690.00	Night Blue	2018
	Alfa Romeo	Spider	5950.00	Black	2018
	Aston Martin	DB2	99990.00	Silver	2018
	Aston Martin	DB2	62500.00	British Racing Green	2018
	Aston Martin	DB2	52500.00	Green	2018
	Aston Martin	DB2	39500.00	Blue	2018
	Aston Martin	DB4	56850.00	Canary Yellow	2018
	Aston Martin	DB4	42500.00	Black	2018
	Aston Martin	DB5	69500.00	Blue	2018

Figure 12.14: *Using a subquery to filter data on several elements*

How it Works

Here you can see how data analysis can be a multistep process. This example shows you how to

First:	Use a subquery to find the colors of vehicles sold in 2015.
Then:	Use this data to filter the results from a simpler "outer" query.

This example is one of those times when a subquery can as complex—and powerful—as the outer query that contains it. Indeed, most of the work is done by the subquery, so it makes sense to look at this first.

The subquery	Joins three tables (Stock, Sales and SalesDetails) so that you can list the colors of vehicles sold in 2015.
The main query	Joins a series of tables so that you can return the make, model, color year of sale and sale price. It then uses this result as the filter in its WHERE clause—which is nothing more than a list of makes and sale prices. However, since the subquery can potentially return *more than one result*, you have to use the *IN* operator in the WHERE clause, and not a simple comparison operator, such as =, <, >, <=, or >= (or even != or <>).

Note: When a subquery returns more than one record you *must* use the IN operator in the WHERE clause. If you do not, you will get an error message.

If you select the code for the SQL that makes up the subquery and run it, you can see that the output returns the list of colors that is shown in Figure 12.15. As you used the DISTINCT operator in the subquery each color is output only once.

Figure 12.15: A subquery that returns multiple elements used to filter a main query

If you scroll down the output from the whole query you will see that these are the only colors returned by the query.

Tricks and Traps

Using subqueries in this way means being aware of some important aspects of SQL

- You should be able to run any subquery independently of the outer query. So, you can select the subquery and execute it at any time, just as you would execute the entire query.

- You can begin a complex query like this by writing the subquery first, if you prefer. That way, you can be sure that it returns the data you need to filter the outer query correctly.

- You can create a subquery using many separate tables that are joined together, just as you would any "ordinary" query.

- You can see in this code that we use different aliases in the inner and outer queries, even when the same tables are used. This is not strictly necessary, because the two queries are totally separate. However, I prefer to do this for a couple of reasons:

  o It highlights the fact that you are dealing with two separate queries.

  o It is less confusing to read because you can easily see which field comes from which table.

- More complex subqueries like this one can take longer to run, so do not be surprised if it takes a few seconds for the results to appear.

8. Using Subqueries to Exclude Data

Some analysis requires you to examine data that lies *outside* a certain range or category. For instance, at Prestige Cars, the CEO now wants a report that shows the colors of vehicles ever sold that were *not* sold in 2015. Subqueries can often be the solution to these requirements, as the following SQL illustrates:

```
SELECT     MK.MakeName, MD.ModelName, SD.SalePrice

           ,ST.Color, YEAR(SA.SaleDate) AS YearOfSale

FROM       make AS MK

JOIN       model AS MD USING(MakeID)

JOIN       stock AS ST USING(ModelID)

JOIN       salesdetails SD ON ST.StockCode = SD.StockID

JOIN       sales AS SA USING(SalesID)

WHERE      Color NOT IN (SELECT     DISTINCT ST.Color

                         FROM       model AS MD

                         JOIN       stock AS ST USING(ModelID)

                         JOIN       salesdetails SD

                                    ON ST.StockCode = SD.StockID

                         JOIN       sales AS SA USING(SalesID)

                         WHERE      YEAR(SA.SaleDate) = 2015

                         )

ORDER BY   YearOfSale DESC, MK.MakeName, MD.ModelName

           ,SD.SalePrice DESC;
```

If you run this piece of SQL you should see the following output shown in Figure 12.16:

MakeName	ModelName	SalePrice	Color	YearOfSale
Aston Martin	DB4	56950.00	Pink	2018
Aston Martin	Virage	103650.00	Pink	2018
Bentley	Continental	89500.00	Dark Purple	2018
Delahaye	135	25500.00	Dark Purple	2018
Delahaye	175	12500.00	Pink	2018
Ferrari	Dino	123500.00	Dark Purple	2018
Ferrari	F40	269500.00	Dark Purple	2018
Jaguar	XK120	68500.00	Dark Purple	2018
Mercedes	350SL	33600.00	Dark Purple	2018
Morgan	Plus 4	18500.00	Pink	2018
Noble	M600	45950.00	Dark Purple	2018
Triumph	TR4	6590.00	Dark Purple	2018
Alfa Romeo	Giulietta	21500.00	Dark purple	2017
Austin	Lichfield	6500.00	Pink	2017
Mercedes	350SL	32675.00	Dark Purple	2017
Porsche	944	15750.00	Pink	2017

Figure 12.16: Using a subquery to exclude data

How it Works

This query extends the concepts that you have seen so far in this chapter. It also tries to show that what appears to be complex or convoluted SQL is, in fact, quite simple.

If you look at the preceding SQL, you can see that it breaks down into two main elements:

First: Create a subquery that uses the tables required to find the colors of cars sold in 2015.

Second: The outer query joins a series of tables so that you can use the MakeName, ModelName, Color, SalePrice and SaleDate fields. This outer query has a WHERE clause to use the subquery as a filter. So, the code must make the Color field accessible in both inner and outer queries, as this is the field that is used for the filter.

Once you have defined these queries, it is simply a question of using the output from the subquery (the colors of vehicle sold in 2015) and *excluding* it from the result that the outer query returns. You do this by using the *NOT IN* operator in the WHERE clause of the outer query. So, what you have done is say, "find me sales where the cars sold are *not* in the colors sold in 2015."

So, a query that seems long and complex is, in fact, relatively simple once you break it down into its constituent parts. Here, as in most SQL, it is largely a question of ensuring that a query or subquery can access *all* the required fields by ensuring that *all* the necessary tables are joined in the FROM clause of each query. This means that the field used to include or exclude records in the outer query must be accessible in both queries.

Tricks and Traps

To finish this introduction to simple subqueries, you should take note of the following:

- Once again, if a subquery is returning potentially more than one element—and because we are asking for four countries, we hope that more than one element is returned—you *cannot* use equals or not equals (=, !=, or <>); you have to use the IN keyword. Then you make it negative by adding NOT to the IN. This way you are excluding from the outer query an element returned from the subquery.

9. Multiple Nested Subqueries

The only downside to making senior managers happy is that it generates even more work for you. This time the sales manager wants you find the top five vehicles sold by value in the color of the most expensive car sold. The following piece of SQL does exactly this:

```
SELECT     MK.MakeName, MD.ModelName, SD.SalePrice

FROM       make AS MK

JOIN       model AS MD USING(MakeID)

JOIN       stock AS ST USING(ModelID)

JOIN       salesdetails SD ON ST.StockCode = SD.StockID

JOIN       sales AS SA USING(SalesID)

WHERE      Color IN (SELECT     ST.Color

                     FROM       model AS MD

                     JOIN       stock AS ST USING(ModelID)
```

```
JOIN        salesdetails SD

            ON ST.StockCode = SD.StockID

WHERE       SD.SalePrice =

                (

                SELECT  MAX(SD.SalePrice)

                FROM    salesdetails SD

                JOIN    sales SA

                        USING(SalesID)

                )

            )

ORDER BY    SD.SalePrice DESC

LIMIT 5;
```

Running this query gives the results that you can see in Figure 12.17.

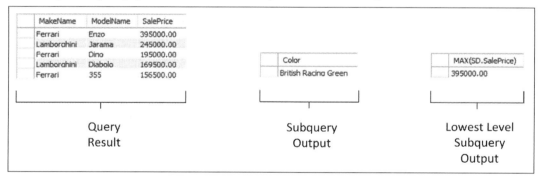

Figure 12.17: A query containing nested subqueries

How it Works

Answering some questions can require more complex queries. This is where MySQL's ability to "nest" subqueries inside subqueries can help you find a solution to even quite tricky problems. The current query is an example of this kind of approach because it contains a subquery inside another subquery. As is often the case with subqueries, it is easiest to start on the inside with the deepest nested subquery and then work outward to explain the SQL.

The innermost (or lowest level) query:	Joins the Sales and SalesDetails tables and returns the highest sale price for a vehicle sold.
The middle (or intermediate) subquery:	Uses the sale price from the deepest nested subquery as a filter (in its WHERE clause) to find any vehicles that have been sold at this price. It then returns the colors of this vehicle, or vehicles.
The outer query:	Lists the Make, Model, and Sale Price for all the vehicles sold in the color returned by the middle subquery. Note that the WHERE clause uses IN and not = (equals) because there is potentially *more than one vehicle of this color returned by the intermediate query.*

When faced with a challenge such as "Find the Top Five Vehicles Sold by Value in the Color of the Most Expensive Car Sold," the hard part can be to analyze the question and then break the solution down into separate parts that can then be answered as separate SQL queries. In these cases, our advice is to look hard at the question before starting to write any SQL. Often the code itself is easier than the analysis—and if the initial analysis is correct, then you are likely to write simpler and better SQL.

Because the concept of using nested subqueries can seem a little daunting at first glance, take a look at Figure 12.18. Here you can see how each query uses the output from the query at a lower level to filter the data that it, in turn, passes up to the query above it. Finally, the topmost query returns the required result.

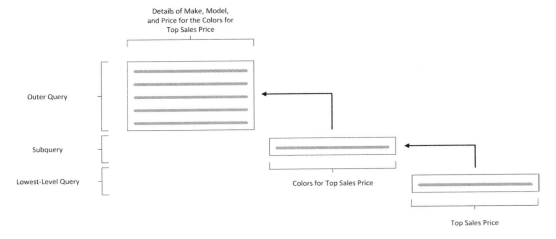

Figure 12.18: Using subqueries to filter data progressively

Tricks and Traps

This approach is best applied when you bear the following points in mind:

- MySQL can nest subqueries to multiple levels. However, this can result in very slow queries—so be warned!

- As you can see in this example, you can easily end up repeating table joins in nested subqueries. This is perfectly normal considering that—as I have mentioned—each query is completely independent of the others.

10. Filtering across Queries and Subqueries

In your analytical career you will probably have to produce reports that do not look at a dataset in its entirety. The following SQL snippet returns each make sold in 2015, along with the total sales figure per make for 2015, and the percentage that this represents of the total sales for that year only.

```
SELECT      MK.MakeName

            ,SUM(SD.SalePrice) AS SalePrice

            ,SUM(SD.SalePrice) /

                        (SELECT     SUM(SD.SalePrice)

                         FROM       SalesDetails SD

                         JOIN       Sales AS SA USING(SalesID)

                         WHERE      YEAR(SaleDate) = 2015

                        ) AS SalesRatio

FROM        make AS MK

JOIN        model AS MD USING(MakeID)

JOIN        stock AS ST USING(ModelID)

JOIN        salesdetails SD ON ST.StockCode = SD.StockID

JOIN        sales AS SA USING(SalesID)

WHERE       YEAR(SA.SaleDate) = 2015

GROUP BY    MK.MakeName;
```

Running this query gives the results that you can see in Figure 12.19—where you can also see the result of the subquery.

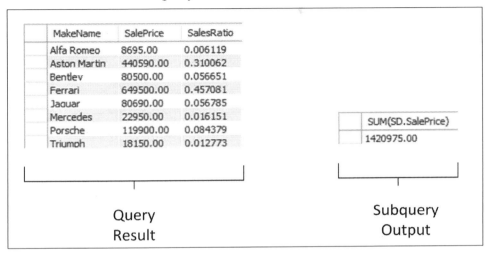

MakeName	SalePrice	SalesRatio
Alfa Romeo	8695.00	0.006119
Aston Martin	440590.00	0.310062
Bentley	80500.00	0.056651
Ferrari	649500.00	0.457081
Jaguar	80690.00	0.056785
Mercedes	22950.00	0.016151
Porsche	119900.00	0.084379
Triumph	18150.00	0.012773

SUM(SD.SalePrice)
1420975.00

Query
Result

Subquery
Output

Figure 12.19: Applying filters to subqueries

How it Works

As you saw earlier in this chapter, a classic analytical requirement is comparing the whole with its constituent parts. Sometimes, however, you need to compare a subset of data with another subset. You do this by applying separate filters to both the main/outer query *and* the subquery (which some people call the inner query). So even if this query does provoke a sense of Déjà vu (it is quite similar to the query that you saw in Section 2), nonetheless, there is a major difference. Each query has a *separate* WHERE clause.

The subquery	Finds the figure for the total sales for 2015.
The outer query	Finds the sales per make for 2015. It then divides this by the total sales figure for the same year to display the percentage sales per make for the year.

I prefer to explain the subquery first, since SQL queries nearly always work from the inside to the outside, and not the other way around. The subquery is calculated first, and it returns the *total* sales for 2015. This query merely provides the total figure with no subsetting of data. It joins the necessary tables (only Sales and SalesDetails are needed to find the annual total) and calculates the SUM() of the sale price field. The outer query finds the sales for each make for the same year and then divides the sales for each make by the yearly total, giving the percentage of sales by value for each make. The outer query needs to return not only the sales total (from the SalesDetails table) but also the year (from the Sales table); it also needs to return the makes of car sold. Consequently, it needs to add joins to the Stock and Make tables.

The really important thing to take away from this example is that each query is truly independent of the other. So, if you want to compare the sales by make for a given year with the total sales for the same year, you must apply *an identical* filter (that is, set the year to be 2015) in both queries.

Tricks and Traps

Obviously, you need to bear a few key points in mind when filtering multiple data sets like this:

- The subquery shown here follows all the same rules and restrictions as the subqueries that you saw earlier in this chapter.

- The fact that the queries are completely independent can work to your advantage by making querying really fluid. For instance, if you want to compare the sales per make for a given year to the total for all vehicles ever sold, all you have to do is omit the WHERE clause from the subquery. The subquery then calculates the value of all cars ever sold by the company, which you still use in the outer query to calculate the percentages of sales per make.

- Remember to test the subquery and to ensure that it gives the result that you expect before you rely blindly on the output that it sends up to the outer query.

- If you are filtering inner and outer queries, you need to pay particular attention to the filters that you apply and ensure that you are using similar filters in both queries if you are attempting to use comparable datasets.

11. Applying Separate Filters to the Subquery and the Main Query

"Like for Like" comparisons are a mainstay of business analysis. Like most companies that make their margin by buying and selling, Prestige Cars needs to see if sales are up or down compared to previous years. Specifically, the CEO wants to see the difference in sale price for each car sold compared to the average price for the previous year. As the following SQL snippet shows, year-on-year sales comparisons are not overly difficult:

```
SELECT     MK.MakeName
           ,MD.ModelName
           ,SD.SalePrice AS ThisYearsSalePrice
           ,SD.SalePrice
             - (SELECT     AVG(SD.SalePrice)
                FROM       stock ST
                JOIN       salesdetails SD
                           ON ST.StockCode = SD.StockID
                JOIN       sales AS SA USING(SalesID)
                WHERE      YEAR(SaleDate) = 2015)
                           AS DeltaToLastYearAverage
FROM       make AS MK
JOIN       model AS MD USING(MakeID)
JOIN       stock AS ST USING(ModelID)
JOIN       salesdetails SD ON ST.StockCode = SD.StockID
JOIN       sales AS SA USING(SalesID)
WHERE      YEAR(SA.SaleDate) = 2016;
```

Running this query gives the results that you can see in Figure 12.20.

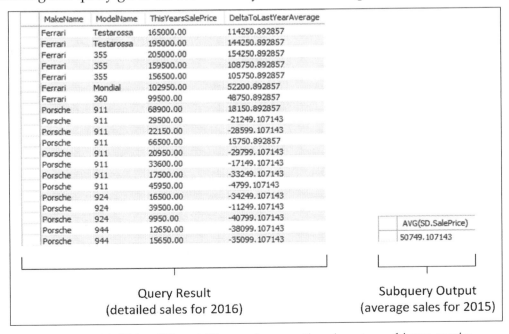

Figure 12.20: Using different filters and aggregations in outer and inner queries

How it Works

Being able to use completely independent queries together is particularly useful when you want to compare data over time. This time the subquery (or the inner query, if you prefer) calculates the average vehicle sale price for *2015*. The outer query, however, filters on *2016*—the following year.

When the outer query returns the list of makes sold in 2016, it calculates for each make the difference between the sale price for 2016 (returned by the outer query) and the average sale price for 2015 (returned by the inner query). This way you can compare data from two separate years.

The fact that the two queries can work together, while remaining completely independent, allows you to see how sales evolve over time from one year to the next.

Tricks and Traps

One important point to remember when applying different filters to queries and subqueries is this:

- Another indication of the fact that subqueries are completely independent of the query that contains them is given by the fact that you can use different filters in each query. In this example, for instance, the outer query uses filters on one year, whereas the subquery uses filters on another year.

Conclusion

In this chapter, you saw how you can nest queries inside queries to deliver far-reaching analytics. As you have learned, a subquery is nothing more than a standard SQL query in its own right. However, the ability to return two or more independent datasets inside a single query opens up the road to much more advanced comparative analysis of your data. You can compare data at different levels of aggregation and calculate percentages of a total with a minimum of effort. Subqueries also let you isolate data in many subtle and surprising ways and can, consequently, help you deliver deeper insights into your data.

Core Knowledge Learned in This Chapter

The concepts and techniques that you have seen in this chapter are

- A subquery is completely independent of the outer query.
- You can refer to the subquery in the SELECT, WHERE, or HAVING clauses of the outer query.
- You must enclose a subquery in parenthesis.
- A subquery must include a SELECT clause and a FROM clause.
- A subquery can include optional WHERE, GROUP BY, and HAVING clauses.
- You can use subqueries to include or exclude data.
- If a subquery returns more than one record, then you *have* to use the IN operator in the WHERE or HAVING clause of the outer query.
- You can nest subqueries inside other subqueries.

CHAPTER 13
Derived Tables

> *Some analytical challenges require you to combine different types of query to get the result that you are looking for. You may need to compare data at different levels of aggregation or carry out calculations that mix and match different ways of grouping data. For these types of problem, SQL has a clear answer—derived tables.*

What Is a Derived Table?

Derived tables let you focus on producing complex datasets inside a single query. You can then use this data to solve your analytical conundrum. As you see during the course of this chapter, whenever you are faced with a challenge that seems to require different types of SQL queries at the same time, it can help to think in terms of derived tables. This is not only because they deliver a technical answer; they also help you analyze a problem by breaking it down into smaller, separate components. This, in turn, assists you in constructing the code that can produce the result that you need.

A derived table is, in many ways, a subquery. However, it is also often the "engine room" where most of the hard work is done. After the work is complete, the derived query may pass its output to the outer query that shapes and presents the final dataset.

Indeed, trying to carry out certain kinds of calculations and aggregations without a derived table is extremely difficult—both conceptually and practically. So, in this chapter, you learn how to use derived tables to

- Define calculated metrics that you can reuse several times without having to redefine the calculation each time

- Create your own ad-hoc classifications that you can use to group data

- Analyze ratios for subgroups of data

- Mix different data sources that have differing levels of data aggregation, such as monthly budgets and daily sales

- Compare values across years

- Isolate maximum, minimum, and average values and use them to analyze data that you have classified

- Filter datasets based on the first or last records output from a derived table

The aim of this chapter is to enhance and extend the knowledge that you have already acquired so far in this book. I also hope to introduce you to ways of juggling data that not only extend your SQL skills but also start you on the road to thinking in datasets as a way of solving analytical challenges.

1. Using a Derived Table to Create Intermediate Calculations

There is no point in being in business unless you are making a profit—at least that is what the boss of Prestige Cars maintains. She wants a printout of the sales, costs, and gross and net profit for every car sold. Fortunately, MySQL makes delivering this kind of output easy, as the following code shows:

```
SELECT

 MakeName

,ModelName

,SaleDate

,SalePrice

,Cost

,SalePrice - IFNULL(Cost, 0) AS GrossProfit

,SalePrice - IFNULL(Cost, 0) - IFNULL(DirectCosts, 0)

        - IFNULL(LineItemDiscount, 0)
```

```
          AS NetProfit
FROM
(
  SELECT
   MK.MakeName
  ,MD.ModelName
  ,SA.SaleDate
  ,SD.SalePrice
  ,ST.Cost
  ,IFNULL(SD.LineItemDiscount, 0) AS LineItemDiscount
  ,(IFNULL(ST.RepairsCost, 0) + IFNULL(ST.PartsCost, 0)
  + IFNULL(ST.TransportInCost, 0)) AS DirectCosts
  FROM      make AS MK
  JOIN      model AS MD USING(MakeID)
  JOIN      stock AS ST USING(ModelID)
  JOIN       salesdetails SD ON ST.StockCode = SD.StockID
  JOIN       sales AS SA USING(SalesID)
) AS DT;
```

Running this query gives the results that you can see in Figure 13.1.

MakeName	ModelName	SaleDate	SalePrice	Cost	GrossProfit	NetProfit
Ferrari	Davtona	2018-03-08 00:00:00	99500.00	79600.0000	19900.0000	17150.0000
Ferrari	Davtona	2018-12-31 00:00:00	145000.00	116000.0000	29000.0000	18100.0000
Ferrari	Testarossa	2016-01-01 08:00:00	165000.00	132000.0000	33000.0000	19900.0000
Ferrari	Testarossa	2015-05-28 00:00:00	195000.00	156000.0000	39000.0000	29550.0000
Ferrari	Testarossa	2015-01-02 08:00:00	65000.00	52000.0000	13000.0000	5875.0000
Ferrari	Testarossa	2016-07-25 10:00:00	195000.00	156000.0000	39000.0000	29950.0000
Ferrari	Testarossa	2017-09-20 12:32:00	250000.00	200000.0000	50000.0000	45350.0000
Ferrari	355	2017-09-20 16:33:00	155000.00	124000.0000	31000.0000	18550.0000
Ferrari	355	2016-07-25 00:00:00	205000.00	164000.0000	41000.0000	29050.0000
Ferrari	355	2017-01-12 18:57:00	125950.00	100760.0000	25190.0000	-710.0000
Ferrari	355	2015-05-10 00:00:00	169500.00	135600.0000	33900.0000	24250.0000
Ferrari	355	2015-01-25 00:00:00	220000.00	176000.0000	44000.0000	-25650.0000
Ferrari	355	2016-01-01 00:00:00	159500.00	127600.0000	31900.0000	24800.0000
Ferrari	355	2016-09-19 00:00:00	156500.00	125200.0000	31300.0000	24000.0000

Figure 13.1: A derived table that creates intermediate calculations

How it Works

It sometimes gets a little laborious to code financial analysis with SQL. The speed at which MySQL can perform calculations on a large set of data is rarely a problem. However, as you have seen in previous examples, because you are required to repeat field names over and over as you create intermediate and final calculations, the process can get rather wearing.

Fortunately, there is a convenient way to minimize the repetitive use of field names. Start by creating a core query that carries out any basic analysis. You can then use the results of these calculations in the outer query without having to repeat the initial arithmetic.

In this example, the derived table (which has the alias DT in the preceding code) calculates the direct costs associated with a sale by adding up the total for the cost of repairs, parts, and transport. This inner query also ensures that any NULLs in the data are handled at the source to avoid them falsifying the results. It does this by applying the IFNULL() function to any numeric field that may contain NULL values. The derived table joins all the tables that we need to output the make, model, date of sale, selling price, and vehicle cost. To see this more clearly, take a look at Figure 13.2, which displays part of the output from the derived table.

	MakeName	ModelName	SaleDate	SalePrice	Cost	LineItemDiscount	DirectCosts
▶	Ferrari	Daytona	2018-03-08 00:00:00	99500.00	79600.0000	0.00	2750.0000
	Ferrari	Daytona	2018-12-31 00:00:00	145000.00	116000.0000	5000.00	5900.0000
	Ferrari	Testarossa	2016-01-01 08:00:00	165000.00	132000.0000	5000.00	8100.0000
	Ferrari	Testarossa	2015-05-28 00:00:00	195000.00	156000.0000	0.00	9450.0000
	Ferrari	Testarossa	2015-01-02 08:00:00	65000.00	52000.0000	2700.00	4425.0000
	Ferrari	Testarossa	2016-07-25 10:00:00	195000.00	156000.0000	0.00	9050.0000
	Ferrari	Testarossa	2017-09-20 12:32:00	250000.00	200000.0000	0.00	4650.0000
	Ferrari	355	2017-09-20 16:33:00	155000.00	124000.0000	500.00	11950.0000
	Ferrari	355	2016-07-25 00:00:00	205000.00	164000.0000	0.00	11950.0000
	Ferrari	355	2017-01-12 18:57:00	125950.00	100760.0000	12500.00	13400.0000
	Ferrari	355	2015-05-10 00:00:00	169500.00	135600.0000	0.00	9650.0000
	Ferrari	355	2015-01-25 00:00:00	220000.00	176000.0000	60000.00	9650.0000
	Ferrari	355	2016-01-01 00:00:00	159500.00	127600.0000	0.00	7100.0000
	Ferrari	355	2016-09-19 00:00:00	156500.00	125200.0000	0.00	7300.0000
	Ferrari	Dino	2018-04-24 00:00:00	195000.00	156000.0000	0.00	11950.0000
	Ferrari	Dino	2018-03-08 00:00:00	123500.00	98800.0000	750.00	4425.0000

Figure 13.2: The output from a derived table

As you can see, the columns that are returned are not the same in the derived table as they are in the outer query. Nonetheless, the columns in the derived table are the basis for any data that is output by the outer query. More specifically, the calculation is carried out in the derived table.

In cases like this, a derived table is a *query in a query*. More precisely, it is a *completely independent piece of SQL* that feeds its output into an outer query that wraps around the derived table. In this example, you can see that the outer query has a FROM clause that does not directly use a table or a set of joined tables. Instead, the outer query refers to a self-sufficient query (the derived table or inner query) to isolate a dataset. This dataset is then used as the data source for the outer query.

The outer query is a straightforward list of the fields that are in the SELECT clause of the derived table. These fields are then extended with a couple of simple calculations to deliver both the gross profit and the net profit.

You could achieve the final calculation of gross and net profit without using a derived table. However, in this case, the query that returns the gross and net profit looks like this:

```
,SD.SalePrice - ST.Cost - (IFNULL(ST.RepairsCost, 0) + IFNULL(ST.
PartsCost, 0) + IFNULL(ST.TransportInCost, 0)) AS GrossProfit
```

```
,SD.SalePrice - ST.Cost - (IFNULL(ST.RepairsCost, 0) + IFNULL(ST.
PartsCost, 0) + IFNULL(ST.TransportInCost, 0) + IFNULL(LineItemDiscount,
0)) AS NetProfit
```

Although this code is not difficult to write, it is more laborious and certainly more repetitive; it is also possibly a greater source of potential errors precisely *because* of its repetitive nature. Defining a derived table not only removes the need to repeat fields (as well as their NULL handling code), it also makes any additional calculations you have to apply to these fields easier.

The derived table we use in this example shows the two basic techniques used to define a derived table:

Enclosed in parentheses	A derived table *must* be enclosed in parentheses. If you forget the parentheses, you get an error message. Think of them as isolating and enclosing the derived table and making it into a separate self-contained table.
Must have an alias	A derived table *must* have an alias. In this example, the derived table is given the alias DT. You can use this alias just as you would use the alias for any "normal" table in a SQL query.

Visualizing a concept can often make it easier to understand, so take a look at Figure 13.3 to see how a derived table works from a high level.

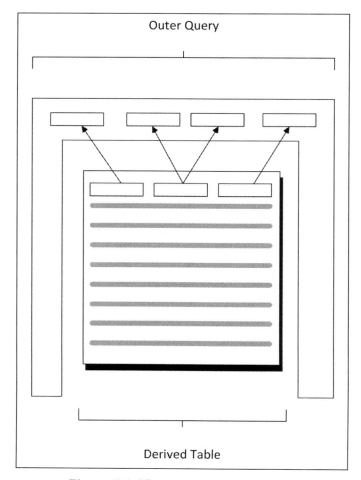

Figure 13.3: *The concept of a derived table*

This technique is similar to the way you might use a spreadsheet to perform financial arithmetic. In a spreadsheet, you carry out basic arithmetic in multiple cells to get an intermediate result that you then use for other calculations. The principle is similar when you use a derived table in SQL:

First: You carry out any essential calculations in a derived table and give the result an alias.

Then: You use the derived table as the basis for any further calculations in the outer query.

Tricks and Traps

Derived tables are a fundamental concept in SQL, so there are, perhaps inevitably, several key points to remember when you begin to use them in your analysis:

- When you use a derived table in a FROM clause, you must include *all* the fields that you wish to return from the outer query in the SELECT clause of the inner derived table. This is because the derived table is the source of *all* the data that is accessible to the outer query. Consequently, you must ensure that *every* field that you want to output from the overall code is part of the inner SELECT clause. If you forget to include a field in the derived table and then try to select it in the main query, MySQL returns an error message. Adding the field to the derived table normally solves this problem.

- A derived table *must* have an alias.

- Another advantage of beginning with a derived table when calculating metrics is that you only have to handle potential NULLs once—in the derived table at the heart of the query.

- Another factor that argues in favor of using a derived table to simplify calculations is that if a core calculation changes, you only make the change *once* in the derived table (just like in a spreadsheet). Any modifications ripple up through the rest of the query. Without a derived table, you have to make the change *every time* the calculation is repeated in the query.

- It is important to ensure that *every field* in a derived table has a name. MySQL does *not* add a name (such as "Column 1") if you forget to add an alias. Indeed, the query does not work if any calculated fields (such as SalePrice and GrossProfit in this example) are not given aliases.

- The AS keyword that introduces the derived table alias is not strictly necessary, but it is good practice to use it, so we have kept it, even if the query would work without it.

2. Grouping and Ordering Data Using a Custom Classification

Suppose the CEO decides that she wants you to classify all your customers by spend. You realize that what she really wants is five categories of customer (tiny, small, medium, large, and mega-rich) according to a series of thresholds of total sales per customer. Then she wants the total spend for customers in each of these spending brackets.

This sounds complicated. Yet we can do it with only a few lines of SQL and the clever use of a derived table:

```
SELECT      DT.CustomerClassification

            ,COUNT(DT.CustomerSpend) AS CustomerCount

FROM

        (

        SELECT      SUM(SD.SalePrice) AS CustomerSpend

        ,SA.CustomerID

        ,CASE

         WHEN SUM(SD.SalePrice) <= 100000 THEN 'Tiny'

         WHEN SUM(SD.SalePrice) BETWEEN 100001 AND 200000

                            THEN 'Small'

         WHEN SUM(SD.SalePrice) BETWEEN 200001 AND 300000

                            THEN 'Medium'

         WHEN SUM(SD.SalePrice) BETWEEN 300001 AND 400000

                            THEN 'Large'

         WHEN SUM(SD.SalePrice) > 400000 THEN 'Mega Rich'

        END AS CustomerClassification

        FROM        salesdetails SD

                    JOIN sales AS SA USING(SalesID)

        GROUP BY    SA.CustomerID

        ) AS DT

GROUP BY    DT.CustomerClassification

ORDER BY    DT.CustomerSpend DESC;
```

Running this query gives the results that you can see in Figure 13.4.

CustomerSpend	CustomerID	CustomerClassification
602850.00	0001	Mega Rich
348950.00	0002	Large
469740.00	0003	Mega Rich
172500.00	0004	Small
201050.00	0005	Medium
316450.00	0006	Large
228500.00	0007	Medium
511675.00	0008	Mega Rich
428000.00	0009	Mega Rich
266500.00	0010	Medium
305950.00	0011	Large
393980.00	0012	Large
497190.00	0013	Mega Rich
361995.00	0014	Large

CustomerClassification	CustomerCount
Mega Rich	18
Large	11
Medium	15
Small	16
Tiny	27

Derived
Table
Output

Query
Result

Figure 13.4: *An aggregated derived table feeding into a separate outer aggregation*

How it Works

It is said that a problem shared is a problem halved. In the case of SQL queries, a problem broken down into smaller parts is often a problem that has become much easier to solve. Using derived tables is a fundamental technique for breaking down seemingly complex challenges into smaller and more comprehensible solutions. This piece of SQL is an example of how a derived table can help you break down analytical tasks into their component parts.

Consequently (as is the case with much SQL), the logic of this code begins at the center and works its way outward. The overall query does two things:

The inner query   Takes the data from the Sales and SalesDetails tables and finds the total value of sales per customer. This query then uses a CASE statement to test the total value of sales for each customer and places each one in one of five custom categories—from the tiny customers to the mega-rich ones. In this kind of statistical query, we do not need to see the customer name because we are not interested in detail-level analysis. We can group on the CustomerID field from the SalesDetails table, and we do not need to refer to the Customer table for any customer data.

The outer query   Aggregates the results of the derived table by counting the number of customers in each category and grouping on the category itself (the field that has been given the alias CustomerClassification). Finally, it sorts the categories in descending order of customer spend–even if this field does not appear in the SELECT clause it can be used as it is defined in the derived table.

As you can see, the main element in this piece of code is the derived table (the inner query), where the core aggregation is carried out. Indeed, you can run the derived table separately if you wish. You can do this by selecting *only* the SQL inside the parentheses, from SELECT SUM(SA.SalePrice) to GROUP BY SA.CustomerID. This way, you can check that the inner query gives you the result that you expect—something like the output from the derived table shown earlier in Figure 13.4.

Now that you can see the output from the derived table, hopefully you have a clearer understanding of the way that the overall query works. The derived table has let you create a classification of your entire customer base where each customer is categorized. The main query then groups and sorts this data to produce the final result set that shows the spend for customers in each classification "bucket."

Tricks and Traps

I have one comment to make here.

- The ranges that you define need to be adjacent but not overlapping. The ranges defined in this query work with integer values. If you were using decimals, you would need to write something like: BETWEEN 100000.01 AND 200000.

3. Joining Derived Tables to Other Tables

When you are buying and selling, it can help to see how an article compares to others in its category. Specifically, say you have decided that you want to look at the purchase and selling price of each vehicle that has been sold and see how this data maps to the average cost and sale price for every similar model. This is all in a day's work for SQL.

```
SELECT      ST.DateBought, MK.MakeName, MD.ModelName, ST.Color

            ,ST.Cost, SD.SalePrice, DT.AveragePurchasePrice

            ,DT.AverageSalePrice

FROM

        (

        SELECT      MakeName

                    ,ModelName

                    ,AVG(Cost) AS AveragePurchasePrice

                    ,AVG(SalePrice) AS AverageSalePrice

        FROM        make AS MK1

        JOIN        model AS MD1 USING(MakeID)

        JOIN        stock AS ST1 USING(ModelID)

        JOIN        salesdetails SD1

                    ON ST1.StockCode = SD1.StockID

        GROUP BY    MakeName, ModelName

        ) AS DT

JOIN        make AS MK

            ON MK.MakeName = DT.MakeName

JOIN        model AS MD

            ON MK.MakeID = MD.MakeID

JOIN        stock AS ST USING(ModelID)

JOIN        salesdetails SD ON ST.StockCode = SD.StockID

ORDER BY    MakeName, ModelName, DateBought;
```

Running this query gives the results that you can see in Figure 13.5.

	DateBought	MakeName	ModelName	Color	Cost	SalePrice	AveragePurchasePrice	AverageSalePrice
▶	2017-11-11	Alfa Romeo	1750	Blue	7960.0000	9950.00	5410.00000000	6762.500000
	2018-06-01	Alfa Romeo	1750	Black	2860.0000	3575.00	5410.00000000	6762.500000
	2015-07-10	Alfa Romeo	Giulia	Red	6956.0000	8695.00	8969.50000000	11211.875000
	2016-01-02	Alfa Romeo	Giulia	British Racing Green	2040.0000	2550.00	8969.50000000	11211.875000
	2016-02-10	Alfa Romeo	Giulia	British Racing Green	4800.0000	6000.00	8969.50000000	11211.875000
	2016-05-02	Alfa Romeo	Giulia	Green	14000.0000	17500.00	8969.50000000	11211.875000
	2016-07-03	Alfa Romeo	Giulia	British Racing Green	10000.0000	12500.00	8969.50000000	11211.875000
	2017-10-29	Alfa Romeo	Giulia	Black	20000.0000	25000.00	8969.50000000	11211.875000
	2017-11-01	Alfa Romeo	Giulia	Black	8400.0000	10500.00	8969.50000000	11211.875000
	2018-07-01	Alfa Romeo	Giulia	Black	5560.0000	6950.00	8969.50000000	11211.875000
	2017-02-04	Alfa Romeo	Giulietta	Dark purple	17200.0000	21500.00	10536.00000000	13170.000000
	2017-05-15	Alfa Romeo	Giulietta	Blue	5200.0000	6500.00	10536.00000000	13170.000000
	2018-01-01	Alfa Romeo	Giulietta	Night Blue	9240.0000	11550.00	10536.00000000	13170.000000
	2018-03-01	Alfa Romeo	Giulietta	Night Blue	4552.0000	5690.00	10536.00000000	13170.000000
	2018-05-01	Alfa Romeo	Giulietta	Blue	14800.0000	18500.00	10536.00000000	13170.000000
	2018-07-01	Alfa Romeo	Giulietta	Black	8400.0000	10500.00	10536.00000000	13170.000000

Figure 13.5: A derived table that is part of a complex join clause

How it Works

MySQL considers derived tables to be just like any "ordinary" tables that exist in a database. This means that you can collate or aggregate data from one or more tables to obtain a derived table and then join the result to another table, or tables, just as you would for any database table.

This is particularly useful when you need to aggregate data and include the *aggregated* result in a query that contains *non-aggregated data*. This example shows how a single query can show—for every sale—the average selling price for that model of car. This opens up a whole spectrum of analytical possibilities that allow you to put each sale into perspective and see how it compares to other, similar sales.

This example differs from those that you have seen so far in this chapter in that it does not have an inner and outer query structure. Instead, it contains a series of table joins, which are

Standard joins	Using regular database tables to return the cost and sale price for every model of car sold.
A derived table join	Where a derived table is joined to existing tables in the query.

The derived table is interesting because it operates on a different level of data granularity than the other tables. More precisely, the derived table is an aggregation that calculates the average cost and selling price of each model of car. The derived table is then joined to the Make and Model tables in the main query perfectly normally.

Because the SQL that underlies this example is a little complex at first sight, take a look at Figure 13.6, which is a visual representation of the joins—including the joins to the derived table.

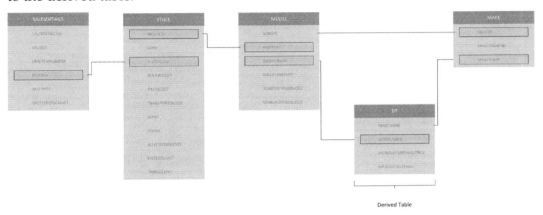

Derived Table

Figure 13.6: *Visualizing a complex join using a derived table*

To help you understand how this works, take a look at Figure 13.7. In it, you can see the output from the derived table (aliased as DT in the SQL code that you used to obtain this output).

MakeName	ModelName	AveragePurchasePrice	AverageSalePrice
Alfa Romeo	1750	5410.00000000	6762.500000
Alfa Romeo	Giulia	8969.50000000	11211.875000
Alfa Romeo	Giulietta	10536.00000000	13170.000000
Alfa Romeo	Spider	7696.00000000	9620.000000
Aston Martin	DB2	45644.00000000	57055.000000
Aston Martin	DB4	32194.28571429	40242.857143
Aston Martin	DB5	40045.33333333	50056.666667
Aston Martin	DB6	58234.00000000	72792.500000
Aston Martin	DB9	51173.33333333	63966.666667
Aston Martin	Rapide	60500.00000000	75625.000000
Aston Martin	Vanquish	41261.71428571	51577.142857
Aston Martin	Vantage	68700.00000000	85875.000000
Aston Martin	Virage	71909.33333333	89886.666667
Austin	Cambridge	18000.00000000	22500.000000

Figure 13.7: *The output from an aggregated derived table*

What is really interesting here is that because the derived table isolates data by two fields (make *and* model), it needs to join to the other tables using *both* these fields. This ensures that any model name for which there could be potentially two make names can be uniquely identified. Consequently, the derived table *has* to contain *both* these fields in its SELECT clause; otherwise you cannot join the derived table to the outer query correctly.

The query then outputs fields from any or all of the tables that make up the FROM clause. It is in all other respects a perfectly standard query. However, using the derived table to calculate the average cost and average sale price allows you to show these aggregated figures in the query output and make some interesting comparisons.

Tricks and Traps

When joining derived tables, you need to remember the following:

- We chose to use independent table aliases in the derived query (ST1 for the Stock table, for instance) even if it is possible to use the same aliases in the derived table subquery as those we used in the main query's FROM clause. This is because it is generally easier to understand and debug queries when all the component elements are separately and uniquely identifiable.

- Although we chose to show you a complex join to a derived table, it is also possible to use the derived table to collate all the information required from the Make, Model, Stock and SalesDetails tables and use these in the outer query. Indeed, if you include the ModelID field in the derived table you can join the derived table on this field alone—as the following SQL shows:

```
SELECT  ST.DateBought, DT.MakeName, DT.ModelName, ST.Color
        ,ST.Cost, SD.SalePrice
        ,DT.AveragePurchasePrice, DT.AverageSalePrice
FROM (
        SELECT  ModelID, AVG(Cost) AS AveragePurchasePrice
                ,AVG(SalePrice) AS AverageSalePrice
        FROM    make AS MK1
        JOIN    model AS MD1 USING(MakeID)
        JOIN    stock AS ST1 USING(ModelID)
        JOIN    salesdetails SD1  ON ST1.StockCode = SD1.StockID
        GROUP BY  MakeName, ModelName
        ) AS DT
JOIN    stock AS ST USING(ModelID)
JOIN    salesdetails SD ON ST.StockCode = SD.StockID
ORDER BY  MakeName, ModelName, DateBought;
```

This code will return exactly the same results as the query at the start of this section. This shows you how subtle and interesting SQL can be. It also shows that you can often find more than one valid solution to a challenge.

4. Using Multiple Results from a Derived Table to Filter Data

The sales director has asked you to find all the sales for the top five bestselling makes. A request like this illustrates that some data analysis challenges require you to output a set of records that uses the result of a derived table as a filter.

The (slightly more complex) SQL to solve this problem is as follows:

```
SELECT     MKX.MakeName, SDX.SalePrice
FROM       make AS MKX
JOIN       model AS MDX ON MKX.MakeID = MDX.MakeID
JOIN       stock AS STX ON STX.ModelID = MDX.ModelID
JOIN       salesdetails SDX ON STX.StockCode = SDX.StockID
JOIN       (
           SELECT     MK.MakeName
           FROM       make AS MK
           JOIN       model AS MD USING(MakeID)
           JOIN       stock AS ST USING(ModelID)
           JOIN       salesdetails SD
                      ON ST.StockCode = SD.StockID
           JOIN       sales SA USING(SalesID)
           GROUP BY   MK.MakeName
           ORDER BY   SUM(SA.TotalSalePrice) DESC
           LIMIT 5
           ) SB
ON MKX.MakeName = SB.MakeName
ORDER BY   MakeName, SalePrice DESC;
```

Running this query gives the results that you can see in Figure 13.8, where you can also see the output from the subquery. Although this list contains five makes (Aston Martin, Bentley, Bugatti, Ferrari, and Lamborghini), it is, nonetheless, fairly long. You have to scroll through the output to ensure that only these five makes are displayed.

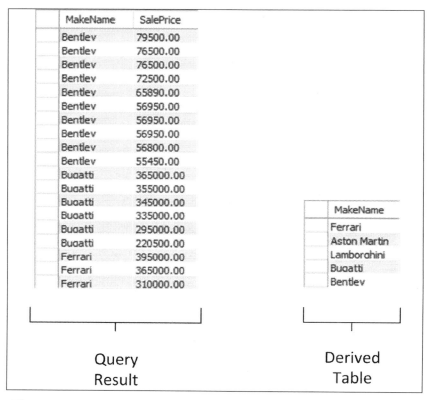

Figure 13.8: *A complex derived table used to restrict data in the outer query*

How it Works

Here you can see how data analysis can be a multistep process. This example shows you how to

First: Use a derived table to find the top five bestselling makes by sale value.

Then: Use this data to filter the results from a simpler "outer" query.

This example is another of those times when a derived table can be a lot more complex—and powerful—than the rest of the query that uses it. Once again, most of the work is done by the derived table.

The derived table	Joins a series of tables so that you can return the make and sale price. It then aggregates sales by make, calculates the total sale price for each make, and finally returns only the top five makes thanks to the LIMIT operator.
The overall query	Uses this result as the filter as it joins the derived table to the Make table on the MakeName field.

It is worth noting that the derived table can be a different type of query to the overall query. In this example, both the overall query and the derived table are aggregate queries. However this does not have to be the case when you are writing your own derived tables.

Tricks and Traps

Handling complex queries like this one inevitably introduces some key points to take away:

- When solving complex analytical problems like this one, you may well find yourself beginning with the derived table (as it contains the key filter for the overall query) and then moving on to the rest of the query.

- You should be able to execute the SQL that defines any derived table independently of the outer query. So, you can select the derived table and execute it at any time, just as you would execute the entire query.

- You can begin a complex query like this by writing the derived table first, if you prefer. That way, you can be sure that it returns the data you need to filter the outer query correctly.

- You can see in this code that we use different aliases in the derived table and the rest of the query, even when the same tables are used. This is not strictly necessary, because the SQL for the derived table and the SQL that joins to the derived table are totally separate. However, I prefer to do this for a couple of reasons:

  o It highlights the fact that you are dealing with two separate queries.

  o It is less confusing to read because you can easily see which field comes from which table.

- More complex queries like this one can take longer to run, so do not be surprised if it takes a while for the results to appear if you are using large datasets.

5. Complex Aggregated Derived Tables

After all the work that you did for the sales director, your reputation as an analyst has hit new heights. Now it is the CEO's turn to request some assistance. She wants to know which makes are generating the most sales, and specifically, how many cars have been sold for the top three bestselling makes. The following code snippet lets you impress her with your SQL abilities:

```
SELECT      MK.MakeName

            ,COUNT(MK.MakeName) AS VehiclesSold

            ,SUM(SD.SalePrice) AS TotalSalesPerMake

FROM        make AS MK

JOIN        model AS MD ON MK.MakeID = MD.MakeID

JOIN        stock AS ST ON ST.ModelID = MD.ModelID

JOIN        salesdetails SD ON ST.StockCode = SD.StockID

JOIN        (

                    SELECT      MK.MakeName

                    FROM        make AS MK

                    JOIN        model AS MD USING(MakeID)

                    JOIN        stock AS ST USING(ModelID)

                    JOIN        salesdetails SD

                                ON ST.StockCode = SD.StockID

                    JOIN        sales AS SA USING(SalesID)

                    GROUP BY    MK.MakeName

                    ORDER BY    COUNT(MK.MakeName) DESC

                    LIMIT 3

            ) DT

ON          DT.MakeName = MK.MakeName

GROUP BY    MK.MakeName

ORDER BY    VehiclesSold DESC;
```

Running this query gives the results that you can see in Figure 13.9.

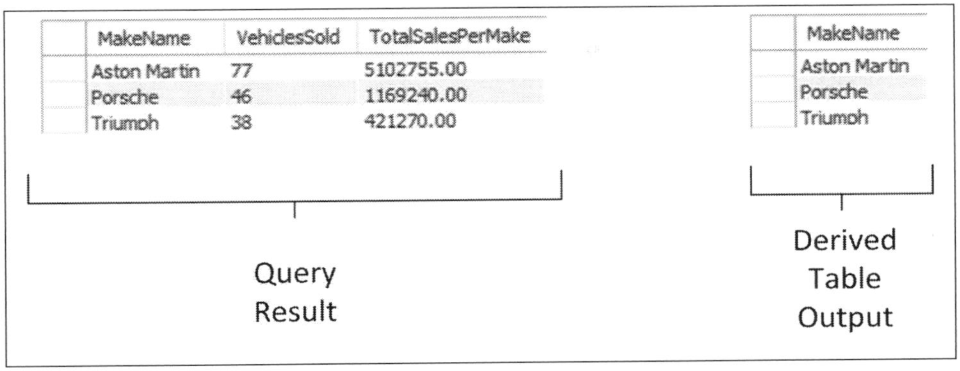

Figure 13.9: Using a complex derived table as a filter in an aggregated query

How it Works

Some queries are really two queries in one. In these cases, derived tables unlock the real power of SQL to allow you to carry out complex filtering that then becomes the basis of further analysis. This example shows that the two queries (the main query and the SQL that produces a derived table) that generate the final result are—and have to be—*totally independent* of one another. Even though the derived table counts the sales per make, you cannot pass this value back to the outer query. You have to count the number of vehicles sold *twice*: once in the *derived table* to act as a filter and once in the *outer query* to display the result.

Otherwise this query is very similar to the previous one. The derived table finds the top three makes sold by quantity. Then these three makes are used as the filter by the outer query.

Tricks and Traps

There are a couple of points to note here:

- In this example, both queries (the "main" query and derived table) aggregate data. As you saw in the previous example, this does not necessarily need to be the case.

- This code applies the *same aliases* for the tables in both the outer query and the derived table. This reinforces the point that the two queries are *completely separate* and that the aliases in the outer query only refer to tables in the outer query and the aliases in the inner query only refer to tables in the inner query—even if the same aliases are used in both queries.

- There is an alternative way to obtain the same result (although I chose to use the method above to illustrate the concept of using complex aggregated derived tables). So, if it is only the result that interests you, the following SQL returns exactly the same output:

```
SELECT    MK.MakeName, COUNT(MK.MakeName) AS VehiclesSold

          ,SUM(SD.SalePrice) AS TotalSalesPerMake

FROM      make AS MK

JOIN      model AS MD USING(MakeID)

JOIN      stock AS ST USING(ModelID)

JOIN      salesdetails SD  ON ST.StockCode = SD.StockID

JOIN      sales AS SA USING(SalesID)

GROUP BY  MK.MakeName

ORDER BY  COUNT(MK.MakeName) DESC

LIMIT     3;
```

The trick here is to sort on the COUNT() of makes in the ORDER BY clause.

6. Joining Multiple Derived Tables

Continuing with the theme of comparisons, let's suppose that you want to see which colors sell the most. Indeed, you want not only to produce this kind of analysis but also find the percentage of cars purchased by value for each color of vehicle. The following SQL does this for you:

```
SELECT

TOT.PurchaseYear

,AGG.Color

,(AGG.CostPerYear / TOT.TotalPurchasePrice) * 100

          AS PercentPerColorPerYear

FROM

    (

      SELECT      Color
```

```
              ,SUM(Cost) AS CostPerYear

              ,YEAR(DateBought) AS YearBought

   FROM       stock


   GROUP BY   Color

              ,YEAR(DateBought)

   ) AGG

JOIN

   (

   SELECT     YEAR(DateBought) AS PurchaseYear, SUM(Cost)

              AS TotalPurchasePrice

   FROM       stock

   GROUP BY   YEAR(DateBought)

   ) TOT

ON TOT.PurchaseYear = AGG.YearBought

ORDER BY PurchaseYear, PercentPerColorPerYear DESC
```

Running this query gives the results that you can see in Figure 13.10.

PurchaseYear	Color	PercentPerColorPerYear
2015	Black	24.38950354
2015	Red	16.76394006
2015	British Racing Green	12.68397680
2015	Blue	11.56636765
2015	Night Blue	10.56465872
2015	Silver	10.28910006
2015	Green	8.53877039
2015	Canary Yellow	5.20368279
2016	Black	29.10594596
2016	Red	12.04842378
2016	Blue	11.32712530
2016	British Racing Green	9.25362042
2016	Green	9.05275248
2016	Silver	7.66411595

Figure 13.10: Using two separate derived tables in a query

How it Works

This query requires you to produce two completely different aggregations and then use them together to deliver the final result.

The first aggregation	Is the total cost of vehicles purchased for each year for each color
The second aggregation	Is the total cost of purchases per year

Using derived tables allows you to handle each aggregation as a separate derived table. Before going any further, it is probably worth taking a look at the output from each of the derived tables so that you can see what each one is doing. Figure 13.11 illustrates how multiple derived tables relate to an outer query. Once again, I hope that this simple illustration makes the concept clearer.

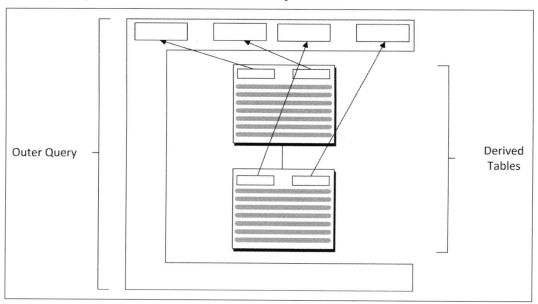

Figure 13.11: *Derived tables and the outer query*

The first derived table (aliased as AGG in this example) shows the year, color, and cost per year for each color of vehicle bought. If you select just the SQL for the first of the two derived tables, you see output similar to that in Figure 13.12.

Color	CostPerYear	YearBought
Black	494944.0000	2015
Black	1275128.0000	2016
Black	2534800.0000	2017
Black	1816476.0000	2018
Blue	234720.0000	2015
Blue	496240.0000	2016
Blue	574696.0000	2017
Blue	807680.0000	2018
British Racing Green	257400.0000	2015
British Racing Green	405400.0000	2016
British Racing Green	749672.0000	2017
British Racing Green	403108.0000	2018
Canary Yellow	105600.0000	2015
Canary Yellow	256456.0000	2016

Figure 13.12: The output from an aggregated derived table

This derived table only needs a single table– the Stock table. Then all it does is aggregate the result by year and color and return the total vehicle cost for all available combinations of these two fields.

Running the second of the derived table queries (aliased as TOT in the SQL code for this section) shows you the data that you can see in Figure 13.13.

PurchaseYear	TotalPurchasePrice
2015	2029332.0000
2016	4380988.0000
2017	7083824.0000
2018	6265020.0000

Figure 13.13: The output from a high-level aggregated derived table

This high-level aggregated derived table also needs only the Stock table to produce the annual cost of cars that have been purchased.

These two derived tables both output the Year field. Consequently, the overall query can use this field to join the two derived tables. Once the derived tables are constructed and joined, you can treat this query just like any other query and use the fields it contains to analyze your data.

In this specific example, the year and color fields are output and the cost per color for each year is divided by the total cost for the same timeframe to return the percentage cost of each color for each year.

Finishing the query with an ORDER BY clause allows you to list the result first by year and second in descending order of sales per color. This makes it easy to see which color tops the sales charts each year.

Once again, we use derived tables to break down the problem into component parts. The challenge is to produce two sets of data that aggregate at different "levels." One requires the year and the color, the other only the year. We build the query to handle these different requirements using the flexibility that derived tables bring to analysis with SQL.

What is interesting here is that the query uses nothing but derived tables to carry out its analysis. Once again, each derived table is a completely separate entity that works independently of the other parts of the overall query.

Tricks and Traps

One point needs to be made about joining derived tables:

- Because derived tables are *always* independent entities in a query, you can reuse tables in separate derived tables. Here, for instance, the Stock table is used twice—once in each derived table. Each derived table makes use of the Stock table separately and in different ways.

7. Using Multiple Derived Tables for Complex Aggregations

Good analysis is about seeing the wood for the trees. This is where SQL really shines. The following code lets you create a report for the CEO that lists sales per customer by volume and value. Not only that, but the output is broken down by country and sorted to make it clear who the best customers are in each country. All of this is possible in a single query that produces an analysis of sales ratios per customer per country—as you can see in the following code:

```
SELECT

 DT2.CountryName

,DT2.CustomerName

,DT2.NumberOfCustomerSales

,DT2.TotalCustomerSales

,DT2.NumberOfCustomerSales / DT1.NumberOfCountrySales

      AS PercentageOfCountryCarsSold

,DT2.TotalCustomerSales / DT1.TotalCountrySales
```

```
            AS PercentageOfCountryCarsSoldByValue
FROM
(
    SELECT       CO.CountryName
                 ,COUNT(*) AS NumberOfCountrySales
                 ,SUM(SD.SalePrice) AS TotalCountrySales
    FROM         stock AS ST
    JOIN         salesdetails SD ON ST.StockCode = SD.StockID
    JOIN         sales AS SA USING(SalesID)
    JOIN         customer CU USING(CustomerID)
    JOIN         country CO ON CU.country = CO.CountryISO2
    GROUP BY     CO.CountryName
) AS DT1
JOIN
(
    SELECT       CO.CountryName
                 ,CU.CustomerName
                 ,COUNT(*) AS NumberOfCustomerSales
                 ,SUM(SD.SalePrice) AS TotalCustomerSales
    FROM         stock AS ST
    JOIN         salesdetails SD ON ST.StockCode = SD.StockID
    JOIN         sales AS SA USING(SalesID)
    JOIN         customer CU USING(CustomerID)
    JOIN         country CO ON CU.country = CO.CountryISO2
    GROUP BY     CO.CountryName, CU.CustomerName
) AS DT2
ON       DT1.CountryName = DT2.CountryName
ORDER BY DT1.CountryName, DT2.NumberOfCustomerSales DESC;
```

Running this query gives the results that you can see in Figure 13.14.

CountryName	CustomerName	NumberOfCustomerSales	TotalCustomerSales	PercentageOfCountryCarsSold	PercentageOfCountryCarsSoldByValue
Belgium	Stefan Van Helsing	6	80900.00	0.6000	0.259420
Belgium	Diplomatic Cars	3	224000.00	0.3000	0.718294
Belgium	Flash Voitures	1	6950.00	0.1000	0.022286
France	Vive La Vitesse	13	1269600.00	0.1884	0.215815
France	Laurent Saint Yves	11	1343950.00	0.1594	0.228454
France	SuperSport S.A.R.L.	9	509630.00	0.1304	0.086630
France	M. Pierre Dubois	8	511675.00	0.1159	0.086978
France	La Bagnole de Luxe	6	497190.00	0.0870	0.084516
France	Capots Reluisants S.A.	6	583115.00	0.0870	0.099122
France	Casseroles Chromes	4	201050.00	0.0580	0.034176
France	Mme Anne Duport	3	162650.00	0.0435	0.027648
France	Khader El Ghannam	2	50500.00	0.0290	0.008584
France	Wladimir Lacroix	2	55100.00	0.0290	0.009366
France	Jacques Mitterand	1	69500.00	0.0145	0.011814

Figure 13.14: A complex use of derived tables to apply different levels of aggregated calculation

How it Works

Given the size of this query, it is probably easier to understand what it does if you begin by looking at the output from the two derived tables that are the core of the SQL.

The first derived table (DT1) shows the number of sales per country and the total value of sales per country, as you can see in Figure 13.15.

CountryName	NumberOfCountrySales	TotalCountrySales
Belgium	10	311850.00
France	69	5882810.00
Germany	13	873040.00
Italy	18	1215280.00
Spain	27	1693060.00
Switzerland	18	839415.00
United Kingdom	165	9236375.00
United States	31	1995620.00

Figure 13.15: An aggregate derived table to produce high-level totals

The second derived table (DT2) goes into greater detail and shows the value and number of sales per customer for each country, as you can see (partially, at least) in Figure 13.16.

CountryName	CustomerName	NumberOfCustomerSales	TotalCustomerSales
Belgium	Diplomatic Cars	3	224000.00
Belgium	Flash Voitures	1	6950.00
Belgium	Stefan Van Helsing	6	80900.00
France	Bling Bling S.A.	1	345000.00
France	Capots Reluisants S.A.	6	583115.00
France	Casseroles Chromes	4	201050.00
France	Francois Chirac	1	25950.00
France	Jacques Mitterand	1	69500.00
France	Jean-Yves Truffaut	1	1950.00
France	Khader El Ghannam	2	50500.00
France	La Bagnole de Luxe	6	497190.00
France	Laurent Saint Yves	11	1343950.00
France	Le Luxe en Motion	1	255950.00
France	M. Pierre Dubois	8	511675.00

Figure 13.16: An aggregate derived table that produces detail-level totals

As a whole, the query builds on the data that is returned from the two derived tables. It joins the derived tables on the country field so that it can then list countries, clients, the number of sales made per client, and the value of those sales. So far, then, it is just an extension of the derived table DT2. However, once the aggregate data at country level is added to the query, it allows you to see the percentage of both the value of sales and the number of sales that each customer represents. This is done simply by dividing the totals for number of sales and sale value by country in the derived table DT1 by the number of sales and sale value for each customer in the derived table DT2.

Because the SQL that creates and uses an aggregated derived table can seem a little dense at first sight, taking a look at a more graphic representation, like the one shown in Figure 13.17, might help you understand how it works.

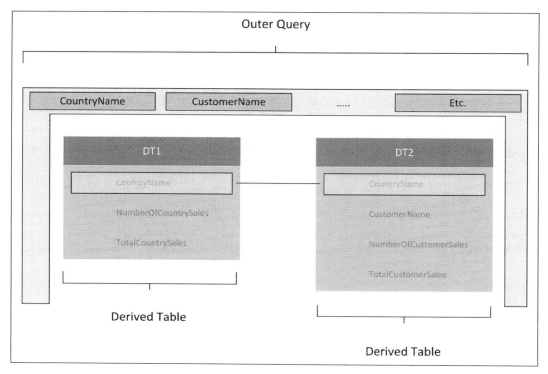

Figure 13.17: Joining on derived tables

Tricks and Traps

When creating complex analyses using multiple derived tables, you need to remain aware of the following key points:

- In this example, we left the figures as "raw" numbers without any formatting. You can use the FORMAT() and CONCAT() functions to display the percentages in a more readable way if you prefer.

8. Using Derived Tables to Join Unconnected Tables

A well-managed business almost certainly defines budgets and then tracks them over time. Fortunately, SQL can be very efficient at monitoring budgets and comparing and forecasts. So, when the financial director comes to your desk requesting a report that compares sales to the budget for each country by year and month, you know there is nothing to worry about. The following SQL is an example of this:

```
SELECT     CO.CountryName

           ,SUM(SD.SalePrice) AS sales

           ,CSQ.BudgetValue

           ,YEAR(SaleDate) AS YearOfSale

           ,MONTH(SaleDate) AS MonthOfSale

           ,SUM(CSQ.BudgetValue)

           - SUM(SD.SalePrice) AS DifferenceBudgetToSales

FROM       salesdetails SD

JOIN       sales AS SA USING(SalesID)

JOIN       customer CU USING(CustomerID)

JOIN       country CO ON CU.country = CO.CountryISO2

JOIN           (

                   SELECT     BudgetValue, BudgetDetail, Year, Month

                   FROM       budget

                   WHERE      BudgetElement = 'country'

               ) CSQ

               ON CSQ.BudgetDetail = CO.CountryName

               AND CSQ.Year = YEAR(SaleDate)

               AND CSQ.Month = MONTH(SaleDate)

GROUP BY CO.CountryName, YEAR(SaleDate), MONTH(SaleDate)

ORDER BY CO.CountryName, YEAR(SaleDate), MONTH(SaleDate);
```

Running this query gives the results that you can see in Figure 13.18.

CountryName	sales	BudgetValue	YearOfSale	MonthOfSale	DifferenceBudgetToSales
Belgium	125000.00	100000.00	2016	8	-25000.00
Belgium	12500.00	15500.00	2017	2	3000.00
Belgium	86500.00	100000.00	2017	3	13500.00
Belgium	45950.00	45950.00	2017	7	0.00
Belgium	34000.00	34000.00	2017	11	0.00
Belgium	950.00	950.00	2018	1	0.00
Belgium	6950.00	6950.00	2018	6	0.00
France	19600.00	19600.00	2015	4	0.00
France	8950.00	8950.00	2015	5	0.00
France	22950.00	22950.00	2015	6	0.00
France	75500.00	75500.00	2015	7	0.00
France	2550.00	2550.00	2016	1	0.00

Figure 13.18: A derived table used to join otherwise unconnected tables

How it Works

Even a well-thought-out database model can have some tables that simply do not link in any conventional way to the core data tables that you are using. Budget data is frequently an example of this. Yet you can use the budget data stored in your database and compare it to the other data that you use to compare sales and budget data and highlight any differences. This only works, however, if you shape the budget data in a way that allows it to be joined to other tables.

This query joins the tables that contain the essential data for make, model, stock, sales details, and sales that you have used so far in this book. Then it also joins data from a new table—the Budget table—to the query so that you can also display data from this source.

The Budget table *cannot be joined directly to the other tables that contain sales and stock data*, however. This is because it contains budget data for many different elements (countries, makes of vehicle, etc.). Moreover the Budget table contains *aggregated* data, whereas the sales data is at a detail level. These different levels of granularity mean that the tables cannot be linked without a little work.

First: You have to query the Budget table and select only the data that you need. In this example, you need to filter the table on the Budget field to limit it to budgets for country sales. If you highlight and run the SELECT query for the derived table, then you will see what the data is like (it is shown in Figure 13.19).

BudgetValue	BudgetDetail	Year	Month
100000.00	Belgium	2016	8
15500.00	Belgium	2017	2
100000.00	Belgium	2017	3
45950.00	Belgium	2017	7
34000.00	Belgium	2017	11
950.00	Belgium	2018	1
6950.00	Belgium	2018	6
19950.00	France	2015	2
19600.00	France	2015	4
8950.00	France	2015	5
22950.00	France	2015	6
75500.00	France	2015	7
2550.00	France	2016	1
39500.00	France	2016	2

Figure 13.19: *A derived table that filters source data*

As you can see from Figure 13.17 the budget data is for country, year, and month. To join the derived table to the other tables in the query, you must perform a complex join using three fields—country, year, and month of sale. This is why the join for the derived table uses the YEAR() and MONTH() functions to isolate these elements from the SaleDate field that is used to join the SalesDetails table to the derived table of budget data.

Finally: The elements that are output from the outer query have to be grouped and aggregated. This is because the data from the tables used in the outer query is at a much more detailed level than the budget data used in the subquery. Mixing data at different levels of detail (or *granularity,* as it is also called) almost never produces coherent results. It is up to you to ensure that the data from all your tables is at the same level of granularity.

Tricks and Traps

I have only one point to stress here:

- Unless you extract the year and month elements from the SalesDate field, the join to the derived tables cannot work correctly because it attempts to match a year (or a month) to a full date. This means that no data matches between the two tables and, consequently, no records are returned by the query.

9. Compare Year-on-Year Data Using a Derived Table

As part of a relentless focus on profitability, the CEO wants to look at all vehicle sales in 2016 and see how each sale compares to the best price achieved in the previous year for the same model of car. All this can be done with one piece of SQL:

```
SELECT     MK.MakeName

           ,MD.ModelName

           ,SD.SalePrice

           ,CSQ.MaxSalePrice AS MaxPrevYear

           ,SD.SalePrice - CSQ.MaxSalePrice

               AS PriceDifferenceToMaxPrevYear

FROM       make AS MK

JOIN       model AS MD ON MK.MakeID = MD.MakeID

JOIN       stock AS ST ON ST.ModelID = MD.ModelID

JOIN       salesdetails SD ON ST.StockCode = SD.StockID

JOIN       sales AS SA ON SA.SalesID = SD.SalesID

JOIN   (

           SELECT     MAX(SDX.SalePrice) AS MaxSalePrice

                      ,YEAR(SAX.SaleDate) AS SaleYear

                      ,MDX.ModelName

           FROM       make AS MKX

           JOIN       model AS MDX USING(MakeID)

           JOIN       stock AS STX USING(ModelID)

           JOIN       salesdetails SDX

                      ON STX.StockCode = SDX.StockID

           JOIN       sales AS SAX USING(SalesID)

           WHERE      YEAR(SAX.SaleDate) = 2015
```

```
       GROUP BY    YEAR(SAX.SaleDate)

               ,MDX.ModelName

    ) CSQ

    ON CSQ.ModelName = MD.ModelName

WHERE       YEAR(SA.SaleDate) = 2016;
```

Running this query gives the results that you can see in Figure 13.20.

	MakeName	ModelName	SalePrice	MaxPrevYear	PriceDifferenceToMaxPrevYear
▶	Ferrari	Testarossa	165000.00	195000.00	-30000.00
	Ferrari	Testarossa	195000.00	195000.00	0.00
	Ferrari	355	205000.00	220000.00	-15000.00
	Ferrari	355	159500.00	220000.00	-60500.00
	Ferrari	355	156500.00	220000.00	-63500.00
	Porsche	911	68900.00	22950.00	45950.00
	Porsche	911	29500.00	22950.00	6550.00
	Porsche	911	22150.00	22950.00	-800.00
	Porsche	911	66500.00	22950.00	43550.00
	Porsche	911	20950.00	22950.00	-2000.00
	Porsche	911	33600.00	22950.00	10650.00
	Porsche	911	17500.00	22950.00	-5450.00
	Porsche	911	45950.00	22950.00	23000.00
	Porsche	924	16500.00	11500.00	5000.00

Figure 13.20: Applying different filters to a "main" query and a derived table

How it Works

In this chapter, you have seen that a derived table is a completely independent dataset relative to the rest of the query. You can use this to your advantage when comparing virtually identical datasets.

In this code the main query is the part of the query that is not a derived table. It lists the makes and models of car sold in 2016 along with their sale price.

The derived table does something fairly similar. It, too, finds models, and sale price, only it finds the maximum sale price for each model for a *different year* to the outer query—the previous year (2015), in fact. The output from this inner query (if you run it separately) is shown in Figure 13.21.

MaxSalePrice	SaleYear	ModelName
22950.00	2015	280SL
220000.00	2015	355
22950.00	2015	911
11500.00	2015	924
19950.00	2015	944
29500.00	2015	DB4
49500.00	2015	DB5
76000.00	2015	DB6
80500.00	2015	Flying Spur
8695.00	2015	Giulia
195000.00	2015	Testarossa
5500.00	2015	TR4

Figure 13.21: Output from a derived table query

As you can see, the derived table shows the maximum sale price per model for one year, yet a close examination of the code shows that the outer query looks at the data for another year. The trick is to join the derived table to the rest of the query using the make as the join element.

You can then output not only the details for sales in 2016, but also the maximum value of each model sold in the previous year. In this example, the current sale price is subtracted from the maximum sale price for the previous year. You can then analyze the difference to compare sales growth from year to year.

Tricks and Traps

I have a single comment for you to take away when using derived tables for data comparison:

- This type of query is extremely extensible and can become a basis for many varied types of comparative analysis. The fact that the derived table and the outer query are completely independent makes derived queries ideal for comparing certain types of data over time.

10. Synchronizing Filters between a Derived Table and the Main Query

Clever buying strategies can make or break a business. Because of this, the finance director wants to ensure that Prestige Cars is not spending too much when buying stock. The following piece of SQL compares the purchase price of every car bought in 2017 with the average price of cars of the same color in 2016.

```
SELECT     ST.Color, ST.DateBought, ST.Cost, CSQ.AveragePurchaseCost

FROM       stock ST

JOIN

           (

           SELECT     Color, AVG(Cost) AS AveragePurchaseCost

                      ,YEAR(DateBought) AS PurchaseYear

           FROM       stock

           WHERE      YEAR(DateBought) = 2016

           GROUP BY   Color, YEAR(DateBought)

           ) CSQ

           ON ST.Color = CSQ.Color

           AND YEAR(ST.DateBought) = CSQ.PurchaseYear + 1;
```

Running this query gives the results that you can see in Figure 13.22; you can also see the output from the derived table.

Color	DateBought	Cost	AveragePurchaseCost
Black	2017-10-29	20000.0000	41133.16129032
Red	2017-12-09	6040.0000	47985.45454545
Dark purple	2017-02-04	17200.0000	48066.66666667
Night Blue	2017-03-29	34360.0000	21377.77777778
Red	2017-04-30	130000.0000	47985.45454545
Black	2017-11-11	40960.0000	41133.16129032
Silver	2017-05-18	7400.0000	41970.50000000
Red	2017-04-05	176400.0000	47985.45454545
Green	2017-03-12	44480.0000	56657.14285714
Blue	2017-05-31	36000.0000	70891.42857143
Pink	2017-09-25	12600.0000	51690.00000000
Pink	2017-02-05	5200.0000	51690.00000000
Red	2017-09-03	124000.0000	47985.45454545
Black	2017-12-09	36760.0000	41133.16129032

Color	AveragePurchaseCost	PurchaseYear
Black	41133.16129032	2016
Blue	70891.42857143	2016
British Racing Green	31184.61538462	2016
Canary Yellow	42742.66666667	2016
Dark Purple	48066.66666667	2016
Green	56657.14285714	2016
Night Blue	21377.77777778	2016
Pink	51690.00000000	2016
Red	47985.45454545	2016
Silver	41970.50000000	2016

Query
Result

Derived
Table
Output

Figure 13.22: Extending the JOIN clause for a derived table

How it Works

This SQL is essentially two pieces of code:

A derived table	That calculates the average price for all the cars bought in 2016
An outer query	That displays the key stock information for all the cars bought in 2017 where cars of the same color were purchased in 2016 and 2017

The interesting tweak is the way that the outer query and the inner derived table are joined. As the grouping for the derived table is by color and year, these are the fields that must be used in the JOIN clause. However, as the derived table contains data for 2016, you can tweak the JOIN clause so that the data from the derived table is mapped not to a year that is specified in the WHERE clause of the outer query, but to a year defined in the ON clause that joins the outer query to the derived table. This is done simply by specifying

```
AND YEAR(ST.DateBought) = CSQ.PurchaseYear - 1
```

This filters the data returned from the outer query so that only data for the following year is returned compared to the derived table.

Of course, you could have specified the year to filter on in the outer query, but this approach is more fluid and extensible because it automatically finds data from the *following* year in the outer query—without the need to filter on the year in the WHERE clause of the outer query.

Tricks and Traps

To end your introduction to derived tables, I suggest that you remember the following points:

- This particular technique can be used in JOIN clauses whenever the fields that are used in a join are numeric.

- It is particularly useful when comparing data across years. It also makes the point that the fields used in a JOIN can themselves be calculated if necessary.

Conclusion

In this chapter, I introduced you to ways of combining data that allow you to answer some tough analytical questions. We did all of this using derived tables—a technique that lets you assemble complex datasets "on the fly" inside other queries.

These virtual tables let you aggregate, filter, and slice data in-depth and then use the results to carry out all sorts of queries. Moreover, derived tables help you think in terms of sets of data and, consequently, learn to adapt your way of tackling data-based problems so that you can handle more complex data analysis. Derived tables also let you aggregate and filter data in a way that allows you to join otherwise incompatible tables and datasets.

Core Knowledge Learned in This Chapter

The concepts that you have seen in this chapter are

Concept	Description
Derived tables	When creating complex joins, you can define any or all of the component tables to be derived tables—that is, SQL that returns a dataset.
Multiple join fields	You can join derived tables to other tables in a query using several fields if you need to.

CHAPTER 14

Common Table Expressions

The previous two chapters have shown you that SQL is all about creating the datasets that allow you to deliver the analysis that you need. As you have probably surmised while reading this book, SQL imposes on its practitioners a particular way of thinking. More specifically, it is a language that wants you to adopt its world view and to think in terms of sets of data that become the building blocks of your analysis. "Thinking in datasets" can, nonetheless, be a skill that takes a while to acquire. Moreover, the way that some SQL solutions nest queries inside other queries can make for complex code that seems to hide—rather than expose—the true simplicity of the approach. The time has come to demonstrate a powerful way to simplify working with complex datasets.

Simplifying Complex Queries with Common Table Expressions

Once again MySQL can come to the rescue if an analytical challenge seems too daunting at first sight. This is because SQL can not only help you create the code that delivers the analysis, it can also help you define the analytical approach and focus on how you structure the datasets based on the underlying tables. This can be accomplished using a technique known as *Common Table Expressions (CTEs)*.

I admit that the name sounds cryptic and gives little indication of the power of this approach. Yet CTEs (as they are normally called) can help you

- Create datasets outside the core of a query to help you think a problem through.

- Reuse datasets so that you do not have to rewrite or copy SQL code several times.

- Create CTEs that use the output from other CTEs. This allows you to break down an analytical challenge into a sequence of coherent steps in which the results created by one CTE ripple through other CTEs in a query to deliver the final output.

Let's now see how CTEs can help you tame even the most complex SQL queries.

Note: Common Table Expressions were introduced in MySQL version 8. If you are using a previous version of MySQL you will have to update to at least version 8.

1. A Basic Common Table Expression

In sales and marketing, it is essential that you understand what your customers want. A first step to this knowledge can be analyzing what they have bought in the past. The following code snippet lets you prepare a report for the CEO of Prestige Cars that displays the make, model, and color combinations of every vehicle sold in 2015.

```
WITH Sales2015_CTE

AS

(

SELECT     MK.MakeName, MD.ModelName, ST.Color

FROM       make AS MK

JOIN       model AS MD USING(MakeID)

JOIN       stock AS ST USING(ModelID)

JOIN       salesdetails SD ON ST.StockCode = SD.StockID

JOIN       sales AS SA USING(SalesID)

WHERE      YEAR(SaleDate) = 2015

)
```

```
SELECT     MakeName, ModelName, Color

FROM       Sales2015_CTE

GROUP BY   MakeName, ModelName, Color

ORDER BY   MakeName, ModelName, Color;
```

Running this query gives the results that you can see in Figure 14.1.

MakeName	ModelName	Color
Alfa Romeo	Giulia	Red
Aston Martin	DB4	Night Blue
Aston Martin	DB5	Black
Aston Martin	DB5	Blue
Aston Martin	DB6	Canary Yellow
Aston Martin	DB6	Silver
Aston Martin	Virage	Black
Bentley	Flying Spur	British Racing Green
Ferrari	355	Black
Ferrari	355	Blue
Ferrari	Testarossa	Green
Ferrari	Testarossa	Red
Jaguar	XJS	Red
Jaguar	XJS	Silver

Figure 14.1: A simple CTE

How it Works

This code snippet takes a two-phased approach to finding all the existing make, model, and color combinations of cars sold in 2015.

First: An independent initial query—a *CTE*—joins the Make, Model, Stock, SalesDetails, and Sales tables. It then selects the MakeName, ModelName, and Color fields from these tables. It also filters on the SaleDate field.

Then: The output from this *CTE* is then used as the data source in the FROM clause of the subsequent SQL statement.

A CTE is really nothing more than a kind of derived table, like those that you saw in the previous chapter. It is a perfectly normal SELECT query that you build to isolate a subset of data. As you can see from this example, a CTE is composed of the following:

A WITH clause   Begins the CTE.

A CTE name	A CTE must have a name. In this example, it is called "Sales2015_CTE." The name can be a single character or something more complex that explains more clearly what the CTE does.
A query	This is the core of the CTE. It must be a valid SQL SELECT query. It can be as complex as your needs require. The query *must* be enclosed in parentheses.
A use for the CTE	By this I mean that you must do something using the CTE—such as using the SELECT clause to extract data from it as we do in this example. This concept is explained visually in Figure 14.2:

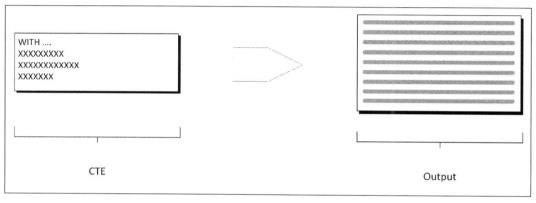

Figure 14.2: *Conceptualizing a CTE*

If you are looking at this example a little quizzically and thinking, "I am sure that I could have done this just by grouping the data without even needing a CTE," then you are right. The CTE that we apply here is not strictly necessary. Either approach delivers the required result. However, as you will see in this chapter, CTEs can be extremely useful in many different ways. I prefer to make the first one as easy as possible so it is as comprehensible as possible. However, there is more to using CTEs than just resolving coding challenges. A CTE like this helps you break down a problem into its component parts. In this specific example, this means

First:	Defining the list of data that you want to aggregate (this is the query inside the CTE).
Finally:	Grouping the data subset from the CTE to achieve the desired result.

So using CTEs is more than merely a variation on a theme; it can also help you think through a problem and enable you to separate out the building blocks that SQL uses to provide a solution in a clear and sequential way.

Tricks and Traps

With a new concept come a few key points to remember:

- You do not have to include the acronym CTE in a Common Table Expression name; however, I have chosen to adopt this approach in this book so that you can identify CTEs more easily among all the other SQL objects that we use.

- If you decide to use a CTE to isolate a subset of data, then you *should* apply the CTE in some way. In other words, you should not "declare" a CTE (as they say in the world of SQL programming) and then not use it. Indeed, if you do not use a CTE that you have created (or at least add a SELECT clause after a CTE), then your code will *not* work.

- The query that makes up a CTE is completely independent of the rest of the query that uses the CTE, so you can always test the CTE by first selecting the SQL inside the parentheses that enclose the query that makes it up, and by then executing it. Figure 14.3 shows the results for the code in the CTE in this example.

MakeName	ModelName	Color
Ferrari	Testarossa	Green
Ferrari	Testarossa	Red
Ferrari	355	Black
Ferrari	355	Blue
Porsche	911	British Racing Green
Porsche	911	Blue
Porsche	911	Black
Porsche	924	British Racing Green
Porsche	924	Black
Porsche	944	Red
Porsche	944	Green
Porsche	944	Blue
Aston Martin	DB4	Night Blue
Aston Martin	DB5	Blue

Figure 14.3: The independent query constituting a CTE

- It is generally easier to avoid spaces and special characters when naming CTEs. This way you avoid the need for backticks or quotes elsewhere in your SQL when you refer to the CTE.

- The name of a CTE can be up to 64 characters.

- CTEs became available in MySQL from version 8.

2. Calculating Averages across Multiple Values Using a CTE

One simple metric can tell many businesses if they are on the path to profitability. This is the average profit for each type of product. A CTE helps you produce this analysis for the CEO of Prestige Cars:

```
WITH Sales_CTE

AS

(

SELECT       MakeName

             ,SalePrice - (

                           ST.Cost

                           + IFNULL(ST.RepairsCost, 0)

                           + IFNULL(ST.PartsCost, 0)

                           + IFNULL(ST.TransportInCost, 0)

                          ) AS Profit

FROM         make AS MK

JOIN         model AS MD USING(MakeID)

JOIN         stock AS ST USING(ModelID)

JOIN         salesdetails SD ON ST.StockCode = SD.StockID

)


SELECT       MakeName, AVG(Profit) AS AverageProfit

FROM         sales_CTE

GROUP BY     MakeName;
```

If you run this query, you see the results that are shown in Figure 14.4.

MakeName	AverageProfit
Alfa Romeo	758.27272727
Aston Martin	10433.06493506
Austin	197.14285714
Bentlev	13831.40000000
BMW	2500.00000000
Buaatti	53890.50000000
Citroen	1962.33333333
Delahave	3473.25000000
Delorean	16910.00000000
Ferrari	29664.10714286
Jaguar	4997.36000000
Lagonda	18175.00000000
Lamborahini	27957.00000000
McLaren	44650.00000000

Figure 14.4: Calculating averages across multiple values using a CTE

How it Works

Calculating averages is fundamental to much data analysis, and this is something that SQL does well. The preceding piece of SQL uses multiple fields to calculate the profit for each car sold, and then it returns the average profit per make.

You may be wondering why you even need a CTE to carry out this calculation. After all, surely you could just average the sale price and the various cost elements and then perform the math?

Indeed, you can do this; however, adding and subtracting overall averages is not the same thing as calculating the average profit. To get this information, you really need to calculate the profit per car and then work out the average of this figure. This is a prime example of how a CTE can prove invaluable. It allows you

First: To calculate the profit figure for *each car* in the Stock table. This metric is worked out at the most detailed level possible—that of each car in the Stock table. Moreover, the CTE allows you to handle NULLs at the most granular level.

Finally: To return the average of the profit figure, aggregated by Make in the main query

3. Reusing CTEs in a Query

When you are trying to control costs, it can help to compare various metrics to a multiple of an average value in order to focus on higher-than-expected values. This is exactly what the finance director wants. In fact, he has asked for a report that finds all makes and models sold where the discount was more than twice the average discount for any vehicle sold in 2015. The following piece of SQL is an example of this type of analysis.

```
WITH Discount2015_CTE (Make, Model, Color, SalePrice, LineItemDiscount)
AS
(
SELECT      MK.MakeName, MD.ModelName, ST.Color
            ,SD.SalePrice, SD.LineItemDiscount
FROM        make AS MK
JOIN        model AS MD USING(MakeID)
JOIN        stock AS ST USING(ModelID)
JOIN        salesdetails SD ON ST.StockCode = SD.StockID
JOIN        sales AS SA USING(SalesID)
WHERE       YEAR(SA.SaleDate) = 2015
)


SELECT      make, model, Color, LineItemDiscount, SalePrice
            ,(SELECT AVG(LineItemDiscount) * 2 FROM Discount2015_CTE)
            AS AverageDiscount2015
FROM        Discount2015_CTE
WHERE       LineItemDiscount > (SELECT AVG(LineItemDiscount) * 2
                        FROM Discount2015_CTE);
```

Running this query gives the results that you can see in Figure 14.5.

Make	Model	Color	LineItemDiscount	SalePrice	AverageDiscount2015
Ferrari	355	Blue	60000.00	220000.00	9655.294118

Figure 14.5: Reusing a CTE in a query

How it Works

This piece of analytical SQL uses a CTE to produce a list of the makes and models of car sold in 2015. It also displays the color, sale price, and sales discount (a column named LineItemDiscount) for each model.

Once the CTE has defined the data subset that will be used by the main query, a few interesting things happen:

First: The rest of the query selects the fields passed into it by the CTE.

Then: A WHERE clause in the main query reuses the CTE to calculate the average sales discount for 2015. This is then doubled and used as a filter so that only sales where a discount greater than twice the average sales discount for the year has been applied appear in the final output.

Finally: The average sales discount for 2015 is recalculated and added to the SELECT clause as a subquery.

The key point here is that a CTE can be reused *several times* in the main query. This approach is based on two fundamental ideas:

- You only have to write the SQL that defines a subset of data *once*, because you can reuse it over and over again. In this example, the main advantage of this approach is that the filter (the WHERE clause that limits the data to the sales for a specific year) is only applied *once*—in the CTE.

- Whenever the CTE is reused to calculate or to display the average value, the filter that it contains is applied *every time*.

There are several clear advantages to this way of working:

Less complexity Subqueries can sometimes be fairly complex, so having to rewrite the same piece of SQL (or adapt it without making any errors) to use in a subquery can become laborious and time-consuming. Reusing a CTE means that you only write the core query *once* to get a reusable dataset.

Avoid repetition This means you are less likely to make a SQL syntax error or enter a wrong value in one of the multiple WHERE clauses that would otherwise be necessary when you reuse the data in the data subset.

Forgetting is harder You do not have to remember to add or update a WHERE clause in multiple subqueries.

Modification is easier

If you want to filter the data on a different year, all you have to do is to change the WHERE clause in the CTE. This change cascades through to the main query everywhere the CTE is used, so you only have to change filter values in one place.

Equally, any other modifications (such as additional fields or calculations) that you make to the CTE are subsequently available whenever the CTE is used in the main query.

Tricks and Traps

A set of key points are worth noting at this point:

- As was the case with derived tables, the SELECT clause of the CTE *must* include all the fields that you want to use in the main query. If you do not select a field in the CTE, then it is completely invisible downstream in the main query that returns the final recordset based on the CTE.

- Although you really should use a CTE if you have added one to your code, you are not obligated to use *all* the fields that you have selected in the CTE elsewhere in your query. In practice, however, it is probably best *only to select the fields that you need* when creating a CTE.

- You can make sure a CTE makes clear the fields that it returns—as the CTE in this example does—by placing a list of fields in parentheses after the CTE name. However, this is not compulsory. Doing so is really nothing more than a way of giving aliases to the fields that the CTE outputs. This can be useful when you are making the column names in underlying tables easier to understand for users.

- If you are adding output field names to the CTE in this way then you must ensure that the aliases inside the parentheses map to the fields in the CTE SELECT clause.

4. Using a CTE in a Derived Table to Deliver Two Different Levels of Aggregation

The sales manager for Prestige Cars wants a slightly subtler analysis of who the most valuable customers are. In this case, she wants a list of customers who bought the most expensive model of car for each make in 2015. The following piece of SQL lets you deliver this information.

```
WITH ExpensiveCar_CTE (

                    MakeName, ModelName, SalePrice

                    ,Color, SaleDate

                    ,InvoiceNumber, CustomerName

                    )

AS

(

SELECT     MK.MakeName, MD.ModelName, SD.SalePrice

           ,ST.Color, SA.SaleDate

           ,SA.InvoiceNumber, CU.CustomerName

FROM       make AS MK

JOIN       model AS MD USING(MakeID)

JOIN       stock AS ST USING(ModelID)

JOIN       salesdetails SD ON ST.StockCode = SD.StockID

JOIN       sales AS SA USING(SalesID)

JOIN       customer CU ON SA.CustomerID = CU.CustomerID

WHERE      YEAR(SaleDate) = 2015

)

SELECT     SLS.MakeName, SLS.ModelName, SLS.Color, SLS.CustomerName

           ,SLS.SalePrice, SLS.SaleDate, SLS.InvoiceNumber

FROM       ExpensiveCar_CTE SLS

           JOIN (

                 SELECT    MakeName

                           ,MAX(SalePrice) AS MaxSalePrice

                 FROM      ExpensiveCar_CTE

                 GROUP BY MakeName

                 ) MX
```

```
ON SLS.MakeName = MX.MakeName

AND SLS.SalePrice = MX.MaxSalePrice;
```

Running this query gives the results that you can see in Figure 14.6.

MakeName	ModelName	Color	CustomerName	SalePrice	SaleDate	InvoiceNumber
Ferrari	355	Blue	Snazzy Roadsters	220000.00	2015-01-25 00:00:00	GBPGB002
Bentley	Flying Spur	British Racing Green	Wonderland Wheels	80500.00	2015-04-30 00:00:00	GBPGB011
Mercedes	280SL	Red	La Bagnole de Luxe	22950.00	2015-06-04 16:37:00	EURFR015
Alfa Romeo	Giulia	Red	Convertible Dreams	8695.00	2015-07-12 10:00:00	GBPGB016
Porsche	911	Black	Convertible Dreams	22950.00	2015-11-10 00:00:00	GBPGB025
Jaguar	XK150	Night Blue	Alexei Tolstoi	22990.00	2015-07-15 00:00:00	GBPGB017
Aston Martin	Virage	Black	Theo Kowalski	123590.00	2015-10-30 00:00:00	USDUS024
Triumph	TR5	Green	Peter McLuckie	12650.00	2015-09-05 00:00:00	GBPGB020

Figure 14.6: Using a CTE in a derived table to deliver two different levels of aggregation

How it Works

The challenge here is to isolate the highest-value car sold for each make as well as return all the important details for each sale. Fortunately, a CTE can really help here:

First: You define a CTE that contains all the key sales information (customer, sale price, make, model, etc.).

Second: You select all the important data from this CTE.

Third: You use the CTE a *second time* in a derived table that groups and aggregates the data from the CTE by make and maximum sale price.

Finally: You join the derived table to the main query on the MakeName and SalePrice fields (or, rather, you join the maximum sale price field from the derived table to the sale price field from the main query).

This way the derived table filters out all cars from the main query where the sale price is not equal to the greatest sale price—in effect isolating the most expensive car sold for each make.

Once again you have reused a CTE. This time, rather than rewrite complex joins in a derived table, you used the CTE as the basis for a simple aggregation. This allowed you to concentrate on getting the initial query (the one used in the CTE) correct and then focus separately on how to use this data twice:

- Once to find the most expensive car for each make
- Once to list the details of that particular sale

To more easily understand this, take a look at Figure 14.7, which provides a visual breakdown of the query used in this example.

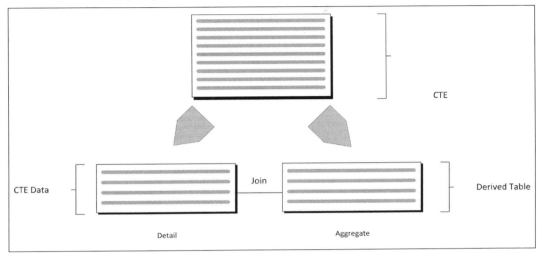

Figure 14.7: *Analyzing a complex CTE*

Tricks and Traps

When creating more complex CTEs, you need to remember

- If you have created a CTE that outputs many fields, then you need to pay attention to the list of column names that you add inside the parentheses that follow the name of the CTE. This involves doing the following:
  - First, make sure that you have the same number of fields as those in the SELECT clause of the CTE.
  - Second, ensure that all the fields are in the same order both in the SELECT clause and inside the parentheses. It is all too easy to mix up the order of the fields—and produce some really bizarre output as a result.

5. Using a CTE to Isolate Data from a Separate Dataset at a Different Level of Detail

The sales manager has asked you to produce a regular report that tracks if the salespeople are meeting their targets. To do so, you need to compare sales figures to budget projections. The SQL that follows is one way of doing this.

```
WITH SalesBudget_CTE

AS

(

SELECT      BudgetValue, BudgetDetail, Year, Month

FROM        budget

WHERE       BudgetElement = 'country'

)


SELECT      CO.CountryName

            ,YEAR(SA.SaleDate) AS YearOfSale

            ,MONTH(SA.SaleDate) AS MonthOfSale

            ,SUM(SD.SalePrice) AS SalePrice

            ,SUM(CTE.BudgetValue) AS BudgetValue

            ,SUM(CTE.BudgetValue)

            - SUM(SD.SalePrice) AS DifferenceBudgetToSales

FROM        make AS MK

JOIN        model AS MD USING(MakeID)

JOIN        stock AS ST USING(ModelID)

JOIN        salesdetails SD ON ST.StockCode = SD.StockID

JOIN        sales AS SA USING(SalesID)

JOIN        customer CU ON SA.CustomerID = CU.CustomerID

JOIN        country CO ON CU.country = CO.CountryISO2

JOIN        SalesBudget_CTE CTE
```

```
ON CTE.BudgetDetail = CO.CountryName

AND CTE.Year = YEAR(SA.SaleDate)

AND CTE.Month = MONTH(SA.SaleDate)
GROUP BY    CO.CountryName, YEAR(SA.SaleDate), MONTH(SA.SaleDate);
```

Running this query gives the results that you can see in Figure 14.8.

CountryName	YearOfSale	MonthOfSale	SalePrice	BudgetValue	DifferenceBudgetToSales
Belgium	2016	8	125000.00	100000.00	-25000.00
Belgium	2017	2	12500.00	15500.00	3000.00
Belgium	2017	3	86500.00	100000.00	13500.00
Belgium	2017	7	45950.00	137850.00	91900.00
Belgium	2017	11	34000.00	68000.00	34000.00
Belgium	2018	1	950.00	950.00	0.00
Belgium	2018	6	6950.00	6950.00	0.00
France	2015	4	19600.00	19600.00	0.00
France	2015	5	8950.00	8950.00	0.00
France	2015	6	22950.00	22950.00	0.00
France	2015	7	75500.00	151000.00	75500.00
France	2016	1	2550.00	2550.00	0.00
France	2016	2	39500.00	39500.00	0.00
France	2016	5	49580.00	49580.00	0.00
France	2016	6	180150.00	720600.00	540450.00
France	2016	8	231500.00	694500.00	463000.00

Figure 14.8: Using a CTE to isolate data from a separate dataset at a different level of detail

How it Works

Once again you are probably thinking, "this is using a CTE like it is a derived table." You are right—this is exactly what we are doing.

More precisely, we are using the CTE to isolate the budget data from the Budget table so that it can be joined to a query in a way that allows us to compare actual and budget data. Now, the budget data does not really fit into the tightly structured "relational" model of the main tables of the Prestige Cars database. However, it *is* possible to produce budget data that returns a list of makes along with the predicted sales for each month and year. The SELECT query that makes up the CTE does exactly this. To get a clearer idea of how this works, take a look at Figure 14.9, which shows you the output from the CTE if you select the SQL and run it independently.

BudgetValue	BudgetDetail	Year	Month
100000.00	Belgium	2016	8
15500.00	Belgium	2017	2
100000.00	Belgium	2017	3
45950.00	Belgium	2017	7
34000.00	Belgium	2017	11
950.00	Belgium	2018	1
6950.00	Belgium	2018	6
19950.00	France	2015	2
19600.00	France	2015	4
8950.00	France	2015	5
22950.00	France	2015	6
75500.00	France	2015	7
2550.00	France	2016	1
39500.00	France	2016	2

Figure 14.9: *The records returned by a CTE that filters data*

As you can see, this is nothing more than a "virtual table" of selected budget data. However, you can now join this data to sales data in the following three fields:

Country Name	Which maps to the BudgetDetail field in the Budget table (once the BudgetDetail table is filtered to show the makes).
Year of Sale	Which requires you to use the YEAR() function to extract the year from the SaleDate field.
Month of Sale	Which requires you to use the MONTH() function to extract the month from the SaleDate field.

The main query in this code snippet then joins the CTE to the other tables as if it is just another table—which it almost is. The main query can then select any necessary fields as well as carry out any required calculations.

Tricks and Traps

When using a CTE to join data from separate data areas at different levels of granularity, be sure to remember that

- In the main query, all the numeric values in the query have to be aggregated (using SUM() functions in this example) and the text fields have to appear in a GROUP BY clause. This is because you are comparing budget data that is aggregated by country, year, and month with data that is at a more detailed level. So, to make the figures meaningful, the detailed sales data also has to be aggregated to country, year, and month, or it cannot be joined to the CTE.

6. Multiple Common Table Expressions

It may be near the end of the day, but the sales manager has appeared at your desk with an urgent request. She wants to see how her budget predictions for sales by color stack up against actual sales for 2016. Fortunately, you can answer this request in a few minutes with the kind of SQL that you can see here:

```
WITH ColorSales_CTE
AS
(SELECT     Color
            ,SUM(SD.SalePrice) AS TotalSalesValue
FROM        stock ST
JOIN        salesdetails SD  ON ST.StockCode = SD.StockID
JOIN        sales AS SA USING(SalesID)

WHERE       YEAR(SA.SaleDate) = 2016

GROUP BY    Color
)
,
ColorBudget_CTE
AS
(
SELECT   BudgetDetail AS Color, BudgetValue
FROM     Budget
WHERE    BudgetElement = 'Color'
            AND YEAR = 2016
)

SELECT      BDG.Color, SLS.TotalSalesValue, BDG.BudgetValue
            ,(SLS.TotalSalesValue - BDG.BudgetValue) AS BudgetDelta
FROM        ColorSales_CTE SLS
JOIN        ColorBudget_CTE BDG
            ON SLS.Color = BDG.Color;
```

Running this code gives you the result that you can see in Figure 14.10. In this figure, you can also see the output of the two separate CTEs.

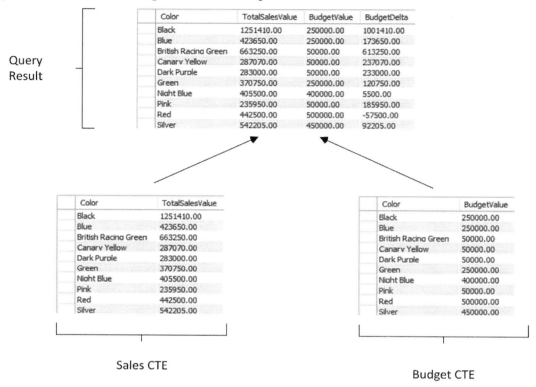

Figure 14.10: Using multiple CTEs in a query

How it Works

This query uses two separate CTEs to isolate two different datasets that are then joined in the final "output" query.

The first CTE   Joins the Sales, Stock, and SalesDetails tables to return all the required sales values per color of vehicle sold for 2016. This CTE is called ColorSales_CTE

The second CTE   Isolates the budget data for colors for 2016 from the Budget table. If you remember, the budget table contains data for many budget elements, and so it needs to be filtered on both the budget element (color, in this example) and the year that you want to get data for. This CTE is called ColorBudget_CTE.

The output query   Joins the two "source" CTEs on the shared color field and returns both the sales and budget values for all the available colors. As a final flourish, it uses the values to calculate any sales that are over—or under—budget values in the BudgetDelta calculated column.

This example illustrates how you can use CTEs to generate completely independent datasets that you can then use together to deliver insight. In the Prestige Cars database, budget data is held completely independently from sales data, and moreover, has its own unique structure. However, using CTEs to isolate the two datasets before you join them shows you that

First: You can isolate separate data elements from each other before attempting to combine them.

Second: The two CTEs are totally separate—neither has any effect on the other.

Indeed, using multiple separate CTEs like this can prove to be a valuable analytical technique. This is because you can concentrate on each dataset individually (and even test the output of each CTE in isolation). Often this can be a valuable way to break down your analysis into smaller, more digestible pieces that you then combine for a final result.

Tricks and Traps

If you decide to use multiple independent CTEs in your queries be aware that

- You can use multiple independent CTEs as a way of testing various approaches to solving data analysis challenges.

- You only need to introduce CTEs with a single WITH keyword. After that, you merely separate each CTE from the others with a comma.

7. Nested Common Table Expressions

As part of your analytical quest to deliver the insight that will lead to increased sales and profits, you want to take a look at the cars that sell more than a minimum quantity. More specifically, you want to display all the makes of car sold in a given year where more than two cars are sold per make. After all, perhaps these are the ones that the company should be pitching to potential buyers. The following SQL shows you how to do this:

```
WITH Outer2015Sales_CTE

AS

(

SELECT     MK.MakeName

FROM       make AS MK

JOIN       model AS MD USING(MakeID)

JOIN       stock AS ST USING(ModelID)

JOIN       salesdetails SD ON ST.StockCode = SD.StockID

JOIN       sales AS SA USING(SalesID)

WHERE      YEAR(SaleDate) = 2015

)

,

CoreSales_CTE (MakeName, NumberOfSales)

AS

(

SELECT     MakeName

           ,COUNT(*)

FROM       Outer2015Sales_CTE

GROUP BY   MakeName

HAVING     COUNT(*) >= 2

)

SELECT     CTE.MakeName, MK2.MakeCountry AS CountryCode

           ,NumberOfSales

FROM       CoreSales_CTE CTE

JOIN       make MK2

           ON CTE.MakeName = MK2.MakeName;
```

Running this query gives the results that you can see in Figure 14.11.

MakeName	CountryCode	NumberOfSales
Ferrari	ITA	4
Porsche	GER	8
Aston Martin	GBR	7
Jaguar	GBR	4
Triumph	GBR	2

Figure 14.11: Nested CTEs

How it Works

This query shows how you can create a short sequence of two CTEs where the second uses the output from the first as its source of data. This way, CTEs can be used as a way of breaking down the initial requirement into a series of successive steps that lead to the solution. What the query does is take a three-phased approach:

First: The initial CTE joins all the tables that are required to produce a list of all makes of vehicle sold in 2015. Even though only two fields are actually used by this query (MakeName and SaleDate), these fields are in the Make and Sales tables, and so several "intermediate" tables must be part of the FROM clause to link the source data tables correctly.

Then: The second CTE (CoreSales_CTE) is built using the first CTE (Outer2015Sales_CTE) as its data source. This query is an aggregate query that only returns makes of car where more than two have been sold. Because this CTE is based on the first CTE, only sales for 2015 are analyzed

Finally: A regular query lists the makes of vehicle returned by the second CTE. It joins this result to the Make table to add further columns to the output.

Once again, it might be easier to grasp this concept with the aid of a more visual representation. Figure 14.12 explains nested CTEs graphically.

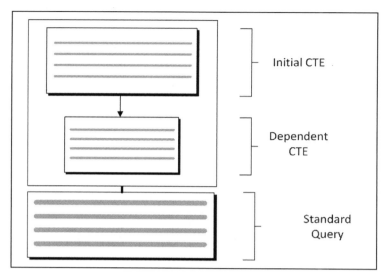

Figure 14.12: The data flow in nested CTEs

Although you could probably arrive at the same result using different approaches, this example shows you that CTEs can be "linked" in a way that lets you make your SQL reflect the analytical challenge that you are faced with. It has the advantage of being more sequential than some other approaches since it lets you see these steps, which are required to produce the final output, more clearly:

First:	Filter the data.
Second:	Aggregate the data.
Finally:	Extend the data selection.

Tricks and Traps

Here are a couple of points to take away:

- When you are writing SQL that uses multiple CTEs, the core principles to using any CTE still apply.

- When writing dependent CTEs like this, you only need to use a single WITH keyword. This serves to introduce any number of CTEs. The CTEs can be independent from one another or derived from one another—it makes no difference. All that matters is that each sucessive CTE is separated from the previous one by a comma.

8. Using Multiple Common Table Expressions to Compare Disparate Datasets

When an existing customer contacts Prestige Cars, the sales director wants to know if they are profitable before starting do discuss discounts. Consequently, she wants to see how much each customer has spent in 2017, and how this relates to Prestige Cars' total annual sales. What is more, she wants to see sales per customer as well as customer sales as a percentage of total sales. The following SQL snippet gives you precisely this information:

```
WITH Initial2017Sales_CTE

AS

(

SELECT     SD.SalePrice, CU.CustomerName, SA.SaleDate

FROM       make AS MK

JOIN       model AS MD USING(MakeID)

JOIN       stock AS ST USING(ModelID)

JOIN       salesdetails SD ON ST.StockCode = SD.StockID

JOIN       sales AS SA USING(SalesID)

JOIN       customer AS CU USING(CustomerID)

WHERE      YEAR(SaleDate) = 2017

)

,

AggregateSales_CTE (CustomerName, SalesForCustomer)

AS

(

SELECT     CustomerName, SUM(SalePrice)

FROM       Initial2017Sales_CTE

GROUP BY   CustomerName

)

,

TotalSales_CTE (TotalSalePrice)
```

```
AS

(

SELECT      SUM(SalePrice)

FROM        Initial2017Sales_CTE

)


SELECT

 IT.CustomerName

,IT.SalePrice

, IT.SaleDate

,CONCAT(FORMAT((IT.SalePrice / AG.SalesForCustomer * 100), 2) , ' %')

        AS SaleAsPercentageForCustomer

,CONCAT(FORMAT((IT.SalePrice / TT.TotalSalePrice * 100), 2), ' %')

        AS SalePercentOverall

        FROM        Initial2017Sales_CTE IT

        JOIN        AggregateSales_CTE AG

        ON          IT.CustomerName = AG.CustomerName

        CROSS JOIN TotalSales_CTE TT

 ORDER BY   IT.CustomerName, IT.SaleDate;
```

Running this query gives the results that you can see in Figure 14.13.

CustomerName	SalePrice	SaleDate	SaleAsPercentageForCustomer	SalePercentO
Alicia Almodovar	12500.00	2017-05-10 16:14:00	4.76 %	0.16 %
Alicia Almodovar	250000.00	2017-09-20 12:32:00	95.24 %	3.15 %
Antonio Maura	12950.00	2017-06-15 18:24:00	11.37 %	0.16 %
Antonio Maura	39500.00	2017-11-01 17:36:00	34.67 %	0.50 %
Antonio Maura	49500.00	2017-11-01 17:36:00	43.44 %	0.62 %
Antonio Maura	11990.00	2017-12-12 14:41:00	10.52 %	0.15 %
Autos Sportivos	65890.00	2017-05-09 12:13:00	100.00 %	0.83 %
Birmingham Executive Prestige Vehicles	335000.00	2017-07-03 19:26:00	100.00 %	4.22 %
Capots Reluisants S.A.	33500.00	2017-05-23 09:19:00	45.44 %	0.42 %
Capots Reluisants S.A.	32675.00	2017-08-06 14:30:00	44.32 %	0.41 %
Capots Reluisants S.A.	7550.00	2017-12-10 12:41:00	10.24 %	0.10 %
Casseroles Chromes	55600.00	2017-03-25 10:07:00	100.00 %	0.70 %
Convertible Dreams	25000.00	2017-11-01 19:35:00	100.00 %	0.31 %
Diplomatic Cars	12500.00	2017-02-12 16:02:00	12.63 %	0.16 %

Figure 14.13: Using multiple CTEs to compare disparate datasets

How it Works

I imagine that when you first see this piece of SQL, you think, "Wow, this is complicated!" After all, this example uses no less than three CTEs to deliver the required analysis. What is more, the second and third CTEs are based on the first CTE. However, before looking at the code, let's see exactly what we are trying to deliver. In essence, the request is for the following pieces of information:

Individual Customer Sales	We need the detail of each sale for each customer for the given period (2017).
Total Customer Sales	We want the total sales figure for each customer for the given period.
Total Sales	We also require the total overall sales for the sales period.

Each of the three CTEs used in this query corresponds to one of these analytical requirements.

Initial2017Sales_CTE	Provides the sales data at a detail level. It joins all the necessary tables needed to output the date of each sale, the customer, and the amount of the sale. This CTE also filters the data to restrict it to a specified year.
AggregateSales_CTE	Takes the data supplied by the initial CTE (Initial.2017Sales_CTE) and aggregates it by customer. This way you also can obtain the total sales per customer
TotalSales_CTE	Also takes the data supplied by Initial2017Sales_CTE and aggregates it, only this time, only the total figure for the dataset is returned, without any grouping.

Once the CTEs have been defined (or "declared" as the techies say), the final query can then assemble the data from all of them. It does this in two ways:

First:	Initial2017Sales_CTE (the detailed list of sales) is joined to AggregateSales_CTE (the total sales per customer). As both contain the CustomerName field, they are joined on this field. This join allows you to return the total sales per customer as well as the detail of each sale for every sale. Dividing the total sales per customer by the value of each sale gives you the percentage of total customer sales that each individual sale represents.

Second: The total overall sales figure is added to the query. This is done using the CROSS JOIN operator. What this does is add the total sales figure to each row that is output. Once the total is there, it can be used to provide the percentage of total sales that each individual sale represents.

This example shows you just how versatile CTEs can be. As you can see, the initial detailed CTE (Initial2017Sales_CTE) is used not only in the final query but also in the other two CTEs. This makes the code much simpler, as it means that you do not have to repeat a series of table joins several times. Instead, you define a source dataset *once* that you then *reuse* on multiple occasions to help deliver different levels of aggregation. Not only that, but if you need to change the filter that underlies the analysis (the year, in this case), you only need to alter it *once* in the top CTE for the filter to be cascaded down through the subsequent, dependent CTEs.

Tricks and Traps

Despite its apparent complexity, this CTE needs only one principal comment:

- In the SQL, we have formatted the percentage output using the FORMAT() and CONCAT() functions—and multiplying the calculated percentage by 100. This merely makes the output more readable, and is certainly not a requirement. If you are feeding this data into another application, you may want to remove this function from the code because it can cause the percentages to be interpreted as text by some programs.

Conclusion

This chapter showed you how to harness the power of SQL to rise to the most daunting data analysis challenges. You did this using Common Table Expressions (CTEs)—a technique that lets you break down data analysis problems into smaller, more manageable parts that you can then join together to obtain the result that you want.

CTEs not only solve technical problems, they also help you handle data analysis one step at a time. This combination makes them one of the most useful SQL techniques available—and, almost certainly, a valuable tool in your armory.

Core Knowledge Learned in This Chapter

The concepts and keywords that you have seen in this chapter are

Concept	Description
Common Table Expressions (CTEs)	A CTE is a separate derived table that allows you to define a dataset outside the main query for use—and reuse—in the body of the query. Multiple CTEs can be used in the same query, CTEs can be chained so that one CTE depends on the output of another CTE and CTEs can be independent from each other.
WITH	This keyword introduces one or more CTEs in a query.
CROSS JOIN	This operator multiplies all the rows in one table with all the rows in another table.

CHAPTER 15

Correlated Subqueries

I realize that the title of this chapter may seem a little hard to understand when you first read it. After all, the term correlated subqueries is more than a little technical—if not incomprehensible—at first sight. However, since it is the term that database people use, I have to use it, too. What this expression means is, quite simply, that certain kinds of subquery can be used to filter the data in the outer query in a particular way. This is done by applying a specific method to join the subquery to the outer query, which means that each query depends on the other. Using correlated subqueries can often enable you to deliver some uniquely powerful data analysis.

Why Use Correlated Subqueries?

As with so many database concepts, this is easier to understand if you see it in action. In this chapter, you see how to

- Calculate ratios and percentages of parts relative to a whole.
- Filter data in a table only if corresponding data exists in another table.
- Filter data based on a calculation that relates to a specific aspect of the data.
- Isolate data according to certain characteristics of another linked dataset.

Since an example is worth a thousand words, let's take a look at a few correlated subqueries that will extend your knowledge of SQL. This will help you take your analytical abilities to a higher level so that you can solve ever more challenging requests.

1. Simple Correlated Subqueries

Most of the clients of Prestige Cars only buy one vehicle at a time; however, some do buy two or more at once. To understand customers better, the sales director wants a list of all invoice items as well as the total for the invoice so that she can do some further analysis. The following SQL provides this:

```
SELECT

        SalesDetailsID

        ,SalePrice

        ,(SELECT TotalSalePrice FROM sales

WHERE   SalesId = SD.SalesId) AS TotalSales

FROM    salesdetails SD

ORDER BY  SalesDetailsID;
```

Running this SQL returns the data that you can see in Figure 15.1. Although the sale price is equal to the total sales in most cases, on occasion—such as in SalesDetailsIDs 11 and 12—two lines make up a single invoice and the sale price is only part of the total sales.

SalesDetailsID	SalePrice	TotalSales
1	65000.00	65000.00
2	220000.00	220000.10
3	19500.00	19500.00
4	11500.00	11500.00
5	19950.00	19900.00
6	29500.00	29500.00
7	49500.00	49500.20
8	76000.00	76000.90
9	19600.00	19600.00
10	36500.00	36500.00
11	8500.00	89000.00
12	80500.00	89000.00
13	169500.00	169500.00
14	8950.00	8950.00
15	195000.00	195000.00
16	22950.00	22950.00
17	8695.00	8695.00
18	22990.00	22990.00

Multiple Invoice Lines (for SalesDetailsIDs 11 and 12)

Figure 15.1: A simple correlated subquery

How it Works

This query is created from an outer query and an inner query, just like many of the examples that you saw in the previous three chapters. Nonetheless, this example has one really important difference. The two queries are *not* independent of each other; they are linked. More specifically, they both can access the *SalesID* field in the tables that they use, and this field is used in the WHERE clause of the subquery to connect the inner and outer queries.

Once the subquery is "connected" to the outer query (or once it becomes a correlated subquery, as it is called in the world of SQL), then the way that the whole query works alters radically. The *outer query now depends on the inner query*, and the inner query is run once for each record in the outer query.

Once again, I prefer to illustrate this concept graphically to help you to understand what exactly a correlated subquery is doing. You can see this in Figure 15.2.

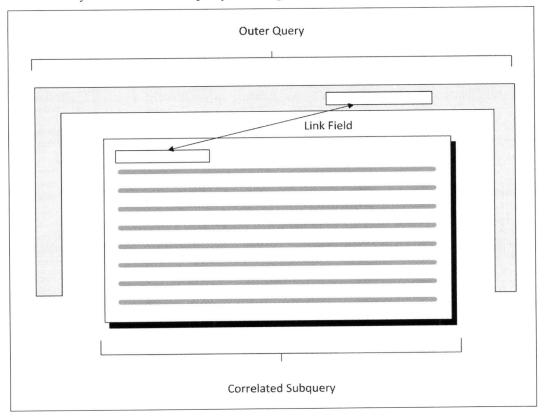

Figure 15.2: The concept of a correlated subquery

This graphic illustrates how the inner and outer queries relate one to the other.

The outer query	Returns the first record that it finds from the SalesDetails table (which is the list of line items in every invoice) and passes a "link" field (SalesID) to the correlated subquery (the inner query).
The inner query	Reads the Sales table (the invoice header table) and returns the total sales price *only* for records containing the SalesID passed in from the outer query.

This is, admittedly, a simple example where we are not doing very much with the data that is returned. In the real world you would probably use this information to provide some deeper analysis and calculate the percentage of line items per invoice, for instance. Just read on and see how to apply the concept of correlated subqueries to deliver precisely the kind of analysis that is often impossible without correlated subqueries.

Tricks and Traps

There is one fundamental point to memorize when creating correlated subqueries:

- You cannot execute the correlated subquery independent of the outer query because the correlated subquery depends on the outer query in its WHERE clause. You can, however, remove the WHERE clause from the correlated subquery and then execute the SQL for the inner query.

2. Correlated Subqueries to Display Percentages of a Specific Total

When she is negotiating each sale, the sales director wants to see a history of all previous sales for every client as well as the percentage of the total value of vehicles sold to the client that each individual sale represents. She says that this will help her develop a discount strategy. The next piece of SQL uses a correlated subquery to deliver this insight:

```
SELECT

 CS.CustomerName

,SA.INVOICENUMBER

,SD.SalePrice
```

```
,SD.SalePrice

/

(

  SELECT      SUM(SDC.SalePrice)

  FROM        salesdetails SDC

  JOIN        sales SAC USING(SalesID)

  JOIN        customer CSC ON SAC.CustomerID = CSC.CustomerID

  WHERE       SAC.CustomerID = CS.CustomerID

) * 100 AS PercentSalesPerCustomer

FROM        salesdetails SD

JOIN        sales AS SA USING(SalesID)

JOIN        customer CS USING(CustomerID)

ORDER BY    CS.CustomerName;
```

Running this piece of SQL displays the percentage of each sale for each client relative to the total sales for the client, as you can see in Figure 15.3. If you add up the total of the percentages of sales records for each client, you will see that they equate to 100 percent per client.

CustomerName	INVOICENUMBER	SalePrice	PercentSalesPerCustomer
Alex McWhirter	GBPGB308	17850.00	100.000000
Alexei Tolstoi	GBPGB017	22990.00	4.408522
Alexei Tolstoi	GBPGB023	22600.00	4.333736
Alexei Tolstoi	GBPGB026	69500.00	13.327197
Alexei Tolstoi	GBPGB046	9950.00	1.907994
Alexei Tolstoi	GBPGB046	39500.00	7.574450
Alexei Tolstoi	GBPGB055	205000.00	39.310437
Alexei Tolstoi	GBPGB063	102500.00	19.655219
Alexei Tolstoi	GBPGB081	3500.00	0.671154
Alexei Tolstoi	GBPGB092	45950.00	8.811291
Alicia Almodovar	EURES098	12500.00	3.271481
Alicia Almodovar	EURES109	39500.00	10.337879
Alicia Almodovar	EURES149	12500.00	3.271481
Alicia Almodovar	EURES185	250000.00	65.429611
Alicia Almodovar	EURES232	5690.00	1.489178
Alicia Almodovar	EURES237	15950.00	4.174409

Figure 15.3: Using a correlated subquery to calculate percentages of a subset

How it Works

This query extends the correlated subquery principle that you saw in the previous example to more complex data sets. More specifically, the code consists of

An outer query	That joins the Sales, SalesDetails, and Customer tables to return the details—the customer name and sale amount—for every sale made by the company.
A correlated subquery	That calculates the total sales per customer. This uses the same tables as the outer query (Sales, SalesDetails, and Customer); however, it groups the data by customer to give the *total* sales for each customer. The correlated subquery is joined to the outer query by the CustomerID field, so the total returned is only for the customer from the outer list and *not* for the whole SalesDetails table.

The overall query essentially works as a whole. When each record of the outer query is returned, the correlated subquery calculates the individual sales *only* for the relevant customer. This figure is then used in the percentage calculation of the sales ratio for this particular sale.

Tricks and Traps

There is one point to note here:

- Since the correlated subquery is linked to the outer query, you cannot just select the SQL for the subquery and run it. Should you wish to test the subquery, I advise that you copy the correlated subquery into a new query tab and replace the reference to the outer query (CS.CustomerID in this example) with a real customer ID. Indeed, you may find it helpful to develop and test a correlated subquery in this way *before* adding it to the outer query.

3. Comparing Datasets Using a Correlated Subquery

Once again, the finance director is determined to reduce the cost of repairs. This time he has asked you to produce a list of vehicle repair costs that are 50 percent higher than the average for each make. The following code lets you deliver this for him:

```
SELECT      MKX.MakeName, STX.RepairsCost, STX.StockCode

FROM        make AS MKX JOIN model AS MDX USING(MakeID)
```

```
JOIN        stock AS STX USING(ModelID)

JOIN        salesdetails SDX ON STX.StockCode = SDX.StockID

WHERE       STX.RepairsCost >

                (

                SELECT      AVG(ST.RepairsCost) AS AvgRepairCost

                FROM        make AS MK

                JOIN        model AS MD USING(MakeID)

                JOIN        stock AS ST USING(ModelID)

                WHERE       MK.MakeName = MKX.MakeName

                ) * 1.5;
```

Running this query gives the results that you can see in Figure 15.4.

MakeName	RepairsCost	StockCode
Ferrari	9250.0000	15108517-AD0C-4FF2-A7D4-57679C374A68
Ferrari	9250.0000	66C9034C-23A3-44F1-B946-2DDA65E684D8
Ferrari	9250.0000	98299E86-0B98-42D8-A549-37D89435B4E3
Ferrari	9250.0000	A326183E-7D45-4CF2-A353-7177A3EAB71F
Ferrari	9250.0000	20041639-9549-415A-AEC2-7159352E8CB7
Ferrari	9250.0000	5D119748-326C-44C5-BA1D-57968CAB0DEE
Ferrari	9250.0000	7392B5F6-783C-4D4B-B687-74A98411A7CB
Porsche	1360.0000	05D4115C-3F27-4059-BDC8-C0C3FFC85E8B
Porsche	2000.0000	1860F37A-EBC7-42E9-B339-3F6D6048322F
Porsche	1360.0000	3F38ED8D-1203-4D3E-8AC0-3ACAC73BDE17
Porsche	1360.0000	518125AE-9A67-45A6-B3FD-557C785796FC
Porsche	2175.0000	6BF8C577-E615-4667-A48C-25E8D825AAC6
Porsche	1360.0000	70C9BE5C-3CCA-4FB2-B4DE-E5F0A61BB84D
Porsche	2000.0000	B165CAEF-FF77-4E63-98C1-59D97F97E7C9
Porsche	1360.0000	896B39D5-8040-4947-94D0-0234B4E78B23
Porsche	1360.0000	10AD713C-C997-48BB-A5FB-F0B5FD26479B

Figure 15.4: *A correlated query used for comparison*

How it Works

Finding exceptions—especially costly exceptions—is a core requirement in data analysis. Correlated subqueries are especially useful when you need to compare values to an aggregated value (such as an average) for a particular category of items. This query begins by calculating the average repair cost for all vehicles in stock and then multiplying this figure by 150 percent. However, since it is a correlated subquery where the inner and outer queries are linked using the MakeName field, this average is calculated for *every* record in the outer query. The result is that the repair cost is evaluated not for *all* vehicles in stock, but as the average for *each make* of vehicle in stock. This changes the calculation completely. Now, for each record in the outer query, the average repair cost is only calculated relative to that particular make of car. If the repair cost for a car is over 1.5 times the average repair cost for that make, then the query output shows the repair cost for the car.

Tricks and Traps

Exception reporting can prove tricky in practice. Be sure to take note of the following points if you want to get better results:

- The "filter" effect of a correlated subquery is not limited to finding records that are (or are not) in a dataset as was the case with the three previous examples. You can use a correlated subquery to compare values using all the traditional comparison operators—greater than (>), less than (<), greater than or equal to (>=), less than or equal to (<=), or not equal to (<>). This example only shows how to compare using less than, but all the others are available if your analysis requires them.

- You are also not limited to comparing results to an average. You can just as easily use the MAX()or MIN() functions to find records that are close to the upper and lower limits of a dataset for a specific element.

- In this example, the two queries—inner and outer—use very similar datasets. This is not always the case with correlated subqueries. It can, however, be a frequent occurrence.

- In a correlated subquery it is vital to create *individual aliases* for any tables that are used in both the inner and outer tables of the query. Because many of the same tables are used in both the outer query and the correlated subquery, we distinguished them by adding an "X" for each outer query table alias.

4. Duplicating the Output of a Correlated Subquery in the Query Results

The finance director was pleased with the data that you just sent him; however, he now wants the average repair cost per make to appear in the resulting data while keeping the filter on the average repair cost per make that you set up previously.

If you want to be absolutely certain that this query is working, the best way to find out is to display the average repair cost per make in the output. This means you need to duplicate the correlated subquery that you use in the WHERE clause in the actual SELECT clause of the query. If you do this, the code looks like the following:

```
SELECT     MKX.MakeName, STX.RepairsCost, STX.StockCode
,(
    SELECT      AVG(ST.RepairsCost) AS AvgRepairCost
    FROM        make AS MK
    JOIN        model AS MD USING(MakeID)
    JOIN        stock AS ST USING(ModelID)
    WHERE       MK.MakeName = MKX.MakeName
  ) AS MakeAvgRepairCost


FROM       make AS MKX
JOIN       model AS MDX USING(MakeID)
JOIN       stock AS STX ON STX.ModelID = MDX.ModelID
JOIN       salesdetails SDX ON STX.StockCode = SDX.StockID
WHERE      STX.RepairsCost >
                (
                    SELECT      AVG(ST.RepairsCost) AS AvgRepairCost
                    FROM        make AS MK
                    JOIN        model AS MD USING(MakeID)
                    JOIN        stock AS ST USING(ModelID)
                    WHERE       MK.MakeName = MKX.MakeName
                ) * 1.5;
```

The output looks like that shown in Figure 15.5.

MakeName	RepairsCost	StockCode	MakeAvgRepairCost
Ferrari	9250.0000	15108517-AD0C-4FF2-A7D4-57679C374A68	4645.00000000
Ferrari	9250.0000	66C9034C-23A3-44F1-B946-2DDA65E684D8	4645.00000000
Ferrari	9250.0000	98299E86-0B98-42D8-A549-37D89435B4E3	4645.00000000
Ferrari	9250.0000	A326183E-7D45-4CF2-A353-7177A3EAB71F	4645.00000000
Ferrari	9250.0000	20041639-9549-415A-AEC2-7159352E8CB7	4645.00000000
Ferrari	9250.0000	5D11974B-326C-44C5-BA1D-57968CAB0DEE	4645.00000000
Ferrari	9250.0000	7392B5F6-783C-4D4B-B687-74A98411A7CB	4645.00000000
Porsche	1360.0000	05D4115C-3F27-4059-BDC8-C0C3FFC85E8B	848.02083333
Porsche	2000.0000	1860F37A-EBC7-42E9-B339-3F6D6048322F	848.02083333
Porsche	1360.0000	3F3BED8D-1203-4D3E-8AC0-3ACAC73BDE17	848.02083333
Porsche	1360.0000	518125AE-9A67-45A6-B3FD-557C785796FC	848.02083333
Porsche	2175.0000	6BF8C577-E615-4667-A48C-25E8D825AAC6	848.02083333
Porsche	1360.0000	70C9BE5C-3CCA-4FB2-B4DE-E5F0A61BB84D	848.02083333
Porsche	2000.0000	B165CAEF-FF77-4E63-98C1-59D97F97E7C9	848.02083333
Porsche	1360.0000	896B39D5-8040-4947-94D0-023484E78B23	848.02083333
Porsche	1360.0000	10AD713C-C997-48BB-A5FB-F0B5FD26479B	848.02083333

Figure 15.5: Using a correlated query in two parts of a query

How it Works

This query extends the SQL from the previous section by repeating the entire content of the subquery in the main query's SELECT clause. Both the identical correlated subqueries are linked to the outer query using the MakeName field.

5. Aggregated Correlated Subqueries

The sales manager has appeared at your desk. She has a new challenge—a report that shows all the customers in the countries where high-spending customers reside.

This kind of challenge proves that there are times when you need to look at multiple categories of data in order to get a better idea of the relative importance of certain data items. The following SQL is an example of this—for each country, it isolates the top customers (defined as those who have bought more than £500,000.00 worth of cars) and then displays all the customers in those countries:

```
SELECT     CUX.CustomerName

           ,CUX.Town

           ,COX.CountryName

FROM       customer CUX
```

```
JOIN      country COX ON CUX.country = COX.CountryISO2

WHERE     COX.CountryISO2 IN

                (

          SELECT      DISTINCT CU.country

          FROM        salesdetails SD

          JOIN        sales AS SA USING(SalesID)

          JOIN        customer CU USING(CustomerID)

          JOIN        country CO

                      ON CU.country = CO.CountryISO2

          WHERE       CU.country = CUX.country

          GROUP BY    CU.CustomerID

          HAVING      SUM(SD.SalePrice) > 500000

                )

ORDER BY   COX.CountryName, CUX.CustomerName;
```

Running this query gives the results that you can see in Figure 15.6.

	CustomerName	Town	CountryName
	Bling Bling S.A.	Paris	France
	Capots Reluisants S.A.	Paris	France
	Casseroles Chromes	Lyon	France
	Francois Chirac	Paris	France
	Jacques Mitterand	Paris	France
	Jean-Yves Truffaut	Paris	France
	Khader El Ghannam	Paris	France
	La Bagnole de Luxe	Paris	France
	Laurent Saint Yves	Marseille	France
	Le Luxe en Motion	Paris	France
	M. Pierre Dubois	Marseille	France
	Mme Anne Duport	Paris	France
	SuperSport S.A.R.L.	Paris	France
	Vive La Vitesse	Marseille	France
	Wladimir Lacroix	Lyon	France
	Glitz	Stuttgart	Germany

Figure 15.6: An aggregate correlated subquery

How it Works

This example is fairly similar to the previous one, but if you look carefully, you see that the correlated subquery is an aggregate query—it uses the GROUP BY and HAVING clauses to find all customers where the total sales are greater than £500,000.

Let's take a closer look at how this query works:

The outer query	Creates a list of customers by town and country. It does this by joining the Customer and Country tables.
The inner query	Joins the SalesDetails, Sales, Customer, and Country tables to obtain a dataset of sales information. This dataset groups the data using the CustomerID field to aggregate the total sales for each customer in the specific country that was passed in from the outer query. It then applies a HAVING clause to restrict the set of customers to only those with over £500,000.00 in sales.
The outer query	Then detects whether the country returned by the correlated subquery matches the country for the record that is being analyzed. If it does, then the record from the outer query is displayed

To resume, because the subquery is linked to the outer query on the Country field, it now finds only customers for the countries where there are high-spending clients. This is because, once again, the inner query runs once for each record in the outer query. Because the country field links the two queries, the inner query only aggregates customers per country.

Once the countries containing lucrative customers have been identified by the subquery—and passed up to the outer query via its WHERE clause—the outer query can select all required fields and order the result just as you would for any standard query.

Tricks and Traps

There are a few points that you may want to take note of when using aggregated correlated subqueries:

- A correlated subquery can be an aggregate query if your query logic requires it to be so. This is also the case for ordinary subqueries. In this respect, the outer and inner queries are structurally independent. Either can be a simple detail query or an aggregate query, no matter what type the other query is.

- If you copy the SQL for the inner query to a new query tab—and remove the WHERE clause—you can run the inner query. It will only return four countries, as you can see in Figure 15.7.

Country
GB
FR
DE
ES

Figure 15.7: *The output from a correlated subquery*

- Because the correlated subquery is potentially passing multiple elements back to the outer query for each make of car, it is important to use the *IN operator* for the outer query WHERE clause, and not the equal (=) operator. Remember that you can only use the equal operator if a *single* value is used in a WHERE clause.

- This example shows that the inner and outer queries can be quite different query types. However, they do share a field that allows them to be linked as well as some way of using the result from the subquery to filter the outer query, and this is all that is really necessary to create a correlated subquery.

6. Using Correlated Subqueries to Filter Data on an Aggregate Value

No firm wants to spend too much when buying goods, so it follows that you have to be able to analyze purchases that exceed certain calculated thresholds. As the finance director is homing in on purchasing costs as part of his drive to control spending, he wants you to create a report that shows all models of car where the maximum purchase cost is more than one and a half times the average purchase price for that model. The following SQL is an example of how to do this:

```
SELECT     MKX.MakeName, MDX.ModelName

FROM       make AS MKX

           JOIN model AS MDX USING(MakeID)

           JOIN stock AS STX USING(ModelID)

GROUP BY   MKX.MakeName, MDX.ModelName

HAVING     MAX(STX.Cost) >=

           (
```

```
SELECT     AVG(ST.Cost) * 1.5 AS AvgCostPerModel

FROM       make AS MK

JOIN       model AS MD USING(MakeID)

JOIN       stock AS ST USING(ModelID)

WHERE      MD.ModelName = MDX.ModelName

           AND MK.MakeName = MKX.MakeName

        );
```

Running this query gives the results that you can see in Figure 15.8.

MakeName	ModelName
Alfa Romeo	Giulia
Alfa Romeo	Giulietta
Aston Martin	DB2
Aston Martin	DB6
Aston Martin	DB9
Austin	Lichfield
Austin	Princess
Citroen	Rosalie
Jaguar	Mark X
Jaguar	XJ12
Jaguar	XK120
Jaguar	XK150
Lamborghini	Countach
Mercedes	280SL
Peugeot	205
Peugeot	404

Figure 15.8: Using a correlated subquery in the HAVING clause of the outer query

How it Works

For a change, let's begin by looking at the outer query in this example.

The outer query generates a list of vehicle makes and models based on the Make, Model, and Stock tables. It uses a GROUP BY to make this into an aggregate list where the make and model name only appear once.

Then the outer query gets interesting. Since it is an aggregate query, it can have a HAVING clause (if you remember, this clause filters data at the level of the aggregation, not at the level of individual records). It applies a HAVING clause to say, "only if the maximum cost for any make and model is greater than or equal to 150 percent of the average cost for this make and model."

It is the correlated subquery that calculates 150 percent of the average cost. Yet again, since this is a correlated subquery, it is filtered on data passed in from the outer query—in this case, the make and model. The subquery calculates the average cost for a specific make and model, then multiplies it by 1.5. This result is, in turn, passed back up to the outer query so it can be compared to the greatest vehicle cost for each make and model combination. Finally, the comparison operator (>=, or greater than or equal to) allows *only* those records that meet the filter criterion to pass through into the final output. That is, only makes and models are shown if any car of this type costs more than one and a half times the average for that particular car.

Tricks and Traps

There are only a few points to take away from this section:

- Correlated subqueries are, at their heart, a filtering mechanism, so you need to analyze what kind of filter you are looking for. If you are filtering data row by row, then you will probably use the correlated subquery in the WHERE clause. If, however, you are filtering records to compare a value with an aggregate result (such as the maximum cost for a vehicle model here), then you will almost inevitably want to apply the correlated subquery to the HAVING clause of the outer query.

- If the outer query is an aggregation query, then you can use any of the classic aggregation functions—SUM(), AVG(), MIN(), or MAX(), for instance—in the HAVING clause. This allows you to compare a result from the subquery to the total, the average, the highest, or the lowest aggregate value for a specific data group.

- Correlated subqueries can be joined to the "outer" query on multiple fields— as you can see in this example.

7. Using Correlated Subqueries to Detect If Records Exist

"Know your customer" is the mantra that resounds throughout businesses across five continents. For many firms, however, the refrain could just as well be "know who your customer is." The following SQL shows you how to create a list of all the active clients of Prestige Cars in 2017:

```
SELECT DISTINCT     CU.CustomerName

FROM                customer CU
```

```
WHERE              EXISTS

                   (

                   SELECT    *

                   FROM      sales SA

                   WHERE     SA.CustomerID = CU.CustomerID

                             AND YEAR(SA.SaleDate) = 2017

                   )

ORDER BY           CU.CustomerName;
```

The list that you can see in Figure 15.9 shows only the customers that have bought a vehicle from Prestige Cars in a specific year—2017, in this example. Any potential customer in the Customer table who did *not* buy a car in 2017 is not displayed.

CustomerName
Alicia Almodovar
Antonio Maura
Autos Soortivos
Birmingham Executive Prestige Vehicles
Capots Reluisants S.A.
Casseroles Chromes
Convertible Dreams
Diplomatic Cars
Eat My Exhaust Ltd
Glittering Prize Cars Ltd
Glitz
Honest Pete Motors
Kieran O'Harris
King Leer Cars
La Bagnole de Luxe
Laurent Saint Yves

Figure 15.9: A simple correlated subquery using EXISTS

How it Works

Correlated subqueries are not just for calculations. They can also be very useful in determining whether data should be included in a result set. In practice, what this means is that you need to apply the EXISTS keyword to the query. When you use this new keyword, the outer query checks to see if any records exist for this specific customer ID. If one does, then the customer name is output. The flip side to this is that if *no* records exist then data for this customer is *not* displayed.

This means that *if* the correlated subquery contains any records for this particular CustomerID, then the customer name is returned by the outer query. This is because the filter in the outer query says, "Where a record exists in the inner query." If there is no corresponding record in the correlated subquery, then no customer name is output. This way the query as a whole only returns data from one dataset when a criterion applied to a second set of data is met.

Tricks and Traps

When using correlated subqueries, you need to be aware that

- Correlated subqueries depend on a link existing between the inner and outer queries, so, if you can use a JOIN to link tables in a query, then you can use the same tables in a correlated subquery.

- When you use the EXISTS keyword, you are looking simply for the existence of a record in the subquery. This means that you can make the SELECT clause of the correlated subquery really simple and not even specify any particular column names. After all, column names in the subquery will not be used in this type of correlated subquery since you are only looking to see if records exist.

8. Using a Correlated Subquery to Exclude Data

No business wants to carry excess stock. Consequently, I am sure that you understand why the company finance director wants to know which vehicles have not yet been sold and are paralyzing valuable cash in the parking lot. The following SQL code shows you how to produce this list for him:

```
SELECT     CONCAT(MakeName, ', ', ModelName) AS VehicleInStock
           ,ST.Stockcode
FROM       make AS MK
JOIN       model AS MD ON MK.MakeID = MD.MakeID
JOIN       stock AS ST ON ST.ModelID = MD.ModelID
WHERE      NOT EXISTS
                    (SELECT   *
                     FROM     salesdetails SD
                     WHERE    ST.StockCode = SD.StockID);
```

Running this query gives the results that you can see in Figure 15.10. You can see all the results if you scroll down this list.

VehicleInStock	STOCKCODE
Ferrari. Testarossa	8BD326B3-8DE8-4DC9-9F96-FD132C5E1BF2
Ferrari. Testarossa	DE3096AD-76F9-4AAF-B2E1-49FA8E2C377F
Ferrari. 355	C82D133F-3442-464B-A16A-D5419A9E1CDF
Ferrari. 308	FBF39066-2C13-469D-B913-EBCF22CCFD63
Ferrari. Dino	F187F74F-3909-4291-A15B-F793AB88DE3B
Ferrari. 360	579AD98F-B7A5-456A-8F17-5B77A5479767
Porsche. 944	52F665EA-2D6D-4ECA-8A14-553522A45B04
Porsche. 944	74F717DA-B4DA-44F2-857A-F062AC60052E
Aston Martin. DB2	51451AC8-A35F-4597-B4BC-94E92C150C3D
Aston Martin. DB2	532B985F-94AC-45DF-AE17-431FBCC66D0C
Aston Martin. DB2	62611547-0F2D-41B1-BA32-E34AB67E10A3
Aston Martin. DB4	4831A9DA-09BD-4AC3-8984-947F284CD4A8
Aston Martin. DB5	2309FF52-564A-4A2C-B6EB-D94AA321D687
Aston Martin. DB6	26A3D067-DCEA-4FF1-9A97-E7AEE0D2BC14
Aston Martin. DB6	373B7D39-B5A3-4018-883C-AC81EF3B5D8F
Aston Martin. DB9	A4A2F089-526E-4C69-AACC-F58488B2E1C7

Figure 15.10: A correlated subquery using NOT EXISTS

How it Works

Just as you may need to know when data exists (as was the case in the previous example), there could be cases when you need to find out when data is *not* present in related tables. In the Prestige Cars data model, the Stock table contains all the vehicles ever bought. The SalesDetails table contains all the vehicles ever sold. A correlated subquery can compare the data in one table with the data in the other.

When you want to run this kind of analysis, it is probably easier to use the table that contains the most data as the outer query and the table that contains a mode-limited set of data as the correlated (or inner) subquery. The code above does exactly this.

The outer query	Joins the Make, Model, and Stock tables so that the required fields can be output—as well as ensuring access to a field that can be shared with the subquery (the StockCode field in this example).
The inner query	Selects all the data from the SalesDetails table, but as this is a correlated subquery, it only finds records where the StockID matches the StockCode of the outer query.

Once again, the subquery is rerun for every record that the outer query finds. If there is a match on the StockCode/StockID fields, then the WHERE clause of the outer query comes into play. This filter says, "tell me if there is not a match," which is the colloquial way of saying WHERE NOT EXISTS. If the two tables do *not* match for a record in the outer query, this record is returned by the query.

Tricks and Traps

It takes a little practice to successfully use the NOT EXISTS function, so when you are applying this concept to your queries, be sure to remember the following key points:

- A correlated subquery that uses NOT EXISTS is also only looking for the existence of data in the subquery—the actual fields selected by the subquery are irrelevant.

- A correlated subquery like this can run much more slowly than a simpler query does. This should not worry you; it is precisely because the inner query has to run once for every record in the outer query. However, you need to be aware that a query like this can take quite a while to run for a large dataset.

9. Complex Joins in Correlated Subqueries

Diligent purchasing can require an in-depth knowledge of your products, so it follows that the buyers for Prestige Cars want to track any vehicles that seem unduly expensive compared to similar models. The following piece of SQL helps you keep tabs on your costs by listing all makes where the maximum purchase cost is over twice the average purchase cost for that make and model for the year:

```
SELECT      MKX.MakeName, MDX.ModelName

            ,YEAR(STX.DateBought) AS PurchaseYear

FROM        make AS MKX JOIN model AS MDX

            ON MKX.MakeID = MDX.MakeID

            JOIN stock AS STX ON STX.ModelID = MDX.ModelID

WHERE       YEAR(STX.DateBought) IN (2015, 2016)

GROUP BY    MKX.MakeName, YEAR(STX.DateBought)

HAVING      MAX(STX.Cost) >=

                        (

            SELECT  AVG(ST.Cost) * 2 AS AvgCostPerModel
```

```
               FROM      make AS MK

                         JOIN model AS MD

                         ON MK.MakeID = MD.MakeID

                         JOIN stock AS ST

                         ON ST.ModelID = MD.ModelID

               WHERE     MK.MakeName = MKX.MakeName

                         AND  MD.ModelName = MDX.ModelName

                         AND YEAR(ST.DateBought) =

                                             PurchaseYear

          );
```

Running this query gives the results that you can see in Figure 15.11.

	MakeName	ModelName	PurchaseYear
▶	Aston Martin	DB4	2015
	Aston Martin	DB2	2016
	Bentley	Continental	2016
	Jaguar	XJ12	2016
	Lamborghini	Countach	2016

Figure 15.11: A correlated subquery with a complex join

How it Works

Some questions require you to be more restrictive in your analysis. You might want to add multiple elements to the calculated comparison, not just one, as was the case in the previous couple of examples. Correlated subqueries allow you to join the inner and outer queries on more than one field. Consequently, this query *also* calculates an average value for a subset of data. This time the value that is passed in to the correlated subquery from the outer query is a calculation—double the average cost for each make. This figure is then compared to the aggregate maximum cost per make in the HAVING clause of the outer query.

What makes this query a little subtler is the use of a more complex link between the outer and inner queries. This time there are three elements:

- The make of vehicle
- The model of vehicle
- The year that the car was bought

A multiple connection like this has the effect of limiting the comparison even further. Now it is the maximum cost per *make* per *year* that is used as the comparison element. The net result is that certain makes of car can appear in the final result more than once, because at least one item in stock costs more than twice the average for that make in any of several years.

The outer query also adds a filter in the form of a WHERE clause. Since the field that is used in the WHERE clause is also used to join the outer query to the correlated subquery, the choice of years is applied in *both* queries, even though it is only added *once*—to the outer query.

Tricks and Traps

When applying complex joins you need to take away a couple of fundamental points concerning correlated subqueries:

- Being able to join the inner and outer queries on several fields is, in fact, a powerful tool for simplifying certain types of analysis. In Chapter 12, you saw that if you filtered an ordinary query that contained a subquery, you *also* had to filter the subquery in certain cases to get the result that you wanted. If you are filtering the outer query on a field that is used to create the correlation between the two queries, then you are automatically applying the WHERE clause of the outer query to the inner query. This avoids repetition—and minimizes the risk of error.

- When you are joining the main query to the correlated subquery on a field that has been wrapped in a function (as is the case for the DateBought field in the outer SELECT query in this example) you *must* add an alias to this field and *also* use this alias in the WHERE clause inside the correlated subquery. Indeed, if you try and write a WHERE clause like this inside the correlated subquery:

  ```
  AND YEAR(ST.DateBought) = YEAR(STX.DateBought)
  ```

  Then the query will simply not work.

10. Using a Correlated Subquery to Verify Values across Tables

No organization wants erroneous data. This is especially true where invoices are concerned. Fortunately SQL is a perfect tool when it comes to data validation. Specifically, let's suppose that you want to check that invoice header totals correspond to invoice line aggregation. The following short piece of SQL shows how to do this:

```
SELECT      SalesID

            ,TotalSalePrice

            ,CASE WHEN

                        (

                          SELECT SUM(SalePrice)

                          FROM    salesdetails

                          WHERE   SalesID = sales.SalesID

                        ) = TotalSalePrice

                              THEN 'OK'

                              ELSE 'Error in Invoice'

                  END AS LineItemCheck

FROM        sales

ORDER BY    SalesID;
```

Running this query gives the results that you can see in Figure 15.12.

SalesID	TotalSalePrice	LineItemCheck
1	65000.00	OK
2	220000.10	Error in Invoice
3	19500.00	OK
4	11500.00	OK
5	19900.00	Error in Invoice
6	29500.00	OK
7	49500.20	Error in Invoice
8	76000.90	Error in Invoice
9	19600.00	OK
10	36500.00	OK
11	89000.00	OK
12	169500.00	OK
13	8950.00	OK
14	195000.00	OK
15	22950.00	OK
16	8695.00	OK

Figure 15.12: Using a correlated subquery to verify values across tables

How it Works

Despite the best efforts of programmers and data entry staff everywhere, errors can creep into data. Fortunately, SQL can also carry out automated checks and balances on your data. This code works because the two tables that it uses—Sales and SalesDetails—are part of a relational structure. More specifically, the Sales table is in a one-to-many relationship with the SalesDetails table. That is, several sales details records can be linked to a single Sales record. What is more, the Sales table contains a field—SalePrice—that should contain the total sales value of all the corresponding detail records for that particular sale in the SalesDetails table.

This query begins with a subquery that returns the sum of the SalePrice for the SalesDetails table. However, to prevent the query from merely returning the total for every record, a correlation is set up between the subquery and an outer query that lists the SalePrice for every record in the Sales table. This forces the inner query to calculate only the total sales for the records that are linked to the Sales table.

The trick in this query is how the output from the correlated subquery is used. Rather than just returning the total sales for each sale from the SalesDetails table, this aggregate figure is compared—using a CASE statement—with the sales figure from the Sales table. If the two are identical, the query returns "OK." Should they not match, it returns "Error in Invoice."

This way the query can verify that the data is as it should be, and if not, bring any erroneous records to your attention for further investigation.

Tricks and Traps

To conclude this chapter I have one final point:

* As the Sales table in the outer query does not have an alias we have to precede the SalesID field from this table with the table name in the WHERE clause of the correlated subquery.

Conclusion

This short chapter introduced you to a new tool to extend your SQL skillset—correlated subqueries. Correlated subqueries let you link subqueries to main queries and filter the data in the outer query by checking every record that it contains against the result of a subquery.

Core Knowledge Learned in This Chapter

The keywords and concepts that you have seen in this chapter are

Concept	Description
Correlated subqueries	Correlated subqueries let you link subqueries to main queries and filter the data in the outer query by checking every record that it contains against the result of a subquery.
EXISTS	This keyword tests for the existence of a record in a subquery that is linked to the outer query.
NOT EXISTS	This keyword tests for the absence of a record in a subquery that is linked to the outer query

CHAPTER 16

Dataset Manipulation

Sometimes the data that you use may not be in a single table (as you might expect it to be) but can be spread across a series of tables with identical structures. Moreover, since much data analysis is comparative, you may want to compare one specific set or subset of data with another separate dataset and isolate any differences—even if both datasets originate in the same source data. You can accomplish this by seeing if two sets of data overlap, for instance. Yet another potential requirement can consist of isolating the data that exists in one dataset but not in another. These challenges involve handling entire datasets.

Using Datasets to Mix and Match Data

This chapter takes you further into the domain of comparative analysis of data using MySQL. It builds on the techniques that you saw in the previous chapters and teaches you how to mix and match datasets in order to delve deep into the information they contain.

More specifically, in this chapter you learn how to

- Read data from several identically structured tables simultaneously.
- Create separate subsets of data that you can use for comparison purposes.

- Compare the data in two tables or subsets of data and only display data that is common to both tables.

- Compare the data in two tables or subsets of data and only display data that is in one table but not the other.

1. Read Data from Multiple Identical Tables Using the UNION Operator

Data comes in a multitude of shapes and forms and is not always available as a relational set of tables that can be joined. Sometimes you may have to query data from two or more tables that have identical structures—meaning each table contains a slice of a total dataset. As an example of this, imagine that you have been asked to look at *three tables* of sales information, one for sales in each of the years 2015, 2016, and 2017. All three tables contain the same columns of data in the same order.

The SQL to query the three tables at once looks like this:

```
SELECT   MakeName, ModelName, CustomerName, CountryName, Cost
         ,RepairsCost, PartsCost, TransportInCost, SalePrice, SaleDate
FROM     sales2015

UNION

SELECT   MakeName, ModelName, CustomerName, CountryName, Cost
         ,RepairsCost, PartsCost, TransportInCost, SalePrice, SaleDate
FROM     sales2016

UNION

SELECT   MakeName, ModelName, CustomerName, CountryName, Cost
         ,RepairsCost, PartsCost, TransportInCost, SalePrice, SaleDate
FROM     sales2017;
```

Running this query gives the results in Figure 16.1. As you can see—if you scroll down through the output—the data is returned for any of the three years, whereas each table only contains data for a single year.

MakeName	ModelName	CustomerName	CountryName	Cost	RepairsCost	PartsCost	TransportInCost	SalePrice	SaleDate
Alfa Romeo	Giulia	Convertible Dreams	United Kingdom	6956.00	400.00	750.00	150.00	8695.00	2015-07-12 00:00:00
Jaguar	XJS	SuperSport S.A.R.L.	France	15600.00	290.00	750.00	150.00	19500.00	2015-07-25 00:00:00
Jaguar	XK150	Alexei Tolstoi	United Kingdom	18392.00	390.00	750.00	150.00	22990.00	2015-07-15 00:00:00
Jaguar	XK150	Alexei Tolstoi	United Kingdom	18080.00	660.00	750.00	150.00	22600.00	2015-10-30 00:00:00
Jaguar	XJS	Alexei Tolstoi	United Kingdom	12480.00	1100.00	500.00	150.00	15600.00	2015-09-15 00:00:00
Jaguar	XK120	Peter McLuckie	United Kingdom	10120.00	320.00	750.00	150.00	12650.00	2015-09-05 00:00:00
Triumph	TR5	Peter McLuckie	United States	4400.00	500.00	750.00	150.00	5500.00	2015-08-02 00:00:00
Triumph	TR4	Theo Kowalski	Germany	79600.00	500.00	750.00	750.00	99500.00	2016-04-30 00:00:00
Ferrari	360	Glitz	United Kingdom	156000.00	3950.00	3150.00	1950.00	195000.00	2016-07-25 00:00:00
Ferrari	Testarossa	Mrs. Ivana Telford	United Kingdom	125200.00	2200.00	3150.00	1950.00	156500.00	2016-09-19 00:00:00
Ferrari	355	Honest Pete Motors	United Kingdom	82360.00	2175.00	2200.00	750.00	102950.00	2016-04-05 00:00:00
Ferrari	Mondial	King Leer Cars	United Kingdom	164000.00	9250.00	750.00	1950.00	205000.00	2016-07-25 00:00:00
Ferrari	355	Alexei Tolstoi	United Kingdom	132000.00	3950.00	2200.00	1950.00	165000.00	2016-01-01 00:00:00
Ferrari	Testarossa	Wonderland Wheels	United States	127600.00	2000.00	3150.00	1950.00	159500.00	2016-01-01 00:00:00
Ferrari	355	Sondra Horowitz	France	53200.00	2175.00	1500.00	750.00	66500.00	2016-08-13 00:00:00
Porsche	911	Casseroles Chromes							

Figure 16.1: Joining data from multiple identically structured queries using the UNION operator

How it Works

SQL lets you read data from multiple tables at once if—and only if—the structure of the queries is identical. You carry out this operation by writing a SELECT query for each table and then by amalgamating the queries using the UNION operator.

Clearly using UNION to merge the data from several tables is only useful if you have a database that contains identically structured tables. Because this is often the case for data analysis and reporting (where the original, relational data is kept separate) or when dealing with data sent from outside suppliers, you could find this technique useful in practice.

In this example, you joined the three tables sequentially (or "vertically") rather than "horizontally," as you have done in many queries so far in this book. Put another way, you have added the contents of one table to the contents of another. Figure 16.2 illustrates conceptually what you have done.

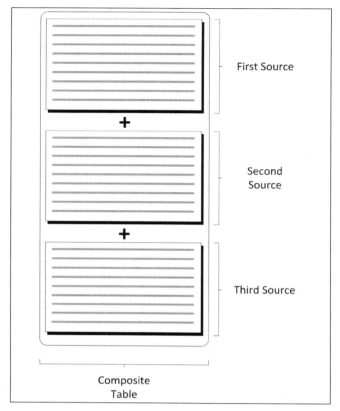

Figure 16.2: Compiling a dataset from multiple identical tables

Tricks and Traps

Although simple enough, the UNION operator does require you to remember that

- You can use aliases to rename the columns in a UNION query just as you can in an SQL query; however, you only need to add aliases to the *first* query in the series—that is, the query for 2015 sales in this example. The other queries use the aliases that you applied to the topmost query. After all, a column can only have one name, so the name is taken from the topmost query.

- In a UNION query, it is vital that you select the columns from each of the separate queries in the same order.

- If the underlying tables do not contain identical columns in the same order you can replace the name of any columns that are missing from a table with NULL in the SELECT statement. For instance, if the table Sales2016 does not contain a TransportInCost field, you can write the following SQL so that the query over the three tables will still work:

```
SELECT    MakeName, ModelName, CustomerName, CountryName, Cost,
RepairsCost, PartsCost, NULL, SalePrice, SaleDate
```

* The UNION operator will remove any duplicates from the output. If you want to let duplicates through into the result, then you should use the UNION ALL operator instead.

2. Isolate Identical Data in Multiple Tables

The sales director is convinced that some clients have bought identical cars two years running. She has even been using yearly data in spreadsheets to look into this. Now she wants you to use yearly data tables to identify all customers that have bought identical makes and models of vehicles in 2015 and 2016.

The following SQL does this for you.

```
SELECT DISTINCT MakeName, ModelName, CustomerName, CountryName

FROM            sales2015

JOIN            sales2016

                USING(MakeName, ModelName, CustomerName, CountryName)

ORDER BY        MakeName, ModelName;
```

Running this tiny piece of SQL will give the result that you can see in Figure 16.3.

MakeName	ModelName	CustomerName	CountryName
Aston Martin	DB5	Birmingham Executive Prestige Vehicles	United Kingdom
Aston Martin	DB6	SuperSport S.A.R.L.	France
Jaguar	XJS	Alexei Tolstoi	United Kingdom

Figure 16.3: Identifying identical data from similarly structured tables

How it Works

Before even considering the code it is important to understand what exactly is happening here.

The aim is to isolate any records from two tables that share a common structure where certain fields contain the same elements. To be even more precise, *each* of the fields that you are using to identify shared records must each contain the *same* element in both tables.

A Venn diagram (see Figure 16.4) can help you better understand how a query that isolates shared data works.

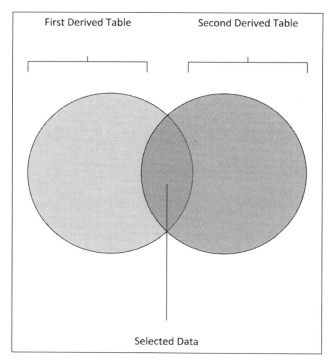

Figure 16.4: How isolating common elements in separate tables works

The query works like this:

First: It joins the two source tables and specifies all the fields that must contain identical data as the JOIN fields. In this example they are the fields inside the parentheses following the USING operator.

Second: It identifies the fields to extract from the two tables. These should be the same fields used in the JOIN clause. The DISTINCT keyword is added to force the result set to show each record once only.

The result is that the query returns all the data that is common in the specified fields from any record across the source tables.

Tricks and Traps

I feel that the following few points are worth noting when juggling separate but similarly or identically structured tables like these:

- Joining datasets like this does not automatically remove any duplicates. So you need to add the DISTINCT operator to the query to avoid displaying identical elements several times.

- The fields that you are using to identify the shared elements have to be identical (or similar) data types.

- You do not have to select *all* the fields that are in each table to isolate data; however, any fields that you do select must be *identical* in all the source tables if the record is to be returned, *and* you must join on these fields.

- You can add fields to the SELECT clause that are not used to join the tables. However in this case you will have to specify which table the data is drawn from—and there is no guarantee that the data will be identical in both tables for these fields.

- You can join using multiple fields with the USING operator. In this case—as you can see in the SQL for this example—you simply separate each join field with a comma inside the parentheses following the USING operator.

- If you want to join the two tables using several fields without the USING operator, the code would look like this:

```
SELECT DISTINCT  S15.MakeName, S15.ModelName

                 ,S15.CustomerName, S15.CountryName

FROM             sales2015 AS S15

JOIN             sales2016 AS S16

                 ON S15.MakeName = S16.MakeName

                 AND S15.ModelName = S16.ModelName

                 AND S15.CustomerName = S16.CustomerName

                 AND S15.CountryName = S16.CountryName

ORDER BY         MakeName, ModelName;
```

3. Isolate Common Elements in Multiple Subsets of Data

The sales director needs to compare elements that are similar across separate time periods. Her exact requirement is to find all the makes bought in 2016 that were also bought the previous year. The following query does exactly this.

```
SELECT DISTINCT TB1.MakeName

FROM

(

SELECT     MK.MakeName
```

```
FROM       make AS MK

JOIN       model AS MD USING(MakeID)

JOIN       stock AS ST USING(ModelID)

WHERE      YEAR(DateBought) = 2015

) TB1

JOIN

(

SELECT     MK.MakeName

FROM       make AS MK

JOIN       model AS MD USING(MakeID)

JOIN       stock AS ST USING(ModelID)

WHERE      YEAR(DateBought) = 2016

) TB2

ON         TB1.MakeName = TB2.MakeName

ORDER BY TB1.MakeName;
```

Running this query gives the results that you can see in Figure 16.5.

MakeName
Alfa Romeo
Aston Martin
Bentlev
Ferrari
Jaquar
Porsche
Triumph

Figure 16.5: Isolating common elements in separate tables

How it Works

In this query you actually have two separate queries:

The first:	Joins the Stock, Make, and Model tables and adds only the MakeName field to the SELECT clause. This query then filters the results so that only vehicles bought in *2015* are returned.
The second:	Duplicates the first query, but sets the year to *2016*.

Combining these two queries with a JOIN (which is, in fact, an inner join) runs both queries and then identifies which results are common to both. This is because you are joining the two datasets using the field that is shared. Only these shared results are finally output.

Finally, the DISTINCT operator ensures that only one of each data element is returned.

Tricks and Traps

As you might imagine, there are several key points to note with a technique as powerful as this:

- The two queries in this example are, technically, subqueries—even if they are both on the same "level." Consequently, they have to be placed inside parentheses. However, they are completely separate subsets of data.

- Joining subsets of data like this does not automatically remove any duplicates in the final result. If you run each query separately, you see that many examples of each make are sold in either of the two years (this is shown in Figure 16.6); however, the final result removes all duplicates from the output due to the application of the DISTINCT operator.

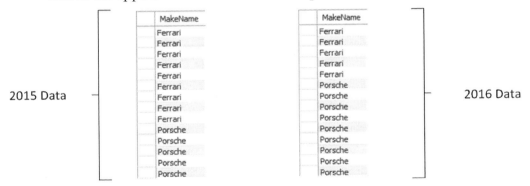

Figure 16.6: Duplicate data before it is removed when isolating identical data

- You are not limited to just two queries in a query that joins separate datasets like this. You can add multiple queries if you need to.

- You do not have to select *all* the fields that are in each table to isolate data; however, any fields that you *do* select must be identical in all the source tables if the record is to be returned, *and* you must join on these fields.

4. Joining Multiple Identical Tables in a Subquery

The CEO has gone back to the sales data that you joined together in the first section of this chapter and is now requesting that you produce a simple list of makes and models from all three tables that were sold to German clients.

After a little thought, you adapt the query that you used previously to satisfy her request. The SQL looks like this:

```
SELECT  MakeName, ModelName

FROM

(

    SELECT  MakeName, ModelName, CustomerName, CountryName, Cost

    ,RepairsCost, PartsCost, TransportInCost, SalePrice, SaleDate

    FROM    sales2015

    UNION

    SELECT  MakeName, ModelName, CustomerName, CountryName, Cost

    ,RepairsCost, PartsCost, TransportInCost, SalePrice, SaleDate

    FROM    sales2016

    UNION

    SELECT  MakeName, ModelName, CustomerName, CountryName, Cost

    ,RepairsCost, PartsCost, TransportInCost, SalePrice, SaleDate

    FROM    sales2017

) SQ

WHERE   CountryName = 'Germany';
```

Running this code produces the output that you can see in Figure 16.7.

MakeName	ModelName
Porsche	924
Ferrari	360
Porsche	944
Lamborghini	Diabolo
Aston Martin	Rapide
Bentley	Flying Spur
Alfa Romeo	Giulia
Lamborghini	Jarama
Aston Martin	DB9
Aston Martin	DB2
Austin	Lichfield

Figure 16.7: Using a derived query with tables joined using the UNION operator

How it Works

The ability of SQL to deliver the output from multiple identical tables is certainly useful in many occasions; however, you need a way to make the resulting data easy to filter. Moreover, undoubtedly you will have times when you want to select only some of the columns that each table contains.

This is a perfect opportunity for wrapping the UNION query inside an outer query and treating the UNION query as a derived table. This simple technique allows you to select only the fields that you require, then filter the data using a single WHERE clause, and even group the data if you so choose.

Tricks and Traps

I have only a couple of comments to make here:

- It is perfectly possible to apply the same SELECT and WHERE clauses to each query that is used in a UNION query. However, this can be both more laborious and more error-prone than making the UNION query into a derived table and filtering on the combined data.

- Extending a query to include a derived table is a great example of code reuse, where just a small tweak can make SQL that you created previously even more applicable. So remember to save your code snippets in case they turn out to be important at a later date.

5. Isolating Nonidentical Records from Two Datasets

Sometimes it is not overlap of data that interests you but the data that is *not* shared between two datasets. A practical example of this is when the CEO requests a list of all the vehicle models sold this year but not in the previous year. The following SQL shows you how to isolate this kind of result:

```
SELECT DISTINCT TB1.MakeAndModel

FROM

(

    SELECT      CONCAT(MK.MakeName, '-', MD.ModelName) AS MakeAndModel

    FROM        make AS MK

    JOIN        model AS MD USING(MakeID)

    JOIN        stock AS ST USING(ModelID)

    WHERE       YEAR(DateBought) = 2016

) TB1

LEFT JOIN

(

    SELECT      CONCAT(MK.MakeName, '-', MD.ModelName) AS MakeAndModel

    FROM        make AS MK

    JOIN        model AS MD USING(MakeID)

    JOIN        stock AS ST USING(ModelID)

    WHERE       YEAR(DateBought) = 2015

) TB2

ON      TB1.MakeAndModel = TB2.MakeAndModel

WHERE   TB2.MakeAndModel IS NULL

ORDER BY TB1.MakeAndModel;
```

Running this query gives the results that you can see in Figure 16.8.

MakeAndModel
Alfa Romeo-Spider
Aston Martin-DB2
Aston Martin-DB9
Aston Martin-Rapide
Aston Martin-Vanquish
Aston Martin-Vantage
Bentley-Arnage
Bentley-Brooklands
Bentley-Continental
Ferrari-360
Ferrari-Mondial
Jaguar-E-Type
Jaguar-XJ12
Lamborghini-Countach
Lamborghini-Diabolo
Porsche-928

Figure 16.8: Isolating nonidentical records from two datasets

How it Works

This query is similar in certain respects to the queries that you saw in previous examples. Once again, you have multiple queries that output identical field sets in the same order. This time, however, a LEFT JOIN is used to link the datasets returned by the individual queries. Then the IS NULL operator is applied in the WHERE clause to the join field in the second derived table to filter out data that is contained in the first derived table but not contained in the second derived table.

This technique finds all the elements (the make and model of vehicles sold in a specific year) in the first derived table and then compares these rows with the make and model of vehicles sold the previous year in the second derived table. Any models of car that are present in *both* datasets are left out of the final result. This way you can see which cars were sold in 2016 but not in 2015.

Figure 16.9 shows you, conceptually, how this approach works.

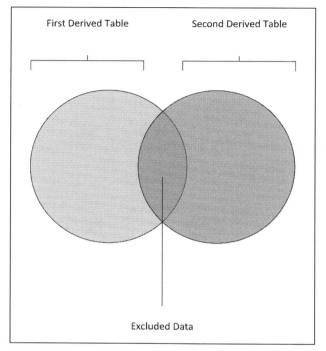

Figure 16.9: Excluding the shared items from two sets of data

Tricks and Traps

I have only one comment to make here:

- The two queries used to create the two derived tables in this example are, once again, completely separate. Indeed, they have to be different for the query to work properly. Consequently, each query has its own WHERE clause, and this is what allows you to specify completely different datasets, even if the two queries are otherwise identical.

6. Displaying the Complete Records for Nonidentical data

The CEO wants you to extend the principle underlying the query that you wrote previously that showed a list of makes and models sold in 2015 but not in 2016. Only this time she wants to see all the details of the sales—not just the makes and models. What is more, she wants to see the data for sales in 2016 were there was no sale in 2017.

It only takes you a few minutes to extend your previous query to look like the following code:

```
WITH MakeAndModel_CTE

AS

(

SELECT DISTINCT TB1.MakeName, TB1.ModelName

FROM

(

SELECT      MakeName, ModelName
FROM        Sales2016
) TB1

LEFT JOIN

(

SELECT      MakeName, ModelName
FROM        Sales2017
) TB2

            USING (MakeName, ModelName)

WHERE       TB2.MakeName IS NULL

            AND TB2.ModelName IS NULL

)

SELECT    *
FROM      Sales2016
JOIN      MakeAndModel_CTE
          USING (MakeName, ModelName);
```

Running this query will produce the output that you can see in Figure 16.10.

ModelName	Color
280SL	Red
355	Red
404	Red
500	Red
57C	Red
600	Red
924	Red
944	Red
DB2	Red
DB5	Red
DB6	Red
DB9	Red
Flying Sour	Red
Ghost	Red
Giulia	Red
Mark X	Red

Figure 16.10: *Displaying full records when isolating datasets by specific fields present in one table but not in another*

How it Works

The principle behind this query is to use the output from your initial query as a filter on the 2016 data set. This way, the makes and models sold in 2016 can be isolated—and then used as the basis for a complete list.

So this requires a two-phased approach:

First: Define a CTE that isolates the data that you will use to filter another dataset.

Then: Create the "main" query that extracts the required data from the source—and joins to the CTE so that the latter acts as a filter on the former.

To appreciate this more clearly, it probably helps if you select the query inside the CTE and run it. Do this and you will see the output shown in Figure 16.11.

	MakeName	ModelName
▶	Ferrari	360
	Ferrari	Mondial
	Lamborghini	Countach
	Bentley	Flying Spur
	Bentley	Brooklands
	Bentley	Continental
	Rolls Royce	Ghost
	Jaguar	XJ12
	Jaguar	XK120
	Jaguar	E-Type
	Jaguar	XJS
	Triumph	TR4

Figure 16.11: The output from a CTE that isolates nonidentical data

This list contains the makes and models sold in 2016 but not in 2017. As I explained this approach in Section 5 I will not explain it again here. The only slight difference between this example and the SQL in Section 6 is that here we are not concatenating the MakeName and ModelName fields, but keeping them separate.

Once this list of makes and models is defined you can create the main query. This query selects all the data from the sales2016 table using a SELECT * clause. It then joins the source table (sales2016) to the CTE on the MakeName and ModelName fields so that the data is filtered and, as a result, *only lists these specific makes and models*. As these two fields were used in the CTE we have to use *both* of these fields in the main query when joining the output data to the CTE. You can then extend the SELECT clause to add any further required fields.

Tricks and Traps

I have only a couple of comments to make here.

- I realize that writing SELECT * is generally considered poor coding practice. However, there are rare occasions when it can be considered a valid approach. In cases like this example, where the structure of tables might be extended to contain other valuable information, using SELECT * can make the code more resilient, as it will gracefully accept many changes to the source structure.

- When dealing with multiple data sets, it can help to try and break down the problem into component parts. Once the challenge is understood, writing the actual code can be much easier. Indeed, it can be really useful if you think in terms of what is required rather than what the data is or how it is shaped.

7. Displaying the Complete Records for Identical data

The sales director has seen the data that you recently produced for the CEO that isolated cars sold in both 2015 and 2016. However, she wants a complete list of all these vehicles—not just the make and model. Oh, and she wants to know which table each record came from, too.

After a few minutes you come up with the following SQL:

```
WITH IdenticalData_CTE

AS

(

SELECT DISTINCT MakeName, ModelName, CustomerName, CountryName
FROM            sales2015
JOIN            sales2016
                USING(MakeName, ModelName, CustomerName, CountryName)
ORDER BY        MakeName, ModelName
)


SELECT  *, '2015 Data'
FROM    sales2015
JOIN    IdenticalData_CTE
        USING (MakeName, ModelName, CustomerName, CountryName)
UNION
SELECT  *, '2016 Data'
FROM    sales2016
JOIN    IdenticalData_CTE
        USING (MakeName, ModelName, CustomerName, CountryName);
```

Executing this code gives the output that is shown in Figure 16.12.

MakeName	ModelName	CustomerName	CountryName	Cost	RepairsCost	PartsCost	TransportInCost	SalePrice	SaleDate	2015 Data
Aston Martin	DB5	Birmingham Executive Prestige Vehicles	United Kingdom	39600.00	2500.00	1500.00	550.00	49500.00	2015-03-24 00:00:00	2015 Data
Aston Martin	DB6	SuperSport S.A.R.L.	France	44800.00	1785.00	500.00	550.00	56000.00	2015-07-25 00:00:00	2015 Data
Jaguar	XJS	Alexei Tolstoi	United Kingdom	18080.00	660.00	750.00	150.00	22600.00	2015-10-30 00:00:00	2015 Data
Aston Martin	DB5	Birmingham Executive Prestige Vehicles	United Kingdom	45512.00	2000.00	750.00	550.00	56890.00	2016-11-03 00:00:00	2016 Data
Aston Martin	DB6	SuperSport S.A.R.L.	France	39664.00	660.00	500.00	550.00	49580.00	2016-05-30 00:00:00	2016 Data
Jaguar	XJS	Alexei Tolstoi	United Kingdom	7960.00	500.00	750.00	150.00	9950.00	2016-05-30 00:00:00	2016 Data

Figure 16.12: *Displaying complete records from separate tables to illustrate shared elements*

How it Works

This query tackles the challenge in a way that reflects how the problem has been analyzed.

First: A CTE is created that isolates the Make, Model, Customer, and Country where all these fields contain *identical* data in records from both source tables. This query is identical to the one explained in Section 2.

Second: The main query joins the output from the CTE to the first source table (sales2015) so that the CTE acts as a filter—only outputting the makes, models, customer and country data for records from both source tables.

Finally: The main query is extended—using a UNION operator—to add the data from the second source table (sales2016) to the output. The data from this table, too, is filtered using the CTE.

To make the output clearer to understand, an extra field is added to the SELECT statement in each of the clauses that make up the UNION query. This added field indicates, as a text, which table the data has come from.

The trick with a challenge like this one is to understand that you are using two levels of data.

First: You are isolating a dataset using the fields that define where the data that is common to the two tables resides. Here, these are the MakeName, ModelName, CustomerName, and CountryName fields. You cannot add further fields to isolate common data without overly restricting the shared data.

Second: This dataset is joined to the source data tables (each in separate queries as part of a UNION query) so that *only* the records containing the information that is shared is output. This operation, however, can use *all* the fields in the source tables.

Tricks and Traps

There are a couple of takeaways of interest here.

- If you want to sort the output from the UNION query—the main query, that is—you will have to make this into a subquery, and sort on the results of the subquery. Doing this will require code like the following to follow the CTE as the main query:

```
SELECT *
FROM
(
    SELECT  *, '2015 Data'
    FROM    Sales2015
    JOIN    IdenticalData_CTE
            USING (MakeName, ModelName, CustomerName, CountryName)
    UNION
    SELECT  *, '2016 Data'
    FROM    Sales2016
    JOIN    IdenticalData_CTE
            USING (MakeName, ModelName, CustomerName, CountryName)
) SQ
ORDER BY  MakeName, ModelName, CustomerName, CountryName;
```

- A query like this shows how a SQL query is often composed of multiple interconnected queries.

Conclusion

Despite being brief, this chapter helped you to extend your knowledge of the way that data analysis in MySQL depends on using datasets correctly. You saw how to filter separate datasets individually in order to effect comparisons over time as well as combine multiple tables to create a single result set.

Finally, you saw how to extract overlapping data from two tables. Then you discovered how to do the opposite and return data that is present in one table but not in another.

Core Knowledge Learned in This Chapter

The concepts that you have seen in this chapter are

Concept	Description
UNION	This operator lets you pull data from multiple tables or views that are identical in structure. It excludes duplicates from the result set.
UNION ALL	This operator lets you pull data from multiple tables or views that are identical in structure including any duplicates.

CHAPTER 17

Using SQL for More Advanced Calculations

In previous chapters you saw how to perform elementary math on the data in a MySQL database. Although SQL is not a language that is designed to carry out advanced mathematical calculations, it can go much further than the simple addition, subtraction, division, and multiplication that you have seen previously. However, these more advanced calculations also require you to understand more completely how SQL handles numbers.

Additional Calculation Techniques

The aim of this chapter is to extend your skills when it comes to performing essential math with MySQL. This does not mean that you will be following a math course in SQL. Instead we take a more real-world approach and show you how MySQL deals with numbers internally. Initially this means showing you how to ensure that SQL accepts data as being numeric. This may be necessary because what appears to be a number to us humans may not be interpreted as a numeric value by SQL. Making sure that numbers are correctly handled will help you to write robust SQL that can handle potentially unpleasant surprises and deliver the results that you expect to see. After you learn this, you begin learning to use SQL to write more complex formulas to analyze your data.

In this chapter you will learn how to

- Ensure that you are using the appropriate data types in certain types of calculation.

- Understand numeric data types.

- Remove currency symbols from source data so that you can calculate columns that are not "pure" numbers.

- Use calculated columns several times in a SQL snippet—without having to copy the calculation.

- Test for non-numeric values in SQL calculations—and deal with them—so that your queries do not return erroneous results, but perform the appropriate calculation where this is feasible.

This chapter is for you, then, if you want to extend the results of your analysis with some more complex calculation techniques. It gives you the confidence to deliver sound and accurate metrics to enhance your analysis with SQL.

1. Calculating the Percentage Represented by Each Record in a Dataset

All businesses like repeat customers, so it is perfectly understandable that the CEO of Prestige Cars wants to know what percentage of individual sales can be attributed to each client. The following SQL does this for you:

```
SELECT      CustomerName

            ,CONCAT(FORMAT(

                COUNT(CustomerName)

                / (SELECT COUNT(*)

                    FROM sales) * 100, 2), ' %')

            AS PercentageSalesPerCustomer

FROM        sales SA

JOIN        customer CU USING(CustomerID)

GROUP BY    CustomerName

ORDER BY    CustomerName;
```

Running this query gives the results that you can see in Figure 17.1. If you scroll down the list, you will see all the customers and the percentage of individual sales for each one. Moreover, if you add up all the percentage sales per customer, you will find that the total is 100 percent.

CustomerName	PercentageSalesPerCustomer
Alex McWhirter	0.31 %
Alexei Tolstoi	2.47 %
Alicia Almodovar	2.16 %
Andrea Tarbuck	0.62 %
Andy Cheshire	0.62 %
Antonio Maura	1.85 %
Autos Sportivos	0.31 %
Beltway Prestige Driving	0.62 %
Birmingham Executive Prestige Vehicles	1.85 %
Bling Bling S.A.	0.31 %
Bling Motors	0.93 %
Boris Sory	0.62 %
Bravissima!	0.62 %
Capots Reluisants S.A.	1.85 %
Casseroles Chromes	1.23 %
Clubbing Cars	0.62 %
Convertible Dreams	2.47 %
Diplomatic Cars	0.93 %

Figure 17.1: Displaying the percentage represented by each record in a dataset

How it Works

Given the SQL experience that you have acquired by now, I imagine that this query is not too hard to understand. Indeed, you might even be wondering exactly what is so "advanced" about it. Take a closer look; this query should draw your attention to an apparently minor point that we first looked at briefly when formatting output in previous chapters.

After joining the Sales and Customer tables, you group on the CustomerName field to see a record for each customer. Then you select

First:	The customer name.
Second:	The number of records for each customer. This is done using the COUNT() function.
Third:	You create a subquery to calculate the total number of records in the joined table set.

Fourth: You divide the number of sales (or records representing an individual sale) by the total number of sales to give the percentage of individual sales per customer.

Finally: To make the result more instantly comprehensible, this is formatted as a percentage using the FORMAT() and CONCAT() functions.

Tricks and Traps

Here is one fundamental point to remember when calculating percentages:

- All calculations have to be carried out on numeric values (that is, on figures). Consequently, you *must* multiply by 100 before formatting the result otherwise the calculation—and even the entire query—could fail.

2. Replacing Multiple Subqueries

The sales manager wants to see a list of all vehicles sold in 2017, with the percentage of sales each sale represents for the year as well as the variation to the average sales figure. You know that this will require adding a couple of subqueries—and then you remember that SQL allows you to use a single subquery in cases like these! After a few minutes, you produce the code that follows:

```
SELECT       SC.MakeName, SC.ModelName, SC.SalePrice

             ,(SC.SalePrice / CRX.TotalSales) * 100 AS PercentOfSales

             ,SC.SalePrice - CRX.AverageSales AS DifferenceToAverage

FROM         salesbycountry AS SC

CROSS JOIN   (SELECT SUM(SalePrice) AS TotalSales

                     ,AVG(SalePrice) AS AverageSales

              FROM   salesbycountry

              WHERE  YEAR(SaleDate) = 2017) AS CRX

WHERE        YEAR(SC.SaleDate) = 2017;
```

Running this code produces the output that is shown in Figure 17.2.

MakeName	ModelName	SalePrice	PercentOfSales	DifferenceToAverage
Triumph	TR6	12500.00	0.157479	-65319.362745
Aston Martin	Rapide	86500.00	1.089753	8680.637255
Peugeot	205	3950.00	0.049763	-73869.362745
Noble	M600	29500.00	0.371650	-48319.362745
Alfa Romeo	Spider	12500.00	0.157479	-65319.362745
Triumph	Roadster	23500.00	0.296060	-54319.362745
Alfa Romeo	Giulia	10500.00	0.132282	-67319.362745
Mercedes	280SL	22500.00	0.283462	-55319.362745
Triumph	TR7	8850.00	0.111495	-68969.362745
Triumph	TR5	8500.00	0.107086	-69319.362745
Citroen	Rosalie	2350.00	0.029606	-75469.362745
Rolls Royce	Wraith	165000.00	2.078721	87180.637255
Aston Martin	DB9	99500.00	1.253531	21680.637255
Lamborghini	Jarama	305000.00	3.842483	227180.637255
Aston Martin	DB2	45000.00	0.566924	-32819.362745
Austin	Lichfield	23600.00	0.297320	-54219.362745
Delahave	145	29500.00	0.371650	-48319.362745
Bentley	Arnage	99950.00	1.259201	22130.637255

Figure 17.2: Replacing multiple subqueries by a CROSS JOIN

How it Works

Some calculations require multiple subqueries. This, potentially, means writing very similar subqueries several times. You might need one subquery to return a total, another to get an average, yet another to find a standard deviation, and so on. Fortunately, you can apply a workaround to make the SQL both more comprehensible and easier to maintain.

The trick is to write a subquery that calculates all the aggregate values that you need in a single query and then uses the CROSS JOIN operator to apply the output from the subquery for every single record returned from the main query.

The overall query works like this:

First:　It begins with a subquery (once again it is the subquery that contains the heart of the solution). The subquery quite simply calculates the total sales and average sales for 2017. It uses the SalesByCountry view as the source of this data.

Then:　The main query extracts the make name, model name, and sale price from the same data source (the SalesByCountry view) for the same year (2017).

The next step:	Is to join the main query to the subquery using the CROSS JOIN function. This ensures that every record can use the output from the subquery in the main query and that the join does not filter the data in any way.
Finally:	The SELECT clause of the main query is extended to use the output from the cross-joined subquery. In this example, we are dividing the sale price of each vehicle sold by the total sales for the year to calculate the percentage of total sales that this figure represents.

As a final flourish, we subtract the average selling price from the sale price of each car to find out how much each sale differs from the average sale price for the year.

If you want to verify that the calculations are accurate, you can always select the SQL for the subquery and run it. You will see the output that is shown in Figure 17.3.

	TotalSales	AverageSales
	7937575.00	77819.362745

Figure 17.3: *The output from the subquery*

Tricks and Traps

Using CROSS JOIN can simplify certain calculations. Nonetheless, you need to be aware that

- The subquery is a perfectly standard subquery. This means that it is completely independent of the main query, so any filters that you apply to restrict the output from the subquery may have to be applied to the main query as well—assuming that you want to use them both to examine similar ranges of data.

- CROSS JOIN does not require an ON clause because it is not attempting to link the tables or queries in any way. Indeed, it specifically wants to use all the fields from both tables and/or queries together.

- Since the subquery is aliased, you need to use the subquery alias when referring to the fields that are output from the subquery in the calculations in the main query's SELECT clause.

- In this example we add an alias to the main table even if the SQL will work without it. However, you can presume that non-aliased fields come from the first table and write the SQL without table aliases for fields from the first table if you want. This gives code like the following:

```
SELECT          MakeName, ModelName, SalePrice
                ,(SalePrice / CRX.TotalSales) * 100 AS PercentOfSales
                ,SalePrice - CRX.AverageSales AS DifferenceToAverage
```

However, I advise always using table aliases with field names if a table is aliased. It is both good practice and makes the code easier to understand.

3. Remove Decimals in Calculations

If you are trading high-value products, you might not need to show pennies (or cents or centimes) in your results. Indeed, the financial director wants a list of vehicles sold that shows core costs without pennies to avoid rounding errors. An easy way to deliver on this requirement is shown in the following SQL:

```
SELECT          MakeName
                ,ModelName
                ,CAST(Cost AS UNSIGNED) AS Cost
                ,CAST(RepairsCost AS UNSIGNED) AS RepairsCost
                ,CAST(PartsCost AS UNSIGNED) AS PartsCost
                ,CAST(SalePrice AS UNSIGNED) AS SalePrice
FROM            SalesByCountry;
```

Running this query gives the results that you can see in Figure 17.4.

MakeName	ModelName	Cost	RepairsCost	PartsCost	SalePrice
Aston Martin	Vantage	100000	500	2200	125000
Triumph	TR6	10000	500	750	12500
Aston Martin	Rapide	69200	2000	1500	86500
Peugeot	205	3160	500	750	3950
Noble	M600	23600	1360	750	29500
Alfa Romeo	Spider	10000	500	750	12500
Triumph	Roadster	18800	1360	500	23500
Alfa Romeo	Giulia	8400	500	750	10500
Peugeot	205	760	500	750	950
Triumph	TR4	5560	500	457	6950
Triumph	TR4	10000	500	225	12500
Aston Martin	DB9	63600	1490	750	79500
Triumph	TR7	3160	500	150	3950
Mercedes	280SL	18000	500	750	22500
Triumph	TR7	7080	500	750	8850
Triumph	TR5	6800	500	750	8500
Porsche	928	14280	1360	150	17850
Aston Martin	Virage	82920	1490	750	103650

Figure 17.4: Using the CAST() function for a specific numeric data type conversion

How it Works

You have seen the CAST() function a few times in previous chapters, but I have never really explained how useful it can be when dealing with numbers. In this example, you take the SalesByCountry view (to avoid having to join seven tables) and selected five key fields. However, in this view, the fields that contain numeric values are all Decimal data types. Since this data type allows decimals, the fastest way to remove any decimals and present only whole number is to convert these fields to integers.

This is done by applying the CAST() function to the numeric fields and specifying that each is converted as an UNSIGNED (which is an integer). The result is that the values are now integers—and the decimals have disappeared.

4. Numeric Data Types

In Chapter 10 you saw how to find out the data type of a field. In previous sections you have seen how to convert numeric data types to other numeric data types as and when required.

As a result, now is probably a good moment to explain all the various ways that MySQL can store and manipulate numbers. In other words, it is time to look at all the numeric data types that MySQL offers. Each has its uses and limitations, and they are given in Table 6-1.

Table 6-1: Numeric Data Types

Data Type	Range	Comments
Bit	*0 or 1*	*Essentially used for true or false (also called Boolean) values*
Tinyint	*0 to 255 (-128 to 127 if signed)*	*An integer value without any decimals*
Smallint	*0 to 65535 (−32,768 to +32,767 if signed)*	*An integer value without any decimals*
Mediumint	*0 to 16777215 (-8388608 to 8388607 if signed)*	*An integer value without any decimals*
Int	*0 to 4294967295 (−2,147,483,648 to +2,147,483,647 if signed)*	*An integer value without any decimals*
Bigint	*0 to 264-1 (−9,223,372,036,854,775,808 to +9,223,372,036,854,775,807 if signed)*	*An integer value without any decimals*

Data Type	Range	Comments
Numeric	*Up to 65 digits (depending on the operating system)*	*You must specify the precision*
Decimal	*Up to 65 digits (depending on the operating system)*	*You must specify the precision and scale (total allowable numbers and numbers after the decimal)*
Float	*−3.40E +38 to −1.18E − 38, 0 and 1.18E −38 to 3.40E +38*	*Potentially huge numbers—but not stored precisely*
Double	*−1.79E+308 to −2.23E–308, 0 and 2.23E–308 to 1.79E+308*	*Potentially huge numbers— but not stored precisely*

You may be wondering why there are so many numeric data types—especially for integers. The reasons are largely a question of the space that data can take up on disk and in memory. Put simply, if a field uses a data type that can contain the maximum value that will ever be stored in that field, it will take up less space. It will also make fetching data from disk into memory faster.

This means that database designers nearly always try and use appropriate numeric data types so that databases run faster and cost less to maintain. It is as simple as that.

Originally this was because disk storage and main memory were extremely expensive. Now, despite ever-lower hardware costs, the exponential growth of data means that it is still important to choose appropriate numeric data types when designing and building databases.

Tricks and Traps

Handling numeric data types can require a little practice. So here are a few essential points to help you:

- When casting numeric data to an integer data type, you *must* always use an integer type that can hold the largest value that you are converting to an integer. So, for example, if the field that you want to cast contains values in the millions, you cannot use the SmallInt data type since it only goes up to 32,767 (or 65535 if it is a signed value). This data type physically cannot store a larger value. Indeed, if you try a data type conversion on a field that contains values that are simply too large for the destination data type to hold, then MySQL refuses to display any output and only shows an error message.

- When casting numbers to the Decimal data type, you should specify the total allowable numbers (including decimals) as well as the number of decimal places.

  So, for instance, the following code

  ```
  CAST(COST AS DECIMAL(10,2))
  ```

  converts the contents of the Cost field to the numeric data type. It allows a maximum value of 99999999.99—ten figures in all, and two decimal places.

- You should only convert to the Float or Real data type if your calculations do not require total accuracy. These data types can handle extremely large values, but they do not necessarily restitute the number that they contain completely accurately, so I do not advise you to use them for business or financial calculations. Remember that these data types were specifically designed for scientific data analysis where precision is less important.

- The CAST() function is very powerful, but it can be rather picky about the data that it converts. If a field that you are trying to convert using CAST() contains a text or a number that cannot be converted (whatever the reason) then the *whole query* can fail to work.

5. Converting Formatted Source Data into Usable Numbers

The IT department has loaded a spreadsheet into the database so that MySQL can read it. Unfortunately, they left the currency symbols in the numeric fields. The good news is that MySQL can handle this without any real difficulty, as you can see from the following code snippet:

```
SELECT      MakeName

            ,ModelName

            ,CAST(REPLACE(RIGHT(VehicleCost,

            LENGTH(VehicleCost) -1), ',', '') AS DECIMAL(12,2))

               AS VehicleCost

FROM        SalesInPounds;
```

Running this query gives the results that you can see in Figure 17.5.

MakeName	ModelName	VehicleCost
Ferrari	F50	204760.00
Ferrari	F50	248000.00
Ferrari	F40	215600.00
Ferrari	Enzo	316000.00
Ferrari	355	124000.00
Ferrari	Enzo	292000.00
Ferrari	Testarossa	132000.00
Ferrari	355	176000.00
Ferrari	355	127600.00
Ferrari	F40	200000.00
Ferrari	F50	156000.00
Ferrari	355	125200.00
Ferrari	Mondial	82360.00
Ferrari	Mondial	124000.00

Figure 17.5: Converting formatted text to numbers

How it Works

Although not strictly a calculation, making numeric data usable by MySQL is often a prerequisite to performing math on the data.

To appreciate this better, you need, perhaps to see the original data. This is shown in Figure 17.6.

Ferrari	F40	£200000.00
Ferrari	F50	£156000.00
Ferrari	355	£124,000.00
Ferrari	Mondial	£82360.00
Ferrari	Mondial	£124000.00
Ferrari	355	£124,000.00

Figure 17.6: Formatted data that can be converted to numeric values

I need to warn you that converting text to numbers consists essentially of applying a set of techniques that remove all the extra characters that will prevent MySQL from treating a text like a "true" number. It follows that you may have to apply a range of techniques depending on the way that the number is formatted.

In this example there are two issues that you have to deal with:

First: You need to remove the thousands separator from the numbers.

Second: You have to remove the British pound symbol (£) from the start of the text.

This piece of SQL tackles the challenge in the following order:

First: It extracts all the characters from the VehicleCost field except the pound symbol. It achieves this by extracting all the characters from the right of the field minus one—the first character. This is done by using the RIGHT() function—and specifying that the number of characters to remove is the length of the field minus 1.

Second: The remaining text (with the currency symbol now removed) is handed over to the REPLACE() function. This function replaces any commas (the thousands separator) with an empty string (defined as a set of single quotes).

Finally: The CAST() function is applied to convert the number (as it is now) to a decimal value. This ensures that the conversion has worked, as any numbers that cannot be confirmed as "real" numbers will show as zeros in the output. You can see this if you scroll down the output until you find records for Aston Martin Vanquish, for instance.

As you can see, the result of using this approach is that the currency symbol is stripped out and any decimal or thousands separator is recognized. Finally, only the number is left.

Tricks and Traps

When converting text to numbers you need to be aware of the following points:

- The techniques that you apply to convert a text to a number will vary depending on the formatting of the number. You may, for instance, have to remove currency symbols from the end of a text rather than from the beginning.

- There are cases when the CAST() function can make a good attempt at converting a text to a number without any need for a more complex set of nested functions. However, I prefer to give you a template that you can adapt to some of the more challenging circumstances that you may meet in the real world.

- If the attempt to strip formatting characters from the source data does not work, then MySQL will return a 0 instead of a value—or an error. You can see this in Figure 17.7. You will then have to decide if you want to apply more complex techniques to remove the formatting from the source data.

MakeName	ModelName	VehicleCost
Aston Martin	Vanquish	0.00
Aston Martin	DB9	37200.00
Aston Martin	Virage	100400.00
Aston Martin	Vanquish	0.00

Figure 17.7: Zero values indicating that formatted text could not be converted to numbers

6. Testing for Failures When Removing Formatting Characters

When removing formatting characters from numbers you need to be careful that no errors occur. One good way to prevent zero values not getting noticed (and causing problems with your users) is to trap these as part of the overall approach to removing formatting characters. The following SQL extends the code that you used in the previous section to add a text to draw your attention to any records where the attempt to remove the formatting and convert the data to numbers has not worked:

```
SELECT      MakeName

            ,ModelName

            ,CASE

                WHEN CAST(REPLACE(RIGHT(VehicleCost

                ,LENGTH(VehicleCost) -1), ',', '') AS DECIMAL(12,2))

                      <> 0

                THEN CAST(REPLACE(RIGHT(VehicleCost

                ,LENGTH(VehicleCost) -1), ',', '') AS DECIMAL(12,2))

                ELSE 'Manual Intervention'

            END AS VehicleCostUnformatted

FROM        SalesInPounds;
```

Running this query gives the output that you can see in Figure 17.8

MakeName	ModelName	VehicleCostUnformatted
Aston Martin	Rapide	69200.00
Aston Martin	DB5	55600.00
Aston Martin	DB4	29200.00
Aston Martin	DB9	62000.00
Aston Martin	Vanquish	Manual Intervention
Aston Martin	Virage	98872.00
Aston Martin	DB9	47600.00
Aston Martin	DB9	44000.00
Aston Martin	Virage	36000.00
Aston Martin	Vanquish	Manual Intervention
Aston Martin	DB6	90872.00
Aston Martin	DB9	52360.00
Aston Martin	DB9	44000.00
Aston Martin	Vanquish	Manual Intervention

Figure 17.8: Using a CASE statement to detect errors when stripping formatting text from numbers

How it Works

This query wraps the code that strips formatting code from the source field in a CASE statement. This way, if the attempt to remove formatting leaves a zero as the result (which means, generally, that the code was unsuccessful for a record) then the ELSE statement is triggered—and outputs "Manual Intervention" instead of the number with the formatting removed. This way you can look at any source data that has failed the conversion, and either correct it manually or extend the SQL to remove the formatting.

7. Testing for Non-Numeric Values

There could be times when you will inherit a table where a field containing numbers has been defined as a text data type (and consequently could contain stray alphabetical or special characters that could make calculations fail). In cases like these you need to be able to check if all the data in the field will be recognized as numeric.

The following SQL does exactly this for you.

```
SELECT      CountryName, CountrySales

FROM        CountrySales

WHERE       CountrySales NOT REGEXP '^[0-9\.]+$';
```

If you execute this code, you will see the output shown in Figure 17.9.

CountryName	CountrySales
Spain	50.000.000.00

Figure 17.9: *Detecting non-numeric values in a text field*

How it Works

To understand the problem more easily, take a look at the source data in the CountrySales table. You can see this in Figure 17.10.

CountryName	CountrySales
Belgium	311850.00
France	5882810.00
Germany	873040.00
Italy	1215280.00
Spain	50.000.000.00
Switzerland	839415.00
United Kingdom	9236375.00
United States	1995620.00

Figure 17.10: *The source data containing numeric values in a text field*

As you can see, the figure for Spain is not a true number. So using this in a calculation could produce either a zero, a NULL or an unreliable result.

So what this code does is to apply a regular expression in the WHERE clause to display any records where the value in the CountrySales field does not map to a regular expression that expects the field to contain numbers and, possibly, decimals. I will not explain the regular expression here, as this would involve a short course on regular expressions. It suffices to say that this particular regular expression will detect most numeric values.

Once you have run the query you can examine any output and correct the source data, as required.

Tricks and Traps

There are a few points of interest here.

- You may find—or develop—much more powerful regular expressions to handle numbers and use this technique with your own regular expression.

- It is simple to reverse the effect of this query and display only data that looks like a true numeric value. All you have to do is to use a WHERE clause like this:

```
WHERE CountrySales REGEXP '^[0-9\.]+$'
```

- In this query the same name is used for a table and a field it contains. This is not best practice—but it can happen in data that you inherit from other users. As you can see, this does not prevent SQL from working—but you have to be careful when writing the code.

8. Finding the Remainder in a Division Using the Modulo Function

The marketing director's latest idea has left you speechless. She wants you to generate a list of clients who will receive a letter saying that they have won a special customer discount on their next purchase of a classic sports car. She insists that this process must produce a list of around one third of the client base.

Once you have recovered from your bemusement at all things concerning marketing wizardry, you write the following code:

```
SELECT      CustomerID

FROM

       (

    SELECT        CustomerID

                 ,CustomerID MOD 3 AS ModuloOutput

                 ,CASE

                       WHEN CustomerID MOD 3 = 1 THEN 'Winner'

                             ELSE NULL

                   END AS LuckyWinner

       FROM        Customer

       ) Rnd

WHERE       LuckyWinner IS NOT NULL

ORDER BY    CustomerID;
```

Running this query gives the results that you can see in Figure 17.11.

CustomerID
0001
0004
0007
0010
0013
0016
0019
0022
0025
0028
0031
0034
0037
0040
0043
0046
0049
0052

Figure 17.11: Using the modulo function to return the remainder in a calculation

How it Works

As befits a language that can carry out basic math, SQL can calculate the remainder after dividing one number by another. This is called a *modulo operation*, and MySQL calls the function that carries out this calculation the *modulo* operator.

What happens is

First:	A field is defined that contains a numeric value. In this example, it is the CustomerID field.
Then:	The modulo operator (MOD) is added after the field name.
Finally:	The value that you are dividing the field by is added.

So, the key part of this code is

```
CustomerID MOD 3
```

However, as merely finding the remainder is of little practical interest, a small amount of logic is added to the calculation. What this logic does is to say, "if the remainder is 1, then flag the record." The logical selection is then used as a subquery so that only winning records are returned in the final output.

To make this clearer, take a look at Figure 17.12 where you can see the (unordered) output from the subquery. This illustrates how the modulo function displays the remainder of a calculation and also shows the output from the CASE statement for every record.

CustomerID	ModuloOutput	LuckyWinner
0034	1	Winner
0049	1	Winner
0067	1	Winner
0006	0	NULL
0024	0	NULL
0058	1	Winner
0084	0	NULL
0004	1	Winner
0023	2	NULL
0055	1	Winner
0080	2	NULL
0032	2	NULL
0039	0	NULL
0042	0	NULL
0048	0	NULL
0064	1	Winner
0074	2	NULL
0005	2	NULL

Figure 17.12: *The modulo function applied to all records*

Tricks and Traps

A couple of interesting aspects to this example are

- The figure that is used by a modulo operator does not have to be a numeric data type, provided that the text value can be converted internally by MySQL to a number.

- You do not have to display the modulo output in a calculation. We did it here to make the use of this operator clearer.

- Instead of the MOD operator you can use the % operator if you prefer. In this case the code would look like the following snippet:

```
CustomerID % 3
```

- Yet another alternative to the MOD operator is to use the MOD() function. In this case the code would look like the following snippet:

```
MOD(CustomerID, 3)
```

When using the MOD() function the first parameter is the field or value to be divided, and the second parameter is the field or value to divide the first parameter by.

9. Creating Financial Calculations

"Money is expensive" is one of the finance director's recurring mantras. It would appear that he has devoted countless hours to developing spreadsheets that count the cost of unsold stock in the showroom. Now, unfortunately, he wants you to adapt his basic compound interest calculation to SQL so that your reports can show how much "dead metal" (to use the term he uses to describe unsold stock) actually costs the company.

To help you in your work he has added that

- You are to use a standard compound interest calculation.

- The interest is to be compounded monthly.

- The rate that he wants to apply is 0.75 percent per month.

- You only need to calculate interest for cars that have been sold.

- You are only to calculate interest when a vehicle was in stock for over two months.

As a further hint, he has kindly emailed you the exact calculation that he wants you to apply. This is the one in Figure 17.13.

$$CI = K * \left(1 + \frac{P}{100} \right)^{t}$$

Figure 17.13: A compound interest calculation

After some thought, you come up with the following SQL that shows not only the interest charge, but also the number of months in stock as well as the cost price and the total cost including interest.

```
SELECT

 InitialCost

,MonthsSincePurchase

,(InitialCost * POWER(1 + (0.75 / 100), MonthsSincePurchase))

- InitialCost AS InterestCharge
```

```
,InitialCost * POWER(1 + (0.75 / 100), MonthsSincePurchase)
 AS TotalWithInterest


FROM

(

   SELECT

     DATEDIFF(SA.SaleDate, ST.DateBought) / 30 AS MonthsSincePurchase

     ,(ST.Cost + ST.PartsCost + ST.RepairsCost) AS InitialCost

     FROM    stock ST

     JOIN    salesdetails SD

             ON ST.StockCode = SD.StockID

     JOIN    sales SA USING(SalesID)

     WHERE   DATEDIFF(SA.SaleDate, ST.DateBought) > 60

) SRC;
```

Running this code snippet gives the result that you can see in Figure 17.14.

InitialCost	MonthsSincePurchase	InterestCharge	TotalWithInterest
7930.0000	9.3333	572.7687079564494	8502.76870795645
130550.0000	12.4667	12745.28244511917	143295.28244511917
11250.0000	4.4667	381.80467089791637	11631.8046708979 16
38000.0000	23.3667	7249.075535643831	45249.07553564383
188650.0000	8.3000	12070.053695291077	200720.05369529108
40600.0000	16.2000	5224.308655761291	45824.30865576129
153600.0000	16.7333	20457.12251909607	174057.12251909607
45075.0000	29.0333	10920.160455910045	55995.160455910045
9210.0000	5.1667	362.50819303807293	9572.508193038073
1725.0000	11.9333	160.8772442766267	1885.8772442766267
6522.0000	11.7000	595.8353190877951	7117.835319087795

Figure 17.14: Calculating compound interest

How it Works

Creating complex calculations in SQL is a vast subject. Indeed, entire books and papers have been written on this subject. So, although I want to show you the basics of using SQL to handle intricate financial mathematics, I am not delving too profoundly into this subject.

Given that this challenge could be complex, we have started by breaking it down into two parts:

An inner query   That calculates the total cost of a vehicle by adding up the purchase cost, cost of spares, and any repair costs. This query then also determines the number of months between the purchase date and the sale date.

                    This query uses the Stock, SalesDetails, and Sales tables to source the required information. Once the joins are in place, it adds a WHERE clause to restrict the output to vehicles where the time between purchase and sale is more than two months. The (inner) join between the Sales and Stock tables ensures that only cars that have been sold are evaluated.

An outer query   That displays the two fields isolated by the inner query (InitialCost and MonthsSincePurchase). The outer query then uses these two fields as core elements in calculating the compound interest.

Essentially you have applied a two-step process to calculating compound interest:

First: Take the arithmetical formula and adapt it so that it can be read on a single line.

Second: Convert the single-line formula to SQL.

Converting the formula from Figure 17.14 to a single line gives you the following:

$$CI = K * (1 + P/100)t$$

where

- CI is the compound interest (including the original capital value)
- K is the initial value
- P is the interest rate
- t is the number of periods

The SQL that delivers the compound interest (CI) takes the initial value (K) to be the purchase cost, cost of spares, and any repair costs. It then "hard-codes" the interest rate as 0.75 and divides by 100 to express it as a percentage. Finally it uses the POWER() function to apply the number of periods (t) as the exponent for the formula. The number of periods is, in fact, the number of months between purchase and sale.

The POWER() function takes two parameters:

First: The base value you wish to raise to the power of the exponent (one plus the percentage interest rate in this example)

Second: The exponent to apply (the number of months in this example)

As a final tweak, this calculation is applied a second time. Only on this occasion, the initial cost is subtracted from the compound interest to leave the actual interest amount. This way you can see the total cost as well as the interest.

This is, of course, only a simple example. Financial calculations can get much more complicated than this one. However, it is a starting point on which you can build to develop much more complex analyses if you need to.

Tricks and Traps

There is one idea that you can take away from this example:

* It is possible to write a query like this one without actually using a subquery; however, I feel that the improved simplification and increased clarity that a subquery brings to both the analysis and the coding make a subquery worth any extra effort.

10. Using a Tally Table to Produce a Sequential List of Numbers

The CFO has come with a request for you. He wants to be able to calculate the straight-line depreciation for any vehicle in stock. After a few minutes' thought, you come up with the following code:

```
SELECT          RowNo AS PeriodNumber

                ,Cost

                ,Cost / 5 AS StraightLineDepreciation

                ,Cost - ((Cost / 5) * RowNo) AS RemainingValue
```

```
FROM                    stock
CROSS JOIN
(
SELECT 1 AS RowNo
UNION
SELECT 2
UNION
SELECT 3
UNION
SELECT 4
UNION
SELECT 5
) Tally
WHERE                   StockCode =
                        'A2C3B95E-3005-4840-8CE3-A7BC5F9CFB5F';
```

Running this piece of code gives the result that you can see in Figure 17.15.

PeriodNumber	Cost	StraightLineDepreciation	RemainingValue
1	176000.0000	35200.00000000	140800.00000000
2	176000.0000	35200.00000000	105600.00000000
3	176000.0000	35200.00000000	70400.00000000
4	176000.0000	35200.00000000	35200.00000000
5	176000.0000	35200.00000000	0.00000000

Figure 17.15: Using a tally table to calculate straight-line depreciation

How it Works

Producing a depreciation table requires a sequence of time periods against which the series of amortization amounts can be calculated. However, MySQL is not a spreadsheet where you can just enter a series of numbers to represent the time periods. You need another solution. The answer is a concept called a *tally table*. This is a recordset (it can be a table but does not have to be) that contains a series of numbers, generally starting from 1, that increment regularly and have no gaps in the series. This suite of numbers can then be used to create sets of records.

In the case of a depreciation table, the first thing that you need is a recordset that contains the number of records corresponding to the number of years over which the vehicle will be amortized. In this example, I presume that this is a five-year period, so a recordset containing five rows is created using a set of UNION queries. You can see this in the CROSS JOIN clause of the SQL. Running the code inside the CROSS JOIN clause produces the result that you can see in Figure 17.16.

RowNo
1
2
3
4
5

Figure 17.16: *The output from a tally table*

Once you have the tally table, you can calculate the depreciation and the residual value of a specific car. Calculating the depreciation each year is as simple as dividing the cost of the vehicle by the number of years. Calculating the residual value means subtracting the accumulated depreciation each year from the cost. So, to work out the accumulated amortization amount, you multiply the depreciation amount by the number of years. This number is provided by the tally table; in effect, it takes the single record for the car cost and makes it into a table of five records by using a CROSS JOIN clause to multiply the number of records in the SELECT clause (one) by the number of records in the CROSS JOIN clause (all five of them). As a final, and necessary, flourish, the row number of the tally table is used as the multiplier to calculate the accumulated depreciation.

Tricks and Traps

I have only a few comments here:

- If you need to include a salvage cost in the calculation for the depreciation, you can subtract the salvage cost from the cost of the vehicle every time the Cost field is used.

- You will discover other ways to create a tally table in a later chapter.

- You can use tally tables in many situations to resolve otherwise seemingly impossible SQL issues. Although they may not be something that you use daily, they can be a valuable resource in certain circumstances.

11. Generating Completely Random Sample Output from a Dataset

The CEO wants to call up a handful of clients at random and ask them about the service that they have received from Prestige Cars. She asks you to produce a totally random list of sales with the relevant customers. It takes you just a few seconds to produce the following piece of SQL to satisfy her request.

```
SELECT      *

FROM        salesbycountry

ORDER BY    RAND()

LIMIT       50;
```

Running this code could deliver the results that you can see in Figure 17.17—but this can vary, given that the output is randomized.

CountryName	MakeName	ModelName	Cost	RepairsCost	PartsCost	TransportInCost	Color	SalePrice	LineItemDiscount	InvoiceNumber	SaleDate	CustomerName	SalesDetailsID
Belgium	Aston Martin	Vantage	100000.0000	500.0000	2200.0000	750.0000	Green	125000.00	1500.00	EURBE074	2016-08-23 00:00:00	Diplomatic Cars	81
Belgium	Triumph	TR6	10000.0000	500.0000	750.0000	150.0000	Red	12500.00	750.00	EURBE125	2017-02-12 16:02:00	Diplomatic Cars	138
Belgium	Aston Martin	Rapide	69200.0000	2000.0000	1500.0000	750.0000	Silver	86500.00	1250.00	EURBE132	2017-03-12 17:06:00	Diplomatic Cars	145
Belgium	Peugeot	205	3160.0000	500.0000	750.0000	150.0000	Black	3950.00	750.00	EURBE171	2017-07-01 10:25:00	Stefan Van Helsing	185
Belgium	Noble	M600	23600.0000	1360.0000	750.0000	150.0000	Black	29500.00	750.00	EURBE171	2017-07-01 10:25:00	Stefan Van Helsing	186
Belgium	Alfa Romeo	Spider	10000.0000	500.0000	750.0000	150.0000	Black	12500.00		EURBE171	2017-07-01 10:25:00	Stefan Van Helsing	187
Belgium	Triumph	Roadster	18800.0000	1360.0000	500.0000	150.0000	Black	23500.00		EURBE193	2017-11-06 21:36:00	Stefan Van Helsing	210
Belgium	Alfa Romeo	Giulia	8400.0000	500.0000	750.0000	150.0000	Black	10500.00		EURBE193	2017-11-06 21:36:00	Stefan Van Helsing	211
Belgium	Peugeot	205	760.0000	500.0000	750.0000	150.0000	British Racing Green	950.00	25.00	EURBE218	2018-01-10 00:00:00	Stefan Van Helsing	237
Belgium	Triumph	TR4	5560.0000	500.0000	457.0000	150.0000	Red	6950.00		EURBE264	2018-06-03 00:00:00	Flash Voitures	287
Switzerland	Triumph	TR4	10000.0000	500.0000	225.0000	150.0000	Silver	12500.00		GBPCH029	2016-01-01 00:00:00	Le Luxe en Motion	29
Switzerland	Aston Martin	DB9	63600.0000	1490.0000	750.0000	750.0000	Red	79500.00	2450.00	GBPCH067	2016-08-13 00:00:00	Le Luxe en Motion	73
Switzerland	Triumph	TR7	3150.0000	500.0000	150.0000	150.0000	Black	3950.00		GBPCH082	2016-09-04 00:00:00	Le Luxe en Motion	89
Switzerland	Mercedes	280SL	18000.0000	500.0000	750.0000	150.0000	Silver	22500.00		GBPCH114	2017-01-11 17:52:00	Le Luxe en Motion	127
Switzerland	Triumph	TR7	7080.0000	500.0000	750.0000	150.0000	Black	8850.00		GBPCH116	2017-01-13 19:58:00	Le Luxe en Motion	129
Switzerland	Triumph	TR5	6800.0000	500.0000	750.0000	150.0000	Green	8500.00		GBPCH164	2017-06-15 21:22:00	Le Luxe en Motion	178
Switzerland	Porsche	928	14280.0000	1360.0000	150.0000	150.0000	British Racing Green	17850.00	750.00	GBPCH223	2018-02-11 00:00:00	Le Luxe en Motion	242
Switzerland	Aston Martin	Virage	82920.0000	1490.0000	750.0000	750.0000	Pink	103650.00		GBPCH223	2018-02-11 00:00:00	Le Luxe en Motion	243
Switzerland	Peugeot	404	1890.0000	500.0000	750.0000	150.0000	British Racing Green	2350.00		GBPCH276	2018-07-30 00:00:00	Le Luxe en Motion	299
Switzerland	Bentley	Arnage	45440.0000	500.0000	750.0000	550.0000	Silver	56800.00	750.00	GBPCH292	2018-08-18 00:00:00	Le Luxe en Motion	315

Figure 17.17: Generating random output from a table using RAND()

How It Works

SQL has a function—RAND()—that generates a random value. This value is between 0 and 1 and is completely random; that is, there is no sequence or order to the way that it is generated.

This query uses RAND() to randomize data selection like this:

First: You write a simple SELECT query to return data from the SalesByCountry view.

Then:	You sort the data by the RAND() function. The RAND() function does not have to be in the SELECT clause to be added to the dataset.
Finally:	You add a LIMIT clause to the SQL to output only the first 50 records from the recordset.

The final result is a random subset of data from a database.

Conclusion

This chapter explained some of the techniques that you may need to use when carrying out more advanced calculations in SQL. These include handling data type conversions, and avoiding other circumstances where SQL can, potentially, prevent some calculations from working properly. You also learned more about numeric data types and how to convert formatted numbers to numeric values when they are stored as text. Finally, you saw a few examples of how you can use SQL to carry out more complex math, such as depreciation and compound interest calculations.

Core Knowledge Learned in This Chapter

The keywords that you have seen in this chapter are

Concept	Description
CAST()	The CAST() function is used to convert data types—where this is possible. It can convert a numeric data type to a different numeric data type or convert a string that is, in effect, a number, to a numeric data type.
CROSS JOIN	Applies all the records returned by one query to another query without filtering the data.
% (modulo)	The % function—called the *modulo function*—returns the remainder after dividing one value by another.
MOD	The MOD operator returns the remainder after dividing one value by another.
MOD()	The MOD() function also returns the remainder after dividing one value by another.
POWER()	POWER() is a math function used to raise one value to the power of another.
RAND()	This function adds a random floating point number between 0 and 1.

CHAPTER 18

Segmenting and Classifying Data

Selecting and filtering information can certainly help you reach a deep insight into your data, yet there are times when you really need to prioritize and classify lists of data in order to analyze the elements that really matter. This chapter will teach you a range of practical techniques to help you to isolate the valuable information hidden inside your data.

Ranking and Segmenting Data

MySQL offers a useful set of functions that can help you when it comes to segmenting datasets. Specifically, it can

- Rank data according to a given criterion
- Break down recordsets into multiple segments
- Isolate the top or bottom elements in multiple data segments
- Return the top percentage of a dataset
- The relative standing of a record in a recordset

Analyzing data in this way is a first step on the path to in-depth statistical analysis. I do not—rest assured—expect you to be an expert in statistics in order to use the SQL functions that you meet in this chapter. However, I hope that, as you learn how to slice and dice data in this chapter, you come to appreciate the power of SQL in data analysis.

In this chapter, then, you see how applying a few analytical functions can help you deliver real insight from your data. This can help both you and your organization stay one step ahead of the competition.

1. Organizing Data by Rank

Turning data into information is what analysis is all about. In order to tailor your offering for your clients you need to see how individual sales compare. In fact, the sales director wants a list that shows each sale per customer for 2018 with an indicator of their relative value. The following SQL can help you deliver this:

```
SELECT        CustomerName
              ,CONCAT(MakeName, ', ', ModelName) AS MakeAndModel
              ,SalePrice
              ,RANK() OVER (ORDER BY SalePrice DESC)
                    AS SalesImportance
FROM          salesbycountry
WHERE         YEAR(SaleDate) = 2018
ORDER BY      SalesImportance;
```

Running this query gives the results that you can see in Figure 18.1. A figure that indicates the relative position of each sale shows the rank for each record.

CustomerName	MakeAndModel	SalePrice	SalesImportance
La Bagnole de Luxe	Bugatti. 57C	365000.00	1
Andrea Tarbuck	Bugatti. 57C	355000.00	2
Bling Bling S.A.	Bugatti. 57C	345000.00	3
Capots Reluisants S.A.	Ferrari. F50	310000.00	4
Laurent Saint Yves	Ferrari. F40	269500.00	5
Kieran O'Harris	Lamborghini. Diabolo	255000.00	6
Smooth Rocking Chrome	Ferrari. Dino	195000.00	7
Stephany Rousso	Ferrari. F50	195000.00	7
Capots Reluisants S.A.	Bentley. Brooklands	189500.00	9
Sondra Horowitz	Rolls Royce. Phantom	182500.00	10
King Leer Cars	Ferrari. Mondial	155000.00	11
Antonio Maura	Lamborghini. 400GT	145000.00	12
Andy Cheshire	Ferrari. Daytona	145000.00	12
Smooth Rocking Chrome	Ferrari. 360	135000.00	14
El Sport	Ferrari. 360	128500.00	15
Ronaldo Bianco	Aston Martin. Virage	123500.00	16

Figure 18.1: The RANK() function

How it Works

This query starts by joining all the tables that are required to let you display the CustomerName, Make, Model, and SalePrice fields, only it does this using the SalesByCountry view to save you from having to join all the tables. Then, once a WHERE clause has been added to filter on a specific year for sales, these fields are added to the SELECT clause. Then, as a final touch, the customers are clearly ranked by order of importance using a new function—RANK().

As its name implies, RANK() indicates where a row stands in a list of elements. We also used the RANK() function to sort the records so that you can see clearly what the relative importance of each row is. In this example we used the alias applied to the RANK() function in the ORDER BY clause to sort the data by rank without repeating the complete calculation.

However, the RANK() function needs to know how to classify the data that it will convert into an ordered hierarchy, so to set up a ranked dataset, you need the following elements at a minimum:

RANK()	This function tells MySQL that you want to classify a dataset.
OVER	This keyword is compulsory and follows the RANK() keyword.
ORDER BY	This statement is added inside parentheses after the OVER keyword and you then add the field that will be used to "grade" the results.

In this example, the vehicle sale price is used as the basis for ranking the output. The final result is a list of sales ordered and ranked by value relative to other sales.

Tricks and Traps

The RANK() function can be a really powerful addition to your SQL toolkit; however, you need to be aware of the following points when using it:

- The RANK() function is one of a group of SQL functions that are known as the *window functions*. You will see many of these in both this chapter and the next.

- The ORDER BY clause in a window function works just like a standard SQL ORDER BY clause. You can use multiple fields separated by a comma, or add the ASC (for ascending) or DESC (for descending) keywords to tell MySQL how to sort your data.

- It is not strictly necessary to add an alias for the column that displays the result of the RANK() function, but it helps make the output clearer. An added benefit is that you can then use this alias to sort the output without repeating the full RANK() calculation in the ORDER BY clause.

- Adding a RANK() function does *not* sort the output data automatically.

- The window functions (such as RANK()) used in this chapter require MySQL version 8 at a minimum. If the examples in this chapter do not work then you may have to upgrade your MySQL version.

2. Creating Multiple Groups of Rankings

Classifying product sales can be essential for an accurate understanding of which products sell best. At least that is what the CEO said when she requested a report showing sales for 2017 ranked in order of importance by make. The following short piece of SQL shows you how to look at the relative sales value of each model for each make of car:

```
SELECT      CONCAT(MK.MakeName, ', ', MD.ModelName) AS MakeAndModel

            ,SD.SalePrice

            ,RANK() OVER (PARTITION BY MK.MakeName

                    ORDER BY SD.SalePrice DESC) AS SalesImportance

FROM        make AS MK

JOIN        model AS MD USING(MakeID)

JOIN        stock AS ST USING(ModelID)

JOIN        salesdetails SD ON ST.StockCode = SD.StockID

JOIN        sales AS SA USING(SalesID)

WHERE       YEAR(SA.SaleDate) = 2017

ORDER BY    MakeName, SD.SalePrice DESC;
```

Running this query gives the results that you can see in Figure 18.2.

MakeAndModel	SalePrice	SalesImportance
Alfa Romeo. Giulia	25000.00	1
Alfa Romeo. Giulietta	21500.00	2
Alfa Romeo. Spider	12500.00	3
Alfa Romeo. Spider	11500.00	4
Alfa Romeo. Giulia	10500.00	5
Alfa Romeo. Giulietta	6500.00	6
Alfa Romeo. Spider	5650.00	7
Aston Martin. DB6	225000.00	1
Aston Martin. Virage	125000.00	2
Aston Martin. Rapide	99500.00	3
Aston Martin. DB9	99500.00	3
Aston Martin. Rapide	86500.00	5
Aston Martin. DB9	77500.00	6
Aston Martin. Vantage	66500.00	7
Aston Martin. DB2	61500.00	8

Figure 18.2: *Applying the PARTITION BY clause to a RANK() function*

How it Works

The core of this code snippet is the set of tables that allows you to access the MakeName, ModelName, SalePrice, and SaleDate fields. Once you have created the required dataset, you can then assemble a query that lists the fields that you need.

With the core elements of the query in place, you can add a RANK() function. As was the case in the previous example, you need the RANK() keyword, the OVER clause, and an ORDER BY statement with the field that you are using to prioritize the data.

This time you want to classify the output in a subtler way. Specifically, you want to grade each model of car, not compared to all the sales for the year, but relative to *all models of the same make* rather than relative to all sales for the year.

This is done—quite simply—by adding the PARTITION BY clause and a field name inside the parentheses that follow the OVER keyword. In this way, you are, in effect, telling SQL that you want to break the data down into *subgroups* by make of car. The PARTITION BY clause is, in effect, creating *subgroups* by make of vehicle. The ORDER BY clause then grades the records for each subgroup on the SalePrice field.

Tricks and Traps

When partitioning—or grouping datasets, if you prefer to think of it like that—you need to remain aware of a few key points:

- MySQL can handle situations where there is a tie that occurs when data is ranked. What it does is give any tied rows the same ranking, and then it makes the next-lowest record two or more places lower. Figure 18.3 shows you an example of this from further down the list.

Aston Martin, Rapide	86500.00	5
Aston Martin, DB9	77500.00	6
Aston Martin, Vantage	66500.00	7
Aston Martin, DB2	61500.00	8
Aston Martin, Vanquish	56950.00	9
Aston Martin, DB9	56500.00	10
Aston Martin, Vanquish	56500.00	10
Aston Martin, DB9	56500.00	10
Aston Martin, Rapide	55000.00	13
Aston Martin, DB2	49500.00	14
Aston Martin, DB4	46900.00	15

Tied Rankings

Next In Sequence

Figure 18.3: The effect of tied records when using the RANK() function

- Most, if not all, of the time, you are likely to find yourself ranking data on a numeric field. You will nearly always partition data using a text field. This is not, however, inevitable, merely likely. You can just as easily partition on a numeric field and order on an alphabetical field.

- You can partition the data by multiple fields if you use a comma-separated list of fields (rather than a single field) after the PARTITION BY clause.

3. Creating Multiple Ranked Groups and Subgroups

The finance director has realized that he does not yet know how to grade customers on a scale of profitability per sale, so he has requested an immediate report that shows the profit per vehicle sold ranked in order of importance by make per customer. After a little thought, you come to the conclusion that what he wants is a list of customers in which you can see which makes and models of vehicle each client bought and where the data is ranked by customer, make and gross profit. The following SQL query uses a window function and a CTE (Common Table Expression) to deliver this essential piece of analysis:

```
WITH

AllSalesProfit_CTE (CustomerName, MakeName

                ,ModelName, SalePrice, GrossProfit)

AS
```

```
(
SELECT      CustomerName, MakeName, ModelName
            ,SalePrice
            ,SalePrice - Cost - IFNULL(RepairsCost, 0)
               - IFNULL(PartsCost, 0)
FROM        salesbycountry
)


SELECT      CustomerName, MakeName, ModelName
         ,SalePrice
         ,RANK() OVER
                    (PARTITION BY CustomerName, MakeName
                    ORDER BY GrossProfit DESC)
                    AS SalesImportance
FROM        AllSalesProfit_CTE
ORDER BY    CustomerName, MakeName, SalesImportance;
```

Running this query gives the results that you can see in Figure 18.4.

CustomerName	MakeName	ModelName	SalePrice	SalesImportance
Alex McWhirter	Jaguar	XJ12	17850.00	1
Alexei Tolstoi	Aston Martin	Virage	102500.00	1
Alexei Tolstoi	Aston Martin	DB6	69500.00	2
Alexei Tolstoi	Ferrari	355	205000.00	1
Alexei Tolstoi	Jaguar	E-Type	39500.00	1
Alexei Tolstoi	Jaguar	XK150	22990.00	2
Alexei Tolstoi	Jaguar	XJS	22600.00	3
Alexei Tolstoi	Jaguar	XJS	9950.00	4
Alexei Tolstoi	Porsche	911	45950.00	1
Alexei Tolstoi	Triumph	GT6	3500.00	1
Alicia Almodovar	Alfa Romeo	Giulietta	5690.00	1
Alicia Almodovar	Aston Martin	DB6	45950.00	1
Alicia Almodovar	Ferrari	Testarossa	250000.00	1
Alicia Almodovar	Porsche	959	39500.00	1
Alicia Almodovar	Porsche	928	15950.00	2
Alicia Almodovar	Porsche	924	12500.00	3

Figure 18.4: Combining a CTE with a RANK() function to create multiple ranked groups and subgroups

How it Works

This piece of code is in two parts:

First: A CTE that calculates the gross profit for every car sold.

Finally: A query that uses the data from the CTE to classify the output.

A CTE can help you define the key data that is required by the overall query. Although not absolutely necessary, it can help isolate the core data that you then use to categorize and hierarchize data. This example uses a CTE to define the data that is required. Once the essential data has been isolated from the SalesByCountry view, the relevant fields (Customer, Make, Model, SalePrice and gross profit) are output and a RANK() function is added to the final query that delivers the categorized output based on the recordset defined by the CTE.

If you think back to Chapter14, you will remember that a CTE can be executed separately from the rest of the query. So if you select the SQL that is contained inside the CTE and execute it, you obtain the sort of output that you can see in Figure 18.5 (remember that the final column is aliased in the CTE header). Of course, the sort order of the data that you see may well be different.

	CustomerName	MakeName	ModelName	SalePrice	SalePrice - Cost - IFNULL(RepairsCost, 0) - IFNULL(PartsCost, 0)
▶	Magic Motors	Ferrari	Testarossa	65000.00	9325.0000
	Magic Motors	Aston Martin	DB4	29500.00	4650.0000
	Magic Motors	Lamborghini	Countach	3650.00	-520.0000
	Magic Motors	Aston Martin	Vanquish	55000.00	10350.0000
	Magic Motors	Ferrari	355	125950.00	13740.0000
	Magic Motors	Austin	Princess	2250.00	-800.0000
	Magic Motors	Aston Martin	Vantage	66500.00	9625.0000
	Magic Motors	Ferrari	Enzo	255000.00	40250.0000
	Snazzy Roadsters	Ferrari	355	220000.00	36300.0000
	Snazzy Roadsters	Aston Martin	Virage	56500.00	9300.0000
	Snazzy Roadsters	Aston Martin	DB2	45950.00	8540.0000
	Snazzy Roadsters	Jaguar	XK150	26500.00	4050.0000

Figure 18.5: CTE output to be used in a ranking query

This dataset calculates sales figures and profit per sale, so it can be used in the final query to group and rank the records by customer and make.

A couple of aspects of this query make it a little subtler than the previous two that you have seen.

First: The output is ranked by customer *and* make. As you can see, the PARTITION BY clause (rather like an ORDER BY clause) can specify multiple fields. All the fields that you use in the PARTITION BY clause must be comma-separated.

Second: You can override the sort order that may be provided by the RANK() function by adding a standard ORDER BY clause in the final query. In this example, the ORDER BY clause is applied to guarantee that the final output is both clear and comprehensible.

Tricks and Traps

I have a couple of remarks to make about using CTEs when ranking datasets:

* You could just as easily use a derived table instead of a CTE. The two techniques are essentially interchangeable, and the approach that you choose is largely a matter of personal preference.

* If the query inside the CTE does not have column names or aliases, then you *must* add names to the output fields inside parentheses at the top of the CTE after the CTE name.

4. Filtering Data by Ranked Items

Buyer psychology is a peculiar thing. To better understand Prestige Cars' clients, the sales director has decided that she wants to find the bestselling color for each make sold. The following short SQL snippet gives you this information:

```
SELECT      MakeName, Color

FROM

            (

            SELECT      DISTINCT MakeName, Color

                        ,RANK() OVER (PARTITION BY MakeName

                                    ORDER BY SalePrice DESC)

                        AS ColorRank

            FROM        make AS MK

            JOIN        model AS MD USING(MakeID)

            JOIN        stock AS ST USING(ModelID)
```

```
        JOIN        salesdetails SD

                    ON ST.StockCode = SD.StockID

        ) SQ

WHERE       ColorRank = 1

ORDER BY MakeName;
```

Running this query gives the results that you can see in Figure 18.6.

MakeName	Color
Alfa Romeo	Black
Aston Martin	Black
Austin	Night Blue
Bentley	Blue
BMW	Black
Bugatti	Red
Citroen	Blue
Delahaye	Night Blue
Delorean	Night Blue
Ferrari	British Racing Green
Jaguar	Canary Yellow
Lagonda	Blue
Lamborghini	Green
McLaren	Silver
Mercedes	Canary Yellow
Morgan	Pink

Figure 18.6: Filtering on the results of a RANK() function in a subquery

How it Works

This query works by breaking down the problem into its two constituent parts, the better to answer the question that is asked.

First: A derived table joins all the required tables to produce a list of sales that displays only the make, color and the hierarchy of each color sold per make using the RANK() function. The OVER clause specifies that the data is partitioned (grouped, if you prefer) by make of car and the value used to rank the data is the selling price.

Finally: The outer query returns the make and color of each car if —and only if—it is ranked *first* for each make. The outer query does this by applying a WHERE clause to the output from the derived table so that only records where the rank equals 1 are allowed through to the final data set.

To make this clearer, Figure 18.7 shows a few of the records from the data that is returned by the derived table to the outer query.

MakeName	Color	ColorRank
Ferrari	Dark Purple	4
Ferrari	Silver	3
Ferrari	Blue	5
Ferrari	Blue	23
Ferrari	Black	27
Ferrari	British Racing Green	22
Ferrari	Black	6
Ferrari	British Racing Green	1
Ferrari	Black	2
Porsche	Black	6
Porsche	Dark Purple	2
Porsche	Black	8
Porsche	Silver	7
Porsche	Black	13

Figure 18.7: Grouping and classifying data using the RANK() function

This output shows you that the derived table has, effectively, classified sales by make for each color. Then the outer query simply discards most of the data that the derived table has returned so that only the top-ranked record for each make is displayed.

Tricks and Traps

There are a couple of points worth noting at this juncture:

- Remember that you *have* to add an alias to all calculated columns that are used in a derived table if you are using this column in the outer query.

- You could have just as easily used a CTE instead of a derived table to perform the initial ranking of the data. It is entirely up to you which you prefer to use.

5. Classifying Data by Strict Order of Rank

Segmenting data in order to deliver real insight is what SQL is all about. Management now wants you to push the envelope and perform a more complex analysis of the Prestige Cars' sales data by finding the ten highest-selling sales values but only when these cars belong to the category of the five bestselling colors by quantity sold. The SQL that does this is slightly longer than some of the code snippets that you have seen so far; however, it is definitely worth a closer look:

```
SELECT      Color, MakeAndModel, SalesImportance
FROM
(
SELECT       ST.Color, CONCAT(MK.MakeName, ', ', MD.ModelName)
                    AS MakeAndModel
         ,SD.SalePrice
         ,DENSE_RANK() OVER (ORDER BY SD.SalePrice DESC)
                    AS SalesImportance
FROM        make AS MK
JOIN        model AS MD USING(MakeID)
JOIN        stock AS ST USING(ModelID)
JOIN        salesdetails SD ON ST.StockCode = SD.StockID
JOIN

            (
            SELECT    Color, COUNT(*) AS NumberOfSales
            FROM      stock AS ST
            JOIN      salesdetails SD
                      ON ST.StockCode = SD.StockID
            GROUP BY Color
            ORDER BY NumberOfSales DESC
            LIMIT 5
            ) CL
            ON CL.Color = ST.Color
) RK
WHERE       SalesImportance <= 10
ORDER BY    SalesImportance;
```

Running this query gives the results that you can see in Figure 18.8.

Color	MakeAndModel	SalesImportance
British Racing Green	Ferrari, Enzo	1
Black	Ferrari, Enzo	2
Red	Bugatti, 57C	2
Blue	Bugatti, 57C	3
Red	Bugatti, 57C	4
Silver	Bugatti, 57C	5
Silver	Ferrari, F50	6
Silver	McLaren, P1	7
Black	Bugatti, 57C	7
Blue	Ferrari, F50	8
Black	Lamborghini, Diabolo	9
Black	Ferrari, Enzo	9
Black	Ferrari, Testarossa	10

Figure 18.8: Using the DENSE_RANK() function to classify items

How it Works

Sometimes an analytical request can seem more complicated than it really is. However, if you break the problem down into its component parts, then it can prove to be easier than you think. This query is case in point. Let's look more closely at what is required and then see how SQL can provide the information that you want to extract from the data.

Top five by color   First you need to isolate the five bestselling colors by quantity. This has to be done first, as it restricts the data only to those vehicles whose color is one of the five bestselling colors.

Top ten bestselling   Then you need to find the bestselling cars that make up the ten best sales by value *if* the vehicle color is one of the five bestselling colors.

Getting this query right requires a nested derived table inside a derived table. Let's begin at the lowest level of the query—the inner derived table that deduces the five bestselling colors by quantity.

The inner derived table finds the five bestselling colors by joining the Stock and SalesDetails tables and then by counting the number of sales per color. Then it selects only the top five records, giving you the list of the five bestselling colors. If you select the query that makes up the inner derived table (the one that is aliased as CL), you see something like the data in Figure 18.9.

Color	NumberOfSales
► Black	115
Blue	38
British Racing Green	34
Silver	33
Red	33

Figure 18.9: *Using a derived table to filter a subset of elements that are passed up to an outer query*

Once you have the list of colors that make up the five bestselling colors, you can build the "main" derived table that returns the make and model of car sold along with its color, the sale price, and the ranking of the sale relative to the selling prices of all vehicles sold. The inner derived table is used in the outer derived table's JOIN clause to filter the colors so that only the five returned by the inner query are used in the outer query. If you select this query (which includes the inner derived table, aliased as RK), you see something like the data in Figure 18.10.

Color	MakeAndModel	SalePrice	SalesImportance
► Red	Ferrari, Testarossa	65000.00	52
Blue	Ferrari, 355	220000.00	15
British Racing Green	Porsche, 911	19500.00	104
British Racing Green	Porsche, 924	11500.00	117
Red	Porsche, 944	19950.00	102
Black	Aston Martin, DB5	49500.00	70
Blue	Porsche, 911	19600.00	103
Blue	Aston Martin, DB5	36500.00	80
Blue	Porsche, 944	8500.00	130
British Racing Green	Bentley, Flying Spur	80500.00	45
Black	Ferrari, 355	169500.00	19
Red	Mercedes, 280SL	22950.00	95

Figure 18.10: *A derived table that filters data based on an inner derived table*

Once you have a list of all the sales of cars in a ranked dataset, it is easy to add the final step. This consists of using this derived table as the data source for the outermost query where you select only those cars whose rank is 10 or less. This is done in the WHERE clause that says, WHERE SalesImportance <= 10. An ORDER BY clause is added as a final tweak to present that data in an order that visually enhances the result by sorting the output in ascending sequence of importance of sale.

Notice that this SQL uses the DENSE_RANK() function rather than the RANK() function. The two are virtually identical but have one vital difference. You saw in previous examples that the RANK() function skips numbers if there is a tie. The DENSE_RANK() function does *not* do this and continues the numbering sequentially. This way, you are sure to get the top ten sales values—even if there are duplicate values for some sales. This is why the final output shows fourteen records when you only asked for the top ten. This is because there are only ten distinct top-selling prices, but these represent fourteen different sales since there can always be more than one sale at the same price.

Tricks and Traps

A query as complex as this one inevitably means that there will be a few key points to take away:

- This query could also be solved by nesting the inner derived table inside a CTE and then using the output from the CTE for the final query. Once again, how you solve it is simply a question of personal preference.

- The inner derived table can be used by the outer derived table either in a JOIN with the outer query (as is the case here) or in a WHERE clause. Either of these approaches gives the same result.

- You might be tempted to use a LIMIT 10 clause in the outer derived table to get the top ten sales. However, this might not give you exactly the top ten values. This is because LIMIT *n* merely returns a specified number of *rows*. In the case of this query, it is perfectly possible that the top ten *values* could represent eleven or more *sales*. Only showing the LIMIT 10 would not exactly answer the question since it might not display a full ten *values*, just ten records.

6. Segment Data into Deciles

While we are still exploring the area of data classification, suppose that the sales director wants to group sales into *deciles* by sale price— that is "buckets" of equal size where each group of data contains one tenth of the records in the total dataset. The first decile contains the most expensive cars sold, the second the subsequent tranche of cars by sale price and so on. The following SQL does this for you:

```
SELECT     ST.Color

           ,CONCAT(MK.MakeName, ', ', MD.ModelName) AS MakeAndModel

           ,SD.SalePrice
```

```
            ,NTILE(10) OVER (ORDER BY SD.SalePrice DESC) AS SalesDecile
FROM        make AS MK
JOIN        model AS MD USING(MakeID)
JOIN        stock AS ST USING(ModelID)
JOIN        salesdetails SD ON ST.StockCode = SD.StockID
ORDER BY    SalesDecile, ST.Color, MakeAndModel;
```

Running this query gives the results that you can see in Figure 18.11. You have to scroll down the result to see how the SalesDecile field changes every 35 records or so.

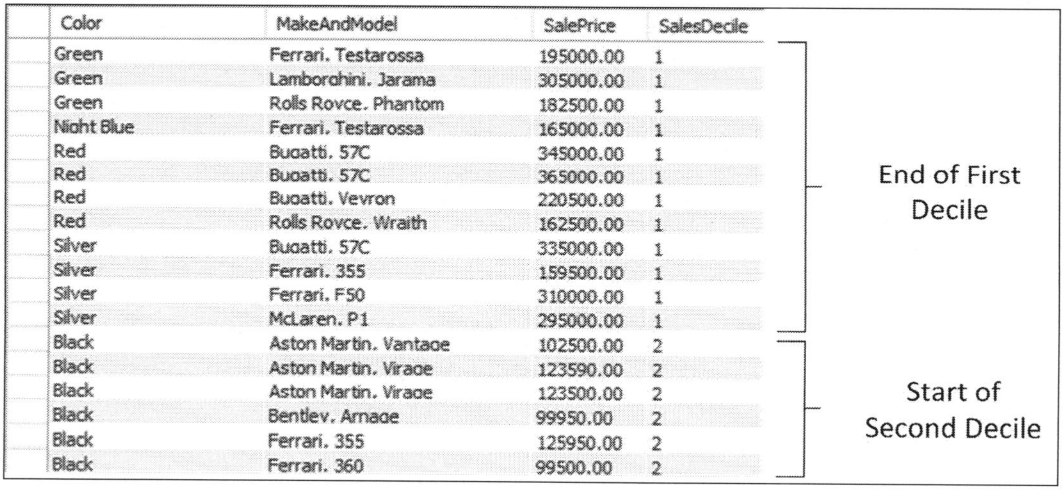

Color	MakeAndModel	SalePrice	SalesDecile
Green	Ferrari, Testarossa	195000.00	1
Green	Lamborghini, Jarama	305000.00	1
Green	Rolls Royce, Phantom	182500.00	1
Night Blue	Ferrari, Testarossa	165000.00	1
Red	Bugatti, 57C	345000.00	1
Red	Bugatti, 57C	365000.00	1
Red	Bugatti, Veyron	220500.00	1
Red	Rolls Royce, Wraith	162500.00	1
Silver	Bugatti, 57C	335000.00	1
Silver	Ferrari, 355	159500.00	1
Silver	Ferrari, F50	310000.00	1
Silver	McLaren, P1	295000.00	1
Black	Aston Martin, Vantage	102500.00	2
Black	Aston Martin, Virage	123590.00	2
Black	Aston Martin, Virage	123500.00	2
Black	Bentley, Arnage	99950.00	2
Black	Ferrari, 355	125950.00	2
Black	Ferrari, 360	99500.00	2

Figure 18.11: Using the NTILE() function to group data into segments

How it Works

You can see from the output that this query has added a field that indicates the decile (or segment, or bucket, if you prefer) that each record belongs to. You can then use this segmentation to pursue your analysis.

This query delivers an easy solution to a potentially complex question—all thanks to the NTILE() function. What this window function does is segment the dataset into as many separate subgroups as you have specified when you apply the function. Quite simply, placing the figure inside the parentheses after the NTILE() function defines the number of data "buckets" that you want to create. Whatever the number of records in the dataset, the NTILE() function subdivides them into the number of groups that you specify as a parameter of the function.

This query is, at its heart, a simple SELECT query where you joined the necessary tables and selected the required fields. Then you added a final field using the NTILE() function.

Just like the RANK() and DENSE_RANK() functions, the NTILE() function requires you to add the OVER keyword and an ORDER BY clause inside parentheses—in addition to a value that is used for classifying the data. The NTILE() function requires one further element—the number of "buckets" that you want to appear in the output. This is defined by adding a number inside the parentheses just after the NTILE() function. The number that you add is the number of groups into which the dataset will be divided.

Tricks and Traps

I have only one comment to make here:

- NTILE() can also contain a PARTITION BY clause to add a further level of segmentation should you need it. It works exactly as it does for the RANK() function as you saw in previous sections.

7. Plot Values for a Percentile

SQL can be particularly useful when it comes to teasing out meaning from statistics. At least, that is what the sales director seems to believe, since she has come to you with this request: provide her with a dataset that contains the total cost for vehicles for each cost percentile and the corresponding repair cost. She wants to use this to create a chart that displays any potential correlation between the cost of a car and its repair cost.

```
WITH PercentileList_CTE

AS

(

SELECT      RepairsCost

            ,Cost

            ,NTILE(100) OVER (ORDER BY Cost DESC) AS Percentile

FROM        stock

)
```

```
SELECT      Percentile
            ,SUM(Cost) AS TotalCostPerPercentile
            ,SUM(RepairsCost) AS RepairsCostPerPercentile
              ,SUM(RepairsCost) / SUM(Cost) AS RepairCostRatio
FROM        PercentileList_CTE
GROUP BY    Percentile
ORDER BY    RepairCostRatio DESC;
```

Execute this code snippet and you obtain the results that you can see in Figure 18.12.

Percentile	TotalCostPerPercentile	RepairsCostPerPercentile	RepairCostRatio
100	1520.0000	1000.0000	0.65789474
99	2312.0000	1500.0000	0.64878893
98	2840.0000	1500.0000	0.52816901
97	3080.0000	1500.0000	0.48701299
96	3748.0000	1500.0000	0.40021345
95	6720.0000	2000.0000	0.29761905
94	7480.0000	2000.0000	0.26737968
93	8036.0000	2000.0000	0.24888004
92	11320.0000	2000.0000	0.17667845
91	13640.0000	2000.0000	0.14662757
90	17600.0000	2000.0000	0.11363636
89	18160.0000	2000.0000	0.11013216
88	19560.0000	2000.0000	0.10224949
72	42592.0000	4190.0000	0.09837528
87	20912.0000	2000.0000	0.09563887
69	55480.0000	5220.0000	0.09408796

Figure 18.12: Purchase cost versus repairs cost per percentile

How it Works

This piece of SQL is essentially in two stages:

A CTE   That attributes each sale to a percentile of sales. It also gives the repair cost for each sale. This CTE uses the NTILE() function and specifies that the function is to distribute the results over 100 groups, in effect segmenting the sales into percentiles.

A query   That aggregates the output from the CTE to obtain the total for each percentile.

The CTE produces the output that you can see in Figure 18.13.

RepairsCost	Cost	Percentile
1360.0000	20000.0000	58
2000.0000	15600.0000	66
500.0000	6040.0000	85
500.0000	17200.0000	64
1490.0000	66072.0000	24
5500.0000	146000.0000	9
500.0000	47600.0000	32
500.0000	4400.0000	91
970.0000	34360.0000	48
3950.0000	130000.0000	10
1360.0000	40960.0000	41
500.0000	2860.0000	92
500.0000	7400.0000	82
3950.0000	124000.0000	12

Figure 18.13: Attributing each sale to a percentile

Once you have the percentile that each sale belongs to, it is simple to aggregate the output so that you are grouping the result on each percentile and using the SUM() function to return the total for sales and repair costs per percentile.

Tricks and Traps

It is well worth noting that

- Although MySQL cannot generate charts, it can isolate the data that you can then export and paste into a spreadsheet. Alternatively, you can connect many applications directly to a MySQL database. Indeed, you can use MySQL Workbench to hone your queries and then copy the query into the application that you are using to display and/or analyze the data.

- In Chapter 21 I will explain how to save query output to a file that you can use in a spreadsheet.

8. Extract Data from a Specific Quintile

Prestige Cars caters to a wide range of clients, and the sales director does not want to forget about the 80 percent that are outside the top 20 percent of customers. She wants you to take a closer look at the second quintile of customers—those making up the second 20 percent of sales. Her exact request is this: "Find the sales details for the top three selling makes in the second 20 percent of sales." Here is the SQL to do this:

```
WITH Top20PercentSales_CTE

AS

(

SELECT SD.SalesDetailsID, MK.MakeName, MD.ModelName, SD.SalePrice

        ,NTILE(5) OVER (ORDER BY SD.SalePrice DESC) AS SalesQuintile

FROM    make AS MK

JOIN    model AS MD ON MK.MakeID = MD.MakeID

JOIN    stock AS ST ON ST.ModelID = MD.ModelID

JOIN    salesdetails SD ON ST.StockCode = SD.StockID

)

SELECT     CTE.MakeName, CTE.ModelName, CTE.SalePrice

FROM       Top20PercentSales_CTE CTE

JOIN       (

                  SELECT    MakeName

                  FROM      Top20PercentSales_CTE

                  WHERE     SalesQuintile = 2

                  GROUP BY MakeName

                  ORDER BY SUM(SalePrice) DESC

                  LIMIT 3

           ) SB

           ON CTE.MakeName = SB.MakeName

ORDER BY   SalePrice DESC;
```

Running this query gives the results that you can see in Figure 18.14.

MakeName	ModelName	SalePrice
Aston Martin	DB6	225000.00
Bentlev	Brooklands	189500.00
Rolls Rovce	Phantom	182500.00
Rolls Rovce	Wraith	165000.00
Rolls Rovce	Wraith	162500.00
Rolls Rovce	Silver Seraoh	139500.00
Rolls Rovce	Silver Shadow	135000.00
Aston Martin	Virage	125500.00
Aston Martin	Vantage	125000.00
Aston Martin	Virage	125000.00
Aston Martin	Virage	123590.00
Aston Martin	Virage	123500.00
Rolls Rovce	Silver Seraoh	120000.00
Rolls Rovce	Phantom	119600.00
Aston Martin	DB6	113590.00
Aston Martin	Virage	103650.00
Aston Martin	Vantage	102500.00
Aston Martin	Virage	102500.00

Figure 18.14: *Using the NTILE() function to isolate a segment of data*

How it Works

The ability to segment and classify your customers can make or break a business. This query shows you how to isolate a segment of sales data to produce exactly this kind of really useful information. The SQL in this example uses a CTE as the core of the query. The CTE uses the NTILE() function to list makes, models, and sale prices for all cars sold. Then it calculates the quintile for each sale.

Once the quintile has been defined, the subsequent query carries out two operations:

First: It uses a derived table to isolate the top three makes belonging to the second quintile. The source data for this derived table is the CTE, *in order to filter the data to the second quintile.*

Then: This derived table is then joined to the source CTE in the "main" query, and filters the output from the CTE by limiting the makes to those found in the second quintile.

Tricks and Traps

Segmenting data can be a challenge—but an interesting one. Be sure to remember the following essential points when you have to deal with this kind of query:

- What is interesting here is that the CTE is used twice. The key technique is first to define the quintile, and then to select a specific quintile from the dataset. However, because the CTE also joins the tables required to list the make, model, and sale price, it can be *reused* in the main query so you don't have to rewrite all the SQL that is needed to produce this specific output.

- You can, of course, isolate deciles, percentiles—indeed any segment of data. All you have to do is enter the appropriate figure inside the parentheses that are part of the NTILE() function. For a decile, you would have entered the following SQL in the preceding example:

```
NTILE(10) OVER (ORDER BY SalePrice DESC) AS SalesDecile
```

9. Returning the Top "N" Percent of a Dataset

The CEO clearly studied statistics as part of her management training. She has now asked for a list of the top ten percent most expensive makes and models ever sold. Fortunately, MySQL can help you deliver this really easily—as the following SQL snippet shows.

```
WITH SalesByPercentile_CTE

AS

(

SELECT MK.MakeName, MD.ModelName, SD.SalePrice

        ,NTILE(100) OVER (ORDER BY SD.SalePrice DESC) AS SalesPercentile

FROM    make AS MK

JOIN    model AS MD ON MK.MakeID = MD.MakeID

JOIN    stock AS ST ON ST.ModelID = MD.ModelID

JOIN    salesdetails SD ON ST.StockCode = SD.StockID

)

SELECT    MakeName, ModelName, SalePrice

FROM      SalesByPercentile_CTE
```

```
WHERE       SalesPercentile <= 10

ORDER BY  MakeName, ModelName, SalePrice;
```

Running this short piece of SQL will give the results given in Figure 18.15. If you scroll down the output you will see that the data is only around 10% of the size of the SalesDetails table.

MakeName	ModelName	SalePrice
Aston Martin	DB6	225000.00
Bentley	Brooklands	189500.00
Bugatti	57C	295000.00
Bugatti	57C	335000.00
Bugatti	57C	345000.00
Bugatti	57C	355000.00
Bugatti	57C	365000.00
Bugatti	Veyron	220500.00
Ferrari	355	155000.00
Ferrari	355	156500.00
Ferrari	355	159500.00
Ferrari	355	169500.00
Ferrari	355	205000.00
Ferrari	355	220000.00
Ferrari	Daytona	145000.00
Ferrari	Dino	195000.00
Ferrari	Enzo	255000.00
Ferrari	Enzo	365000.00
Ferrari	Enzo	395000.00
Ferrari	F40	250000.00
Ferrari	F40	269500.00
Ferrari	F50	195000.00

Figure 18.15: Using the NTILE() function to return the top "n" percent of records

How it Works

This query splits neatly into two parts:

First: A CTE that joins the Make, Model, Stock and SalesDetails tables so that you can extract the makes and models along with the sale price for all vehicles sold.

Second: A SELECT statement that uses the CTE as the source of its data.

The real trick, however, is in the addition of the NTILE() function to the CTE. What is more, as we have set a value of 100 as the NTILE() parameter it will attribute each record in the dataset to a percentile, based on the sale price of each car. In other words, it has divided the dataset into 100 separate buckets. The top percentile (1) contains the 1 percent of the most expensive cars, and the bottom percentile (100) contains the 1 percent of the least expensive cars.

The main query can then use the percentile figure in a WHERE clause to filter the data coming from the CTE. In specifying that the SalesPercentile column is less than or equals to 10, it has limited the query output to the top ten percent of the records in the source data by sale price.

If you want to see how the CTE attributes a percentile indicator to each record in the source data, you can select and execute the query inside the CTE. Doing this gives the output that you can see in Figure 18.16.

MakeName	ModelName	SalePrice	SalesPercentile
Ferrari	Davtona	99500.00	17
Ferrari	Davtona	145000.00	10
Ferrari	Testarossa	165000.00	9
Ferrari	Testarossa	195000.00	6
Ferrari	Testarossa	65000.00	28
Ferrari	Testarossa	195000.00	7
Ferrari	Testarossa	250000.00	4
Ferrari	355	155000.00	10
Ferrari	355	205000.00	6
Ferrari	355	125950.00	12
Ferrari	355	169500.00	8
Ferrari	355	220000.00	6
Ferrari	355	159500.00	9
Ferrari	355	156500.00	10
Ferrari	Dino	195000.00	7
Ferrari	Dino	123500.00	14
Ferrari	Mondial	155000.00	10
Ferrari	Mondial	102950.00	15

Figure 18.16: Using the NTILE() function to specify the percentile of a dataset

Tricks and Traps

The key points to take away here are:

- When breaking down the dataset defined by the CTE into 100 buckets the NTILE() function will attempt to place the same number of records into each bucket. However, this cannot always be done precisely—and is impossible with smaller datasets. So the percentage returned is likely to be only approximately the required percentage of the underlying data if the dataset is very small.

10. Calculating Cumulative Distribution

This time a sales person wants to know the relative standing of each sale by make. In other words, she expects to see a list with a column that shows what percentage of sales were made for less than the current record for each make of car. The following piece of SQL does exactly this:

```
SELECT     MK.MakeName, MD.ModelName, SA.InvoiceNumber, SD.SalePrice
           ,ROUND(CUME_DIST()
           OVER (PARTITION BY MK.MakeName ORDER BY SD.SalePrice), 2)
           AS RelativeStanding
FROM       make AS MK
JOIN       model AS MD USING(MakeID)
JOIN       stock AS ST USING(ModelID)
JOIN       salesdetails SD ON ST.StockCode = SD.StockID
JOIN       sales AS SA USING(SalesID)
ORDER BY   MK.MakeName, SD.SalePrice, RelativeStanding;
```

Running this query gives the results that you can see in Figure 18.17. I have scrolled down the data that is returned to give you a better idea of what the output looks like for a couple of makes of car.

MakeName	ModelName	InvoiceNumber	SalePrice	RelativeStanding
BMW	Isetta	GBPGB182	5500.00	0.33
BMW	Alpina	EURFR226	21500.00	0.67
BMW	E30	EURFR158	33500.00	1.00
Bugatti	Vevron	EURFR143	220500.00	0.17
Bugatti	57C	GBPGB142	295000.00	0.33
Bugatti	57C	GBPGB173	335000.00	0.50
Bugatti	57C	EURFR282	345000.00	0.67
Bugatti	57C	GBPGB230	355000.00	0.83
Bugatti	57C	EURFR221	365000.00	1.00
Citroen	Rosalie	GBPGB139	990.00	0.17
Citroen	Rosalie	GBPGB252	1350.00	0.33
Citroen	Rosalie	GBPCH161	2350.00	0.50
Citroen	Rosalie	EURFR322	5500.00	0.67
Citroen	Traction A...	EURFR300	25000.00	0.83
Citroen	Torpedo	EURES147	65890.00	1.00
Delahave	175	EURIT302	12500.00	0.25
Delahave	135	EURFR300	25500.00	0.50
Delahave	145	EURES140	29500.00	0.75

Figure 18.17: Displaying cumulative distribution with the CUME_DIST() function

How it Works

Putting things into perspective is what data analysis can be all about, so it can help if you are able to see the relative position of a value compared to other values. In this window function, you used the CUME_DIST() function to see how each sale is situated relative to all other sales for the same make of car. Only this time you do not see a strict ranking, but the percentage of cars sold for a lower price. This means that the bestselling car for a specific make will display 1 (100 percent) with all other cars showing a smaller percentage figure.

This query initially requires that you join all the tables that you need to select the required fields. In this case, the tables are Make, Model, Sales, SalesDetails, and Stock.

Then you can add the CUME_DIST() function to the SELECT clause. As is the case with the other window functions that you have seen so far in this chapter, you need to specify an ORDER BY element (the sale price in this example). Then you extend the window function with a PARTITION BY clause that uses the make of vehicle to group the records into multiple subsets. This lets you isolate the sale price for each record relative to cars of the same make.

The end result is that for each make of car, you can see which is the most expensive sale and what percentage of cars sells for each sale per make.

Tricks and Traps

Creating a cumulative distribution with the CUME_DIST() function does require some attention to detail. The key points to take away are

- The PARTITION BY clause is optional with this function. If you want, you can remove it and instead display the percentage of vehicles that sell for less than the current car for *all* sales, irrespective of make.

- The field that you use in the ORDER BY function of the OVER clause to establish the relative standing must be numeric.

- We have added the ROUND() function to the CUME_DIST() function to prevent the display of the 15 decimal places that otherwise appear by default. You can, of course, leave this function out of the query if you prefer.

- You may prefer to sort a dataset such as this by the sale price in descending order so that you can see the most expensive sale per make first. In any case, the sort order that is applied to the overall query is independent of the ORDER BY clause that is applied inside the CUME_DIST() function.

11. Classifying Data Using the PERCENT_RANK() Function

To conclude her analyses of vehicle sales, the sales manager not only wants to see vehicle sales for each country by value but also wants to get an idea of the percentile in the sale hierarchy for each vehicle sold. The next piece of SQL delivers exactly what she is looking for:

```
SELECT      CO.CountryName, SA.SaleDate, SA.InvoiceNumber

            ,CONCAT(FORMAT(PERCENT_RANK()

            OVER (PARTITION BY CO.CountryName

            ORDER BY SA.TotalSalePrice), 2) * 100, ' %')

                AS PercentageRanking
FROM        sales AS SA
JOIN        customer CU USING(CustomerID)
JOIN        country CO ON CU.country = CO.CountryISO2
ORDER BY    CO.CountryName, SA.TotalSalePrice DESC;
```

Running this query gives the results that you can see in Figure 18.18.

CountryName	SaleDate	InvoiceNumber	PercentageRanking
Belgium	2016-08-23 00:00:00	EURBE074	100 %
Belgium	2017-03-12 17:06:00	EURBE132	83 %
Belgium	2017-07-01 10:25:00	EURBE171	67 %
Belgium	2017-11-06 21:36:00	EURBE193	50 %
Belgium	2017-02-12 16:02:00	EURBE125	33 %
Belgium	2018-06-03 00:00:00	EURBE264	17 %
Belgium	2018-01-10 00:00:00	EURBE218	0 %
France	2017-02-08 13:01:00	EURFR122	100 %
France	2017-02-07 20:00:00	EURFR121	98 %
France	2018-01-15 00:00:00	EURFR221	97 %
France	2018-07-31 00:00:00	EURFR282	95 %
France	2018-03-15 00:00:00	EURFR235	93 %
France	2017-05-21 16:18:00	EURFR156	92 %
France	2018-05-15 00:00:00	EURFR254	90 %
France	2017-05-12 13:15:00	EURFR151	89 %
France	2017-10-15 18:34:00	EURFR189	87 %

Figure 18.18: *Using the PERCENT_RANK() function to classify groups of data*

How it Works

One useful analytical technique is to indicate the relative rank of a row inside a group of rows. This query starts when you select the necessary tables (Sales, Customer, and Country). Then you add any fields that you want to display and use the ORDER BY clause so that the data that is returned is more comprehensible.

Finally, you add the PERCENT_RANK() function to the SELECT clause. It requires the OVER clause and an ORDER BY function that takes a numeric value as the field to sort on (TotalSalePrice). In this example (although this is optional), you added a PARTITION BY clause to the window function to subset the relative sale position by country.

The end result is an ordered list of sales per country. Starting with the highest-value sale, the list displays each vehicle sale in descending order by value and where each record stands in relation to all the other sales for the country. This "ranking" is expressed as a percentage of the number of records that appear below the current record. This means that the top record shows 100 percent, and the bottom record shows 0 percent.

Tricks and Traps

When using PERCENT_RANK() be sure to note that

- The field that you use in the ORDER BY function of the OVER clause to establish the relative standing must be numeric.

- You do not need to add the field used as the basis for the PERCENT_RANK() function to the SELECT clause; however, adding it can make the output easier to understand.

- You do not need to format the output for the PERCENT_RANK() function as a percentage; however, I feel that it makes the output easier to comprehend.

Conclusion

This chapter introduced you to some of the ways that you can use SQL to segment and classify data. You saw how to deliver hierarchies of data that can also segment the output according to the criteria that you specify. You also saw how to subset data into deciles and quintiles that you can extract for further analysis—as well as ranking records by their relative standing and returning the top percentage of records in a data set.

Core Knowledge Learned in This Chapter

The keywords that you have seen in this chapter are

Concept	Description
RANK()	The RANK() function hierarchizes data according to the criterion that you define.
OVER	The OVER keyword is used by the RANK() function to introduce the ranking criteria.
PARTITION BY	The PARTITION BY keyword is used by the RANK() function to separate the data into multiple hierarchies.
DENSE_RANK()	The DENSE_RANK() function hierarchizes data without any gaps in the ranking.
NTILE()	The NTILE() function distributes the rows in an ordered partition into a specified number of groups.
CUME_DIST()	This function returns a *cumulative distribution*—the relative position of a value compared to other values.
PERCENT_RANK()	This function returns a figure indicating what percentage of a subgroup of records can be found with smaller values than a defined column in a recordset or subgroup of records.

CHAPTER 19

Rolling Analysis

> *Few metrics exist in isolation. Most of the time, you not only want to compare these metrics with other figures, but you also want to see how they evolve over time. This lets you discern trends, track growth, and establish a solid factual base that you can use to make projections.*

Running Totals, Running Averages, Running Counts, and Comparative Values

MySQL provides a range of functions that can help you show how data evolves over time—or, indeed, over any sequence or progression. These functions are both simple and easy to use. They help you deliver a range of running calculations, including

- Running totals
- Running averages
- Running counts

Fortunately, MySQL does not require you to learn any new functions in order to deliver this kind of rolling analysis. It simply extends the use of a handful of functions that you know already, such as SUM(), AVG(), and COUNT(). Once you have mastered these extensions, you are also able to use this new approach with a few new functions to isolate

- Comparative values across a range of records
- The first or last element in a series
- The most recent element in a series for comparison

Indeed, the great thing about these calculations is that they all work in a very similar way. The upshot is that once you have mastered the basics of how these functions work, you can apply them to your queries to give your analysis a new power and depth.

This set of functions are a further extension of the window functions that you first encountered in Chapter 18. These functions group datasets into "windows" of data behind the scenes. They also allow you to specify what elements are calculated and exactly how they are grouped. This means that you can ask MySQL to restart the running total at specific breakpoints. Consequently, you can restart a running calculation with every new year, month, or day if you want—and, in so doing, you can track how metrics evolve over time.

1. Adding a Running Total

The sales manager does not always want complex analyses; sometimes she wants fairly simple lists as well. This time she has requested a list of sales for 2017 that includes running totals of both sales to date and average sales. Fortunately, window functions make this not too difficult, as the following code snippet displays:

```
SELECT      SA.InvoiceNumber
            ,DATE_FORMAT(SA.SaleDate, '%e %M %Y')  AS DateOfSale
            ,SD.SalePrice
            ,SUM(SD.SalePrice)
            OVER (ORDER BY SA.SaleDate ASC) AS AccumulatedSales
            ,AVG(SD.SalePrice)
            OVER (ORDER BY SA.SaleDate ASC) AS AverageSalesValueToDate
FROM        salesdetails SD
JOIN        sales AS SA USING(SalesID)
WHERE       YEAR(SA.SaleDate) = 2017
ORDER BY    SA.SaleDate;
```

Running this query gives the results that you can see in Figure 19.1.

InvoiceNumber	DateOfSale	SalePrice	AccumulatedSales	AverageSalesValueToDate
EURFR110	1 January 2017	22500.00	22500.00	22500.000000
GBPGB111	5 January 2017	125000.00	147500.00	73750.000000
GBPGB112	10 January 2017	85000.00	232500.00	77500.000000
GBPCH114	11 January 2017	22500.00	255000.00	63750.000000
GBPGB115	12 January 2017	125950.00	380950.00	76190.000000
GBPCH116	13 January 2017	8850.00	389800.00	64966.666667
GBPGB117	14 January 2017	9950.00	399750.00	57107.142857
EURFR113	21 January 2017	1250.00	401000.00	50125.000000
EURFR118	30 January 2017	56500.00	457500.00	50833.333333
GBPGB119	31 January 2017	55000.00	512500.00	51250.000000
GBPGB120	31 January 2017	56950.00	569450.00	51768.181818
EURFR121	7 February 2017	365000.00	934450.00	77870.833333
EURFR122	8 February 2017	395000.00	1329450.00	102265.384615
USDUS123	9 February 2017	21500.00	1350950.00	96496.428571

Figure 19.1: Generating running totals with the OVER clause

How it Works

A classic analytical requirement is to see how values change over time. This short piece of SQL shows not only how to list sales values, but also how the running total and average sale price change with each new sale.

The core of this query is a list of sales dates and values taken from the Sales and SalesDetails tables. The data is filtered to limit the result to sales for a given year. Finally, to give this initial list some coherence, it is sorted by sales date.

Then two window functions are added to enhance the output and to turbo-charge the level of information that the query delivers. They do this by extending the use of two functions that you have come to know well: SUM() and AVG().

Each of these functions is extended with an OVER clause that causes the function to be applied to the field that you are calculating from the beginning of the dataset up to and including the current record. This way, both the SUM() function and the AVG() function perform their tasks (adding up the total sales and averaging the sale price, respectively) for each record, up to and including the current record. The final result is a mixture of the detailed sales information for each sale and the overall data up to that date. Essentially, the OVER clause ensures that the functions are only applied to a *part* of the dataset, and not to the entire set, as has been the case up until now.

As you analyze how data evolves over time, it is important to ensure that the OVER function orders the data using a field, or fields, that sequence the records over time. In this example, we are using the SaleDate field so that the OVER function essentially says, "from the start of the filtered dataset up to the current record where the dataset is ordered by sale date."

Since this is a new use of the SUM() and AVG() functions, you may find that looking at an image makes it easier for you to grasp the concepts that are being applied. Figure 19.2 shows how window functions work more graphically.

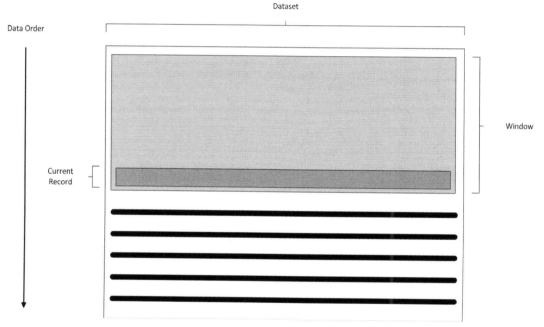

Figure 19.2: Window functions used to create running totals described conceptually

Tricks and Traps

Window functions are extremely powerful; however, they do require you to remain aware of a few key points if you are to use them correctly:

- Because you are listing the individual records for each sale, it helps if you display some piece of information (such as the invoice number in this example) that lets the reader see what makes each record unique.

- In this example, we formatted the date purely for presentation purposes. You can, of course, leave the date data in its raw state when you output the query results.

- When using several running totals in a single query, it is important to make sure that they use the same ORDER BY clause in the OVER operator or you could get results that are not what you are looking for.

- A running total, just like any other aggregation, needs an alias if you want a column title to be displayed in the output.

- MySQL workbench might indicate potential errors with these more recent functions. For instance it might show a red cross on left of a line with a window function, or maybe certain keywords such as OVER could be underlined in red. This is nothing to worry about (and may even no longer be the case by the time that you read this).

2. Using Window Functions in an Aggregated Query

Because Prestige Cars is perfectly capable of buying several cars on the same day, the CFO wants a report that displays the purchase cost per day with the cumulative cost for the year for 2016. This is exactly what the following SQL code achieves:

```
SELECT      DateBought

            ,SUM(Cost) AS PurchaseCost

            ,SUM(SUM(Cost))

                OVER (ORDER BY DateBought ASC) AS CostForTheYear

FROM        stock

WHERE       YEAR(DateBought) = 2016

GROUP BY    DateBought

ORDER BY    DateBought;
```

Running this query gives the results that you can see in Figure 19.3.

DateBought	PurchaseCost	CostForTheYear
2016-01-02	35760.0000	35760.0000
2016-01-10	45560.0000	81320.0000
2016-01-31	44800.0000	126120.0000
2016-02-01	52712.0000	178832.0000
2016-02-10	4800.0000	183632.0000
2016-02-11	38280.0000	221912.0000
2016-02-27	125560.0000	347472.0000
2016-03-15	31600.0000	379072.0000
2016-03-19	2920.0000	381992.0000
2016-04-17	176400.0000	558392.0000
2016-04-26	82360.0000	640752.0000
2016-04-29	14000.0000	654752.0000
2016-05-02	93600.0000	748352.0000
2016-05-11	10000.0000	758352.0000
2016-05-25	7960.0000	766312.0000
2016-05-28	93384.0000	859696.0000
2016-06-01	62000.0000	921696.0000
2016-06-02	28000.0000	949696.0000

Figure 19.3: Using window functions in an aggregated query

How it Works

Sometimes you might need to see an aggregated value, such as the cost of goods bought per day, alongside the running total over time of these same costs. You do this by grouping data from the Stock table on the DateBought field and by displaying this field alongside the SUM() of the Cost field. To avoid getting drowned in data, make sure the output is restricted to only purchases for 2016.

After this, ask MySQL to provide a running total using a SUM()...OVER window function. However, because this function is a grouped query (or an *aggregated query*, if you prefer), it needs to be aggregated as well. You have to make the SUM(Cost) function into an aggregate function by writing it as SUM(SUM(Cost)).

Tricks and Traps

I have only one point that really needs your attention here, but it is a very important one. This example is based on a simple technique that you must bear in mind when aggregating data using window functions:

- It may seem peculiar, and even counterintuitive, to wrap a SUM() function inside another SUM() function. But if you write this query as

```
SUM(Cost)) OVER (ORDER BY DateBought ASC)
```

then the query will give an incorrect result. This is because you are grouping data in a query. Consequently, you must *also* group data used in running totals.

3. Restarting Running Totals

You can use running totals to get an idea of how your key metrics evolve. Sometimes, however, you want to reset a grouping element so that you can start over when some key piece of data changes—like beginning a new year, for instance. So, when the sales manager requests a list that shows all sales to date with a running count of sales per year, you are relieved that you can use a window function to answer her query. The following SQL snippet shows you how to reset a counter or a running total:

```
SELECT     DATE(SA.SaleDate) AS DateOfSale

           ,CU.CustomerName, CU.Town

           ,SD.SalePrice

           ,COUNT(SD.SalesDetailsID)

             OVER (PARTITION BY YEAR(SA.SaleDate)

                 ORDER BY SA.SaleDate, SalesDetailsID ASC)

               AS AnnualNumberOfSalesToDate

FROM       salesdetails SD

JOIN       sales AS SA USING(SalesID)

JOIN       customer CU ON SA.CustomerID = CU.CustomerID

ORDER BY   SA.SaleDate;
```

Running this query gives the results that you can see in Figure 19.4.

Figure 19.4: Grouped running totals using OVER and PARTITION BY

How it Works

This query begins by joining the Customer, Sales, and SalesDetails tables so that you can return sales and customer information—such as the date of sale, customer name, and sale price—for each sale. No filter is applied because you want to see all sales since Prestige Cars began trading. The query is sorted by date to ensure that the data appear in a clear and comprehensible way.

You can now add the running counter of sales over time. You build it like this:

First: Work out the number of sales by adding a COUNT()function.

Second: Extended this function to make it a window function by adding an OVER clause.

Third: Order the resulting counter by the date as well as a *unique* field—the SalesDetailsID field—so there is *no aggregation* of the data and each individual record displays, while showing the progression over time.

Finally: Add a PARTITION BY clause so that the counter *restarts* when the field specified after the PARTITION BY clause (the year) changes.

The end result is a list of all sales over time where you can see not only the accumulated sales as the year progresses, but also the total sales for the year at year end.

Once again, a visual representation may help you understand this better. Figure 19.5 shows you how a PARTITION BY clause works with a window function.

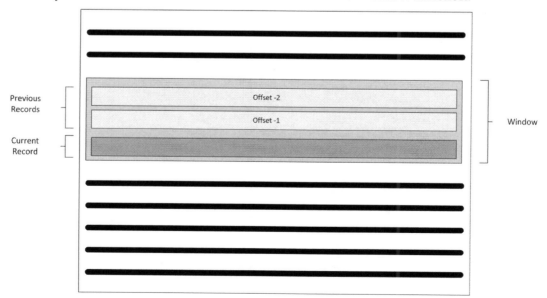

Figure 19.5: *A PARTITION BY clause with a window function*

Tricks and Traps

When you add a PARTITION BY clause to a window function, you need to remember the following key points:

- It is important to use the appropriate fields in the ORDER BY clause of the OVER function to achieve your desired output. If you use the wrong fields, it probably will not return the result that you expect. In practice, this means you need to select a field that contains the finest level of granularity of the data that is meaningful. In this example, each individual sale is what matters, so you use the SalesDetailsID field in both the COUNT() function and the ORDER BY clause because it contains a unique value for each record. This ensures that all records are output individually and not aggregated in any way.

- If you use the SaleDate field instead of the SalesDetailsID field in this query, MySQL counts the days with sales throughout the year. Since there may well be days with multiple sales—or no sales at all—the resulting recordset will not give the same results.

- Generally, you want to make sure that you are repeating the field(s) that you are using to sort the data in the query (that is, the field or fields that you are using in the main ORDER BY clause) in the OVER clause. This ensures that the output is visually coherent with the actual data analysis.

4. Applying Window Functions to a Subquery

The CEO has become obsessed with analyzing key metrics over time. Her latest request is that you obtain the total sales to each date and then display the running total of sales by value for each year. The following code snippet shows how to do this:

```
SELECT      DATE(SaleDate) AS DateOfSale

            ,DailyCount AS NumberOfSales

            ,SUM(DailyCount) OVER

                    (PARTITION BY YEAR(SaleDate) ORDER BY SaleDate ASC)

                    AS AnnualNumberOfSalesToDate

            ,SUM(DailySalePrice) OVER
```

```
                    (PARTITION BY YEAR(SaleDate) ORDER BY SaleDate ASC)

                    AS AnnualSalePriceToDate
FROM        (
            SELECT      SaleDate

                        ,COUNT(SD.SalesDetailsID) AS DailyCount

                        ,SUM(SD.SalePrice) AS DailySalePrice

            FROM        salesdetails SD

            JOIN        sales AS SA USING(SalesID)

            GROUP BY    SaleDate

            ) DT

ORDER BY    SaleDate;
```

Running this query gives the results that you can see in Figure 19.6.

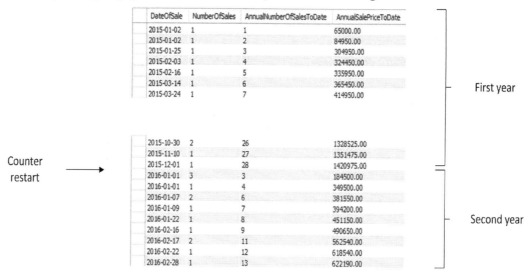

Figure 19.6: Using window functions and a subquery

How it Works

Possibly the easiest way to achieve the objectives that you have set yourself in this query is to break the task into two parts:

First: Create a derived table that counts the number and value of sales per day for each individual date.

Second: Create an outer query that returns the cumulative sales over the year in addition to the running total of sales revenue from the derived table.

In this example, the subquery is an aggregate query that groups the result by date and provides a COUNT() of sales and a SUM() of sales value. We did not apply any filters so that all sales from the start of trading are included. To get a clearer idea of what is included, take a look at Figure 19.7, which shows the output from the subquery.

MakeName	Color	ColorRank
Ferrari	Dark Purple	4
Ferrari	Silver	3
Ferrari	Blue	5
Ferrari	Blue	23
Ferrari	Black	27
Ferrari	British Racing Green	22
Ferrari	Black	6
Ferrari	British Racing Green	1
Ferrari	Black	2
Porsche	Black	6
Porsche	Dark Purple	2
Porsche	Black	8
Porsche	Silver	7

Figure 19.7: Subquery output

The outer query can then take the three fields that are generated by the inner query (sale date, daily sales count, and daily sales value) and use them as follows:

SaleDate Is displayed in the output "as is" and is also used to sort the query results.

DailyCount Is also output "as is" to display the number of sales for each day that there are sales.

DailyCount Is reused in a window function to provide the running total of sales to date. We achieve the running total by applying the COUNT() function over the sale date. In this example, this aggregate value is also partitioned by year using the PARTITION BY clause so that the count restarts with each new year.

DailySalePrice   Is reused (and output as AnnualNumberOfSalesToDate) in a separate window function that is also ordered by sale date and partitioned by the year. This allows you to show the cumulative sales to date for each year.

Using a derived table to perform the initial aggregation is an effective way of preparing the initial data that you then use to provide the running totals. It also allows you to test the initial data simply by selecting and executing the query that constitutes the derived table; this way you can check each part of the process as you build the query.

5. Adding Unique IDs on the Fly Using ROW_NUMBER()

None of the sales staff like using the complex identifiers that appear in the billing system. They have asked you to create your own numbering system to identify sales sequentially. The following SQL shows how to add this kind of distinguishing feature without changing the source data:

```
SELECT       SA.SaleDate

             ,SD.SalePrice, CU.CustomerName, CU.Town, MK.MakeName

             ,COUNT(SD.SalesDetailsID)

               OVER (PARTITION BY YEAR(SaleDate) ORDER BY SaleDate ASC)

               AS AnnualNumberOfSalesToDate

             ,ROW_NUMBER() OVER (ORDER BY SaleDate ASC) AS SalesCounter

FROM         make AS MK

JOIN         model AS MD ON MK.MakeID = MD.MakeID

JOIN         stock AS ST ON ST.ModelID = MD.ModelID

JOIN         salesdetails SD ON ST.StockCode = SD.StockID

JOIN         sales AS SA ON SA.SalesID = SD.SalesID

JOIN         customer CU ON SA.CustomerID = CU.CustomerID

ORDER BY     SaleDate;
```

Running this query gives the results that you can see in Figure 19.8.

SaleDate	SalePrice	CustomerName	Town	MakeName	AnnualNumberOfSalesToDate	SalesCounter
2015-01-02 08:00:00	65000.00	Magic Motors	Birmingham	Ferrari	1	1
2015-01-02 10:33:00	19950.00	Casseroles Chromes	Lyon	Porsche	2	2
2015-01-25 00:00:00	220000.00	Snazzy Roadsters	Birmingham	Ferrari	3	3
2015-02-03 10:00:00	19500.00	Birmingham Executive Prestige Vehicles	Birmingham	Porsche	4	4
2015-02-16 08:00:00	11500.00	WunderKar	Berlin	Porsche	5	5
2015-03-14 00:00:00	29500.00	Magic Motors	Birmingham	Aston Martin	6	6
2015-03-24 00:00:00	49500.00	Birmingham Executive Prestige Vehicles	Birmingham	Aston Martin	7	7
2015-03-30 00:00:00	76000.00	Eat My Exhaust Ltd	Liverpool	Aston Martin	8	8
2015-04-04 00:00:00	36500.00	Sondra Horowitz	Los Angeles	Aston Martin	9	9
2015-04-06 00:00:00	19600.00	M. Pierre Dubois	Marseille	Porsche	10	10

SaleDate	SalePrice	CustomerName	Town	MakeName	AnnualNumberOfSalesToDate	SalesCounter
2018-11-15 00:00:00	11590.00	Matterhorn Motors	Lausanne	Triumph	116	340
2018-11-22 00:00:00	8500.00	Posh Vehicles Ltd	Manchester	Triumph	117	341
2018-12-05 00:00:00	59500.00	Jason B. Wight	Washington	Aston Martin	119	342
2018-12-05 00:00:00	123500.00	Ronaldo Bianco	Milan	Aston Martin	119	343
2018-12-08 00:00:00	99500.00	Andrea Tarbuck	Birmingham	Aston Martin	122	344
2018-12-08 00:00:00	1590.00	Boris Sorv	Birmingham	Trabant	122	345
2018-12-08 00:00:00	54500.00	Boris Sorv	Birmingham	Aston Martin	122	346
2018-12-16 00:00:00	11500.00	Antonio Maura	Madrid	Triumph	123	347
2018-12-17 00:00:00	17950.00	Screamin' Wheels	Los Angeles	Alfa Romeo	124	348
2018-12-31 00:00:00	145000.00	Andy Cheshire	Stoke	Ferrari	127	349
2018-12-31 00:00:00	950.00	Mrs. Ivana Telford	Liverpool	Reliant	127	350
2018-12-31 00:00:00	5500.00	Laurent Saint Yves	Marseille	Citroen	127	351

Figure 19.8: Using the ROW_NUMBER() window function to add unique IDs to a recordset

How it Works

Source data does not always come with all the elements that you need. At times, you may require a way of numbering records to identify each row individually. The ROW_NUMBER() function lets you do just this, and it has no effect on the underlying data.

This query starts by joining all the tables that are necessary, which allows you to display the fields that you want to output (SaleDate, SalePrice, CustomerName, Town, and MakeName). Then it adds these fields—with any necessary formatting and aliases—to the SELECT clause.

Then two window functions are added:

COUNT()   To display the number of sales per day per year. This function is partitioned by year (so that the counter restarts each time the year changes) and ordered by date.

ROW_NUMBER()   To show an individual and progressively incrementing number to identify each record that is output.

The special feature in this query is the use of the ROW_NUMBER() window function. This function lets you add a series of numbers to an output dataset. The series starts at 1 and increases by one for each record in the windowed dataset.

The ROW_NUMBER() also requires you to add an OVER clause containing an ORDER BY statement. To ensure that these virtual IDs are numbered sequentially in a comprehensible manner, the ROW_NUMBER() function is ordered by the sale date. Since we want a continuous range of numbers defined for all the source data, we choose *not* to add a PARTITION BY clause to the window function. The result is a series of numbers that are consecutively incremented in the query output, even if there is no numbering in the source data.

Tricks and Traps

There is one important point to remember when you are applying the ROW_NUMBER() function:

- ROW_NUMBER() is not the same as COUNT()—despite the superficial similarities. If you look at the output for this query for April 30, 2015, you see two records for this date. The COUNT() window function shows a total of 12 sales to date for this day—and this is the same for either of the day's sales (as it should be). The ROW_NUMBER() function attributes a different number to each record, even if the ORDER BY clause for the function is the SaleDate field.

  So the ROW_NUMBER() function *always* differentiates the records that are returned. This can mean applying the numbering sequence arbitrarily to certain rows. You can see this in the two sales for April 30, 2015.

  Of course, if you really want to specify a completely comprehensive numbering system, you can extend the sort order that is applied by the ROW_NUMBER() function. So, you could, for instance, tweak the SQL to read

  ```
  ROW_NUMBER() OVER (ORDER BY SaleDate, MakeName, ModelName ASC) AS
  SalesCounter
  ```

6. Displaying Records for Missing Data

The CEO has just had another idea; you can tell by the smile on her face as she walks over to your desk. Hiding your trepidation, you listen as she tells you that she needs a weekly calendar of sales for 2016. She makes it clear that she wants to see a list of all the weeks in the year, whether there were any sales in that week or not.

After a little effort, you produce the following SQL to deliver the sales report that she was hoping for:

```
WITH Tally_CTE
AS
(
SELECT      ROW_NUMBER() OVER (ORDER BY StockCode) AS Num
FROM        stock
ORDER BY    Num
LIMIT 52
)


SELECT          Num, SalesForTheWeek
FROM            Tally_CTE CTE
LEFT OUTER JOIN
                (
                SELECT      SUM(TotalSalePrice) AS SalesForTheWeek
                            ,WEEK(SaleDate) + 1 AS WeekNo
                FROM        sales
                WHERE       YEAR(SaleDate) = 2016
                GROUP BY    WEEK(SaleDate)
                ) SLS
                ON CTE.Num = SLS.WeekNo;
```

Running this SQL produces output like that shown in Figure 19.9.

Num	SalesForTheWeek
1	349500.00
2	44700.00
3	NULL
4	56950.00
5	NULL
6	NULL
7	NULL
8	111390.00
9	56000.00
10	3650.00
11	NULL
12	NULL
13	220500.00
14	NULL
15	102950.00
16	NULL
17	NULL
18	155800.00

Figure 19.9: Displaying missing data using a sequence list

How it Works

Delivering output when the data exists is rarely an issue; however, you may need to apply slightly different querying techniques if you need to show "missing" data. By this, we mean that SQL does not naturally create complete lists of dates, or date elements such as weeks, where there is no corresponding data in a database.

To understand this problem more clearly, run the SQL from the preceding snippet that returns the total sales per week for 2016, which is contained in the derived table with the alias SLS. The output from the derived table looks like that shown in Figure 19.10.

SalesForTheWeek	WeekNo
349500.00	1
44700.00	2
56950.00	4
111390.00	8
56000.00	9
3650.00	10
220500.00	13
102950.00	15
155800.00	18
99030.00	23
237300.00	25
15650.00	27

Figure 19.10: *The source data with missing values*

Although the figures are accurate, the data contains "holes" since there are no sales for certain weeks. Since these holes could be precisely the data that you want to focus on, it is important to return a *full* list of weeks—whether they contain data or not.

Forcing MySQL to return a complete sequence (whether it is dates, weeks, or any other series of information) requires you to extend the SQL with a list that contains an unbroken and consecutive list of all the elements that you need to view. You can then use this list as the basis for a query that adds the aggregated output that you require.

A sequence like this is often called a *tally table* or a *numbers list*. What you have done in this SQL is

First:	Created a CTE (Common Table Expression) that contains a numbers list.

| *Second:* | Joined the CTE to a query (the derived subquery in this example) that calculates the sales per week. |

Let's begin by looking at the numbers table. Although we call this a table, it is really a dataset generated by a CTE. If you run the code inside the CTE named Tally_CTE, you see the output in Figure 19.11.

Num
1
2
3
4
5
6
7
8
9
10

Figure 19.11: A sequence list or tally table

As you can see, this CTE simply returns a sequence of numbers. You obtain this sequence by

First:	Choosing a table that contains more records than you need in the numbers table (the CTE output).
Then:	Selecting the first *n* records from this table that correspond to the number of items in the sequence that you require. In this example, there are 52 weeks in the year, so you use LIMIT 52 to limit the number of elements in the tally table.
Finally:	The CTE at the start of the SQL serves *only* to provide a sequential list that provides a row for each week in the year.

Once you have the tally table set up, join this to the derived table that returns the actual data for each week of sales. Because you have extracted the week number from the SaleDate field using the WEEK() function, you can join the week number for each week of sales to the corresponding record in the tally table. Defining the join as a LEFT join from the tally table (the CTE) to the derived query ensures that every record from the CTE is displayed, whether or not any corresponding data is in the derived query.

The result is the output from Figure 19.9, shown previously, that shows all the weeks in 2016 with the sales figures, even if there are no sales for a specific week.

Note: If you use a single table as the basis for the tally table, it must contain at least as many records as you need for the sequential list. The next section explains a technique you can use to guarantee enough rows if you are worried that a single source table will not contain enough records.

7. Displaying a Complete Range of Dates and Relevant Data

You really impressed the CEO with your calendar of weekly sales. The only downside is that she clearly told the sales manager to look at increasing sales and avoiding days with no sales, because the sales manager has just requested a list of daily sales for a six-month period (from January 1 to June 30, 2017, to be precise).

After a little head-scratching, you come up with the following piece of SQL:

```
WITH Tally_CTE

AS

(

SELECT      ROW_NUMBER() OVER (ORDER BY ST1.StockCode) - 1 AS Num

FROM        stock ST1

CROSS JOIN stock ST2

LIMIT 10000

)

,DateRange_CTE

AS

(

SELECT      DATE_ADD('20170101', INTERVAL Num DAY) AS DateList

FROM        Tally_CTE

WHERE       Num <= DATEDIFF('20170630', '20170101')

)


SELECT          DATE(DateList) AS SaleDate, SalesPerDay

FROM            DateRange_CTE CTE
```

```
LEFT JOIN

        (

SELECT          DATE(SaleDate) AS DateOfSale

                ,SUM(TotalSalePrice) AS SalesPerDay

FROM            sales

GROUP BY        DATE(SaleDate)

        ) SLS

        ON CTE.DateList = SLS.DateOfSale;
```

Running this code delivers the output that you can see in Figure 19.12.

SaleDate	SalesPerDay
2017-01-01	22500.00
2017-01-02	NULL
2017-01-03	NULL
2017-01-04	NULL
2017-01-05	125000.00
2017-01-06	NULL
2017-01-07	NULL
2017-01-08	NULL
2017-01-09	NULL
2017-01-10	85000.00
2017-01-11	22500.00
2017-01-12	125950.00
2017-01-13	8850.00

Figure 19.12: A complete range of dates including dates without any corresponding data

How it Works

Once again, the source data used in this example does not necessarily contain records for empty values—that is, there is not necessarily a sale every day during the relevant period. Once again, you need to ensure that you have a sequence of a range of dates where there are no missing values.

You accomplish this using two CTEs:

The first CTE: Is a tally table (or a numbers list if you prefer) that ensures a large sequence of numbers. This guarantees that you can request a range of dates over several years if necessary.

The second CTE: Uses the tally table to create a sequence of dates between a start date and an end date.

As each of these CTEs carries out a specific task, it is probably easier to look at each of them in turn.

The tally table CTE works like this:

First: It specifies a large incremented list of a range of numbers (10,000 in this case—enough for nearly 30 years of individual days) using the ROW_NUMBER() function. Because the tally table begins at 1 by default, in this example, we tweaked it to start at 0 by subtracting 1 from the output of the function. This way, the DATE_ADD() and DATEDIFF() functions begin and end with the actual start and end dates the SQL snippet uses (DATE_ADD() starts the list of dates by adding 0 days to the start date—effectively beginning at the date used in the code).

Second: It uses two tables (or the same table twice with two different aliases) that are joined using the CROSS JOIN operator. This approach multiplies the number of records in the first table by the number of records in the second table producing a large set of records that become the basis for the number sequence.

The DateRange CTE works like this:

First: The DATE_ADD() function is used to increment a start date (January 1, 2017) with a sequence of days. This CTE is based on the value in the first CTE, which it, in effect, converts to a date by adding the value in the first CTE to the start date

Second: A WHERE clause filters the upper limit of the date range to June 30, 2017. It does this by using the DATEDIFF() function to calculate the number of days between the start and end dates, which are also specified in the DATEDIFF() function. The number of days becomes the upper threshold for the largest record number from the tally dataset.

If you run the following code snippet just after the two CTEs (in line 15 of the code, on the blank line before the final SELECT clause), you can see the range of continuous calendar dates shown in Figure 19.13.

```
SELECT * FROM DateRange_CTE
```

DateList
2017-01-01
2017-01-02
2017-01-03
2017-01-04
2017-01-05
2017-01-06
2017-01-07
2017-01-08
2017-01-09
2017-01-10
2017-01-11
2017-01-12

Figure 19.13: *A complete range of dates based on a tally table*

Finally, the second CTE—DateRange_CTE—is joined to the derived query that aggregates daily sales. As was the case in the previous example, it is the range of dates that is the "core" table in the query so that an unbroken range of dates is output. A LEFT join to the derived table ensures that a complete range of dates is output. Joining the derived table and the second CTE join on their respective date fields allows the query to return sales data where there is a sale date.

Tricks and Traps

I have a couple of comments worthy of note at this point:

- The cross join to get a large number of records from two tables is called, technically, a *Cartesian join*. This kind of join shows each record from one table joined to each record from the other table. Although this is dangerous—given the sheer amount of data that can be generated— when you are carrying out precise queries, this approach is useful when you need to create a tally table.

- Although we used the DATE_ADD() function here to increment the list of dates by one day starting with the 1st of January 2017, this could just as easily have been achieved using code like the following:

```
SELECT '20170101' + Num AS DateList FROM Tally_CTE
```

  This is possible because days are the basic element in dates in MySQL, and adding a number to a date will add that number of days to a date. For any other intervals (weeks, months and years, for instance) you will have to use the DATE_ADD() or DATE_SUB() functions.

- Unless you are sure that the date fields that you are using to join the derived table and the tally dataset are of the DATE data type, it is worth converting the date fields to DATEs. This ensures that the join is successful.

8. Comparing Data with the Data from a Previous Record

Prestige Car's sales director is keen to track customer spend. She wants you to track sales over time and highlight the difference between previous and current sale values per customer for each sale. The following piece of SQL lets you satisfy her demand:

```
SELECT      CU.CustomerName

            ,SA.SaleDate

            ,SA.TotalSalePrice

            ,SA.TotalSalePrice - LAG(SA.TotalSalePrice,1)

                    OVER (PARTITION BY CU.CustomerName

                    ORDER BY SA.SaleDate)

            AS DifferenceToPreviousSalePrice

FROM        sales SA

JOIN        customer CU USING(CustomerID)

ORDER BY    SA.SaleDate;
```

Running this query gives the results that you can see in Figure 19.14.

CustomerName	SaleDate	TotalSalePrice	DifferenceToPreviousSalePrice
Magic Motors	2015-01-02 08:00:00	65000.00	NULL
Casseroles Chromes	2015-01-02 10:33:00	19900.00	NULL
Snazzy Roadsters	2015-01-25 00:00:00	220000.10	NULL
Birmingham Executive Prestige Vehicles	2015-02-03 10:00:00	19500.00	NULL
WunderKar	2015-02-16 08:00:00	11500.00	NULL
Magic Motors	2015-03-14 00:00:00	29500.00	-35500.00
Birmingham Executive Prestige Vehicles	2015-03-24 00:00:00	49500.20	30000.20
Eat My Exhaust Ltd	2015-03-30 00:00:00	76000.90	NULL
Sondra Horowitz	2015-04-04 00:00:00	36500.00	NULL
M. Pierre Dubois	2015-04-06 00:00:00	19600.00	NULL
Wonderland Wheels	2015-04-30 00:00:00	89000.00	NULL
London Executive Prestige Vehicles	2015-05-10 00:00:00	169500.00	NULL
M. Pierre Dubois	2015-05-20 00:00:00	8950.00	-10650.00

Figure 19.14: Comparing data between records using the LAG() function

How it Works

Although we have seen how to compare individual pieces of data with groups of data, so far in this book, we have not compared individual records to other records. As a first example of how to look at how a sequence of records varies from record to record, this piece of SQL shows how each sale compares to the previous one for the same customer.

In this piece of code you meet the LAG() function for the first time. This function allows you to look back over a subset of records and return data from a previous record, or records.

The query works like this:

First:	A perfectly normal query is constructed that returns a list of individual sales with the sale price and the customer who bought the car using the Sales and Customer tables.
Then:	A LAG() function is added that goes back through the recordset until it finds the previous sale for the same customer as the one in the current record. It returns the previous sale price and, for this customer, subtracts this figure from the current record's sale price to give the difference between the two sale prices for the vehicles.

Just like the other window functions that you have seen, the LAG() function requires a few parameters to work properly. In this example they are

OVER	This operator introduces a window function.
PARTITION BY	This operator tells MySQL how to group the data when searching for a previous record. Since this example has PARTITION BY CustomerName inside the OVER clause, SQL only jumps back to records that have the same customer name as the current record.
ORDER BY	This clause sorts the subset of data (that is grouped by customer) in chronological order, since it is the SaleDate field that provides the sort order.
Field	This indicates the data to return from the preceding record. In this example, it is the SalePrice field.
Offset Value	This is the number of records to jump back for this customer. The value is set to 1 in this example because we want the *previous* record for the same customer.

Once all these elements are in place, the LAG() function can "subset" the data into an invisible group based on the customer field. Since this data subset is a list of records over time relative to the current record, the function steps back into the preceding record for the customer and returns the previous sale price. As you can see in the output, there is, by definition, no previous sale for the first sale for each customer. This is why the LAG() function returns a NULL value.

If you can visualize what is happening, it may help you deal with previous records. Take a look at Figure 19.15; in it, you can see a high-level overview of how the LAG() value works.

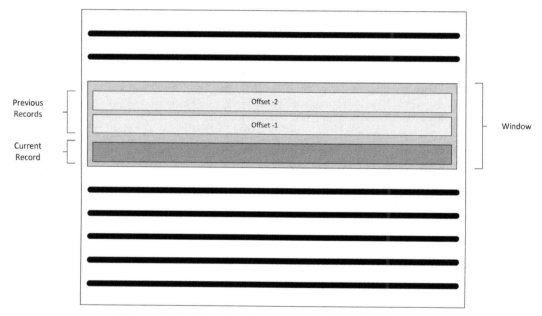

Figure 19.15: Conceptual overview of the LAG() function

Tricks and Traps

The LAG() function is extremely powerful. This inevitably means that you have to master a few subtleties if you want to apply it constructively:

- The field that you place inside the LAG() function does *not* have to appear in the SELECT clause; however, it must be in one of the tables contained in the FROM clause of the query.

- If you do *not* want to see records where there is no difference with any previous sale (because this was the first sale), you can use nearly all of this query as a derived table and wrap it in an outer query. This query then selects the columns from the derived table and adds a WHERE clause to eliminate the PreviousSalePriceDifference records that contain NULLs. The code looks like this:

```
SELECT *
FROM
(
SELECT      CU.CustomerName
            ,SA.SaleDate
            ,SA.TotalSalePrice
            ,SA.TotalSalePrice - LAG(SA.TotalSalePrice,1)
                        OVER (PARTITION BY CU.CustomerName
                            ORDER BY SaleDate)
                            AS PreviousSalePriceDifference
FROM        sales SA
            JOIN customer CU USING(CustomerID)
) SQ
WHERE PreviousSalePriceDifference IS NOT NULL
ORDER BY    SaleDate;
```

Running this query gives the output that you can see in Figure 19.16.

CustomerName	SaleDate	TotalSalePrice	PreviousSalePriceDifference
Magic Motors	2015-03-14 00:00:00	29500.00	-35500.00
Birmingham Executive Prestige Vehicles	2015-03-24 00:00:00	49500.20	30000.20
M. Pierre Dubois	2015-05-20 00:00:00	8950.00	-10650.00
Peter McLuckie	2015-09-15 00:00:00	15600.00	2950.00
Alexei Tolstoi	2015-10-30 00:00:00	22600.00	-390.00
Theo Kowalski	2015-10-30 00:00:00	123590.00	118090.00
Convertible Dreams	2015-11-10 00:00:00	22950.00	14255.00
Alexei Tolstoi	2015-12-01 08:00:00	69500.00	46900.00
Sondra Horowitz	2016-01-01 00:00:00	159500.00	123000.00
Eat My Exhaust Ltd	2016-01-01 00:00:00	12500.00	-63500.90
Wonderland Wheels	2016-01-01 08:00:00	165000.00	76000.00
M. Pierre Dubois	2016-01-07 00:00:00	2550.00	-6400.00
Posh Vehicles Ltd	2016-01-07 00:00:00	29500.00	20550.00
SuperSport S.A.R.L.	2016-02-16 00:00:00	39500.00	-36000.00
Magic Motors	2016-02-28 10:10:00	3650.00	-25850.00
Silver HubCaps	2016-04-30 00:00:00	8800.00	-48150.00

Figure 19.16: Using a subquery with a LAG() function in a derived table

You cannot simply apply the WHERE clause inside the original query to filter the recordset and remove any records with NULL values for the sale price. This is because window functions can *only* be used in SELECT or ORDER BY clauses. Consequently, you have to move the WHERE clause from the derived table to the outer query.

- A PARTITION BY function is not required when using the LAG() function. However, without one, the LAG() function returns data from a record that precedes the current record in the overall dataset without attempting to group the comparative dataset by a specific element—such as the customer in this example.

9. Comparing Data over Time Using the FIRST_VALUE() and LAST_VALUE() Functions

Prestige Cars is continuing its drive to maximize revenue per customer. This time, the sales manager wants to find the initial and final sale prices for each car sold to each customer and then compare these prices with the current selling price. You create the following piece of SQL to do this for him:

```
SELECT     CU.CustomerName

           ,SA.SaleDate

           ,SA.TotalSalePrice AS CurrentSale

           ,FIRST_VALUE(SA.TotalSalePrice)

            OVER (PARTITION BY CU.CustomerName

                  ORDER BY SA.SaleDate, SA.SalesID)

                  AS InitialOrder

           ,LAST_VALUE(SA.TotalSalePrice)

            OVER (PARTITION BY CU.CustomerName

                  ORDER BY SA.SaleDate, SA.SalesID

            ROWS BETWEEN CURRENT ROW AND UNBOUNDED FOLLOWING)

            AS FinalOrder

FROM       sales SA

JOIN       customer CU USING(CustomerID);
```

Running this query gives the results that you can see in Figure 19.17.

MakeName	ModelName	InvoiceNumber	SalePrice	RelativeStanding
BMW	Isetta	GBPGB182	5500.00	0.33
BMW	Alpina	EURFR226	21500.00	0.67
BMW	E30	EURFR158	33500.00	1.00
Bugatti	Veyron	EURFR143	220500.00	0.17
Bugatti	57C	GBPGB142	295000.00	0.33
Bugatti	57C	GBPGB173	335000.00	0.50
Bugatti	57C	EURFR282	345000.00	0.67
Bugatti	57C	GBPGB230	355000.00	0.83
Bugatti	57C	EURFR221	365000.00	1.00
Citroen	Rosalie	GBPGB139	990.00	0.17
Citroen	Rosalie	GBPGB252	1350.00	0.33
Citroen	Rosalie	GBPCH161	2350.00	0.50
Citroen	Rosalie	EURFR322	5500.00	0.67
Citroen	Traction A...	EURFR300	25000.00	0.83
Citroen	Torpedo	EURES147	65890.00	1.00
Delahave	175	EURIT302	12500.00	0.25
Delahave	135	EURFR300	25500.00	0.50
Delahave	145	EURES140	29500.00	0.75

Figure 19.17: Using the FIRST_VALUE() and LAST_VALUE() functions to compare sale prices

How it Works

A useful way to analyze how data evolves over time is to see how a record compares to the first or last record for a common element. This query starts by joining the Customer and Sales tables so that it can access customer and sale data. Then it outputs the CustomerName, SaleDate, and TotalSalePrice fields.

Then a new twist is added. Two output fields are added that are based, respectively, on the FIRST_VALUE() and LAST_VALUE() functions. These act like the LAG() function that you saw in the previous example in that for each record, they create an invisible dataset that is grouped on a shared field (CustomerName in this example). However, in this case, it is not a selected preceding record that is selected, but the very first (or very last) record in this virtual subgroup.

FIRST_VALUE() and LAST_VALUE() require the following elements to work correctly:

OVER　　　　　　This clause starts the window function.

PARTITION BY	This function tells MySQL how to subset the data when searching for the first record; in this example, this means the first value for the customer of the current record. The PARTITION BY function is not strictly necessary, but it is used to compare data that share a common element rather than merely returning the first or last value from the entire dataset.
ORDER BY	This clause sorts the data subset.
Field	This indicates the data to return from the preceding record. In this example, it is the TotalSalePrice field.

The FIRST_VALUE(), LAST_VALUE(), and LAG() functions can be particularly useful because by using them, you avoid having to create multiple, complex subqueries or derived tables to isolate values from the data. These functions traverse the data for each element that is specified in the PARTITION BY clause (the client in this example) and return the record that you are looking for.

Figure 19.18 illustrates how these functions work.

Figure 19.18: *The way that the FIRST_VALUE(), LAST_VALUE(), and LAG() functions operate*

10. Displaying Rolling Averages over a Specified Number of Records

This time the sales manager thinks he has a real challenge for you. He wants to see how average sale prices evolve over time for each customer in a report that shows the rolling average sale value for the last three sales per customer. You do not have to tell her that SQL makes such reports easy as the following code shows:

```
SELECT      CU.CustomerName

            ,SA.SaleDate

            ,SA.TotalSalePrice

            ,AVG(SA.TotalSalePrice)

            OVER (PARTITION BY CU.CustomerName ORDER BY SA.SaleDate

            ROWS BETWEEN 3 PRECEDING AND CURRENT ROW)

                AS AverageSalePrice

FROM        sales AS SA

JOIN        customer CU USING(CustomerID)

ORDER BY    CU.CustomerName, SA.SaleDate;
```

Running this query gives the results that you can see in Figure 19.19.

CustomerName	SaleDate	TotalSalePrice	AverageSalePrice	
Alex McWhirter	2018-10-31 00:00:00	17850.00	17850.000000	
Alexei Tolstoi	2015-07-15 00:00:00	22990.00	22990.000000	Average of Last Two Rows
Alexei Tolstoi	2015-10-30 00:00:00	22600.00	22795.000000	
Alexei Tolstoi	2015-12-01 08:00:00	69500.00	38363.333333	
Alexei Tolstoi	2016-05-30 00:00:00	49450.00	41135.000000	
Alexei Tolstoi	2016-07-25 00:00:00	205000.00	86637.500000	
Alexei Tolstoi	2016-08-02 00:00:00	102500.00	106612.500000	
Alexei Tolstoi	2016-09-04 00:00:00	3500.00	90112.500000	
Alexei Tolstoi	2016-09-16 00:00:00	45950.00	89237.500000	
Alicia Almodovar	2016-10-30 00:00:00	12500.00	12500.000000	Average of Last Three Rows
Alicia Almodovar	2016-12-31 10:00:00	39500.00	26000.000000	
Alicia Almodovar	2017-05-10 16:14:00	12500.00	21500.000000	
Alicia Almodovar	2017-09-20 12:32:00	250000.00	78625.000000	
Alicia Almodovar	2018-03-05 00:00:00	5690.00	76922.500000	

Figure 19.19: Using the ROWS window function to display a rolling average

How it Works

A classic analytical metric is the *rolling average*. A rolling average requires you to isolate a certain number of records up to and including a current record and then calculate the average of a value in all the specified records. The ROWS window function lets you do exactly this. This approach requires you to specify no fewer than seven different elements as part of the window function in order for it to work correctly:

AVG()	Is defined as the aggregation function to apply in the query.
OVER	Indicates that this is a window function that is being applied to a set of records.
PARTITION BY	Specifies how records are assembled into a subgroup inside the overall recordset. In this example, the CustomerName field is used so that a rolling average per customer can be calculated.
ORDER BY	Is used inside the OVER operator to define how the records for the subset are sorted. This is essential to define the sequencing for the range of records used for the rolling average.
ROWS BETWEEN	Indicates that this operator applies to a set of records relative to the current record.
PRECEDING	Says how many rows back the function must go to find the starting row for the running average.
AND CURRENT ROW	Tells the window function to stop at the current record and include it in the total.

In effect, using all these elements to create the rolling average says, "create virtual groups of records for each customer, order them by date, then calculate the average from three rows up to and including the current row."

So, in this example, you begin by creating the basic query to show the customer name, sales date, and the selling price for each vehicle sold by Prestige Cars. You then add a final column to the query that calculates the running average using the ROWS function.

Tricks and Traps

A few points are worth remembering when you use the ROWS() window function:

- A rolling total can be created in exactly the same way as a rolling average. Just use the SUM() function instead of the AVG() function and you have a rolling total.

- Once again, I prefer to add an ORDER BY clause at the end of the query to guarantee that the output is sorted exactly as we want. This is because the ORDER BY clause inside the OVER function is not guaranteed to sort the final output correctly, as it only applies to the data inside the window function.

- You may prefer to apply a totally different sort order to the final output. Doing so has no effect on the way the running average is calculated. To make this clearer, try tweaking the sort order code to read

```
ORDER BY   SA.SaleDate, CU.CustomerName
```

This returns a list rather like the one in Figure 19.20.

CustomerName	SaleDate	TotalSalePrice	AverageSalePrice
Magic Motors	2015-01-02 08:00:00	65000.00	65000.000000
Casseroles Chromes	2015-01-02 10:33:00	19900.00	19900.000000
Snazzy Roadsters	2015-01-25 00:00:00	220000.10	220000.100000
Birmingham Executive Prestige Vehicles	2015-02-03 10:00:00	19500.00	19500.000000
WunderKar	2015-02-16 08:00:00	11500.00	11500.000000
Magic Motors	2015-03-14 00:00:00	29500.00	47250.000000
Birmingham Executive Prestige Vehicles	2015-03-24 00:00:00	49500.20	34500.100000
Eat My Exhaust Ltd	2015-03-30 00:00:00	76000.90	76000.900000
Sondra Horowitz	2015-04-04 00:00:00	36500.00	36500.000000
M. Pierre Dubois	2015-04-06 00:00:00	19600.00	19600.000000
Wonderland Wheels	2015-04-30 00:00:00	89000.00	89000.000000
London Executive Prestige Vehicles	2015-05-10 00:00:00	169500.00	169500.000000
M. Pierre Dubois	2015-05-20 00:00:00	8950.00	14275.000000
Glittering Prize Cars Ltd	2015-05-28 00:00:00	195000.00	195000.000000

Figure 19.20: Using a different sort order in the window function and the overall query

As you can see, the output is based on the sale date, not on the customer name. However, the calculation for the running average has *not* changed. It still calculates the average from last three records per customer, up to and including the current record for that customer; however, the output is less intuitively comprehensible and shows no clear pattern, even if it is arithmetically accurate.

- If you want to show a running average or a running total that does *not* include the current row, you can replace CURRENT ROW with 1 PRECEDING in the SQL. This carries out the calculation up to but *not* including the current row.

- You can specify any row range relative to the current row for a running total—you can even cover rows that are further down the display list (or at a later date than the current record if you prefer). You do this by replacing CURRENT ROW with 3 FOLLOWING in the SQL. You can specify any number for the range of records that you want to use as a basis for your calculation.

11. Show the First Sale and Last Four Sales per Client

Sales at the company are increasing and senior management is convinced that effective analytics is a key factor of corporate success. The latest request to arrive in your inbox is for a report that shows both the first order and the last four sales for each customer. One way of doing this is shown using the following SQL:

```
SELECT
 CU.CustomerName
,SA.SaleDate
,SA.TotalSalePrice
,FIRST_VALUE(TotalSalePrice) OVER (PARTITION BY CU.CustomerName
                                  ORDER BY SA.SaleDate)
                                  AS FirstOrder
,LAG(TotalSalePrice, 3) OVER (PARTITION BY CU.CustomerName
                                  ORDER BY SA.SaleDate)
                                  AS LastButThreeOrder
,LAG(TotalSalePrice, 2) OVER (PARTITION BY CU.CustomerName
                                  ORDER BY SA.SaleDate)
                                  AS LastButTwoOrder
,LAG(TotalSalePrice, 1) OVER (PARTITION BY CU.CustomerName
                                  ORDER BY SA.SaleDate)
                                  AS LastButOneOrder
,LAST_VALUE(TotalSalePrice) OVER (PARTITION BY CU.CustomerName
```

```
                              ORDER BY SA.SaleDate) AS LatestOrder

FROM       sales AS SA

JOIN       customer CU USING(CustomerID)

ORDER BY CU.CustomerName, SA.SaleDate;
```

Running this query gives the results that you can see in Figure 19.21.

CustomerName	SaleDate	TotalSalePrice	FirstOrder	LastButThreeOrder	LastButTwoOrder	LastButOneOrder	LatestOrder
Alex McWhirter	2018-10-31 00:00:00	17850.00	17850.00	NULL	NULL	NULL	17850.00
Alexei Tolstoi	2015-07-15 00:00:00	22990.00	22990.00	NULL	NULL	NULL	22990.00
Alexei Tolstoi	2015-10-30 00:00:00	22600.00	22990.00	NULL	NULL	22990.00	22600.00
Alexei Tolstoi	2015-12-01 08:00:00	69500.00	22990.00	NULL	22990.00	22600.00	69500.00
Alexei Tolstoi	2016-05-30 00:00:00	49450.00	22990.00	22990.00	22600.00	69500.00	49450.00
Alexei Tolstoi	2016-07-25 00:00:00	205000.00	22990.00	22600.00	69500.00	49450.00	205000.00
Alexei Tolstoi	2016-08-02 00:00:00	102500.00	22990.00	69500.00	49450.00	205000.00	102500.00
Alexei Tolstoi	2016-09-04 00:00:00	3500.00	22990.00	49450.00	205000.00	102500.00	3500.00
Alexei Tolstoi	2016-09-16 00:00:00	45950.00	22990.00	205000.00	102500.00	3500.00	45950.00
Alicia Almodovar	2016-10-30 00:00:00	12500.00	12500.00	NULL	NULL	NULL	12500.00
Alicia Almodovar	2016-12-31 10:00:00	39500.00	12500.00	NULL	NULL	12500.00	39500.00
Alicia Almodovar	2017-05-10 16:14:00	12500.00	12500.00	NULL	12500.00	39500.00	12500.00
Alicia Almodovar	2017-09-20 12:32:00	250000.00	12500.00	12500.00	39500.00	12500.00	250000.00
Alicia Almodovar	2018-03-05 00:00:00	5690.00	12500.00	39500.00	12500.00	250000.00	5690.00
Alicia Almodovar	2018-04-02 00:00:00	15950.00	12500.00	12500.00	250000.00	5690.00	15950.00
Alicia Almodovar	2018-04-15 00:00:00	45950.00	12500.00	250000.00	5690.00	15950.00	45950.00

Figure 19.21: *Using the FIRST_VALUE(), LAST_VALUE(), and LAG() functions over time*

How it Works

In order to compare sales (or other metrics) you need to extract elements from several records and place them on the same row. The idea behind this query is to give the recipient an idea of how much each client is spending and see how sales are evolving over time. The output displays

- The first sale made by a customer
- The most recent sale
- The three sales before the most recent sale

Each sale is a separate record in a SQL database. The SQL used here uses three more window functions to extract data from a subset of data. In this case, it is the successive sales per customer. The query selects the customer name and the date for each sale using the Sales and Customer tables. It then uses the following functions to compare the current sale with other sales for the same customer:

FIRST_VALUE   Shows the sale price for the first-ever purchase made by this customer.

| *LAST_VALUE* | Shows the sale price for the latest purchase made by this customer. |
| *LAG* | Shows a previous specific sale—it can be the preceding sale or any previous sale. |

Because you are once again dealing with window functions to output data from multiple records in the same row, these functions also need you to apply the following keywords:

OVER	To indicate to MySQL that you are using a window function.
PARTITION BY	To group records by a criterion so that you can compare values .meaningfully
ORDER BY	To specify how the records are being sorted in a subset

In this example, you are partitioning by the client name so that you can see the sales per client. The ORDER BY clause in the OVER function uses the SaleDate field so that you can compare sales over time.

The FIRST_VALUE and LAST_VALUE functions do what their names imply. They look at all the sales for a common element (defined in the PARTITION BY clause—in this case the customer) and find the oldest and most recent purchases, respectively. The LAG() function lets you go back in time over a set of sales for a customer and return the item in the list that matches the figure that you used in the LAG() function. This way, if you say LAG(SalePrice,1), you display the previous sale to a customer.

Conclusion

This chapter allowed you to focus on running totals when analyzing your data. You saw how to create running totals, running averages, and running counts using SQL. You then learned how to segment the output so that the "rolling" result restarted when a specified element changed.

Finally, you saw how to extend these techniques to show the first or last element in a series. You also saw how to compare records with the previous elements in a data window.

Core Knowledge Learned in This Chapter

The keywords that you have seen in this chapter are

Concept	Description
ROW_NUMBER()	This function adds a system-generated sequential number to each record in the dataset.
LAG()	This function lets you reach back over the previous records in a recordset or subgroup of records to calculate metrics over a defined series of rows relative to the current record.
FIRST_VALUE()	This function returns the starting value in a field in a recordset or subgroup of records.
LAST_VALUE()	This function returns the final value in a field in a recordset or subgroup of records.
ROWS	Used with a window function, this operator lets you define the range of records used in a running calculation.
ROWS BETWEEN	Indicates that this operator applies to a set of records relative to the current record.
PRECEDING	Used with a window function, this operator also lets you define the range of records used in a running calculation
CURRENT ROW	Used with a window function, this operator helps you specify a range of records including the current row.

C<small>HAPTER</small> 20

Analyzing Data over Time

This chapter is all about enhancing your analytical abilities so that you can compare and contrast data over time. Here, I build on the core techniques that you saw earlier in this book and extend your knowledge to make you completely at ease when slicing and dicing data that contains a time element. Of course, when I talk about dealing with time, I mean looking at both date and time elements in MySQL. Mastering these techniques helps you track the evolution of sales, profits, or any metric over any time period—from years to days to hours and seconds.

Time Analysis

Analyzing data over time has the potential to be a vast subject. This is because no two people's requirements are ever going to be identical. So, to give you an idea of what to expect, the kinds of time analysis that you learn in this chapter include

- Month-to-date, quarter-to-date, and year-to-date calculations
- Comparing metrics with those from previous time periods
- Parallel period calculations—comparing figures for the same month in the previous year

- Comparing values for a current month to date with the same month to date from the previous year
- Displaying timespans as years, months, and days
- Calculating weekdays and weekend days
- Displaying time differences in hours and minutes
- Grouping data by time slots

Once you have mastered the essentials of adding a time factor to your SQL queries, you will probably be pleasantly surprised at the new analytical horizons that are available for you to apply in your queries. Admittedly, you need to pay close attention to some of the techniques that are used; however, I am sure that you will find that the investment is well worth the sheer power of the analysis that is now possible when you use SQL to slice and dice data over time.

1. Aggregating Values for the Year to Date

The sales manager keeps one eye firmly on the accumulated sales by make for the year so that she can quickly take any corrective actions that may prove necessary. SQL makes giving her the data that she wants really easy, as the following code shows (for sales in 2017):

```
SELECT      MK.MakeName, SUM(SD.SalePrice) AS CumulativeSalesYTD

FROM        make AS MK

JOIN        model AS MD USING(MakeID)

JOIN        stock AS ST USING(ModelID)

JOIN        salesdetails SD ON ST.StockCode = SD.StockID

JOIN        sales AS SA USING(SalesID)

WHERE       SA.SaleDate BETWEEN

            STR_TO_DATE(YEAR(CURDATE())-1-1, '%Y-%d-%m')

            AND CURDATE()

GROUP BY    MK.MakeName

ORDER BY    MK.MakeName ASC;
```

Figure 20.1 shows the results returned by this query (for a query run on the 31st of October 2017).

MakeName	CumulativeSalesYTD
Alfa Romeo	97200.00
Aston Martin	2532870.00
Austin	8750.00
Bentley	732140.00
BMW	39000.00
Bugatti	850500.00
Citroen	69230.00
Delahaye	29500.00
Delorean	99500.00
Ferrari	3135350.00
Jaguar	408915.00
Lagonda	156500.00
Lamborghini	1082150.00
McLaren	295000.00
Mercedes	180275.00
Noble	129500.00

Figure 20.1: *Calculating aggregate values for the year to date*

How it Works

Collating the sales for the year to date is a fairly regular requirement in many organizations. In this sort of query, all the effort goes (once again) into the WHERE clause. This is because what you do in this clause is set a range of dates in a BETWEEN...AND operator in order to specify a precise date range. The timespan is defined by

A lower boundary	The first of January for the current year that you passed into the query as STR_TO_DATE(YEAR(CURDATE())-1-1, '%Y-%d-%m'). This is another way of saying "January 1, 2017" (assuming you run the query anytime in 2017).
An upper boundary	The date that the query was run, defined by the CURDATE() function. Since the CURDATE() function only returns the date, you do not need to strip out a time part from this date.

The trick that you are using here is finding the *current year*, since the query needs to be dynamic (that is, you want to be able to run it in any year to get the sales for the year to date). It follows that you do not want to enter a fixed year, so you are using the YEAR function to extract the current year from the CURDATE() function. The

CURDATE() function, after all, returns the current date from the computer hosting the MySQL database.

Tricks and Traps

Working with dates can involve using several different SQL functions all at the same time. Be sure to remember that

- The actual results vary depending on the date that you run the query. This example was run in November 2017.

- You can write the following code to return January 1 for the current year if you prefer:

```
SELECT CONCAT(YEAR(CURDATE()), '-01-01')
```

This code snippet extracts the year part from the current date and converts it to a string of four characters. It then adds -01-01 (to represent the month and day, which is January 1) to the year to give the date in the format YYYY-MM-DD for the current year using the CONCAT() function.

- MySQL is very tolerant as far as leading zeros for the month and day parts of a date are concerned. So you can use -01 or -1 for the month and day elements when assembling dates.

- If you are using the BETWEEN ... AND keywords to set a range, you must *always* place the lower boundary after BETWEEN and the upper boundary after AND. This query would not have worked if you typed the WHERE clause as

```
BETWEEN   DATE(CURDATE())   AND   STR_TO_DATE(YEAR(CURDATE())-1-1,
'%Y-%d-%m')
```

- Isolating parts of dates is an essential technique for defining date ranges in SQL. I admit that it can get a little laborious at times separating out the year from the month from the day elements that make up a date. The upside, however, is that this approach does give you unprecedented control and precision when it comes to setting date ranges.

- Instead of using the BETWEEN...AND operator you can use >= and <= instead.

2. Aggregating Values for the Month to Date

Since the sales staff has monthly targets to meet, you have been asked to write a query that can show sales for the month to date. SQL can do this, of course, as the following piece of code shows:

```
SELECT     MakeName, SUM(SD.SalePrice) AS CumulativeSalesMTD

FROM       make AS MK JOIN model AS MD

           ON MK.MakeID = MD.MakeID

JOIN       stock AS ST ON ST.ModelID = MD.ModelID

JOIN       salesdetails SD ON ST.StockCode = SD.StockID

JOIN       sales AS SA ON SA.SalesID = SD.SalesID

WHERE      SA.SaleDate

           BETWEEN

           DATE_SUB(CURDATE(), INTERVAL DAYOFMONTH(CURDATE()) -1 DAY)

           AND CURDATE()

GROUP BY   MakeName

ORDER BY   MakeName ASC;
```

This SQL gives the following result for mid September 2018 as you can see in Figure 20.2. You might see something completely different if you are running this query on a different date.

	MakeName	CumulativeSalesMTD
▶	Bentley	218950.00
	Mercedes	183490.00

Figure 20.2: Aggregate metrics for the month to date

How it Works

If you (or other staff) have monthly targets to meet, then you are likely to want to track metrics for the month to date. This type of query, like its predecessor, sets a date range. This time the range is from the start of the current month to the current date.

First:	You need to find the date that corresponds to the first day of the current month and set this as the lower date threshold for the range of dates. The technique that we are using here is, I admit, a bit of an SQL insider's trick, but it works beautifully and, consequently, is well worth learning. You use the DATE_SUB() function to subtract the current day in the month from the current date to obtain the date of the first day of the month. As using this approach lands on the last day of the previous month, you need to add 1 to this date—by subtracting 1 from the current day of the month.
Second:	You define the upper date threshold using the CURDATE() function.

The technique to find the first day of the month probably needs a more detailed explanation. What you are doing is to subtract a specified number of days from a date using the DATE_SUB() function. This involves four parameters

First:	The date which is the starting point for the calculation. In this case it is the current date (represented by the CURDATE() function and a comma), as you want to subtract the number of days in the month for the current date from this date to obtain the first of the month.
Second:	You add the keyword INTERVAL and a space. This is compulsory.
Third:	You add the number of intervals to subtract from the initial parameter—the starting date. This could be a figure, but in this example it is a calculated value, defined as `DAYOFMONTH(CURDATE())` - `1`. What this says is "find the number of the day for today's date and subtract 1".
Fourth:	You define what the interval actually is from those available in MySQL. In this example it is the day.

You can run this query at any time without having to adjust date parameters because it always adjusts the WHERE clause to look at the sales for the current month.

The principal available interval types that you can use with the DATE_SUB() function are shown in Table 20-1.

Table 20-1: Interval Types

Interval
DAY
WEEK
MONTH
QUARTER
YEAR
SECOND
MINUTE
HOUR

There are several other interval types in MySQL, but I prefer to focus on the key variants here.

Tricks and Traps

There are a couple of key points to take away when aggregating values over time:

- You can enter the interval definition (Day, Month, Year) in uppercase or lowercase. However it should *not* be enclosed in quotes. This holds true for the INTERVAL keyword, too.

- You can also write the beginning of month in other ways if you prefer. One classic way is to use code like the following SQL snippet:

  ```
  CONCAT(YEAR(CURDATE()), '-' ,MONTH(CURDATE()), '-1')
  ```

  This approach re-creates a date by isolating the year, month, and day from the current date. It does this by concatenating the year, month and day—separated by dashes. The year is obtained from applying the YEAR() function to the current date. A dash is then added—in quotes, of course. The month is obtained from applying the MONTH() function to the current date. Then the day is hard-coded as the figure 1—with the dash separator added for good measure.

3. Returning Aggregate Values for the Quarter to Date

Not content with a one-click solution that displays monthly sales, the sales team has now requested a report showing quarterly sales to date as well. The SQL that follows lets you keep them happy:

```
SELECT      MakeName, SUM(SD.SalePrice) AS CumulativeSalesQTD

FROM        make AS MK JOIN model AS MD

            ON MK.MakeID = MD.MakeID

JOIN        stock AS ST ON ST.ModelID = MD.ModelID

JOIN        salesdetails SD ON ST.StockCode = SD.StockID

JOIN        sales AS SA ON SA.SalesID = SD.SalesID

WHERE       QUARTER(SA.SaleDate) = QUARTER(CURDATE())

            AND YEAR(SA.SaleDate) = YEAR(CURDATE())

GROUP BY    MakeName

ORDER BY    MakeName ASC;
```

Figure 20.3 shows what happens when you run this code snippet on September 8, 2018.

MakeName	CumulativeSalesQTD
Alfa Romeo	17450.00
Aston Martin	784820.00
Bentley	375250.00
Bugatti	345000.00
Citroen	25000.00
Delahaye	77500.00
Ferrari	128500.00
Jaguar	68500.00
Mercedes	216940.00
Morgan	18500.00
Noble	5500.00
Peugeot	6000.00

Figure 20.3: Aggregating a metric for the quarter to date

How it Works

To end this short period-to-date trilogy of solutions, this example shows one way to calculate the sales for the quarter to date.

First, as is the case with just about any query, you join the required tables to ensure that you can access the fields that you need. Then you add the GROUP BY and ORDER BY clauses to make this an aggregated query that displays the output in the correct sort order.

Finally, you need to concentrate on getting the WHERE clause right, since this is the key to achieving the desired result.

First: You specify the current quarter. This is as simple as saying "where the quarter for the date of sale is the same as the quarter for the current date". You extract the quarter for both of these dates using the QUARTER() function.

Finally: You specify that we are only interested in the current year by adding a second filter element that makes the query only return information for the current year. You do this using the YEAR() function applied to both the current date and the date of sale.

Tricks and Traps

There are only a few short points to remember at this stage:

- Another function that returns the current date is CURRENT_DATE. This function, however, does not need opening and closing parentheses after the function name. So, in this example, you could write:

```
YEAR(SA.SaleDate) = YEAR(CURRENT_DATE)
```

- Instead of using the QUARTER() function you may prefer to use the EXTRACT() function to identify the quarter. In this example, for instance, you could write:

```
EXTRACT(QUARTER FROM CURDATE())
```

- Instead of using the YEAR() function you may prefer to use the EXTRACT() function to identify the year as well. In this example, for instance, you could enter:

```
EXTRACT(YEAR FROM CURDATE())
```

Of course, the EXTRACT() function could equally be applied to the SaleDate field.

- This technique presumes that there is no available data beyond the current date. If this is not the case then you will need to add a third AND clause to the WHERE clause to restrict the data to less than or equal to the current date.

- You can also use this approach to find the data for the current month to date or year to date if you wish. To do this you would use the MONTH() function instead of the QUARTER() function.

4. Isolating Data for the Previous Month

In his push for increased profits, the CFO always wants to know how this month's purchases compare to last month's figures. As a result, he wants to see purchases by make for the previous calendar month. SQL can help you produce data like this really easily as the following code shows:

```
SELECT      MakeName, SUM(Cost) AS TotalCost

FROM        make AS MK JOIN model AS MD

            ON MK.MakeID = MD.MakeID

JOIN        stock AS ST ON ST.ModelID = MD.ModelID

WHERE       YEAR(DateBought) = YEAR(CURDATE() - INTERVAL 1 MONTH)

            AND

            MONTH(DateBought) = MONTH(CURDATE() - INTERVAL 1 MONTH)

GROUP BY    MakeName;
```

Running this code displays the data that you can see in Figure 20.4 (for November 2017—it will, of course, be different if run on another date).

MakeName	TotalCost
▶ Aston Martin	206840.0000
Bentley	300200.0000

Figure 20.4: Filtering on data for the previous month using the INTERVAL function

How it Works

You might be called on at any time to calculate metrics for the preceding month—such as, for instance, when you compile the month end figures at the start of the following month. Once again, in this kind of time-based query you are defining a date range. On this occasion, however, the WHERE clause uses the INTERVAL function to simplify date and time calculations.

In essence, the INTERVAL function is an alternative to the DATE_ADD() and DATE_SUB() functions. It allows you to add or subtract a number of intervals (or periods, if you prefer) to or from a date.

In this example the objective is to isolate data for the preceding month in a query that can run at any time—without having to specify the date elements. It works by using the WHERE clause to define the filters on the year and month to map to the date for the previous month automatically.

The Year	Is calculated by finding the year for the previous month (which could be December of the previous year).
The Month	Is defined once again by finding the previous month.

What is important is how the INTERVAL function is applied to move backwards in time relative to the current date. It works in a very similar way to how you used it previously in a DATE_SUB() function.

First:	You enter an arithmetic operator. In this case it is the minus sign as you want to *subtract* a specified number of intervals from a date.
Second:	You add the keyword **INTERVAL** and a space.
Third:	You add the number of intervals to subtract from the initial parameter—the starting date. This could be a figure or the result of a calculation. What this says here is "find the date for today's date and subtract 1 month to give me the same date a month ago".
Fourth:	You define what the interval actually is from those available in MySQL. In this example it is the month.

By using these two date calculations in the WHERE clause, you set the entire previous month as the date range. This works no matter how many days are in the month as well as going back across year boundaries.

Tricks and Traps

The interval function can make time period comparisons really simple. However, it is worth noting the following.

- The INTERVAL function must be applied to a date or datetime field or an element that MySQL can interpret as a date or datetime.

- You can, of course use either of the other techniques that you saw in previous examples to calculate the first and last days of the month—even for the previous month—and then calculate date ranges if you prefer. However, this is generally a much more complex approach.

- The interval types that you can use are those that you saw in Table 20-1.

- If you want to test the calculation of an interval you can write SQL like this:

```
SELECT CURRENT_DATE + INTERVAL 1 MONTH
```

5. Using a Derived Table to Compare Data with Values from a Previous Year

Seasonal variations can often be very revealing, or at least this is what the CFO thinks. He has asked you to provide some analysis of like-for-like sales so he can see the average sales by color for the same month in both the previous year and the current year. The following code lets you keep him happy:

```
SELECT      ST.Color, AVG(SA.TotalSalePrice) AS AverageMonthSales

            ,AveragePreviousMonthSales

FROM        make AS MK

JOIN        model AS MD ON MK.MakeID = MD.MakeID

JOIN        stock AS ST ON ST.ModelID = MD.ModelID

JOIN        salesdetails SD ON ST.StockCode = SD.StockID

JOIN        sales AS SA ON SA.SalesID = SD.SalesID

LEFT OUTER JOIN

            (

            SELECT      Color, AVG(SA.TotalSalePrice)

                        AS AveragePreviousMonthSales

            FROM        make AS MK

            JOIN        model AS MD

                        ON MK.MakeID = MD.MakeID

            JOIN        stock AS ST
```

```
                        ON ST.ModelID = MD.ModelID

            JOIN        salesdetails SD

                        ON ST.StockCode = SD.StockID

            JOIN        sales AS SA

                        ON SA.SalesID = SD.SalesID

            WHERE       YEAR(SA.SaleDate) = YEAR(CURDATE()) - 1

                        AND MONTH(SA.SaleDate) = MONTH(CURDATE())

            GROUP BY    Color

            ) SQ

            ON SQ.Color = ST.Color

WHERE       YEAR(SA.SaleDate) = YEAR(CURDATE())

            AND MONTH(SA.SaleDate) = MONTH(CURDATE())

GROUP BY    St.Color;
```

Running this query gives the results that you can see in Figure 20.5—if you run the code in September 2018. For other dates, you get different results.

Color	AverageMonthSales	AveragePreviousYearMonthSales
British Racing Green	72500.000000	NULL
Canary Yellow	62500.000000	NULL
Dark Purple	57866.666667	NULL
Green	50500.000000	49500.000000
Night Blue	39500.000000	NULL
Pink	12500.000000	15750.000000
Red	56950.000000	155000.000000
Silver	43695.000000	NULL

Figure 20.5: *Displaying figures for a parallel time period using a derived table*

How it Works

This query is in two main parts:

A derived table   That calculates the sales by color for the same month in the previous year.

An outer query   That calculates the sales by color for the current month and year.

Each of these elements uses the same core query. First the Make, Model, Stock, SalesDetails, and Sales tables are joined. Then the Color field is added to the SELECT and GROUP BY clauses to aggregate data by color. Finally, the average sale price is calculated. The only real difference is that the derived table (the inner query) looks at last year's data. This is done by adjusting the CURDATE() function for the year so that it reads

```
YEAR(CURDATE()) - 1
```

Then the two parts of the query are joined. We do this using a LEFT JOIN to ensure that all the colors for sales this year will be shown. If you use a simple JOIN (which is an INNER JOIN) instead, then you will not see any colors that sold this year but not last year. Remember that the LEFT JOIN means "all records from the first dataset, including any that match from the second dataset."

Finally, you added the average sale price for last year's sales from the derived table to the outer query.

Using derived tables in subqueries is a standard technique for comparing data over time in SQL. Figure 20.6 explains this concept more visually.

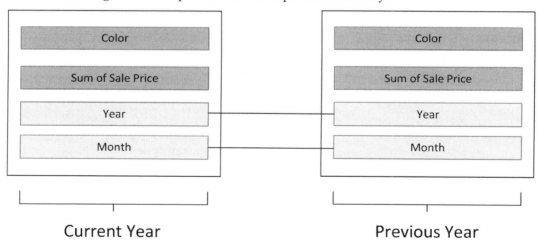

Figure 20.6: *Comparing data over time using a derived table*

Tricks and Traps

To extend your SQL knowledge, you might like to note the following points:

- Any colors that were not sold in the previous months return NULLs using this approach.

- As an alternative way to having the derived table return only the data for the previous year, you can use the DATE_SUB and INTERVAL techniques that you have seen in previous sections.

- Instead of writing LEFT JOIN you can write LEFT OUTER JOIN if you prefer. This is longer, but has the advantage of reminding you that you are applying an outer join.

6. Finding the Total Amount for Each Weekday over a Year

The sales manager is on a mission to find out if certain weekdays are better for sales than others. You have prepared the following query for her so she can analyze sales for each day of the week (but not weekends) in 2017 where there was a sale.

```
WITH TallyTable_CTE
AS
(
SELECT      ROW_NUMBER() OVER (ORDER BY StockCode) AS ID
FROM        stock
ORDER BY    ID
LIMIT       366
)
,DateList_CTE
AS
(
SELECT      DATE_ADD(STR_TO_DATE('2016-12-31', '%Y-%m-%d')
                ,INTERVAL ID DAY)
            AS WeekdayDate
            ,DAYNAME(DATE_ADD(STR_TO_DATE('2016-12-31', '%Y-%m-%d')
                ,INTERVAL ID DAY))
            AS WeekdayName
FROM        TallyTable_CTE
WHERE       DAYOFWEEK(DATE_ADD(STR_TO_DATE('2016-12-31', '%Y-%m-%d')
                ,INTERVAL ID DAY))
```

```
                BETWEEN 2 AND 6
                AND
                DATE_ADD(STR_TO_DATE('2016-12-31', '%Y-%m-%d')
                   ,INTERVAL ID DAY)
                <= '20171231'
)
SELECT          CTE.WeekdayDate
                ,CTE.WeekdayName
                ,SUM(SLS.SalePrice) AS TotalDailySales
FROM            salesbycountry SLS
JOIN            DateList_CTE CTE
                ON CTE.WeekdayDate = DATE(SLS.SaleDate)
GROUP BY        CTE.WeekdayDate
ORDER BY        CTE.WeekdayDate;
```

If you run this query you see the result shown in Figure 20.7.

WeekdayDate	WeekdayName	TotalDailySales
2017-01-05	Thursday	125000.00
2017-01-10	Tuesday	85000.00
2017-01-11	Wednesday	22500.00
2017-01-12	Thursday	125950.00
2017-01-13	Friday	8850.00
2017-01-30	Monday	56500.00
2017-01-31	Tuesday	111950.00
2017-02-07	Tuesday	365000.00
2017-02-08	Wednesday	395000.00
2017-02-09	Thursday	21500.00
2017-02-10	Friday	6500.00
2017-02-14	Tuesday	2250.00
2017-03-10	Friday	213000.00
2017-03-30	Thursday	305000.00
2017-03-31	Friday	313940.00
2017-04-05	Wednesday	29500.00
2017-04-06	Thursday	139500.00
2017-04-07	Friday	515500.00
2017-05-01	Monday	242000.00
2017-05-09	Tuesday	145390.00

Figure 20.7: The total sales for weekdays

How it Works

This query is built in three stages. For the moment, let's take a closer look at the first two parts of the code.

First: A tally CTE is created to provide a list from 0 to 366. The exact number is irrelevant as long as it is at least 365—the number of days in the year (or 366 if you are dealing with a leap year). In this example, we are creating a *tally CTE* by creating an initial CTE (Common Table Expression) that uses the Stock table to create a sequential list using the ROW_NUMBER() function. You can base the tally list on any table that contains enough records (or even more than one table if you need a lot of records in the list). If you select the code for the first CTE (named TallyTable_CTE) and run it, you see a list like the one shown in Figure 20.8

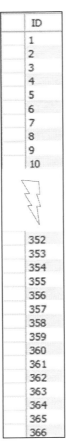

Figure 20.8: The output from a tally table CTE

Second: A second CTE that uses the tally CTE to generate a sequential list of every date in the year. This is done by using the DATE_ADD() function, which is applied to every record in the tally table.

What the DATE_ADD() function does is take January 1, 2017—defined using the STR_TO_DATE() function—and add to this the number in the ID column of the tally table. This gives a sequence of dates.

This technique is then used a total of four times:

First: To give the date resulting from the DATE_ADD() sequence.

Second: Inside a DAYNAME() function to return the name of the day of the week.

Third: Inside the WHERE clause of the second CTE. Specifically the DATE_ADD() sequence is enclosed in a DAYOFWEEK() function to return the number of the day in the week. Because day 1 and day 7 (Sunday and Saturday, respectively) are not weekdays, the WHERE clause excludes these. One way of doing this is to filter so that only day numbers between 2 and 6 (Monday to Friday) pass the conditions set by the WHERE clause.

Then: The WHERE clause adds an upper limit to the list that is generated by the two CTEs by setting the date of the last day of 2017.

Finally: The output is sorted on the weekday date for visual coherence.

To get an idea of how these two CTEs work, you can replace the entire final query with a SELECT statement to show the output of the second CTE using the following code.

```
SELECT * FROM DateList_CTE
```

If you run the two CTEs followed by the SELECT statement, you see the output from the second CTE (which uses the date from the first CTE) as shown in Figure 20.9. Saturdays and Sundays, as you can see, are excluded from the list of dates.

WeekdayDate	WeekdayName
2017-01-02	Monday
2017-01-03	Tuesday
2017-01-04	Wednesday
2017-01-05	Thursday
2017-01-06	Friday
2017-01-09	Monday
2017-01-10	Tuesday
2017-01-11	Wednesday
2017-01-12	Thursday
2017-01-13	Friday
2017-01-16	Monday
2017-01-17	Tuesday
2017-01-18	Wednesday
2017-01-19	Thursday
2017-01-20	Friday
2017-01-23	Monday

Figure 20.9: *Using a CTE to isolate the weekdays*

The output from the second CTE then becomes the basis for the final query, since it displays the dates and weekday names for all the days in the year 2017. The final query joins the CTE output to the SalesByCountry view using the SaleDate field. Because there could be several sales on a single day—and we want the aggregate value for the sales for each weekday—the final query uses a GROUP BY clause on the date and weekday fields and wraps the sales value in a SUM() function.

Tricks and Traps

Given that this is a fairly complex sequence of SQL, I have a few points to make here:

- If you are looking at a list of weekdays for several years, be sure to create a tally table that contains at least as many records as there are consecutive days in the total number of years.

- You can choose to limit the initial tally table to the exact number of days in the year (or between the two dates if you are using a date range); however, this means calculating the exact number of days and adding this to a WHERE clause in the first CTE or using a LIMIT clause (as is the case in this example).

- This piece of SQL displays all weekdays where there is a sale. If you want a complete list of dates, including any days where there were *no sales*, you can change the JOIN to a RIGHT JOIN in the final query. You can see this in the following SQL snippet (since the two CTEs remain the same, I am not showing them again).

```
SELECT              CTE.WeekdayDate
                    ,CTE.WeekdayName
                    ,SUM(SLS.SalePrice) AS TotalDailySales
FROM                salesbycountry SLS
RIGHT JOIN          DateList_CTE CTE
                    ON CTE.WeekdayDate = CAST(SLS.SaleDate AS DATE)
GROUP BY            CTE.WeekdayDate
ORDER BY            CTE.WeekdayDate;
```

Running this altered query gives the output that you can see in Figure 20.10, where the weekdays *without* sales are also displayed.

WeekdayDate	WeekdayName	TotalDailySales
2017-01-02	Monday	NULL
2017-01-03	Tuesday	NULL
2017-01-04	Wednesday	NULL
2017-01-05	Thursday	125000.00
2017-01-06	Friday	NULL
2017-01-09	Monday	NULL
2017-01-10	Tuesday	85000.00
2017-01-11	Wednesday	22500.00
2017-01-12	Thursday	125950.00
2017-01-13	Friday	8850.00
2017-01-16	Monday	NULL
2017-01-17	Tuesday	NULL
2017-01-18	Wednesday	NULL
2017-01-19	Thursday	NULL
2017-01-20	Friday	NULL
2017-01-23	Monday	NULL

Figure 20.10: Using an OUTER JOIN with a tally table to display NULL date records

- If you suspect that the date field that you are using contains a time element then you may need to strip out the time part by applying the DATE() or CAST() functions.

- Remember that sorting the output by the name of the weekday will output the days in alphabetical order.

7. Count the Number of Weekend Days between Two Dates

As a prelude to delivering some more complex analysis of staff deployment, the HR department wants to know how many weekend days there are in March and April 2018. This requires some clever SQL, as you can see in the following code snippet.

```
WITH TallyTable_CTE
AS
(
SELECT      ROW_NUMBER() OVER (ORDER BY StockCode) AS ID
FROM        stock
ORDER BY    ID
LIMIT       90
)
,WeekendList_CTE
AS
(
SELECT      DATE_ADD('20180301', INTERVAL ID - 1 DAY) AS WeekdayDate
FROM        TallyTable_CTE
WHERE       DAYOFWEEK(DATE_ADD('20180301', INTERVAL ID - 1 DAY))
                IN (1,7)
                AND ID <= DATEDIFF('20180430', '20180301')
)
```

```
SELECT      COUNT(*) AS WeekendDays FROM WeekendList_CTE;
```

When you run this query, you should see the output that is shown in Figure 20.11.

WeekendDays
▶ 18

Figure 20.11: *Counting the number of non-weekdays for a date range*

How it Works

What this query does is create a table of all the days between two dates (March 1 and April 30, 2017, in this example). It then deduces the number of the day for each date and excludes Mondays through Fridays. Finally, it counts the number of records remaining.

The code works like this:

First: A tally CTE is created to provide a sequential list of numbers starting with 1. It is limited to slightly more than the required number of records to speed up the query and avoid a full query on the (potentially huge) table used as a basis for the numbers list.

Then: A second CTE uses the tally list as part of a DATE_ADD() function to create a list of dates. This list begins with 0 to give the starting date —by subtracting one day from the lower date threshold that is the third parameter of the DATE_ADD() function—and then continues adding one day for each record in the tally list. The WHERE clause of the second CTE filters out any weekdays by:

- Reusing the same DATE_ADD() expression and enclosing this in a DAYOFWEEK() function that returns the number of the weekday. The filter only allows days 1 and 7 (Sundays and Saturdays) to appear in the second CTE output.

- Limiting the number of records from the tally list that are used. It does this by creating a DATEDIFF() function that returns the number of days between the lower and upper threshold dates. This number of days is the number of records that the subquery should return. Consequently, the maximum number of records in the weekend list is set by filtering on the maximum ID value for the second CTE output.

Finally: A simple SELECT clause using the data from the second CTE counts the number of weekend days between the two dates.

Tricks and Traps

I have a couple of points to make here:

- Once again, you may have to repeat the date thresholds several times in queries like this one. The essential thing is to be careful and consider whether you should be using the lower or upper date thresholds in each case.

- Date tally lists are often fairly short; however, remember that you can make quite large tally lists if you need them by using the same table name two or even three times. This approach gives you code like this:

```
SELECT     ROW_NUMBER() OVER (ORDER BY Y.StockCode) - 1 AS ID
FROM       stock Y
CROSS JOIN Stock Z
```

8. Aggregate Data for the Last Day of the Month

The sales manager is still convinced that some days deliver better sales than others, so now she wants to see the sales for the last day of each month in 2016. SQL can handle this fairly easily, as the following piece of SQL shows:

```
WITH TallyTable_CTE

AS

(

SELECT     ROW_NUMBER() OVER (ORDER BY StockCode) AS ID

FROM       stock

ORDER BY   ID

LIMIT      12

)

,LastDayOfMonth_CTE

AS

(

SELECT     LAST_DAY(CONCAT('2016-', ID, '-01')) AS LastDayDate

FROM       TallyTable_CTE

)


SELECT     CTE.LastDayDate

           ,SUM(SLS.SalePrice) AS TotalDailySales
```

```
FROM        salesbycountry SLS

JOIN        LastDayOfMonth_CTE CTE

            ON CTE.LastDayDate = DATE(SLS.SaleDate)

GROUP BY    CTE.LastDayDate

ORDER BY    CTE.LastDayDate;
```

If you run this query, you see the output that is shown in Figure 20.12.

	LastDayDate	TotalDailySales
▶	2016-04-30	155800.00
	2016-12-31	39500.00

Figure 20.12: Showing aggregate data for the last day of the month

How it Works

This query is composed of three fundamental elements.

A tally CTE   That delivers a list of incremental numbers. This CTE uses the ROW_NUMBER() function to create the list of numbers, starting with 1. The row number field is aliased as ID. The table that the set of numbers is based on is completely irrelevant, as it only serves as a basis for the records that are created, and none of the actual data in the underlying table is required. The list is limited to 12 as we are dealing with a maximum of 12 months in the year.

A second CTE   That uses the tally CTE as the source for its data. This second CTE extracts the 12 records from the tally CTE that correspond to the 12 months in the year. Then the second CTE creates a list of the 12 months of a year (2016 in this case) by applying the CONCAT() function to the tally list. Since the tally list ID field is defined as being the second parameter of the CONCAT() function (the month in other words), the second CTE generates a list of the12 months in the year. The last day of each month is then extracted from the month date using the LAST_DAY() function. This function automatically returns the number of the last day of the month from a DATE or DATETIME field.

A query That uses the second CTE as its data source. This query joins to the SalesByCountry view on the SaleDate field so that any sales that occurred on the last day of any month are returned. Once again a DATE() function is applied to ensure that the fields used to join the two tables are only using date elements for the join and that any time elements of the data are discarded.

This sequence of datasets is probably easier to understand if you display the output from the second CTE. You can do this by placing the following piece of code under the second CTE and deleting the final query.

```
SELECT * FROM LastDayOfMonth_CTE
```

Figure 20.13 shows you the output from the second of two CTEs.

LastDayDate
2016-01-31
2016-02-29
2016-03-31
2016-04-30
2016-05-31
2016-06-30
2016-07-31
2016-08-31
2016-09-30
2016-10-31
2016-11-30
2016-12-31

Figure 20.13: Displaying the last day of the month

Because the LastDayDate is used as the field that joins the second CTE to the SalesByCountry view only the data for the last day of the month is returned. This is because the second CTE is, in fact, acting as a filter on the source view.

Tricks and Traps

You might find this tip about small tally lists useful.

- When creating a small tally list (for days of the week, for instance) you may prefer to use an approach like this:

```
WITH TallyTable_CTE (ID)
AS
```

```
(
SELECT      1 UNION
SELECT      2 UNION
SELECT      3 UNION
SELECT      4 UNION
SELECT      5 UNION
SELECT      6 UNION
SELECT      7
)
```

9. Aggregate Data for the Last Friday of the Month

The HR director has indicated that she is going to want you to calculate sales commissions for payment on the last Friday of every month. However, before you actually carry out the math, she wants a list of the last Friday for every month of 2018. You can deliver this using the following piece of SQL:

```
WITH TallyTable_CTE

AS

(

SELECT      ROW_NUMBER() OVER (ORDER BY StockCode) AS ID

FROM        stock

ORDER BY    ID

LIMIT       12

)

,LastDayOfMonth_CTE

AS

(

SELECT      LAST_DAY(CONCAT('2018-', ID, '-01')) AS MonthEndDate

            ,WEEKDAY(LAST_DAY(CONCAT('2018-', ID, '-01'))) + 1
```

```
             AS MonthEndDay
FROM         TallyTable_CTE
)


SELECT       MonthEndDate
             ,CASE
                 WHEN MonthEndDay >= 5 THEN DATE_ADD(MonthEndDate
                     ,INTERVAL 5 - MonthEndDay DAY)
                 ELSE DATE_SUB(MonthEndDate
             ,INTERVAL (2 + MonthEndDay) DAY)
             END AS LastFridayOfMonth
FROM         LastDayOfMonth_CTE;
```

Running this code snippet produces the output that is shown in Figure 20.14.

MonthEndDate	LastFridayOfMonth
2018-01-31	2018-01-26
2018-02-28	2018-02-23
2018-03-31	2018-03-30
2018-04-30	2018-04-27
2018-05-31	2018-05-25
2018-06-30	2018-06-29
2018-07-31	2018-07-27
2018-08-31	2018-08-31
2018-09-30	2018-09-28
2018-10-31	2018-10-26
2018-11-30	2018-11-30
2018-12-31	2018-12-28

Figure 20.14: Displaying the last Fridays of 2017

How it Works

This query (much like the last one) is based on

- A tally CTE to provide a sequence of numbers
- A second CTE that uses the tally list to produce a series of dates composed of the last day of the month

- A final query that takes the data from the second CTE and delivers the required result

Because the first two elements (the tally list and the CTE of month-end dates) are the same as those used in the previous section, I do not explain them again here.

The output query is a little different, however. It takes the date for the last day of the month and subtracts the required number of days necessary to discover the previous Friday using either a DATE_ADD() function or a DATE_SUB() function. These functions add or subtract a specified number of days from the month-end date. The trick here is to remember that Friday is normally day 5 for MySQL. However in this piece of code it is considered as day 6 because we are adding 1 to the last day calculation in the Common table expression LastDayOfMonth_CTE.

This requires first testing whether the last day is a Friday, Saturday or Sunday. If it is (and this is the first part of the CASE statement), then the number of days to add is calculated to go back one or two days to jump back to the preceding Friday—or remain on the Friday of the date actually is a Friday.

If the last day is Monday through Thursday, then a slightly different calculation is used. In this case the value for the month end day is incremented by 2 (the two remaining days of the week) and then subtracted from the last day of the month to jump back to the preceding Friday.

This sequence of datasets is also probably easier to understand if you display the output from the second CTE. You can do this by placing the following piece of code under the second CTE and deleting the final query.

```
SELECT * FROM LastDayOfMonth_CTE
```

Adding this line of code after the second CTE and then running the SQL gives the result that you can see in Figure 20.15.

MonthEndDate	MonthEndDay
2018-01-31	3
2018-02-28	3
2018-03-31	6
2018-04-30	1
2018-05-31	4
2018-06-30	6
2018-07-31	2
2018-08-31	5
2018-09-30	7
2018-10-31	3
2018-11-30	5
2018-12-31	1

Figure 20.15: Displaying the day number of the Friday of the month

Once you have the day of the week for the last day of the month you can apply a little logic and a simple calculation. What the CASE statement in the final part of the query does is:

First: Decide if the last day of the month is a Friday, Saturday or Sunday (weekday 5, 6 or 7). If it is, then the DATE_ADD() function moves the required date back to the previous Friday.

Then: If the last day of the month is a weekday from 1 through 4 then DATE_SUB() is used to move the required date back to the previous Friday.

10. Analyzing Timespans as Years, Months, and Days

The CEO of Prestige Cars is adamant. "Idle stock is a waste of resources," she maintains. To make sure no vehicles are waiting too long between being bought and sold, she has asked you to produce a report that shows the total number of years, total number of months, and total number of days each car remains in stock. This has required some clever SQL, as you can see:

```
SELECT      ST.StockCode

            ,ST.DateBought

            ,SLS.SaleDate

            ,TIMESTAMPDIFF(YEAR, ST.DateBought

              ,IFNULL(SLS.SaleDate, CURDATE())) AS Years

            ,TIMESTAMPDIFF(MONTH, ST.DateBought

              ,IFNULL(SLS.SaleDate, CURDATE())) AS Months

            ,TIMESTAMPDIFF(DAY, ST.DateBought

              ,IFNULL(SLS.SaleDate, CURDATE())) AS Days

FROM        stock ST

LEFT JOIN   (

            SELECT SA.SaleDate

                  ,SD.StockID
```

```
            FROM    salesdetails SD

            JOIN    sales SA USING(SalesID)

            ) SLS

            ON ST.StockCode = SLS.StockID

ORDER BY    Years DESC, Months DESC, Days DESC;
```

Running this query gives the results that you can see in Figure 20.16. I have scrolled down the output so that you can see a selection of cars sold and cars that have not yet been sold.

	StockCode	DateBought	SaleDate	Years	Months	Days
▶	DE3096AD-76F9-4AAF-B2E1-49FA8E2C377F	2015-03-03	NULL	3	42	1291
	8BD326B3-8DE8-4DC9-9F96-FD132C5E1BF2	2015-04-04	NULL	3	41	1259
	373B7D39-B5A3-4018-883C-AC81EF3B5D8F	2016-02-11	NULL	2	31	946
	A6FCB276-6311-4B3E-9C99-23F197952F1C	2015-09-30	2018-02-17 00:00:00	2	28	871
	62611547-0F2D-41B1-BA32-E34AB67E10A3	2016-06-05	NULL	2	27	831
	18974E49-6B03-4C6E-BA0C-D564CFF868E0	2016-06-01	NULL	2	27	835
	86450D0C-EAA5-4B83-A9DA-55D742E9C2D8	2015-10-29	NULL	2	34	1051
	F0235F1B-636C-4E8B-8617-927F45DA97DB	2016-08-03	NULL	2	25	772
	74F717DA-B4DA-44F2-857A-F062AC60052E	2016-08-11	NULL	2	25	764
	C82D133F-3442-464B-A16A-D5419A9E1CDF	2016-02-27	NULL	2	30	930
	26A3D067-DCEA-4FF1-9A97-E7AEE0D2BC14	2015-10-29	NULL	2	34	1051
	837C835A-5341-46C7-A282-14612449DDB0	2017-01-02	NULL	1	20	620
	E9FE6FE1-1957-4BD4-8643-D8326BC43255	2017-01-02	NULL	1	20	620
	2319EA77-F4D9-4E34-9771-C42DCA3E210C	2016-10-03	2018-02-17 00:00:00	1	16	502
	2866BF16-7A79-4DB7-8657-30958E4035A9	2017-06-23	NULL	1	14	448
	4831A9DA-09BD-4AC3-8984-947F284CD4A8	2017-03-29	NULL	1	17	534
	579AD98F-B7A5-456A-8F17-5B77A5479767	2017-02-02	NULL	1	19	589
	5F898C04-BDFB-437B-A640-AE520F14031E	2017-03-12	NULL	1	18	551

Figure 20.16: *Using TIMESTAMPDIFF() function to calculate time in years, months, and days*

How it Works

What this query does is take advantage of the possibilities the TIMESTAMPDIFF() function offers to take a timespan between two dates and calculate the following metrics:

- The total number of elapsed years
- The total number of elapsed months.
- The total number of elapsed days .

To begin with, this query joins the tables that are required to access the purchase and sales dates. That means joining the Stock and Sales tables using the SalesDetails table as a connecting "bridge" table.

However, there is an interesting tweak here. As you are not just looking for cars that have sold, but also those that are sitting on the lot waiting for a buyer you need to extend the SQL to handle vehicles without a sale date.

This requires two extensions to the SQL.

First:	The Stock table needs to be joined to the SalesDetails table using a LEFT join. This is to ensure that cars in stock but without a corresponding record in the SalesDetails table are found. However, the Sales and SalesDetails tables need a simple JOIN. As the underlying logic of this query will not let you add a simple JOIN after a LEFT JOIN, you need create a derived table to join the Sales and SalesDetails tables with a simple JOIN. This derived (or inline) table is aliased as SLS.
Then:	You need to enclose the SaleDate field from the SalesDetails table in the IFNULL() function and set today's date (using the CURDATE() function) as the value to use if there is no sale date.

This piece of SQL also introduces the TIMESTAMP_DIFF() function. This function requires you to enter three parameters.

First:	The time element that you want to extract from the timespan between two dates.
Second:	The lower—or start—date.
Finally:	The higher—or end—date.

At this point, you can add the three time-based calculations that deliver the information that interests you:

Years elapsed	This calculation uses the YEAR parameter to the TIMSTAMPDIFF() function to give the number of whole years elapsed between the two dates.
Months elapsed	This calculation uses the MONTH parameter to the TIMESTAMPDIFF() function to give the number of complete months that have passed.

Days elapsed　　　This calculation uses the DAY parameter to the TIMESTAMPDIFF() function to give the number of complete days that have passed.

You may not necessarily need all of these individual calculations when you are analyzing your time-related data; however, having them at hand might prove useful one day!

Table 20-2 gives some of the TIMESTAMPDIFF() parameters that you can use when calculating elapsed periods of time in MySQL.

Table 20-2: Period Elements Used with the TIMESTAMPDIFF() Function

Interval Code	Description
DAY	*Extracts the number of whole days between two dates*
WEEK	*Extracts the number of whole weeks between two dates*
MONTH	*Extracts the number of whole months between two dates*
QUARTER	*Extracts the number of whole quarters between two dates*
YEAR	*Extracts the number of whole years between two dates*

Tricks and Traps

There are a couple of extra points to make here.

- Once again, the date elements used in the TIMESTAMPDIFF() function must either be DATE or TIMESTAMP data types or data that MySQL can interpret as a date.
- TIMESTAMPDIFF() calculates complete periods between two dates.

11. Isolate Time Periods from Date and Time Data

The sales team has been vying to sell cars faster and faster, so they want to know which cars have spent the shortest time in stock in 2017. This can sometimes prove to be only a matter of minutes or even seconds, as the following SQL illustrates:

```
SELECT      ST.DateBought

            ,SA.SaleDate

            ,CONCAT(MK.MakeName, '-', MD.ModelName) AS MakeAndModel
```

```
            ,TIMEDIFF(SA.SaleDate, CAST(ST.DateBought AS DATETIME))
               AS TimeDifference
            ,HOUR(TIMEDIFF(SA.SaleDate, CAST(ST.DateBought
               AS DATETIME))) AS Hours
            ,MINUTE(TIMEDIFF(SA.SaleDate, CAST(ST.DateBought
               AS DATETIME))) AS Minutes
            ,SECOND(TIMEDIFF(SA.SaleDate, CAST(ST.DateBought
               AS DATETIME))) AS Seconds
            ,CONCAT(FLOOR(HOUR(TIMEDIFF(SA.SaleDate
                    ,CAST(ST.DateBought AS DATETIME))) / 24)
                    ,' Days - '
                    ,HOUR(TIMEDIFF(SA.SaleDate, CAST(ST.DateBought
               AS DATETIME))) MOD 24
                    ,' Hours')
               AS DaysAndHours
FROM        stock ST
JOIN        model MD
            ON ST.ModelID = MD.ModelID
JOIN        make MK
            ON MD.MakeID = MK.MakeID
JOIN        salesdetails SD
            ON ST.StockCode = SD.StockID
JOIN        sales SA
            ON SD.SalesID = SA.SalesID
WHERE       YEAR(SA.SaleDate) = 2017
ORDER BY    Hours DESC, Minutes DESC, Seconds DESC;
```

Running this query gives the results that you can see in Figure 20.17.

DateBought	SaleDate	MakeAndModel	TimeDifference	Hours	Minutes	Seconds	DaysAndHours
2015-04-30	2017-03-31 13:08:00	Aston Martin-DB6	838:59:59	838	59	59	34 Days - 22 Hours
2016-07-03	2017-11-01 17:36:00	Porsche-911	838:59:59	838	59	59	34 Days - 22 Hours
2016-07-25	2017-03-31 16:08:00	Aston Martin-DB6	838:59:59	838	59	59	34 Days - 22 Hours
2016-10-01	2017-02-12 16:02:00	Triumph-TR6	838:59:59	838	59	59	34 Days - 22 Hours
2017-08-31	2017-09-20 14:32:00	Aston Martin-DB2	494:32:00	494	32	0	20 Days - 14 Hours
2017-01-02	2017-01-21 13:56:00	Peugeot-203	469:56:00	469	56	0	19 Days - 13 Hours
2017-03-12	2017-03-30 13:07:00	Lamborghini-Jarama	445:07:00	445	7	0	18 Days - 13 Hours
2017-09-02	2017-09-20 12:32:00	Ferrari-Testarossa	444:32:00	444	32	0	18 Days - 12 Hours
2017-09-03	2017-09-20 16:33:00	Ferrari-355	424:33:00	424	33	0	17 Days - 16 Hours
2017-03-12	2017-03-25 10:07:00	Porsche-959	322:07:00	322	7	0	13 Days - 10 Hours
2017-01-02	2017-01-14 09:58:00	Triumph-TR5	297:58:00	297	58	0	12 Days - 9 Hours
2017-01-02	2017-01-13 19:58:00	Triumph-TR7	283:58:00	283	58	0	11 Days - 19 Hours

Figure 20.17: Using TIMEDIFF() and arithmetic operators to calculate time in hours, minutes, and seconds

How it Works

This query begins by joining the tables that are needed to source the Make, Model, DateBought, and SaleDate fields. Then a WHERE clause is added that filters the records so that only vehicles that are sold in 2017 are displayed.

Five formulas are added to the SELECT clause to return:

- The time difference in hours, minutes and seconds that the vehicle is in stock
- The hours in stock
- The minutes in stock after any hours are subtracted from the total time in stock
- The seconds in stock after any hours and minutes are subtracted from the total time in stock
- The days and hours in stock

These five formulas work like this:

TIMEDIFF()   The TIMEDIFF() function is used to return the time difference in hours, minutes and seconds between the sale date and the purchase date. AS I explained in the previous section, this function takes two parameters. Firstly, the later date (the sale date) and secondly the earlier date (the purchase date).

Hour	The HOUR()function calculates the number of hours in the time difference (calculated again using the TIMEDIFF() function) between the purchase date and the sale date (which is, in fact, midnight since the DateBought field does not contain hours, minutes, or seconds.
Minute	Here the MINUTE() function calculates the number of minutes in the time difference (calculated again using the TIMEDIFF() function) between the purchase date and the sale date.
Second	The SECOND() function also calculates the number of seconds in the time difference (calculated again using the TIMEDIFF() function) between the purchase date and the sale date.
Days and Hours	The number of hours returned by a TIMEDIFF() function is divided by 24 to calculate the number of whole days between the two dates. The number of hours remaining after the elapsed days is calculated by using the MOD function to return the remainder of the time difference in hours once the number of hours are divided by 24. These two figures are wrapped inside the CONCAT() function to make them more readable—and to add some illustrative text so that the days and hours are presented as a single output column.

12. Listing Data by Time of Day

Now the sales manager wants to look at exactly when cars are sold to see if there are certain times of the day that are better for sales. You produced a list of vehicles sold in 2017 that includes the exact time the sale was made. The code for this is shown here:

```
SELECT     MakeName, ModelName, SalePrice

           ,DATE_FORMAT(SaleDate, '%H:%i') AS TimeOfDaySold

FROM       salesbycountry

WHERE      YEAR(SaleDate) = 2017

ORDER BY   TimeOfDaySold;
```

If you run this code you see the output displayed in Figure 20.18.

	MakeName	ModelName	SalePrice	TimeOfDaySold
▶	BMW	E30	33500.00	09:19
	Jaguar	XK150	29500.00	09:25
	Triumph	TR5	9950.00	09:58
	Aston Martin	Rapide	55000.00	09:59
	Porsche	959	55600.00	10:07
	Rolls Royce	Wraith	162500.00	10:12
	Aston Martin	DB4	36500.00	10:20
	Aston Martin	DB9	77500.00	10:20
	Peugeot	404	19500.00	10:23
	Peugeot	205	3950.00	10:25
	Noble	M600	29500.00	10:25
	Alfa Romeo	Spider	12500.00	10:25
	Porsche	944	15750.00	10:33
	Bentley	Arnage	99950.00	10:39

Figure 20.18: Displaying records by time

How it Works

As long as the source data contains a time element, you can display the time of an event (such as a sale) when querying data. Fortunately, the Sales table (which is used in the SalesByCountry view) contains the SaleDate field that contains both a date and a time element. This query simply selects core information—including the SaleDate—from the SalesByCountry view.

Isolating the time part of a field like this (in fact, it is a DATETIME field) is as simple as selecting the SaleDate field and formatting the output from this field. The trick is to use the DATE_FORMAT() function. As you may have seen previously, the DATE_FORMAT() function requires two parameters:

First:	The field to format
Second:	The format code to apply

In this example, we used the %H and %i format codes. These codes displays the output in a shortened time format with the hour, minutes, and AM/PM indicator.

The DATE_FORMAT() function lets you apply a series of built-in time formats. These are shown in Table 20-3.

Table 20-3: Time Format Codes

Date Structure	Date Format	Example
Hour—24 hour clock with leading zero	*%H*	*14*
Hour—12 hour clock with leading zero	*%h*	*02*
Hour—24 hour clock without leading zero	*%k*	*2*
Hour—12 hour clock without leading zero	*%l*	*2*
Minutes	*%i*	*55*
Seconds—with leading zero	*%S*	*09*
Seconds—with leading zero	*%s*	*09*
AM or PM	*%p*	*AM*
Time in 12 hour format with AM/PM		*10:33:00 PM*
Time in 24 hour format	*%T*	*22:33:00*

Tricks and Traps

Inevitably, I have a few points to make here:

- You can extract the time element from DATETIME, TIMESTAMP, and TIME fields.

- The formatted output is converted to text. This means that you should not use it to sort the data or in-time calculations. Use the underlying data field to carry out these operations.

- If you want to extract the time element from a DATETIME, TIME or TIMESTAMP field, you can use code like this, which removes the date element from the field:

```
SELECT      CAST(SaleDate AS TIME) FROM salesbycountry;
```

Or alternatively:

```
SELECT      TIME(SaleDate) FROM salesbycountry;
```

Once a DATETIME or TIMESTAMP field has been converted to a TIME field in this way, you can use it to sort the data.

13. Aggregating Data by Hourly Bandings

The CEO has been looking at some of the output that you have prepared for the sales manager and is convinced that sales staff need to be aware that certain times of the day produce better sales, so she has asked for a list of 2017 sales aggregated by hour bands. The following SQL delivers this.

```
SELECT

        CONCAT(HourOfDay, '-', HourOfDay + 1) AS HourBand

        ,SUM(SalePrice) AS SalesByHourBand

FROM

    (

    SELECT      SalePrice

                ,HOUR(SaleDate) AS HourOfDay

    FROM        salesbycountry

    WHERE       YEAR(SaleDate) = 2017

    ) A

GROUP BY    HourOfDay

ORDER BY    HourOfDay;
```

Running this piece of code produces the output that you can see in Figure 20.19.

HourBand	SalesByHourBand
9-10	127950.00
10-11	569750.00
11-12	617400.00
12-13	1218390.00
13-14	1052700.00
14-15	106905.00
15-16	85000.00
16-17	854400.00
17-18	672900.00
18-19	605450.00
19-20	668530.00
20-21	1117500.00
21-22	240700.00

Figure 20.19: Displaying data grouped and aggregated for hour bands

How it Works

The heart of this piece of SQL is a subquery that isolates the hour when a sale was made. It does this by applying the HOUR() function to the SaleDate field of the SalesByCountry view. This function can extract the hour from a DATETIME or TIME field.

To make this clearer, take a look at Figure 20.20 where you can see the output from the subquery (aliased as A in the SQL code).

SalePrice	HourOfDay
12500.00	16
86500.00	17
3950.00	10
29500.00	10
12500.00	10
23500.00	21
10500.00	21
22500.00	17
8850.00	19
8500.00	21
2350.00	21
165000.00	21
99500.00	20
305000.00	13
45000.00	17
23600.00	11

Figure 20.20: *Extracting the hour part of a DATETIME field using the HOUR() function*

Once the subquery has delivered the sale price and the hour of the sale, the outer query can take this information and use it as the basis for the final result.

The outer query simply aggregates the sale price by hour. As a final flourish, it displays the hour band as a range by displaying the hour twice—by simply adding 1 to the hour figure. It does this using the CONCAT() function with the following three elements as parameters:

First: The hour of the day taken from the derived table.

Second: A dash (in quotes). This is purely decorative

Finally: The hour of the day taken from the derived table and incremented by 1

Tricks and Traps

I have one idea to add:

- You can wrap the whole query in a CTE or a subquery and then order by the aggregate amount to see most profitable hours of the day if you want to extract even more analysis from the data.

14. Aggregate Data by Quarter of Hour

As a final part of the sales focus, the CEO wants to know which part of the hour is best for sales. You prepare the following piece of code to show sales for 2017 in quarter-hourly tranches.

```
SELECT      QuarterOfHour

            ,SUM(SalePrice) AS SalesByQuarterHourBand

FROM

    (

    SELECT      SalePrice

                ,FLOOR((MINUTE(SaleDate) / 15) + 1) AS QuarterOfHour

    FROM        salesbycountry

    WHERE       YEAR(SaleDate) = 2017

    ) A

GROUP BY    QuarterOfHour

ORDER BY    QuarterOfHour;
```

Running this code snippet produces the output that you can see in Figure 20.21.

	QuarterOfHour	SalesByQuarterHourBand
▶	1	3086360.00
	2	2694100.00
	3	1667115.00
	4	490000.00

Figure 20.21: Data grouped in quarter-hour bands

How it Works

This piece of SQL consists of two queries:

An inner query   That looks at every sale date and time for 2017 (using the SalesByCountry view as the source of the data). This subquery extracts the minute at which each sale took place using the MINUTE() function. Then the number of minutes is divided by 15 to give each quarter of an hour. The 15-minute slot is then incremented by 1, since otherwise it would begin with 0. The entire calculation is then rounded down (to avoid fractions) using the FLOOR() function.

An outer query   That aggregates the sales amount from the inner query (aliased as A) and groups the amounts by each quarter of an hour.

Conclusion

This chapter showed you a more advanced set of techniques that you can use to analyze data over time. You have learned how to compare data across different time periods, to analyze how metrics accumulate over time, and to break down timespans into their constituent parts. Using these kinds of advanced time analysis can really help you discover trends in your source data.

When analyzing data over time you need to be aware that MySQL can often solve a challenge in several different ways. This is why I have shown you alternative solutions to problems in some cases. Indeed, you can also try using the solution suggested for one section in this chapter to other sections. In any case, what matters is the result. If you are obtaining the correct output in a way that you are comfortable with then that is all that matters.

It is only fair to warn you that there are many more ways of analyzing data over time in MySQL that we have not covered in this chapter. This is because an exhaustive overview of every time analysis challenge would require an entire book. I hope, nonetheless that you have learned enough in this chapter to cover all your essential needs.

Core Knowledge Learned in This Chapter

The keywords that you have seen in this chapter are listed here. I have included those that you may already have seen previously.

Concept	Description
LAST_DAY()	This function returns the date for the last day of the month.
DAYOFWEEK()	This function returns the number of the day of the week from a date.
DATEDIFF()	This function finds the number of hours, minutes, and seconds two given dates.
TIMEDIFF()	This function finds the number of days, months, years, and so on between two given dates.
CAST()	This function converts between data types. In this chapter it is used specifically to convert a datetime data type to a date.
DATE()	This function converts a datetime data type to a date.
YEAR()	This function isolates the year part of a date.
MONTH()	This function isolates the month part of a date.
DAY()	This function isolates the day part of a date.
DATE_ADD()	This function adds a specified number of defined time periods to a date.
DATE_SUB()	This function subtracts a specified number of defined time periods from a date.
MINUTE()	This function extracts the number of minutes from a datetime field.
HOUR()	This function extracts the number of hours from a datetime field.
SECOND()	This function extracts the number of seconds from a datetime field.
EXTRACT	This function allows you to isolate a date or time element from a DATE or DATETIME field.
INTERVAL	This parameter specifies the time interval to apply in a timespan calculation.
FLOOR()	This function rounds down to the nearest integer.

CHAPTER 21

Complex Data Output

Often the way data is presented is perceived as more important than the data itself. So you need to know not only how to analyze the data and deliver accurate results, but also how to shape the output so that the essence of your analysis is immediately comprehensible. The techniques covered in this chapter help you present your results in various ways that can make them easier to read and understand.

Presenting Complex Output with SQL

The techniques that you discover in this chapter include

- Pivoting data to create crosstab tables
- Unpivoting data from crosstabs to lists
- Adding multiple separate subtotals and a grand total to an aggregate query
- Creating indented output
- Displaying data from multiple records in separate columns in a single query
- Carrying out search and replace operations on the final output
- Assembling concatenated lists of results

- Exporting comma-delimited format text files from queries
- Exporting fixed-length text files from queries

These ways of enhancing the output from a query are as practical as they are useful. They can make your results as alluring as they are revelatory. In the real world, you may not use all of these techniques on a daily basis; nonetheless, it is probably best to know that they are available so that you can apply them when the need arises. What is more, these presentation techniques can only enhance your SQL skills. Indeed, you can apply several of the approaches that you see in this chapter to solve many other data challenges.

1. Creating a Pivot Table

The finance director has given you a new challenge—deliver a simple, compact table of sales by color for all the years that Prestige Cars has been trading. He was adamant that the results must be presented as a crosstab—or pivot table. SQL can pivot data in this way, as the following code snippet shows:

```
SELECT    Color

          ,SUM(CASE WHEN YEAR(SaleDate) = 2015 THEN SD.SalePrice

                  ELSE NULL END) AS '2015'

          ,SUM(CASE WHEN YEAR(SaleDate) = 2016 THEN SD.SalePrice

                  ELSE NULL END) AS '2016'

          ,SUM(CASE WHEN YEAR(SaleDate) = 2017 THEN SD.SalePrice

                  ELSE NULL END) AS '2017'

          ,SUM(CASE WHEN YEAR(SaleDate) = 2018 THEN SD.SalePrice

                  ELSE NULL END) AS '2018'

FROM      stock ST

JOIN      salesdetails SD

          ON ST.StockCode = SD.StockID

JOIN      sales SA

          ON SA.SalesID = SD.SalesID

GROUP BY Color;
```

Running this query gives the results that you can see in Figure 21.1.

Color	2015	2016	2017	2018
Black	374490.00	1251410.00	3112550.00	1983695.00
Blue	284600.00	423650.00	708420.00	1186400.00
British Racing Green	111500.00	663250.00	872340.00	566385.00
Canary Yellow	132000.00	287070.00	104750.00	134045.00
Dark Purple	NULL	283000.00	219175.00	662640.00
Green	216600.00	370750.00	655090.00	599540.00
Night Blue	57990.00	405500.00	457500.00	600830.00
Pink	NULL	235950.00	54700.00	191600.00
Red	154795.00	442500.00	659150.00	932450.00
Silver	89000.00	542205.00	1093900.00	926030.00

Figure 21.1: *Creating a pivot table*

How it Works

Sometimes a simple list of data is not what you want. Comparing data in a list can be much harder than when it is presented as a table of intersecting rows and columns, as is the case with a pivot table. This table style of data presentation is also called a *crosstab*.

What matters when creating a pivot table is realizing that it is there to display *three* pieces of data in different ways. It needs

Row headers   These are the data elements that appear in the left-hand column of the output table.

Column headers   These are the data elements that appear at the top of each column. Only one field is drawn directly from the database—the Color field. It is important to understand that all the other column headers are *not* field names, but *data* from the database.

Table data   These are the aggregated numeric values that appear inside the final pivoted output table.

Therefore, the art of making a pivot table involves assembling these three pieces of data so that they can be used correctly to give you the result you are looking for. Here is what is actually done in this example:

Initially: The source tables—Stock, SalesDetails and Sales—are joined to allow access to the three fields that are used in the pivot table. These are SaleDate, SalePrice and Color.

Then: You add a GROUP BY clause to ensure that each color will appear on a separate row.

Finally: You create a SELECT clause where each column is defined as the output from a CASE statement.

The hard work in this query is carried out by the CASE statements in the SELECT clause. So let's take a closer look at one of these to see how it works.

First: An aggregate function is entered. We are using SUM() in this example.

Then: A CASE statement is added *inside* the parentheses of the SUM() function. This CASE statement finds (or filters, if you prefer) a specific year from the SaleDate field. This way the SUM() function finds the total of another field—the SalePrice field—*only* for a defined year.

Finally: An alias is added to the "virtual field" that is created using the CASE statement. In this example the alias is the year that is used to filter data.

Once the principle is defined, you can copy and tweak each output field so that it displays the totals for a different year. Each year is, consequently, a column in the pivot table.

A pivot table has to use an aggregation function to handle the values that are displayed in the table. This is because each intersection of a row and a column (several black cars sold in 2015, for instance) can have more than one value. You can use any of the SQL aggregation functions in a pivot table; consequently, you can just as easily use AVG() or COUNT() here to return the average sale price or the number of vehicles. If you are using SUM() or AVG(), then the field that you are aggregating has to be numeric. COUNT() can also be applied to text fields to return the number of values rather than the sum of the values.

Writing pivot table SQL is easier once you understand the process that the code represents. To help conceptualize this technique, take a look at Figure 21.2.

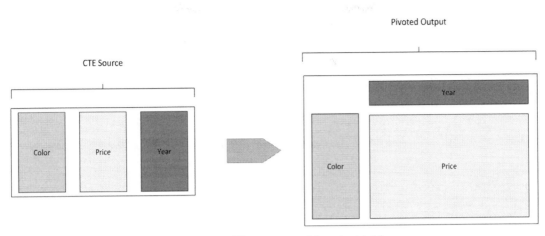

Figure 21.2: *The concept of the pivot table*

Tricks and Traps

Pivot tables require you to pay careful attention to the SQL that you are writing, so be sure to remember the following points when you create your own pivot tables:

- The only tricky part of writing the SQL that creates a pivot table is selecting the data that will constitute the column headers. It helps if you start by isolating this list of individual data elements before you start writing the rest of the code. In this example, you can return the list of years used in the SELECT clause with the following SQL snippet:

```
SELECT DISTINCT YEAR(SaleDate) FROM Sales;
```

This returns the years (as you can see in Figure 21.3) that you can then copy and paste to create the list of column headers.

YEAR(SaleDate)
2015
2016
2017
2018

Figure 21.3: *Preparing the data for the column titles of a pivot table*

- The field aliases used must be entered in quotes or backticks as they are only decorative text, as far as SQL is concerned.
- This is something of a "manual" technique, it has to be admitted. Consequently you need to be really careful that you are adding *all* the required column headers (the years in this example) when you are setting up the pivot table. This can mean first taking a close look at the source data.

2. Creating a Pivot Table Displaying Multiple Row Groupings

Fortunately, the finance director was delighted with your first pivot table. Unfortunately, this has created further demands from him for yet more analysis from you. What he would like now is another pivot table, only this time he wants to see the number of colors purchased by make *and* model. The following code shows how this can be done:

```
WITH PivotDataSource_CTE (Make, Model, Color)

AS

(

SELECT    MK.MakeName, MD.ModelName, ST.Color

FROM      make MK

JOIN      model MD ON MK.MakeID = MD.MakeID

JOIN      stock ST ON ST.ModelID = MD.ModelID

)


SELECT    make, model

          ,COUNT(CASE WHEN Color = 'Black' THEN Color

                    ELSE NULL END)

AS 'Black'

          ,COUNT(CASE WHEN Color = 'Blue' THEN Color

                    ELSE NULL END)

AS 'Blue'

          ,COUNT(CASE WHEN Color = 'British Racing Green'

                  THEN Color ELSE NULL END) AS 'British Racing Green'

          ,COUNT(CASE WHEN Color = 'Canary Yellow' THEN Color

                    ELSE NULL END) AS 'Canary Yellow'
```

```
        ,COUNT(CASE WHEN Color = 'Dark Purple' THEN Color

               ELSE NULL END) AS 'Dark Purple'

        ,COUNT(CASE WHEN Color = 'Green' THEN Color

               ELSE NULL END) AS 'Green'

        ,COUNT(CASE WHEN Color = 'Night Blue' THEN Color

               ELSE NULL END) AS 'Night Blue'

        ,COUNT(CASE WHEN Color = 'Pink' THEN Color

               ELSE NULL END)

AS 'Pink'

        ,COUNT(CASE WHEN Color = 'Red' THEN Color

               ELSE NULL END) AS 'Red'

        ,COUNT(CASE WHEN Color = 'Silver' THEN Color

               ELSE NULL END) AS 'Silver'

FROM     PivotDataSource_CTE

GROUP BY Make, Model;
```

Running this query gives the results that you can see in Figure 21.4.

Make	Model	Black	Blue	British Racing Green	Canary Yellow	Dark Purple	Green	Night Blue	Pink	Red	Silver
Alfa Romeo	1750	1	1	0	0	0	0	0	0	0	0
Alfa Romeo	Giulia	3	0	3	0	0	1	0	0	1	0
Alfa Romeo	Giulietta	1	2	0	0	1	0	3	0	0	0
Alfa Romeo	Spider	4	1	0	0	0	1	0	0	0	0
Aston Martin	DB2	2	1	1	1	0	2	1	0	1	2
Aston Martin	DB4	3	0	0	1	0	1	1	1	0	1
Aston Martin	DB5	2	2	0	0	0	0	1	0	1	1
Aston Martin	DB6	4	0	3	2	0	1	2	0	2	2
Aston Martin	DB9	4	1	1	1	1	2	1	0	1	5
Aston Martin	Rapide	1	0	0	0	0	0	1	0	1	1
Aston Martin	Vanquish	2	0	0	0	1	1	2	0	1	1
Aston Martin	Vantage	2	0	1	0	0	1	0	0	0	0
Aston Martin	Virage	3	2	0	0	1	1	1	2	2	0
Austin	Cambri	1	0	0	0	0	0	0	0	0	0
Austin	Lichfield	0	0	0	0	0	0	1	1	0	0
Austin	Princess	2	0	0	1	0	0	0	0	1	0

Figure 21.4: A complex pivot operation based on a CTE

How it Works

Pivot tables can be more complex than the simple table that you saw in the previous example. For more detailed output where more than one column of aggregated data is required, a CTE (Common Table Expression) can help you simplify both the SQL and the way that you approach the problem. This query follows the same pivot function principles that you saw previously:

- Identify and select the columns to display.
- Identify the data to pivot as column headers.
- Identify the value to aggregate and display in the table.

This query also begins by defining the source data for the pivot operation. This time, however, a CTE is used to do this. The CTE is based on the Make, Model, and Stock tables. If you select the query used in the CTE, you see a result like that shown in Figure 21.5.

MakeName	ModelName	Color
Ferrari	Daytona	Silver
Ferrari	Daytona	Black
Ferrari	Testarossa	Night Blue
Ferrari	Testarossa	Red
Ferrari	Testarossa	Green
Ferrari	Testarossa	Red
Ferrari	Testarossa	Black
Ferrari	Testarossa	Black
Ferrari	Testarossa	Black
Ferrari	355	Red
Ferrari	355	Black
Ferrari	355	Black
Ferrari	355	Black
Ferrari	355	Blue
Ferrari	355	Silver
Ferrari	355	British Racing Green

Figure 21.5: *Using a CTE to return the data used in a pivot operation*

This CTE isolates the two fields that appear as row headers (MakeName and ModelName) as well as the field that contains the data elements that are to be pivoted as column headers (Color).

The query is then built in four sections:

SELECT	This clause is where the output fields are defined: first the two fields that make up the row headers are specified (Make and Model). Then, a COUNT() function is added for each color as a separate output field. The parameter for the COUNT() function is a CASE statement that isolates a single color from the data— and so only counts cars of that specific color. Once again, an alias is added for each output field. In this example the color is used as the column header in the pivot table.
FROM	This clause uses the CTE as the data source.
ORDER BY	Although optional, this clause guarantees comprehensible results by sorting the output.

All these elements together create the pivot SQL that you saw in boldface at the start of this section.

3. Unpivoting Data

Data is not always perfectly organized. Suppose that someone in the company comes to you with an already pivoted dataset. Let's imagine that it looks exactly like the pivot table that you can see in Figure 10.1 (and is available as a data table). The challenge this time is to unpivot the data and display multiple records in fewer columns. The code to do this is as follows:

```
SELECT      Color, YearOfSale

            ,CASE CJ.YearOfSale

                WHEN '2015' THEN '2015'

                WHEN '2016' THEN '2016'

                WHEN '2017' THEN '2017'

                WHEN '2018' THEN '2018'

            END AS SalesValue

FROM        pivottable

CROSS JOIN

            (
```

```
SELECT '2015' AS YearOfSale

UNION

SELECT '2016' AS YearOfSale

UNION

SELECT '2017' AS YearOfSale

UNION

SELECT '2018' AS YearOfSale

) CJ

ORDER BY    Color, YearOfSale;
```

Running this piece of code gives the output that you can see in Figure 10.6.

Color	YearOfSale	SalesValue
Black	2015	374490.00
Black	2016	1251410.00
Black	2017	3112550.00
Black	2018	1983695.00
Blue	2015	284600.00
Blue	2016	423650.00
Blue	2017	708420.00
Blue	2018	1186400.00
British Racing Green	2015	111500.00
British Racing Green	2016	663250.00
British Racing Green	2017	872340.00
British Racing Green	2018	566385.00
Canary Yellow	2015	132000.00
Canary Yellow	2016	287070.00
Canary Yellow	2017	104750.00
Canary Yellow	2018	134045.00
Dark Purple	2015	NULL
Dark Purple	2016	283000.00

Figure 21.6: Unpivoting data

How it Works

You may occasionally acquire data as pivot tables that you need to restructure as more conventional tables of data. This could be, for instance, to allow you to join the output to other tables.

The challenge here is to take a series of columns that contain data from different years and assemble them all into a single column named YearOfSale that contains the year—while placing the sales value from that year into the SalesValue column.

First:　　A derived table containing the list of years has to be created. As the column headers in the original pivot table are not data, you cannot query the table to return them. Consequently they have to be "hand-crafted". This is done using the code that constitutes the derived table in the SQL in this section. Selecting and executing this piece of code gives the output shown in Figure 21.7:

	YearOfSale
▶	2015
	2016
	2017
	2018

Figure 21.7: Creating a derived table of years

Finally:　　The SELECT clause defines the three fields that must appear in the result set—color, year and value. The color is straightforward as it is the record from the color column in the source table. The year is the output from the derived table that has been cross-joined to the source table. The value is pulled from the SalesValue field for the year that matches the year of sale.

The interesting trick here is the application of the CROSS JOIN operator. What this does is to combine every row from the two source tables. Consequently, each year in the derived table containing the list of years becomes a record in the output from the query. So each year (that is: each column in the source table) now becomes a row in the query output. To see this more clearly, take a look at the SQL if you remove the CASE statement:

```
SELECT    Color, YearOfSale
```

Running the query now gives the output shown in Figure 21.8:

Color	YearOfSale
Black	2015
Black	2016
Black	2017
Black	2018
Blue	2015
Blue	2016
Blue	2017
Blue	2018

Figure 21.8: *The derived table of years applied to a query using a CROSS JOIN*

Once this structure is in place the CASE statement can come in to play. However it does something interesting. It chooses the field from the source data that will be used to present the sales value. This is why the year used after the THEN keyword is in backticks—because it refers to a field, and not a value. So, as there is now a row for each year the data from the source column for each year is placed in the SalesValue field in the output.

To make this final part off the query easier to understand, take a look at the original SQL extended to include the output from each of the year fields (2015, 2016, 2017 and 2018) from the source table.

```
SELECT    Color, YearOfSale

          ,'2015'

          ,'2016'

          ,'2017'

          ,'2018'

          ,CASE CJ.YearOfSale

              WHEN '2015' THEN '2015'

              WHEN '2016' THEN '2016'

              WHEN '2017' THEN '2017'

              WHEN '2018' THEN '2018'

          END AS SalesValue
```

Running the entire query with this SELECT clause gives the result in Figure 21.9:

Color	YearOfSale	2015	2016	2017	2018	SalesValue
Black	2015	374490.00	1251410.00	3112550.00	1983695.00	374490.00
Black	2016	374490.00	1251410.00	3112550.00	1983695.00	1251410.00
Black	2017	374490.00	1251410.00	3112550.00	1983695.00	3112550.00
Black	2018	374490.00	1251410.00	3112550.00	1983695.00	1983695.00
Blue	2015	284600.00	423650.00	708420.00	1186400.00	284600.00
Blue	2016	284600.00	423650.00	708420.00	1186400.00	423650.00
Blue	2017	284600.00	423650.00	708420.00	1186400.00	708420.00
Blue	2018	284600.00	423650.00	708420.00	1186400.00	1186400.00
British Racing Green	2015	111500.00	663250.00	872340.00	566385.00	111500.00
British Racing Green	2016	111500.00	663250.00	872340.00	566385.00	663250.00

Figure 21.9: *All the fields from the source data with a CROSS JOIN applied*

Tricks and Traps

There are a few really important points to remember when you are unpivoting data.

- You need to be aware that while this approach will unpivot the source table, it will *not* reconstitute the full source records that were originally used to make the pivot table. This is because the original "unpivoted" data was at a detail level of granularity, whereas the pivot table has aggregated this source data. Once aggregated, it is impossible to "un-aggregate" the output and return to a copy of the source.

- This is something of a "manual" technique, it has to be admitted. Consequently you need to be really careful that you are not forgetting any of the column headers (the years in this example) when you are setting up the derived table that creates rows from columns. You will get no error messages from MySQL if you miss out a year or two—only inaccurate results.

- The years used in both the derived table and the CASE statement may be numbers or text. However, as they are not used in any arithmetic, I prefer to define them as text.

4. Adding Totals to Aggregate Queries

Although pleased with the lists of data that you can now deliver at the drop of a hat, the finance director wants one more thing. He prefers a more spreadsheet-like output that includes subtotals and a grand total; this will save him extra work in a spreadsheet. The following SQL snippet delivers exactly what he is looking for—a list of purchase costs by color and make including the grand total and subtotals:

```
SELECT      MakeName, Color, SUM(Cost) AS Cost

FROM        make MK

JOIN        model MD ON MK.MakeID = MD.MakeID

JOIN        stock ST ON ST.ModelID = MD.ModelID

GROUP BY    MakeName, Color WITH ROLLUP;
```

Running this query gives the results that you can see in Figure 21.10 (if you scroll down to the bottom of the query output).

MakeName	Color	Cost
Rolls Royce	Dark Purple	211600.0000
Rolls Royce	Green	241680.0000
Rolls Royce	Night Blue	48400.0000
Rolls Royce	Red	239192.0000
Rolls Royce	Silver	108000.0000
Rolls Royce	NULL	1355192.0000
Trabant	Black	1272.0000
Trabant	Blue	2000.0000
Trabant	Red	4756.0000
Trabant	NULL	8028.0000
Triumph	Black	208056.0000
Triumph	Blue	45824.0000
Triumph	British Racing Green	8920.0000
Triumph	Canary Yellow	4544.0000
Triumph	Dark Purple	35632.0000
Triumph	Green	32120.0000
Triumph	Night Blue	4400.0000
Triumph	Pink	7960.0000
Triumph	Red	28360.0000
Triumph	Silver	29072.0000
Triumph	NULL	404888.0000
NULL	NULL	19759164.0000

Figure 21.10: Creating totals with the ROLLUP operator

How it Works

Producing aggregations is something that you are now used to with MySQL. So far, you have only seen how to deliver levels of aggregation or totals in *separate* queries; however, sometimes you need to see not just the subtotals, but also the grand total in a single query. This query extends the GROUP BY clause with the ROLLUP operator. This new operator allows you to *add totals and subtotals* to the final output.

First:	You begin with a perfectly normal aggregation query. In this example, the Make, Model, and Stock tables are joined and the make name and color fields are output along with the total for the cost of vehicles purchased. Since this is an aggregation query, any fields that are not aggregated must be added to a GROUP BY clause. In this example, these are the MakeName, and Color fields.
Then:	WITH ROLLUP is added to the GROUP BY clause. In this example, the totals for the make name and color fields will be added calculated for each combination of make and color. The ROLLUP operator will also return the grand total for the dataset as well.

Reading the final result set is not completely intuitive, so I prefer to explain it. The total for each aggregated set of make and color is probably self-evident. However, the record without either a make or a color is probably less easy to understand. This is the grand total, and it is represented by NULLs in the make name and color fields of the output.

Tricks and Traps

There is one fundamental point to remember when applying a ROLLUP operator to the GROUP BY clause:

- If you want to apply a specific sort order to the output you should, ideally, make the current query into a derived table, and then sort the output in the outer query that uses the derived table as its data source. So the final SQL would look like this:

```
SELECT      MakeName, Color, Cost

FROM

(

SELECT      MakeName, Color, SUM(Cost) AS Cost

FROM        make MK

JOIN        model MD ON MK.MakeID = MD.MakeID

JOIN        stock ST ON ST.ModelID = MD.ModelID

GROUP BY    MakeName, Color WITH ROLLUP

) SB

ORDER BY  MakeName, Color
```

Running this query gives the output that you can see in Figure 21.11.

MakeName	Color	Cost
NULL	NULL	19759164.0000
Alfa Romeo	NULL	207248.0000
Alfa Romeo	Black	74500.0000
Alfa Romeo	Blue	37160.0000
Alfa Romeo	British Racing Green	16840.0000
Alfa Romeo	Dark purple	17200.0000
Alfa Romeo	Green	26440.0000
Alfa Romeo	Night Blue	28152.0000
Alfa Romeo	Red	6956.0000
Aston Martin	NULL	4470956.0000
Aston Martin	Black	1212008.0000
Aston Martin	Blue	284400.0000
Aston Martin	British Racing Green	250508.0000
Aston Martin	Canary Yellow	239880.0000

Figure 21.11: Sorting the output from a derived table using the ROLLUP operator

5. Creating Clear Tables That Include Totals and Subtotals

The good news is that the speed with which you delivered the previous subquery impressed the CEO. The bad news is that she now wants the same information in a more comprehensible format so that the board of directors will understand it. She is worried that the top executives will not understand NULLs in columns and wants something more explicit.

After shaking your head in disbelief at the intellectual limitations of senior executives, you come up with the following code:

```
WITH GroupedSource_CTE

AS

(

SELECT

MakeName

,Color

,Count(*) AS NumberOfCarsBought
```

```
FROM        make MK

            JOIN model MD ON MK.MakeID = MD.MakeID

            JOIN stock ST ON ST.ModelID = MD.ModelID

WHERE       MakeName IS NOT NULL OR Color IS NOT NULL

GROUP BY    MakeName, Color WITH ROLLUP

)


SELECT AggregationType

,Category

,NumberOfCarsBought


FROM

(

SELECT    'GrandTotal' AS AggregationType, NULL AS Category
          ,NumberOfCarsBought, 1 AS SortOrder

FROM      GroupedSource_CTE

WHERE     MakeName IS NULL and Color IS NULL

UNION

SELECT    'make Subtotals', MakeName, NumberOfCarsBought , 2

FROM      GroupedSource_CTE

WHERE     MakeName IS NOT NULL and Color IS NULL

) SQ

ORDER BY SortOrder, NumberOfCarsBought DESC;
```

Running this query gives the results that you can see in Figure 21.12.

AggregationType	Category	NumberOfCarsBought
GrandTotal	NULL	394
Make Subtotals	Aston Martin	87
Make Subtotals	Porsche	48
Make Subtotals	Triumph	45
Make Subtotals	Ferrari	35
Make Subtotals	Jaguar	31
Make Subtotals	Alfa Romeo	23
Make Subtotals	Bentley	21
Make Subtotals	Mercedes	17
Make Subtotals	Rolls Royce	15
Make Subtotals	Peugeot	12
Make Subtotals	Lamborghini	10
Make Subtotals	Noble	8
Make Subtotals	Austin	7

Figure 21.12: Displaying subtotals and grand total only with the ROLLUP operator

How it Works

Whatever the data that you are producing, it is essential that you and your audience are able to understand what you are looking at. Consequently, this piece of SQL harnesses the power of the ROLLUP operator and adds some extra presentation tweaks to make the data easier to understand at first sight.

This query is essentially in three parts:

A CTE   That aggregates the number of cars bought for each make, each color, and a grand total for all cars purchased. This CTE uses the Make, Model, and Stock tables to isolate the cars that have been bought by Prestige Cars.

A subquery   This is a derived table in the FROM clause of the main query. It isolates each type of aggregation (color, make, grand total) by filtering on the NULLs in the MakeName column. Each type of total is a separate query that also adds a column specifying the aggregation type as text. The two queries are then joined in a UNION query so that they all appear in the same table structure. This table has three columns: the aggregation type, the make or color, and finally, the metric.

An outer query   That selects the three columns from the derived table .

This query shows, then, how you can use CTEs, derived tables, and UNION queries all together in a practical and useful way. It also shows how you can create your own table output on the fly and combine different data elements (colors and makes of car in this example) in a single column using UNION queries.

6. Handling Hierarchical Data

The CEO wants a list of staff and their managers that also displays each person's level in the company structure (with her at the top, obviously). A long time ago, you came across the Staff table, so you decide to use this data to display staff details along with their manager and the level of each manager and staff member in the corporate hierarchy. You use the following code to do this:

```
WITH RECURSIVE HierarchyList_CTE

AS

(

SELECT    StaffID, StaffName, Department, ManagerID, 1 AS StaffLevel

FROM      staff

WHERE     ManagerID IS NULL

UNION ALL

SELECT    ST.StaffID, ST.StaffName

          ,ST.Department, ST.ManagerID, StaffLevel + 1

FROM      staff ST

JOIN      HierarchyList_CTE CTE

          ON ST.ManagerID = CTE.StaffID

)


SELECT        STF.Department

              ,STF.StaffName

              ,CTE.StaffName AS ManagerName

              ,CTE.StaffLevel
```

```
FROM            HierarchyList_CTE CTE

JOIN            staff STF

                ON STF.ManagerID = CTE.StaffID;
```

Running this code produces the output that you can see in Figure 21.13.

Department	StaffName	ManagerName	StaffLevel
Finance	Gerard	Amelia	1
Marketing	Chloe	Amelia	1
Sales	Susan	Amelia	1
Sales	Andy	Susan	2
Sales	Steve	Susan	2
Sales	Stan	Susan	2
Sales	Nathan	Susan	2
Sales	Maggie	Susan	2
Finance	Jenny	Gerard	2
Finance	Chris	Gerard	2
Marketing	Megan	Chloe	2
Finance	Sandy	Chris	3

Figure 21.13: Hierarchical output

How it Works

This query shows the levels of the staff hierarchy, despite the fact that these levels are not given in the source data. It does this by using a technique known as *recursion*. This means that at some point, a process repeats itself and references itself in a loop that is repeated.

In the case of this particular query, the core is a piece of code called a *recursive CTE*. This means that the CTE runs repeatedly, starting at the highest level of the staff hierarchy and progressing down through the personnel pyramid until it stops when it reaches the bottom.

What the code does is this:

Specify a recursive CTE	This is done by adding the keyword RECURSIVE before the name of the CTE.
Define a root query	This is the starting point for the CTE code. This is the first query inside the actual CTE. It defines the starting point for the hierarchy of numbers that define the level of each staff member. You can see the output from this query in Figure 21.14.

StaffID	StaffName	Department	ManagerID	StaffLevel
1	Amelia	NULL	NULL	1

Figure 21.14: The output from the root query in a recursive CTE

Add a recursive query

This query is independent of the root query. It joins two datasets: the Staff table and the CTE itself. These are joined on the StaffID and the ManagerID so that the reference to each staff member's manager creates the hierarchy. It then increments the counter each time a new level is found in the Staff table, thus returning the depth of the staff hierarchy as a number. When a manager has no further lower levels of staff, the recursion stops.

To see this more clearly, take a look at Figure 21.15 where the recursive CTE is explained graphically. Specifically, you can see that the second query in the CTE refers to the name of the CTE. This means that the second query is repeated each time a match exists between the join fields. In other words, for every match between a manager ID and a staff member ID, the query runs again.

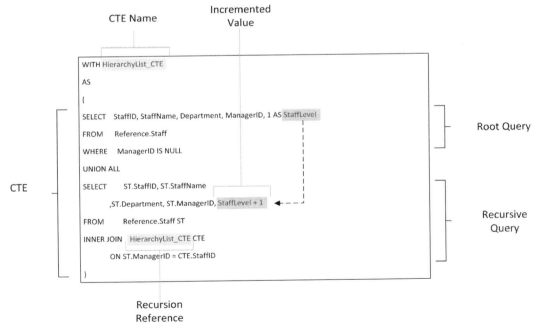

Figure 21.15: The concept of a recursive CTE

Finally, the output query takes the result from the CTE and joins it yet again to the staff table to obtain the manager of each staff member—just like you did in Chapter 14.

Tricks and Traps

There are two useful points to remember here:

- One cool use of this query is that you can easily extend it to show only the staff in a particular department if you add a final couple of lines of code like these:

```
WHERE      STF.Department = 'Finance'
ORDER BY   CTE.StaffLevel
```

Running the whole query now gives the result for the Finance department that you can see in Figure 21.16.

Department	StaffName	ManagerName	StaffLevel
Finance	Gerard	Amelia	1
Finance	Chris	Gerard	2
Finance	Jenny	Gerard	2
Finance	Sandy	Chris	3

Figure 21.16: Filtering hierarchical output

- Recursive CTEs only became available with version 8 of MySQL.

7. Producing Indented Hierarchies

The CTO likes the staff hierarchy that you produced. Nonetheless, he wants you to add a fresh tweak. He wants the names of the staff to be indented so that the level in the hierarchy is more intuitively apparent. You can deliver this using the following piece of SQL.

```
WITH RECURSIVE HierarchyList_CTE

AS

(

SELECT     StaffID, StaffName, Department, ManagerID, 1 AS StaffLevel
FROM       staff
WHERE      ManagerID IS NULL
UNION ALL
```

```
SELECT      ST.StaffID, ST.StaffName
            ,ST.Department, ST.ManagerID, StaffLevel + 1
FROM        staff ST
JOIN        HierarchyList_CTE CTE
            ON ST.ManagerID = CTE.StaffID

)


SELECT      STF.Department
            ,CONCAT(SPACE(StaffLevel * 2)
                ,STF.StaffName)
            AS StaffMember
            ,CTE.StaffName AS ManagerName
            ,CTE.StaffLevel
FROM        HierarchyList_CTE CTE
JOIN        staff STF
            ON STF.ManagerID = CTE.StaffID
ORDER BY    Department, StaffLevel, CTE.StaffName;
```

Running the modified code gives the output that you can see in Figure 10.17.

Department	StaffMember	ManagerName	StaffLevel
Finance	Gerard	Amelia	1
Finance	Jenny	Gerard	2
Finance	Chris	Gerard	2
Finance	Sandy	Chris	3
Marketing	Chloe	Amelia	1
Marketing	Megan	Chloe	2
Sales	Susan	Amelia	1
Sales	Andy	Susan	2
Sales	Steve	Susan	2
Sales	Stan	Susan	2
Sales	Nathan	Susan	2
Sales	Maggie	Susan	2

Figure 21.17: Indenting output

How it Works

As you have probably noticed by now, SQL is not very interested in the way that lists are presented. Delivering accurate output is what good SQL is all about. However, if you are concerned with the visual presentation of the output as we are in this example, you can trick SQL into producing indents in a column by forcing the code to add extra spaces before the data.

This is done using a new function—SPACE(). This function allows you to repeat spaces a specified number of times. This effectively indents the following text. SPACE() requires a single parameter: a figure that tells the SPACE() function exactly how many spaces to add.

The trick in this specific example is to make the indentation depend on the level in the hierarchy of each staff member. Here, we are using the StaffLevel field as the second parameter in the SPACE() function and then multiplying it by two to create a more visible indent. This way, staff at level 1 are indented by two spaces, staff at level 2 are indented by four spaces, and so on. The end result is a series of indentations that correspond to each person's level in the corporate hierarchy.

8. Replace Acronyms with Full Text in the Final Output

The sales manager needs a quick report of all the company's clients. However, she wants you to make the list more presentable by standardizing some of the output to compensate for some shortcomings in the source data. He has suggested that it would be much better to see Limited instead of Ltd after a company name. SQL makes this really easy, as the following code snippet shows:

```
SELECT     REPLACE(CustomerName, 'Ltd', 'Limited') AS NoAcronymName

FROM       customer

WHERE      LOWER(CustomerName) LIKE '%ltd%';
```

Running this query gives the results that you can see in Figure 21.18.

NoAcronymName
Eat My Exhaust Limited
Glittering Prize Cars Limited
Posh Vehicles Limited
My Shiny Sports Car Limited.

Figure 21.18: Using the REPLACE() function when outputting results

How it Works

Corporate data policies may prevent you from altering the data in a table; however, you may need to clean it up for presentation in some way. This is where the REPLACE() function becomes useful. It replaces specified text anywhere in a field with other text. All in all, it is a little like the search-and-replace function in a word processor. You can add some data cleansing at the query output stage without affecting the source data. This SQL snippet uses the Customer table and then applies the REPLACE() function to the data in the CustomerName field.

REPLACE() is another SQL function that needs you to specify three elements for it to work. Geeks call this *taking three arguments*. The arguments are

First:	The field whose data you want to modify
Second:	The text that you are looking for (Ltd in this example)
Third:	The text that you want to replace the search text with (Limited in this example)

As you can see from the code sample, these three arguments are separated by commas in the function.

You may have times when you want to replace multiple words with another word (or even with several words). In these cases, you need to nest several REPLACE() functions inside one another. The following example replaces Ltd with Limited, S.A. with Société Anonyme, and Corp with Corporation:

```
SELECT     REPLACE(

                REPLACE(

                     REPLACE(CustomerName, 'Ltd', 'Limited')

                     ,'S.A.', 'Société Anonyme')

           ,'Corp', 'Corporation')

FROM       customer;
```

Although not difficult, this nesting of functions does require you to be attentive to the structure and to ensure that each opening parenthesis has a corresponding closing parenthesis. All in all, this is a little like handling nested IF() statements.

Tricks and Traps

The REPLACE() function is really quite simple. Nonetheless, be aware of the following when you apply it:

- Since this technique only applies to a SELECT clause here, it has absolutely no effect on the underlying data, which is not altered in any way.

9. Replacing a Specified Number of Characters with Other Text

Sales personnel at Prestige Cars are having difficulty using the complicated stock codes that the system uses. You want to make the codes easier to use in practice. The following piece of SQL shows you how to display a revamped stock code when outputting vehicles:

```
SELECT
INSERT(StockCode,1,23,'PrestigeCars-') AS NewStockCode
,Cost
,RepairsCost
,PartsCost
,TransportInCost
FROM stock;
```

Running this query gives the results that you can see in Figure 21.19.

NewStockCode	Cost	RepairsCost	PartsCost	TransportInCost
PrestigeCars--BA94E1897419	20000.0000	1360.0000	750.0000	150.0000
PrestigeCars--E4F8BC3C9B24	15600.0000	2000.0000	750.0000	150.0000
PrestigeCars--76A312BEEF5D	6040.0000	500.0000	750.0000	150.0000
PrestigeCars--B4B5BC1E344D	17200.0000	500.0000	500.0000	150.0000
PrestigeCars--BA854855A664	66072.0000	1490.0000	457.0000	750.0000
PrestigeCars--F538494D1FAE	146000.0000	5500.0000	1500.0000	1950.0000
PrestigeCars--B0BAA41D7F24	47600.0000	500.0000	500.0000	550.0000
PrestigeCars--29F5C1C1C48E	4400.0000	500.0000	750.0000	150.0000
PrestigeCars--5A1099B0476D	34360.0000	970.0000	750.0000	550.0000
PrestigeCars--615956C94EC2	130000.0000	3950.0000	3150.0000	1950.0000
PrestigeCars--C0C3FFC85E8B	40960.0000	1360.0000	500.0000	550.0000
PrestigeCars--FDBC0A7CEDCE	2860.0000	500.0000	750.0000	150.0000
PrestigeCars--B98BEFB7E490	7400.0000	500.0000	750.0000	150.0000
PrestigeCars--1520460A5631	124000.0000	3950.0000	3150.0000	1950.0000
PrestigeCars--6CEAC851FBC3	14000.0000	1360.0000	225.0000	150.0000
PrestigeCars--2DF054FF73E2	176400.0000	9250.0000	2200.0000	1950.0000

Figure 21.19: Using the INSERT() function to replace a specified number of characters with other text

How it Works

Occasionally you may need to tweak the output that a query returns so that the output is more comprehensible. In this example, you have decided that the first sets of letters and numbers that uniquely identify each vehicle in stock are superfluous (for the moment, anyway). You want to remove them from the invoices and lists that you produce and show something else instead.

This is where the INSERT() function can come in useful. It replaces a certain number of characters with another string of characters beginning at a specified position. So, unlike with the REPLACE() function, SQL is not looking for a specific character, but for *any* character at a specific place in a field.

In this example, the function is saying, "Take the Stock table then, starting at the first character in the StockCode field, replace the initial 23 characters with the text PrestigeCars."

Tricks and Traps

You need to be aware of a couple of points when applying a INSERT() function to your SQL:

- You may be wondering why you need to use the INSERT() function when you also have the REPLACE() function. The two are, in fact, different. The INSERT() function does not look for a specific character or series of characters; it only looks at *where* a character is inside a string. It always replaces a character or characters at the *same position* inside a text field, no matter what the actual characters are. The REPLACE() function looks for a specific text to replace anywhere inside a string.

- The INSERT() function can replace one or more characters with any number of other characters. The replacement string can contain fewer or more characters than the initial string of characters that you are replacing.

10. Creating a Comma-Separated List from Multiple Records

As your final task for the day, you have been asked to produce a list of cars sold by color. However—and this is the potential problem—you need to show the colors for each make and model combination as a comma-separated list, and not as a list of elements over multiple rows. The following code snippet shows how you can do this:

```
WITH ConcatenateSource_CTE (MakeModel, Color)

AS

(

SELECT DISTINCT   CONCAT(MakeName, ' ', ModelName), Color

FROM              make MK

JOIN              model AS MD USING(MakeID)

JOIN              stock AS ST USING(ModelID)

JOIN               salesdetails SD ON SD.SalesDetailsID = ST.StockCode)


SELECT    MakeModel, GROUP_CONCAT(DISTINCT Color) AS ColorList

FROM      ConcatenateSource_CTE

GROUP BY MakeModel;
```

Running this query gives the results that you can see in Figure 21.20. You might, however, see a slight variation in the sequence of colors for each make and model.

	MakeModel	ColorList
▶	Alfa Romeo 1750	Black
	Alfa Romeo Giulia	Green,Red,Black,British Racing Green
	Alfa Romeo Giulietta	Night Blue,Dark purple,Black
	Alfa Romeo Spider	Green,Black
	Aston Martin DB2	British Racing Green,Black
	Aston Martin DB4	Black,Canary Yellow,Pink
	Aston Martin DB5	Red,Blue
	Aston Martin DB6	Night Blue,Canary Yellow,Green,British Racing Green,Black
	Aston Martin DB9	Black,Canary Yellow,Silver,Night Blue
	Aston Martin Rapide	Red,Silver
	Aston Martin Vanqu	Black,Green,Dark Purple
	Aston Martin Vantage	Black,Green,British Racing Green
	Aston Martin Virage	Pink,Blue,Red,Green,Black
	Austin Cambridge	Black

Figure 21.20: Concatenating text using the GROUP_CONCAT() function

How it Works

Tables are not the only way that MySQL can deliver its output. It can also join together a series of elements as a list separated by commas (or, indeed, any other character or characters). SQL "thinks" in terms of tables, and naturally it delivers its results in tabular form. Nonetheless, at times you may not want to see a long table of output, or even a pivot table, but instead a simpler list that shows all the data that interests you in a single column. This is what has been done with this particular query. It has output a single record for each individual model of vehicle and then added a second column that lists every color of car sold for the model in question. On this occasion, however, the colors are shown as a simple comma-separated list.

This code snippet is in two parts:

A CTE   That delivers a unique list of makes and models of car ever sold along with each individual color sold for each model.

A query   That takes the output from the CTE and tweaks it to return a comma-separated list of the colors of vehicle sold by make and model using the GROUP_CONCAT() function.

The CTE is really quite simple. It is a standard SELECT query that returns the Make and Model amalgamated as a single field and then adds a second column containing the color of each vehicle sold. Since the query contains the DISTINCT keyword, only one record is output for each combination of make, model, and color.

Running the SQL that makes up the CTE gives the results that you can see in Figure 21.21.

CONCAT(MakeName, ' ', ModelName)	Color
Ferrari Davtona	Silver
Ferrari Davtona	Black
Ferrari Testarossa	Night Blue
Ferrari Testarossa	Red
Ferrari Testarossa	Green
Ferrari Testarossa	Black
Ferrari 355	Red
Ferrari 355	Black
Ferrari 355	Blue
Ferrari 355	Silver

Figure 21.21: *The output from a CTE used to generate a comma-separated list*

The main query (under the CTE) is simply a SELECT query that uses the CTE as its source. The query does the following:

Groups data   On the make and model and selects the field containing the make and model.

Creates a list   Of colors for each make and model. It does this using the GROUP_CONCAT() function.

The GROUP_CONCAT() function only needs a single parameter. This is the field that you will use as the source for all the data that will be amalgamated into a list.

Just remember that you will need

An identification field   Which is similar to the list of makes and models of car that we are using here.

A list field   That will be used as the basis for the concatenated list of elements, which is similar to the color field that we are using here.

An optional list separator   In this example a comma is a list separator—so no specific list separator is required as the comma is the default separator for the GROUP_CONCAT() function.

If you wanted a hyphen as a list separator you would write the GROUP_CONCAT function like this:

```
GROUP_CONCAT(DISTINCT Color SEPARATOR '-')
```

Tricks and Traps

The ability to create concatenated lists is extremely useful in practice. Just be sure to remember the following points:

- This technique can be slow when applied to large datasets; however, it is extremely useful and can be a valuable way of delivering the information that you need.

- You can use any character to separate the elements in the concatenated list, even spaces. Some character is necessary, though, or the list will be unreadable.

- If the source data is simple, you may not need a CTE to prepare the data, but you can query the source table(s) directly.

11. Exporting Comma-Separated Lists

Data rarely exists for ever inside a single database. So there is every chance that you will, one day, have to export data from MySQL into a spreadsheet or even another database.

One classic format for data transfer is the comma-separated list—or CSV file. MySQL can create these kinds of file extremely easily. The following SQL shows how to export the make, model, purchase cost and sale data of all vehicles sold into a file named SalesList.txt in the C:\MySQLQueriesSampleData folder on your computer (assuming that you are using a Windows computer).

```
SELECT        MK.MakeName, MD.ModelName

              ,TRUNCATE(ST.Cost, 0), DATE(SA.SaleDate)

INTO OUTFILE  'C:\\MySQLQueriesSampleData\\SalesList.txt'

              FIELDS TERMINATED BY ','

              LINES TERMINATED BY '\r\n'

FROM          make AS MK

JOIN          model AS MD USING(MakeID)

JOIN          stock AS ST USING(ModelID)

JOIN          salesdetails SD ON ST.StockCode = SD.StockID

JOIN          sales AS SA USING(SalesID)

ORDER BY      MK.MakeName, MD.ModelName;
```

Running the code produces no output on screen—but if you navigate to the directory that you specified in the INTO OUTFILE clause you will see the file that has been created.

If you open this file you should see something like the example shown in Figure 21.22. As we are working on Windows, the text file here is opened in Notepad:

Figure 21.22: A text file created by an INTO OUTFILE query

How it Works

The query in this example is, at its heart, a perfectly standard SQL query that joins the Make, Model, Stock, SalesDetails and Sales tables. It then adds four fields to the SELECT clause (MakeName, ModelName, Cost and SaleDate) and adds a couple of presentation touches using functions that you are already familiar with—DATE() and TRUNCATE(). The former ensures that the time part is removed from the sale date and the latter strips the decimals from the cost.

The new element to this query is the OUTFILE clause. This clause is added after the SELECT clause and before the FROM clause and it tells MySQL not to return the data in the tool that you are using, but to output the results to disk instead.

The OUTFILE clause consists of three elements in this example:

First:	The INTO OUTFILE keyword followed by the path and file name where you want to create the data extract.
Second:	The FIELDS TERMINATED BY keyword and—also in quotes—the separator character that you want to add between each field in the output. In this example it is a comma.
Third:	The LINES TERMINATED BY keyword and—in quotes again—the codes for the line ending code that you want to add to ensure that each record from the dataset appears on a new line. As we are extracting data to a Windows system in this example, you need to add both the "\r" (carriage return) and the "\n" (new line) codes.

Tricks and Traps

While creating output files to extract data is not difficult, there are a myriad of small points that can affect the output.

- The path and file must be enclosed in quotes (and on most systems these can be single or double quotes).

- You can name the file just about anything (depending on the limits of the operating system) and can add any extension—or none.

- On Unix and Macintosh platforms the "\r" code for a carriage return is not required. So the following will suffice:

```
LINES TERMINATED BY '\n'
```

- On a Unix system you should use standard unix path structures to specify where the output file will be placed.

- You must ensure that the file does not exist already or you will receive an error message. Should this occur then simply delete the existing file manually before rerunning the SQL query.

- On Windows you have to use a *double backslash* to separate drive, directory and file name in the INTO OUTFILE clause.

- Before exporting a potentially large file you can always test the core SQL that defines the source data without the INTO OUTFILE statement. You should preferably also add a LIMIT clause to show only a few records from the query. In this example, the "test" query could look like this:

```
SELECT      MK.MakeName, MD.ModelName

            ,TRUNCATE(ST.Cost, 0), DATE(SA.SaleDate)
FROM        make AS MK
JOIN        model AS MD USING(MakeID)
JOIN        stock AS ST USING(ModelID)
JOIN        salesdetails SD ON ST.StockCode = SD.StockID
JOIN        sales AS SA USING(SalesID)
LIMIT 5;
```

And the output would simply be the results that you can see in Figure 21.23.

MakeName	ModelName	TRUNCATE(ST.Cost, 0)	DATE(SA.SaleDate)
Ferrari	Davtona	79600	2018-03-08
Ferrari	Davtona	116000	2018-12-31
Ferrari	Testarossa	132000	2016-01-01
Ferrari	Testarossa	156000	2015-05-28
Ferrari	Testarossa	52000	2015-01-02

Figure 21.23: Testing query output before exporting data

- Sorting output is not always necessary. I chose to add an ORDER BY clause to this example merely to illustrate that the query is standard SQL except for the addition of the INTO OUTFILE clause.

12. Exporting Lists with Headers

Exporting lists to transfer data into other systems is not difficult. However, occasionally, the recipients of the file will ask you to add headers to the file contents. The following SQL extends the previous example to show you how this can be done.

```
SELECT      'MakeName', 'ModelName', 'Cost', 'SaleDate'

UNION ALL

SELECT      MK.MakeName, MD.ModelName

            ,TRUNCATE(ST.Cost, 0), DATE(SA.SaleDate)
INTO OUTFILE 'C:\\MySQLQueriesSampleData\\SalesList.txt'

            FIELDS TERMINATED BY ','
```

```
                 LINES TERMINATED BY '\r\n'

FROM             make AS MK

JOIN             model AS MD USING(MakeID)

JOIN             stock AS ST USING(ModelID)

JOIN             salesdetails SD ON ST.StockCode = SD.StockID

JOIN             sales AS SA USING(SalesID)

WHERE            MK.MakeName = 'Bentley';
```

If you execute this SQL snippet and then open the resulting file (assuming that you have deleted any previous file with this name in the destination directory if one exists) you should see the kind of output shown in Figure 21.24.

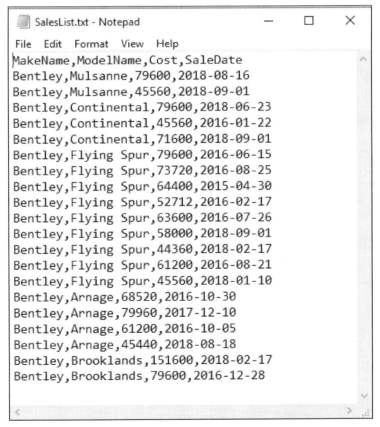

Figure 21.24: File output from a MySQL query with column headers

How it Works

This piece of SQL extends the query that you used in the previous section in two ways.

First: It adds a WHERE clause to the previous query so that only Bentleys are output to the destination file. This is purely to show you that you can write standard SQL using the techniques that you have learned in this book when exporting data.

Second: It precedes the "core" query that extracts the data with a list of field names and the UNION ALL operator. If you remember from Chapter 16, this operator allows you to add the results of one query to the results of another. In this case the first query simply defines the column headers. As the column headers are purely text they are enclosed in single quotes.

The result is that the output file now contains an initial line that defines the column headers. This can help destination systems and programs to load the data mode easily.

Tricks and Traps

There are a few fundamental points to emphasize here:

- You must ensure that both the queries (above and below the UNION ALL operator) contain the *same number of columns*. So be careful in the initial SELECT query to specify the exact number of separate column headers (each enclosed in quotes and separated from the others by a comma) that exist the output from the core query.

- If the output data contains commas (or the character that you have defined as the separator in the INTO OUTFILE clause) then you may want to enclose the data for each field in quotes. MySQL can do this for you automatically by adding the ENCLOSED BY operator to the INTO OUTFILE clause. You can see an example of this in the following piece of SQL:

```
INTO OUTFILE 'C:\\MySQLQueriesSampleData\\SalesList.txt'
        FIELDS TERMINATED BY ','
        ENCLOSED BY '"'
        LINES TERMINATED BY '\r\n'
```

Running the code from this section with the ENCLOSED BY operator will give the file contents that you can see in Figure 21.25. You can, should you prefer, choose another character to enclose the data for each field simply by entering the character to use inside the quotes that follow the ENCLOSED BY operator.

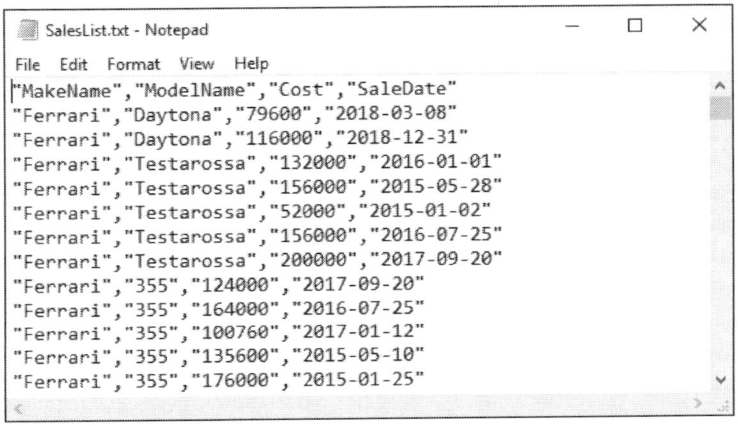


```
"MakeName","ModelName","Cost","SaleDate"
"Ferrari","Daytona","79600","2018-03-08"
"Ferrari","Daytona","116000","2018-12-31"
"Ferrari","Testarossa","132000","2016-01-01"
"Ferrari","Testarossa","156000","2015-05-28"
"Ferrari","Testarossa","52000","2015-01-02"
"Ferrari","Testarossa","156000","2016-07-25"
"Ferrari","Testarossa","200000","2017-09-20"
"Ferrari","355","124000","2017-09-20"
"Ferrari","355","164000","2016-07-25"
"Ferrari","355","100760","2017-01-12"
"Ferrari","355","135600","2015-05-10"
"Ferrari","355","176000","2015-01-25"
```

Figure 21.25: *File output from a MySQL query with fields enclosed in quotes*

- If you wish to use another character—rather than the comma—to separate each field in the destination file, then all you have to do is to specify the character that you require in the FIELDS TERMINATED BY clause of INTO OUTFILE. So, for instance, to use a pipe character you would write code like this:

```
FIELDS TERMINATED BY '|'
```

Making this tweak to the code from this section (and running it, of course) will give the file contents that you can see in Figure 21.26.

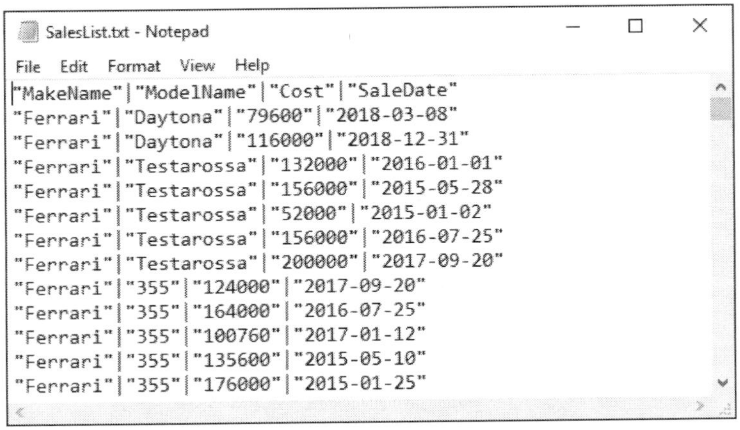


```
"MakeName"|"ModelName"|"Cost"|"SaleDate"
"Ferrari"|"Daytona"|"79600"|"2018-03-08"
"Ferrari"|"Daytona"|"116000"|"2018-12-31"
"Ferrari"|"Testarossa"|"132000"|"2016-01-01"
"Ferrari"|"Testarossa"|"156000"|"2015-05-28"
"Ferrari"|"Testarossa"|"52000"|"2015-01-02"
"Ferrari"|"Testarossa"|"156000"|"2016-07-25"
"Ferrari"|"Testarossa"|"200000"|"2017-09-20"
"Ferrari"|"355"|"124000"|"2017-09-20"
"Ferrari"|"355"|"164000"|"2016-07-25"
"Ferrari"|"355"|"100760"|"2017-01-12"
"Ferrari"|"355"|"135600"|"2015-05-10"
"Ferrari"|"355"|"176000"|"2015-01-25"
```

Figure 21.26: *File output from a MySQL query with fields enclosed in quotes*

- You cannot sort the output without including the headers in the sorted data (that is, the header will appear inside the data. In this example this means that "MakeName" will appear after "Lamborghini" And before "McLaren".

- You can use virtually any character to separate the fields. Generally it helps if you can find a character (such as the pipe character used here) that is not found anywhere in the actual data.

13. Exporting Fixed-Width Lists

There may be times when you need to export data into another system—but the destination program cannot read comma-delimited files. Indeed, some systems require data without any delimiter at all. However they frequently need you to export a list where each column begins after a specified number of characters. Files like these are called "fixed-width" files.

The following SQL snippet shows how you can create files like these.

```
SELECT        RPAD('MakeName', 35, ' ')

              ,RPAD('ModelName', 35, ' ')

              ,RPAD('Cost', 15, ' ')

              ,RPAD('SaleDate', 15, ' ')

UNION ALL

SELECT        RPAD(MK.MakeName, 35, ' ')

              ,RPAD(MD.ModelName, 35, ' ')

              ,LPAD(TRUNCATE(ST.Cost, 0), 15, ' ')

              ,LPAD(DATE(SA.SaleDate), 15, ' ')

INTO OUTFILE 'C:\\MySQLQueriesSampleData\\SalesListFixed.txt'

              LINES TERMINATED BY '\r\n'

FROM          make AS MK

JOIN          model AS MD USING(MakeID)

JOIN          stock AS ST USING(ModelID)

JOIN          salesdetails SD ON ST.StockCode = SD.StockID

JOIN          Sales AS SA USING(SalesID);
```

If you run this code and then open the file that it creates, you will see something like the results in Figure 21.27 (in Notepad, again).

MakeName	ModelName	Cost	SaleDate
Ferrari	Daytona	79600	2018-03-08
Ferrari	Daytona	116000	2018-12-31
Ferrari	Testarossa	132000	2016-01-01
Ferrari	Testarossa	156000	2015-05-28
Ferrari	Testarossa	52000	2015-01-02
Ferrari	Testarossa	156000	2016-07-25
Ferrari	Testarossa	200000	2017-09-20
Ferrari	355	124000	2017-09-20
Ferrari	355	164000	2016-07-25
Ferrari	355	100760	2017-01-12
Ferrari	355	135600	2015-05-10
Ferrari	355	176000	2015-01-25
Ferrari	355	127600	2016-01-01
Ferrari	355	125200	2016-09-19
Ferrari	Dino	156000	2018-04-24
Ferrari	Dino	98800	2018-03-08
Ferrari	Mondial	124000	2018-04-10
Ferrari	Mondial	82360	2016-04-05
Ferrari	F40	215600	2018-05-15
Ferrari	F40	200000	2017-05-13
Ferrari	F50	248000	2018-03-15
Ferrari	F50	204760	2017-05-12
Ferrari	F50	156000	2018-05-15
Ferrari	360	102800	2018-07-31
Ferrari	360	79600	2016-04-30
Ferrari	360	108000	2018-05-25
Ferrari	Enzo	204000	2017-05-10
Ferrari	Enzo	316000	2017-02-08
Ferrari	Enzo	292000	2017-02-07
Porsche	911	40960	2017-11-12
Porsche	911	55120	2016-09-11
Porsche	911	36760	2017-12-10
Porsche	911	39600	2017-11-01

Figure 21.27: Fixed width file output from a MySQL query

How it Works

This query introduces two new functions —the RPAD() and LPAD(). Either of these functions lets you specify:

As the first parameter:	The field that you want to pad out with other characters
As the second parameter:	The total number of characters that the field and the padding should make up.
As the third parameter:	The character to add to the field at the left or right. In this example we defined the space character as the text to pad the output—in quotes, of course.

In this example the "main" query (the one that extract the data) applies the RPAD() or LPAD() function to all the fields that will be extracted from the PrestigeCars database. Each field is set to a different length. When the query is run MySQL adds the required number of spaces to the output for each field to make up the length that you specified as the second parameter for each LPAD() or RPAD() function.

Tricks and Traps

I have a few of points to make here.

- You can if you prefer, simply add the correct number of spaces after the header text (but inside the single quote that ends the text) for each header element rather that repeating the RPAD() and/or LPAD() functions.

- A fixed-length output field can be any number of characters long. However, it is usually better practice to keep the field length as short as possible.

- You can add any character as padding to a field. All you must do is to ensure that the character is in single quotes as the third parameter of the LPAD() or RPAD() function.

14. Removing Extra Spaces from Output

Sometimes, the data that you will find in the databases that you have to work with might not be absolutely perfect. It follows that you might need to tweak it to get an acceptable output when you query certain tables. The following SQL shows you how to remove any extra spaces that have been added to fields in a table.

```
SELECT      TRIM(MK.MakeName), TRIM(MD.ModelName)

            ,TRIM(TRUNCATE(ST.Cost, 0)), TRIM(DATE(SA.SaleDate))

INTO OUTFILE 'C:\\MySQLQueriesSampleData\\SalesList.txt'

            FIELDS TERMINATED BY ','

            LINES TERMINATED BY '\r\n'

FROM        make AS MK

JOIN        model AS MD USING(MakeID)

JOIN        stock AS ST USING(ModelID)

JOIN        salesdetails SD ON ST.StockCode = SD.StockID
```

```
JOIN        sales AS SA USING(SalesID)

ORDER BY    MK.MakeName, MD.ModelName;
```

I am not going to show any output from this query here—because the PrestigeCars data does not have any extraneous leading or trailing spaces to show you!

How it Works

One frequent requirement is to remove all the spaces that appear at both the start and the end of a text. Fortunately MySQL makes this really easy, as all you have to do is to wrap any field containing less than perfect data in the TRIM() function. This will remove any leading or trailing spaces.

Tricks and Traps

I have a few mercifully simple points to add concerning the TRIM() function.

- If all you need to do is to strip out spaces from the left of a field you can use the LTRIM() function instead of TRIM().

- If all you need to do is to strip out spaces from the right of a field you can use the RTRIM() function instead of TRIM().

- If you want to remove a character—or even a series of characters—from the beginning or end of a field you can extend the TRIM() function to specify the character(s) to remove. For instance, to remove leading and trailing asterisks from a field you would write:

  ```
  TRIM(BOTH '*' FROM MD.ModelName)
  ```

  In this case "BOTH" means "leading and trailing"—and the asterisk is placed inside single quotes.

Conclusion

This chapter has taken you on a whirlwind tour of some of the SQL virtuoso techniques that you can use to hone your query output. From pivoting and unpivoting data via concatenated lists to adding complex subtotals in your reports or even replacing and cleansing text in the final output, you have learned a useful variety of advanced data presentation techniques.

Core Knowledge Learned in This Chapter

The keywords and concepts that you have seen in this chapter are

Concept	Description
Pivot	This concept allows you to create pivot tables.
Unpivot	This concept allows you to unpivot tables.
ROLLUP	This operator lets you add multiple subtotals and a grand total to aggregate queries.
SPACE()	This function is used to add multiple spaces in the output.
INSERT()	This function is used to replace text at a specified position in a field.
GROUP_CONCAT()	This function can be used to create comma-separated lists from the data in a column.
Recursion	A programming technique that iterates several times through, referring to itself.
Recursive CTE	A common table expression that is joined to itself to loop through a hierarchy or sequence.
TRIM()	This function removes any leading and trailing spaces from a field.
LTRIM()	This function removes any leading spaces from a field.
RTRIM()	This function removes any trailing spaces from a field.
LPAD()	This function adds extra white space at the left of the contents of a field.
RPAD()	This function adds extra white space at the right of the contents of a field.

Appendix A:
Installing MySQL

> *The only way to learn SQL is to practice using it. Unless you already have a SQL database that is available for you to use, you will need your own MySQL instance. In this appendix, you will see how to set up your own personal MySQL on your laptop or personal workstation. Then, in Appendixes B and C, you will see how to install MySQL Workbench to query MySQL as well as the sample database that is used in the examples in this book.*

Installing MySQL

The MySQL Foundation has made it easy for anyone to learn SQL on a current version of its database software. Not only that, but it has made the latest version of the database freely available. This version is currently not time-limited and will allow you to test all the code that is available in this book.

Note: We will describe how to install MySQL on the Windows platform and Macintosh as well as CentOS 7 here. If you want to set up MySQL on other Linux or UNIX distributions, then please consult the MySQL website.

1. Installing MySQL on Windows

Here, then, is how to access, download, and install the database software on Windows:

1. Browse to the MySQL downloads page. It is currently at https://dev.mysql.com/downloads/windows/installer/8.0.html. It should look something like the one in Figure A-1.

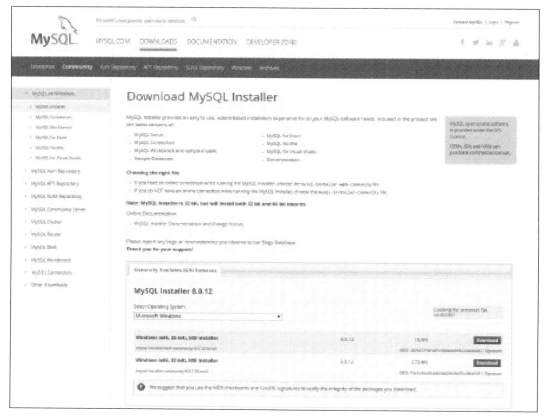

Figure A-1: The MySQL downloads page

Note: If the URL has changed since this book was published, then use your preferred search engine and look for MySQL database.

2. Click the Download button. You will be asked to log in, or sign up.

3. Click the "No thanks, just start my download" link.

4. After a few seconds, the executable will appear at the bottom of the browser window, or a pop-up window will ask you if you want to run the download. This will depend on the browser you are using.

5. Click the executable link or the Run button (depending on your browser). The initial installer window will appear like the one shown in Figure A-2.

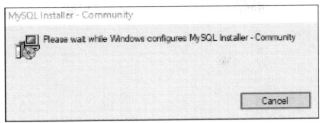

Figure A-2: *The MySQL initial installer dialog*

6. Confirm (if asked) that you want this app to make admin-level changes to your system. The installation dialog will appear. It should look something like the one in Figure A-3.

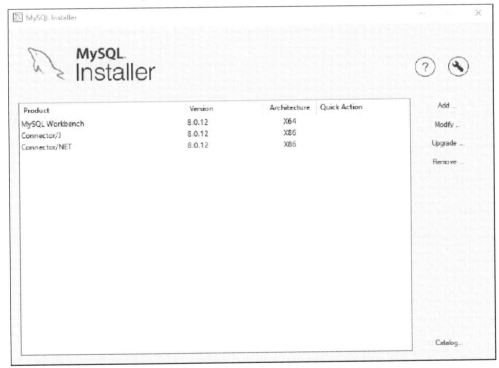

Figure A-3: *The MySQLInstaller dialog*

7. Click Add. The select products and features dialog will appear

8. Expand MySQL Servers, MySQL Server, MySQL Server 8.0 and select MySQL Server 8.0.12 - x64 (or whatever the latest version is) and click the right arrow to select this server version. The dialog will look like the one in Figure A-4.

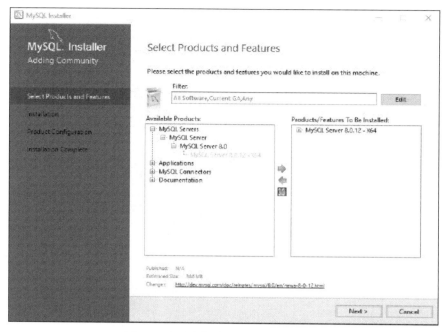

Figure A-4: *The license terms dialog*

9. Click Next. The Installation dialog will appear, as shown in Figure A-5..

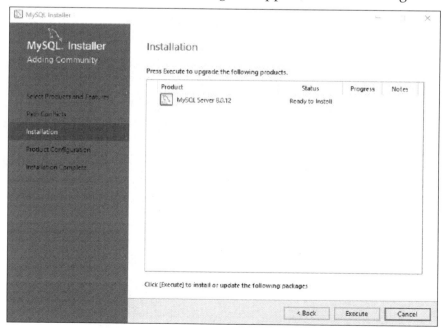

Figure A-5: *The license terms dialog*

10. Click Execute.

11. Once the installation is complete, click Next. The Product Configuration dialog will be displayed, like the one in Figure A-6.

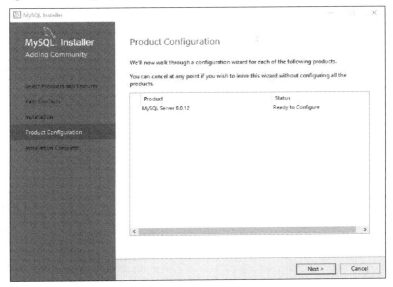

Figure A-6: The Product Configuration dialog

12. Click Next. The Group Replication dialog will appear, as shown in Figure A-7.

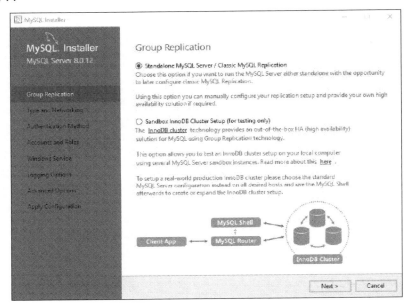

Figure A-7: The Group Replication dialog

13. Leave Standalone MySQL Server selected and click Next. The Type and Networking dialog will appear, as shown in Figure A-8.

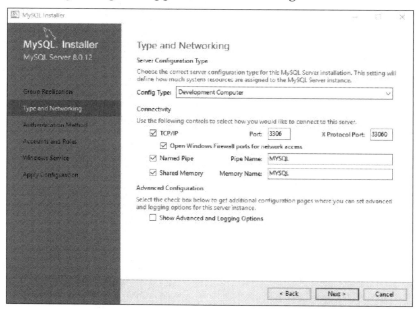

Figure A-8: The Type and Networking dialog

14. Click Next. The Authentication mentod dialog will appear, as shown in Figure A-9.

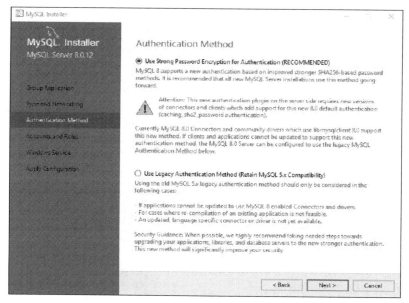

Figure A-9: The Type and Networking dialog

15. Click Next. The Accounts and Roles dialog will appear.

16. Enter and confirm the "root" user password and click Next. The dialog will look like the one in Figure A-10.

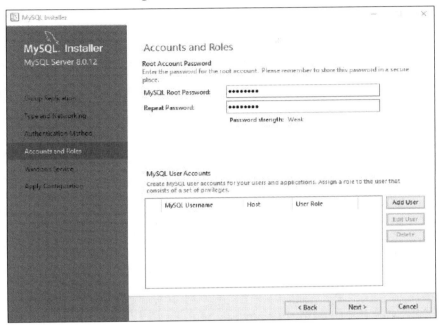

Figure A-10: *The Accounts and Roles dialog*

17. Click Add User. Add the root user and password. You can see this in Figure A-11.

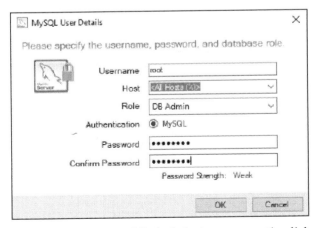

Figure A-11: *The second Default instance properties dialog*

18. Click OK to return to the Accounts and Roles dialog.

19. Click Next. The Windows Service dialog will appear, as shown in Figure A-12.

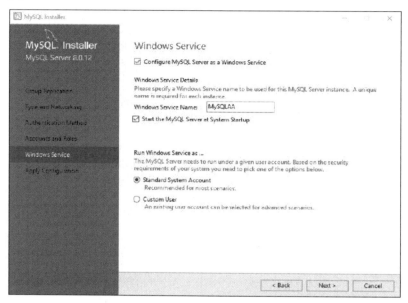

Figure A-12: *The Windows Service dialog*

20. Choose a service name and click Next. The Apply Configuration dialog will appear. You can see this in Figure A-13.

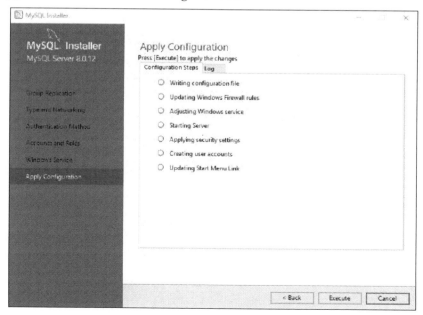

Figure A-13: *The Apply Configuration dialog*

21. Click Execute.

22. The installation process will then begin, Once the installation is complete, you will see the dialog that is shown in Figure A-14.

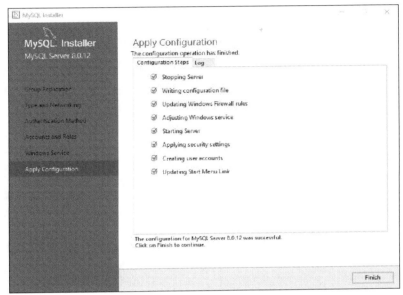

Figure A-14: *The successful completion dialog*

23. Click Finish.

24. Click Next. You will see the Installation Complete dialog shown in Figure A-15.

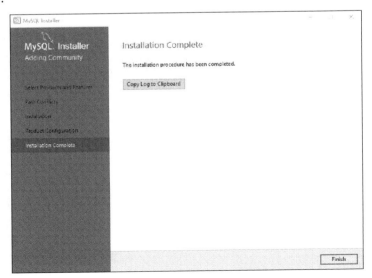

Figure A-15: *The Installation Complete dialog*

25. Click Finish.

Assuming that all ran smoothly, MySQL is now installed on your computer. You can start using it to host databases.

2. Installing MySQL on a Macintosh

Installing MySQL on a Macintosh is mercifully simple.

1. Browse to the MySQL downloads page. It is currently at https://dev.mysql.com/downloads/mysql/. You can see this page in Figure A-1.

2. Select MySQL Community Server.

3. Select MacOS.

4. Download the DMG archive version.

5. Click the "No thanks, just start my download" link (unless you really want to crete an Oracle account, of course).

6. Go to the downloads folder where the dmg file was downloaded to.

7. Double-click the file icon to mount the .dmg archive.

8. Double-click the MySQL package icon to open the MySQL package installer.

9. When the initial dialog opens click Continue. The license terms dialog will appear.

10. Click Continue.

11. Click Agree.

12. Click Install.

13. Note safely the temporary password that displays during the installation process. You must save it. After you log in to MySQL, you are prompted to create a new password and for this you will need the installation password.

14. Press Close.

3. Installing MySQL on Linux

Here is how you can install MySQL Workbench on CentOS.

1. Download the correct version of teh software from: https://dev.mysql.com/downloads/repo/yum/.

2. For CentOS this will be as shown in Figure B-8.

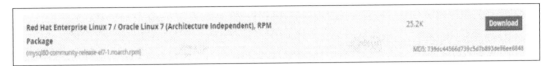

Figure B-8: The CentOS download

3. Click Download. You will be prompted to log into (or create) a free Oracle account to access the software.

4. If you do not want to create an account or log in, click the No thanks, just start my download link and run the download (this will depend on the browser you are using). You will see the Begin your Download dialog shown in Figure B-9.

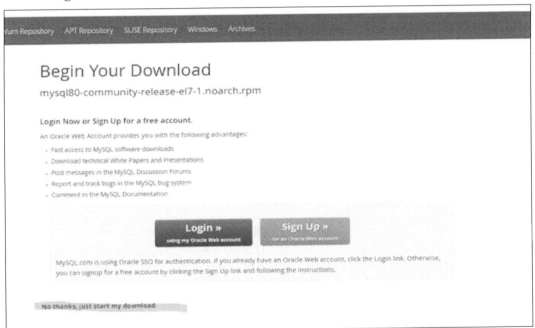

Figure B-8: The Begin your Download dialog

5. Copy the link: https://dev.mysql.com/get/mysql80-community-release-el7-1.noarch.rpm.

6. In CentOS 7 open up a new Shell.

7. To download the file type in

```
$ wget https://dev.mysql.com/get/mysql80-community-release-el7-1.
noarch.rpm
```

8. Now to install the RPM to the package manager in CentOS 7, type in

   ```
   $ sudo rpm  -ivh mysql80-community-release-el7-1.noarch.rpm
   ```

9. Once you have done that you can now install MySQL by typing

   ```
   $ sudo yum install - y mysql-server
   ```

10. Now we can check the status of MySQL. (the daemon will be inactive). Type in

    ```
    $ sudo systemctl status mysqld
    ```

11. To start the daemon up type in

    ```
    $ sudo systemctl start mysqld
    ```

12. Re typing $ sudo systemctl status mysqld will now show MySQL as active.

Appendix B: Installing MySQL Workbench

Having a version of MySQL that you can access is a good start, but you will nonetheless need an application that you can use to enter queries and see the results. In this appendix, you will see how to install MySQL Workbench, the application that we recommend using to enter and run queries when you are learning SQL with MySQL.

1. Installing MySQL Workbench on Windows

As we explained in Chapter 1, one widely used tool for querying MySQL is MySQL Workbench. Here is how you can download and install this particular piece of software, which Oracle (the owner of MySQL) has, fortunately, made free to download and use. The installation is similar on all platforms, so here is an example on Windows.

1. Search for MySQL Workbench in your preferred search engine or click or use the following link: https://dev.mysql.com/downloads/workbench. You should see a page like the one shown in Figure B-1.

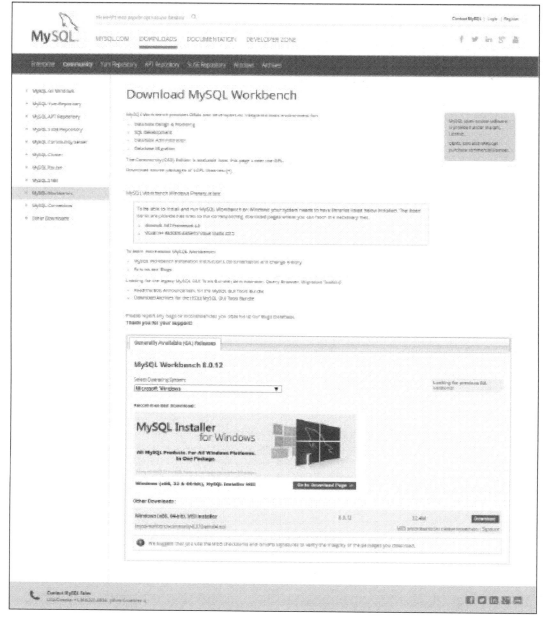

Figure B-1: The MySQL Workbench download page

2. Select the operating system that you are using.

3. Click Download. You will be prompted to log into (or create) a free Oracle account to access the software.

4. If you do not want to create an account or log in, click the "No thanks, just start my download link" and run the download (this will depend on the browser you are using). You may be asked to confirm that you want to allow the package to make changes to your system. Then you will see the Setup Wizard dialog shown in Figure B-2.

Figure B-2: *The MySQL Workbench Setup Wizard*

5. ClickNext. The Destination Folder dialog will appear, as shown in Figure B-3.

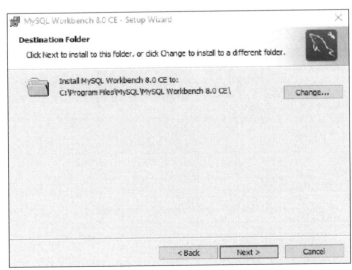

Figure B-3: *The MySQL Workbench destination folder dialog*

6. Click Next. The Setup Type dialog will appear, looking like the one in Figure B-4.

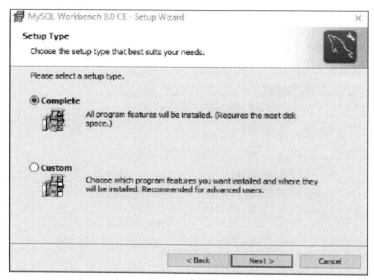

Figure B-4: *The MySQL Workbench Setup type dialog*

7. Select Complete.

8. Click Next. The Installation dialog will appear, as shown in Figure B-5.

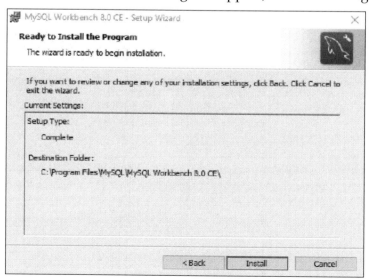

Figure B-5: *The MySQL Workbench Installation dialog*

9. Click the Install button. The Installing MySQL Workbench dialog will appear during the installation process. You can see this in Figure B-6.

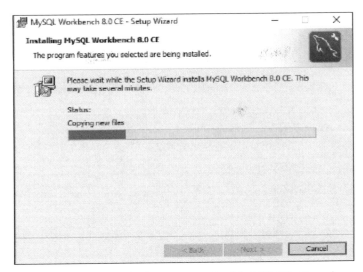

Figure B-6: Installation progress for MySQL Workbench

10. You might be asked to confirm that you want the application to make changes to your system. You will have to confirm this to continue the installation. Once the installation has finished, the Wizard Completed dialog will be displayed, as shown in Figure B-7.

Figure B-7: The Wizard Completed dialog

11. Click Finish.

You can now launch MySQL Workbench and connect to the server you installed previously.

2. Installing MySQL Workbench on a Macintosh

Here is how you can install MySQL Workbench on a Macintosh.

1. Search for MySQL Workbench in your preferred search engine or click or use the following link: https://dev.mysql.com/downloads/workbench. You should see a dialog like the one shown in Figure B-1.

2. Select MacOS as the operating system.

3. Click the Download button. This will only allow you to download a DMG file.

4. Drag the MySQL Workbench icon onto the Applications icon as instructed. MySQL Workbench is now installed.

3. Running MySQL Workbench

To launch MySQL Workbench using Windows, click the Start Menu button at the bottom left of the screen and scroll down the list of installed applications until you find MySQL. Expand this and you will see MySQL Workbench, as shown in Figure B-8. Click on this to run MySQL Workbench.

Figure B-8: Running MySQL Workbench

MySQL Workbench will open and you should see a screen like the one shown in B-9

On a Macintosh you can launch MySQL Workbench from the Applications folder.

Figure B-9: Running MySQL Workbench

4. Creating a Connection to MySQL

Once MySQL Workbench is running, you will need to create a connection to your MySQL database. Fortunately this only needs to be done once.

1. Click the plus symbol next to MySQL connections. The New Connection dialog will appear like the one shown in Figure B-10.

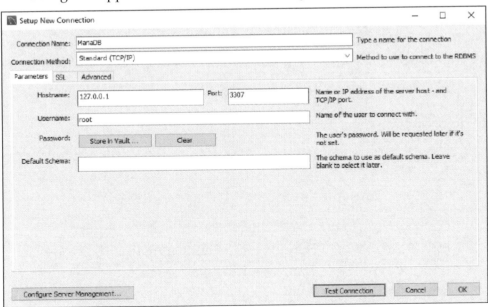

Figure B-10: The New Connection dialog

2. Enter the name that you want to give this connection, leave the Hostname as 127.0.0.1 if you are connecting to a MySQL database that you just installed on your local computer, and ensure that the port corresponds to the port that you set when installing MySQL.

3. Click the Test Connection button. The Connection dialog will appear, as shown in Figure B-11.

Figure B-11: *The Connection dialog*

4. Enter the password that you set when installing the MySQL database. You may get a connection warning. This is irrelevant. You will then see the Successful connection dialog will appear, as shown in Figure B-12.

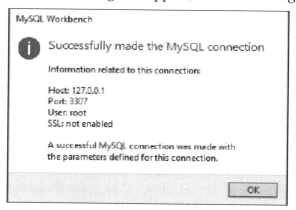

Figure B-12: *The Successful Connection dialog*

5. Click OK to return to Setup New Connection dialog.

6. Click OK to close the Setup New Connection dialog. The new connection appears in the MySQL Workbench window.

7. Click on the Connection name to open MySQL Workbench connected to the MySQL database.

Appendix C: Setting Up the Sample Database

To practice the SQL examples that you have seen (or will discover) in the course of this book, you will need to download and install the sample database that is the basis for learning SQL with the aid of this book.

This appendix will explain how to download the sample data, create the PrestigeCars database, and load the sample data into the PrestigeCars database so that you can practice your SQL.

1. Downloading the Sample Data on Windows

First you will need to download the sample data to a local directory.

1. In Windows Explorer, create a folder named C:\ MySQLQueriesSampleData.

2. Download the sample data file (MySQLQueriesSampleData.zip) from the BPB website (www.XXX) .

3. Extract the contents of the compressed file into the folder C:\MySQLQueriesSampleData (if you are using Windows). If you are using a Macintosh or Linux workstation, then create and choose an appropriate folder. The folder contents should look something like Figure C-1.

Name	Date modified	Type	Size
Chapter01.sql	16/09/2018 15:55	Microsoft SQL Ser...	1 KB
Chapter02.sql	16/09/2018 15:59	Microsoft SQL Ser...	2 KB
Chapter03.sql	16/09/2018 16:02	Microsoft SQL Ser...	2 KB
Chapter04.sql	16/09/2018 16:05	Microsoft SQL Ser...	3 KB
Chapter05.sql	16/09/2018 16:09	Microsoft SQL Ser...	3 KB
Chapter06.sql	16/09/2018 16:22	Microsoft SQL Ser...	3 KB
Chapter07.sql	16/09/2018 16:24	Microsoft SQL Ser...	4 KB
Chapter08.sql	16/09/2018 16:31	Microsoft SQL Ser...	6 KB
Chapter09.sql	16/09/2018 16:34	Microsoft SQL Ser...	3 KB
Chapter10.sql	16/09/2018 16:36	Microsoft SQL Ser...	2 KB
Chapter11.sql	16/09/2018 16:47	Microsoft SQL Ser...	7 KB
Chapter12.sql	05/10/2018 17:02	Microsoft SQL Ser...	6 KB
Chapter13.sql	05/10/2018 17:18	Microsoft SQL Ser...	10 KB
Chapter14.sql	05/10/2018 17:21	Microsoft SQL Ser...	7 KB
Chapter15.sql	05/10/2018 17:24	Microsoft SQL Ser...	6 KB
Chapter16.sql	05/10/2018 17:58	Microsoft SQL Ser...	4 KB
Chapter17.sql	05/10/2018 18:01	Microsoft SQL Ser...	4 KB
Chapter18.sql	06/10/2018 11:47	Microsoft SQL Ser...	6 KB
Chapter19.sql	05/10/2018 17:45	Microsoft SQL Ser...	7 KB
Chapter20.sql	05/10/2018 17:49	Microsoft SQL Ser...	9 KB
Chapter21.sql	05/10/2018 17:53	Microsoft SQL Ser...	8 KB
prestigecars.sql	20/09/2018 15:51	Microsoft SQL Ser...	256 KB

Figure C-1: The sample data folder contents

2. Loading the Sample Data into the PrestigeCars Database

Finally, you need to load the sample data and all the database tables and views into the newly created PrestigeCars database.

1. Run MySQL Workbench.

2. In MySQL MySQL Workbench, click File⇨OpenSQLScript.

3. Browse to the file C:\MySQLQueriesSampleData\PrestigeCars.sql (or the folder where you downloaded the source file on Macintosh or Linux).

4. Click Open. The script will appear in a new query window.

5. Select Query⇨Execute All or Selection to run the script and load the data.

You can now start querying the sample data contained in the PrestigeCars database.

3. Opening the Sample Queries

To save you having to type out all the sample queries in this book, hey are available in the download from the BPB web site. If you have already downloaded the sample data as described in Section 1 of this Appendix, then you can jump directly to step 3.

1. In your web browser, navigate to www.BPB.com/MySQL.

2. Download the sample data file (MySQLQueriesSampleData.zip) from the BPB website and extract the contents into the folder C:\MySQLQueries SampleData. If you are using a Macintosh or Linux workstation, then create and choose an appropriate folder.

3. Launch MySQL Workbench.

4. Click File⇨Open⇨File and navigate to C:\MySQLQueriesSampleData (on Windows) (or the folder where you downloaded the source file on Macintosh or Linux).

5. Double-click the file containing the sample queries for the chapter that you are working on.

Index

C